Another remarkable work from Torkil Lauesen. At a time when capitalism spells the doom of man and nature, this book addresses the difficulties and necessity of socialist transformation. Its message is that the fight for universal emancipation is long, yet delay is a crime. Essential reading to anyone wishing to understand the ascent of socialism and socialist thought. Its incisive examination of the history of imperialist aggression against states that adopt socialist principles covers areas rarely discussed in the mainstream.

—Ali Kadri, Sun Yatsen University, PRC

Torkil Lauesen's *The Long Transition Towards Socialism and the End of Capitalism* is a profound exploration of the global and historical dynamics of the past 150 years of the trajectory of socialism. Employing a historical materialist framework, the book challenges the reductionist "purity politics" lens prevalent in much left analysis of socialism today. A failure to grasp the political economy of imperialism and how it has undermined the material conditions of socialist transition has led to defeatism and pessimism in Western Marxist circles. Lauesen, instead, provides reasons for optimism on the left, deftly tracing the "fundamental contradiction" between the development of productive forces and the capitalist mode of production, demonstrating how this core conflict propels the global struggle towards socialism. The book provides a detailed historical overview of revolutionary movements, from the revolutions of 1848 to the Paris Commune and the Russian, Chinese, and decolonization revolutions of the 20th century. Lauesen emphasizes how each revolution has contributed to the long transition from capitalism to socialism, serving as critical learning experiences for future movements. The discussion of China's strategic use of "market socialism" highlights how the country navigated these contradictions by leveraging the dynamics of capitalism to develop its productive forces, illustrating a significant example of a transitional state adapting to global conditions. With the decline of neoliberalism and the rise of China, Lauesen highlights how Global South states have been provided "breathing space" to remove the boot of imperialism from their necks, challenge historically polarized accumulation in the world-system, and provide support for socialist movements. This masterful analysis makes Lauesen's work essential reading for anyone interested in developing the theoretical tools required to understand "the long transition" and ultimately to achieve socialism on a world scale.

—Corinna Mullin, The New School, author, *Constructing Political Islam as the New Other: America and its Post-War on Terror Politics*

The Long Transition Towards Socialism and the End of Capitalism is a theoretically sophisticated and erudite tour de force that is among the most significant works on the transition from capitalism to socialism over the past 150 years. Lauesen provides a clear-sighted roadmap for a socialist future that is rooted in reality, rejecting idealistic and utopian models proffered by Western Marxist thinkers who view socialism as a seemingly magical and supernatural phenomenon. *The Long Transition* is a project that recognizes, and is grounded in, a pragmatic and learned understanding of past and existing socialist endeavors. This book is essential reading for all who are searching for a concrete pathway towards socialism, and offers a grounded hope now underway in Socialist China, a project that is deepening its original, foundational Marxism for the present era.

—Immanuel Ness, City University of New York and University of Johannesburg, author, *Migration as Economic Imperialism*

A compelling and historically grounded analysis of socialist revolutions, Torkil Lauesen audaciously invites us to think about socialism in longue durée perspective. He masterfully brings together Parisian street barricaders, Soviet red army units, Chinese peasants, and Cuban *guerrilleros*, to narrate the making of a global struggle of humanity for emancipation. His book turns world history as we know it upside down, showing that the history that matters is the one that traces the arduous road towards a socialism still in the making.

—Jeannette Graulau, Lehman College, author, *The Underground Wealth of Nations*

Studies in Anti-Imperialist Marxism

Studies in Anti-Imperialist Marxism (AIM)

Series Editors
Immanuel Ness, Jennifer Ponce de León, and Gabriel Rockhill

International Advisory Board
Amiya Kumar Bagchi, Radhika Desai, Cheng Enfu, John Bellamy Foster, Georges Gastaud, Ali Kadri, Annie Lacroix-Riz, Maxwell Lane, Torkil Lauesen, Linda Matar, Jacques Pauwels, Raúl Delgado Wise, and Helmut-Harry Loewen

Editorial Review Board
Daniel Benson, Jared Bly, Larry Busk, Daniel Cunningham, Salvatore Engel-Di Mauro, Bruno Guigue, Timothy Kerswell, Carlos Martinez, Aymeric Monville, Corinna Mullin, Nima Nakhaei, Eli Portella Perreras, Yin Xing, and Liu Zixu

Critical Theory Workshop's AIM series provides a platform for scholarly research and popular-form essays from around the world that challenge the widespread assumption, including within the Western left, that there is no real-world alternative to capitalism. Refusing to shy away from serious scholarly engagements with actually existing socialism, it opens up the spectrum of analysis to explore histories and contemporary developments that have either been ignored or misrepresented. In order to do so, it promotes innovative, non-Eurocentric research that overcomes the siloing effects of the disciplines and the ideological horizons of imperial knowledge production in favor of resolutely internationalist scholarship that deploys an anti-imperialist framework of analysis. The overall objective is thus to foster non-dogmatic theoretical work that has real use-value, precisely because of its relevance to concrete struggles for a more egalitarian and sustainable world.

Forthcoming AIM Titles:

From France's Royal City to Bourgeois Babylon: How Paris Made the Revolution and the Revolution (Re)Made Paris 1789-1889
Jacques Pauwels

The Accumulation of Waste: A Political Economy of Systemic Destruction
Ali Kadri

The Poverty of Left-Wing Nietzscheanism
Aymeric Monville

The Long Transition Towards Socialism and the End of Capitalism

Published by *Iskra Books* © 2024, 2025

All rights reserved.
The moral rights of the author have been asserted.

Iskra Books
www.iskrabooks.org
US | England | Ireland

Iskra Books is an independent scholarly publisher—publishing original works of revolutionary theory, history, education, and art, as well as edited collections, new translations, and critical republications of older works.

ISBN-13: 979-8-3304-0431-5 (Softcover)
ISBN-13: 979-8-3304-0655-5 (Hardcover)

British Library Cataloguing in Publication Data
A catalogue record for this book is available from the British Library.

Library of Congress Cataloging-in-Publication Data
A catalog record for this book is available from the Library of Congress

Studies in Anti-Imperialist Marxism
Series Editors: Jennifer Ponce de León, Gabriel Rockhill, and Immanuel Ness

Editing by Taylor R. Genovese
Copyediting by David Peat, Ruehl Muller, and Nick Troy
Typesetting by David Peat
Cover Art by Ben Stahnke

THE LONG TRANSITION TOWARDS SOCIALISM AND THE END OF CAPITALISM

TORKIL LAUESEN

ISKRA BOOKS
us | england | ireland

Contents

INTRODUCTION
    WHY THIS BOOK? 1

PART I. PERSPECTIVE, METHODS, AND CONCEPTS
    1. MY METHOD 15
    2. WHAT IS THE DIFFERENCE BETWEEN CAPITALISM AND SOCIALISM? 28
    3. MORALS AND POLITICS 42

PART II. THE HISTORY OF REVOLUTIONS
    4. THE COMMUNIST SPECTER OF 1848 54
    5. THE FRANCO-PRUSSIAN WAR AND THE PARIS COMMUNE 64
    6. FROM REVOLUTIONARY FRANCE TO GERMAN REFORMISM 69
    7. THE ESTABLISHMENT OF THE SECOND INTERNATIONAL 83
    8. THE RUSSIAN REVOLUTION OF 1917 89
    9. THE ATTEMPT TO BUILD SOCIALISM UNDER LENIN 92
    10. EUROPE—THE REVOLUTIONS THAT FAILED 109

11. THE THIRD INTERNATIONAL: COMINTERN 116

12. STALIN: FROM THE WORLD REVOLUTION TO SOCIALISM IN ONE COUNTRY 134

13. THE CHINESE REVOLUTION 162

14. THE THIRD WORLD ON THE RISE 194

15. THE CULTURAL REVOLUTION 204

16. USSR 1956–90: THE END OF "ACTUALLY EXISTING SOCIALISM" 229

17. THE CHINESE ENCOUNTER WITH NEOLIBERAL GLOBALIZATION 237

18. XI JINPING 260

PART III. THE TRANSITION TO SOCIALISM

19. ADDITIONAL HISTORICAL LESSONS 278

20. THE END GAME 315

CONCLUSION

TOWARDS A STRATEGY FOR THE TRANSITION TO SOCIALISM 340

APPENDIX 365

BIBLIOGRAPHY 366

Figures

Figure 1
    China and Russia's Shares (in percent) in World GDP, 1990–2017 **244**
Figure 2
    The History of the Development of Productive Forces in Capitalism **365**

I want to thank the known and unknown reviewers of the manuscript for their valuable comments, and Immanuel Ness, Joseph Mullen, Taylor Genovese, and the Iskra Books staff for the huge work of editing the book.

—Torkil Lauesen, 2024

INTRODUCTION

Why this Book?

Let me begin on a personal note—my motivation to write the book. I have been studying the political economy and history of capitalism since the late 1960s, collecting a pile of puzzle pieces of information. When one gets old, there is a tendency to move towards "grand theory." One wants to assemble the puzzle and get the full picture and understand the process, trying to envision in which direction it is moving.

Most of my writing has been concerned with critiquing capitalism and imperialism. Sometimes I have been challenged with this question: "I share your critique of capitalism, but what about the alternative? There have been many attempts to build socialism in the past, but they have not been very successful, neither in terms of delivering material goods nor democracy." In this book, I respond to this line of argument. When one tries to write the history of the efforts to build socialism, one writes not only against hundreds of years of the European sense of superiority and anticommunism, but also against the disillusioned socialists whose ideals have been betrayed. However, the establishment of socialism is not some kind of ingenious social engineering. Socialism is developed based on technology and knowledge—the productive forces of capitalism. When the capitalist mode of production—the way it manages society—stands in the way of the development of the productive forces, then the transformation to socialism becomes possible. How is this contradiction expressed? In the form of structural political and economic crises and in the current destruction of the foundation of human life itself. These crises give rise to class struggles, which contain within them the transformative power towards socialism. Industrial capitalism has now lasted for two hundred years and is reaching a turning point where it has become a serious burden for the development of humanity on earth.

Unfortunately, we have inherited more than just technology and scientific knowledge from capitalism: its culture of selfishness and greed will not simply disappear, nor will the ecological problems it has created. Socialism is not destined to succeed capitalism. Capitalism can collapse in a brutal, chaotic endgame of wars and natural disasters. To avoid this is our task; and to accomplish that task, we must fulfill the transition to socialism. To do this, we need to learn from the past and mobilize, organize, and develop a strategy for future struggles. The purpose of analyzing the attempts to build socialism is not just to understand the world as it is; but to develop the strategies to produce the world as it should be.

To see the struggle for socialism as a long process of global transformation since the mid-nineteenth century is also somehow comforting on a psychological level for an old man. The struggle and suffering of millions of communists and socialists for the past two hundred years have not been in vain, but are contributions to this long process of creating a better world. To be part of this process—a tiny cogwheel in the machinery of transformation—and give it a little push in the right direction seems to be "the meaning of life." Not founded in some religion or a belief in life after death, but founded in historical materialism and the meaning of life before death—to hand over a world more equal and in balance with nature to future generations. The problem for the next generation, however, is that we are running out of time. Our task—as the subjective forces—is to work for a transformation of the system into a more democratic and equal world order, in balance with nature, in the next several decades.

In this book, I examine the major revolutionary attempts from 1848 to the present to see what can be learned in terms of building an organization and developing political and economic strategies. There are many revolutions and struggles that I do not cover, or which are only mentioned in passing, due to space constraints of a book that is already long.

To see the transition as a long and global process is not only a matter of theory: it also has practical political implications. The current lack of confidence in socialism is to a great extent due to the disappointment with the experiences of socialism in the Soviet Union, China, Eastern Europe, Cuba, Algeria, Vietnam, Mozambique, and so on. However, these experiences were not experiences of socialism. They were a series of efforts to build socialism within the sea of capitalism. In fact, only Stalin claimed that socialism was established in the Soviet Union in 1936.

These transformations towards socialism have taken place within the framework of, and in dialectical relations with, capitalism. The different stages of the development of capitalism have had a huge impact on the attempt to build socialism, and the attempts to build socialism have modified the development of capitalism. I have described the history of capitalism in my book *The Global Perspective*; however, in this book, I focus instead on socialism itself to draw some lessons for the development of a strategy for the coming struggle.[1]

The quest for socialism is as old as capitalism, and the idea of a society without exploitation is much older. Thomas More (1478–1535) wrote *Utopia* in 1516 about a society where the community came before profit, private property was unknown, and in which workers controlled the means of production. The French author Pierre Leroux (1797–1871) is credited for coining the term "socialism," derived from the Latin word *socialis*, meaning sociable. In the beginning, it was connected to the idea of a "social contract." Robert Owen (1771–1858) used the word as early as 1835. In the 1840s the word socialism was used to mean a social system based on state or other forms of collective ownership of the means of production and regulation of distribution to common benefit for all members of society. The word "communism" derived from the Latin *communis*, meaning common, and appeared in the 1840s as a theory that promotes the abolition of private property and the organization of work to the benefit of all members of society.

In the first part of the 1840s, Karl Marx and Frederich Engels were not very accommodating to these early utopian forms of socialism and communism. Theorists such as Moses Hess (1812–1875) and Wilhelm Weitling (1808–1871) dragged Marx and Engels toward socialism. Weitling, a prominent figure in early German communism, was a tailor. As opposed to the utopians, he did not believe in reforms from the ruling classes; instead, the workers should organize themselves and carry out the revolution. Later, in April 1846, Marx broke off his relationship with Weitling due to differences over how to organize the working class. In

---

1   Lauesen, Torkil. *The Global Perspective*. Kerrsplebedeb, 2018.

1890, Engels, in a new preface to the *Communist Manifesto*, described the socialist and communist movement in 1847:

> Nevertheless, when it appeared, we could not have called it a socialist manifesto. In 1847, two kinds of people were considered socialists. On the one hand were the adherents of the various utopian systems, notably the Owenites in England and the Fourierists in France, both of whom, at that date, had already dwindled to mere sects gradually dying out. On the other, the manifold types of social quacks who wanted to eliminate social abuses through their various universal panaceas and all kinds of patch-work, without hurting capital and profit in the least. In both cases, people who stood outside the labor movement and who looked for support rather to the "educated" classes. The section of the working class, however, which demanded a radical reconstruction of society, convinced that mere political revolutions were not enough, then called itself Communist. It was still a rough-hewn, only instinctive and frequently somewhat crude communism. Yet, it was powerful enough to bring into being two systems of utopian communism—in France, the "Icarian" communists of Cabet, and in Germany that of Weitling. Socialism in 1847 signified a bourgeois movement, communism a working-class movement. Socialism was, on the Continent at least, quite respectable, whereas communism was the very opposite. And since we were very decidedly of the opinion as early as then that "the emancipation of the workers must be the task of the working class itself," we could have no hesitation as to which of the two names we should choose. Nor has it ever occurred to us to repudiate it.[2]

During their lifetimes, Marx and Engels developed their perception of socialism and communism without pointing out or explaining the differences, perhaps because they did not believe in a fixed and ideal definition of socialism. It was a mode of production that would originate out of a specific historical situation which to a large extent would define its content.

Engels, in *Socialism: Utopian and Scientific*, identifies the founders of socialism as Henri de Saint-Simon (1760–1825), Owen, and Charles Fourier (1772–1837), and he refers to the "actual communistic theories" of Étienne-Gabriel Morelly and Gabriel Bonnot de Mably.[3] Proudhon and Louis Blanc both produced plans for a communist organization of society in the first part of the nineteenth century. Marx was familiar with

---

2   Engels, Friedrich. "Preface to the New 1890 German Edition of the Communist Manifesto." Marx, Karl and Engels, Friedrich. *Selected Works*. Vol. 1. Progress Publishers, 1969. p. 102.

3   Engels, Friedrich. "Socialism: Utopian and Scientific." Marx, Karl and Engels, Friedrich. *Selected Works*. Vol. 3. Progress Publishers, 1970.

this tradition and assimilated, criticized, and modified many of his predecessors' ideas. From Saint-Simon stems the idea of a planned economy; from Proudhon Marx heard that "property is theft"; from Louis Blanc the precept "from each according to his ability, to each according to his needs." Lenin states that Marx's ideas are a synthesis of French socialism, German idealist philosophy, and British political economy.[4] However, there is something more to add.

Marx's work was part of the scientific breakthroughs of the mid-nineteenth-century and the subsequent organization of knowledge into modern academic disciplines. Besides the significant developments in the social sciences, there were major discoveries in natural science, the earth's geological history, biological cells, the origins of species, and energy transformation. Marx's ideas were highly influenced by natural science. One example is Marx's theory of the metabolic rift.[5] It was built on the German chemist Justus von Liebig's observations of how nutrients were systematically removed from the soil in the form of agricultural products and shipped hundreds and even thousands of miles to the new urban centers. The result was pollution in the cities and less fertile soil. Based on Liebig's research, Marx's critique of political economy included an ecological critique dialectically connected to his overall analysis of capitalist production. The capitalist mode of production disrupted human relations to nature and thereby "provoke[d] an irreparable rift in the interdependent process of social metabolism, a metabolism prescribed by the natural laws of life itself."[6] Marx also developed the notion of sustainability, arguing that humans do not own the earth but need to sustain it for future generations as "good heads of the household." Socialism was defined in Volume III of *Capital* as the rational regulation by the associated producers of the metabolism of nature and society to conserve energy and promote human development.[7]

The new scientists, such as Charles Darwin and Liebig, shared the

---

4   Lenin, Vladimir Ilyich. "Karl Marx: A Brief Biographical Sketch with an Exposition of Marxism." *Granat*. Progress Publishers, 1914. https://www.marxists.org/archive/lenin/works/1914/granat/ch02.htm

5   Foster, John Bellamy and Golemis, Harris. "The Planetary Rift." *Monthly Review*. Vol. 73, no.6, 2021. https://monthlyreview.org/2021/11/01/the-planetary-rift/

6   Marx, Karl. *Capital: Volume III*. Penguin. 1991. p. 949.

7   Foster. "The Planetary Rift."

same materialist perception of how and why things happen. Marx was an empirical scientist par excellence. He used statistics, reports, parliamentary proceedings, figures, and trade and shipping logs as empirical support for his theories. What makes Marx special among contemporaneous scientists was that he connected different parts of science into a systemic theory: history, sociology, economics, and different parts of natural science.

What distinguished Marx and Engels from their predecessors is that communism was no utopian dream but a realistic endeavor based on a scientific theory of history: historical materialism. Just as the rising bourgeoisie had overthrown feudalism to create capitalism, the working class would overthrow capitalism and construct communism. Marx did not specify how a socialist society should be run. However, he reckoned that progress in technology would upend classes, abolish capitalism, and make an equitable and prosperous future possible and likely. One of the first times that Marx and Engels wrote about communism is in *The German Ideology*, written in 1845-46:

> This 'alienation' (to use a term which will be comprehensible to the philosophers) can, of course, only be abolished given two practical premises. For it to become an "intolerable" power, i.e. a power against which men make a revolution, it must necessarily have rendered the great mass of humanity "propertyless," and produced, at the same time, the contradiction of an existing world of wealth and culture, both of which conditions presuppose a great increase in productive power, a high degree of its development. And, on the other hand, this development of productive forces (which itself implies the actual empirical existence of men in their world-historical, instead of local, being) is an absolutely necessary practical premise because without it want is merely made general, and with destitution the struggle for necessities and all the old filthy business would necessarily be reproduced; and furthermore, because only with this universal development of productive forces is a universal intercourse between men established, which produces in all nations simultaneously the phenomenon of the "propertyless" mass (universal competition), makes each nation dependent on the revolutions of the others, and finally has put world-historical, empirically universal individuals in place of local ones. Without this, (1) communism could only exist as a local event; (2) the forces of intercourse themselves could not have developed as universal, hence intolerable powers: they would have remained home-bred conditions surrounded by superstition; and (3) each extension of intercourse would abolish local communism. Empirically, communism is only possible as the act of the dominant peoples "all at once" and simultaneously, which presupposes the

universal development of productive forces and the world intercourse bound up with communism. Moreover, the mass of propertyless workers – the utterly precarious position of labour – power on a mass scale cut off from capital or from even a limited satisfaction and, therefore, no longer merely temporarily deprived of work itself as a secure source of life – presupposes the world market through competition. The proletariat can thus only exist world-historically, just as communism, its activity, can only have a "world-historical" existence. World-historical existence of individuals means existence of individuals which is directly linked up with world history. Communism is for us not a state of affairs which is to be established, an ideal to which reality [will] have to adjust itself. We call communism the real movement which abolishes the present state of things. The conditions of this movement result from the premises now in existence.[8]

What Marx and Engels are doing here is giving a credible forecast of the possible development of communism. As it does not exist, one cannot analyze it. The premise for the development of communism is that the vast majority of the masses are proletarians: propertyless wage laborers. A certain level in the development of the productive forces is also necessary. Socialism with less developed productive forces would only mean the generalization of poverty. Another strategic insight is that it is hard to imagine that communism can exist as a local project: it would produce hostility with the surrounding capitalist world. And finally, that communism is not "an ideal to which reality [will] have to adjust itself," it is a "movement which abolishes the present state of things" on the conditions of the existing world. All these thoughts were presented in the *Communist Manifesto* in 1848. Communism and socialism are no longer utopian ideas of a better society, but a prognosis built on an analysis of history, sociology, and a critique of political economy.

ABSTRACT OF THE BOOK

I take a long and global perspective in my investigation of the struggle for socialism. Since capitalism was born, developed, and accumulated as a world system, the analytic perspective has to be global. In addition, the transformation towards socialism must comprise the vast majority of the world system to be effective. The many local and national attempts to build socialism in the past two centuries have to be seen as part of a long

---

8   Marx, Karl. "The German Ideology." Marx, Karl and Engels, Friedrich. *Collected Works*. Vol. 5. Progress Publishers, 1976. p. 49.

transition process rather than failures, attempts which have contributed to the progress of the transition by modifying capitalism, as well as to the learning process of how to develop socialism. Historical periods do not follow one another as one step follows the other. "History moves often in leaps and bounds and in a zigzag line," as mentioned by Engels, and the different modes of production interpenetrate and coexist over a long period of time.[9] Any national revolution is a factor in changing the nature of not only a single nation, but also the entire world system. The way capitalism works today is a product of the Russian Revolution and Soviet industrialization, the anti-colonial uprisings in the Third World, the 1968 uprising, and the current Chinese development of socialism.

This book is divided into three parts. In the first part, I present my method, its core concepts and some theoretical and philosophical reflections to be used in the analysis. As the development of capitalism is a global process, this process has a principal contradiction, which shapes the transformation towards socialism. The principal contradiction is the specific historical presentation of the general contradiction in capitalism between the development of the productive forces and the mode of production. The principal contradiction changes over time as the balance of its aspects changes, through feedback from class struggle generated by the contradiction. Since the theme of the book is the transition from capitalism to socialism, I also discuss the basic difference between the two modes of production. The first part ends with a discussion of some moral aspects of political struggle.

In the second part, I use these methods and concepts to analyze the history of major revolutions and their interactions with the capitalist world system. The Russian and Chinese revolutions and their subsequent attempts to construct socialism are of course important elements of my analysis. So are the revolutionary spirit of "the long sixties" and the various other attempts to build socialism in the Third World. However, this is not primarily a history book. I focus on forms of political action, types of movements and their form of organization, strategies, and tactics. What are the lessons to be learned from different struggles?

---

9   Engels, Friedrich. "Review: Karl Marx, 'A Contribution to the Critique of Political economy.'" *Das Volk*. No. 16, 1859. https://www.marxists.org/archive/marx/works/1859/critique-pol-economy/appx2.htm

Marx and Engels had a general vision of the transition from capitalism to socialism as a series of revolutions starting in Western Europe and spreading globally driven by a proletarian struggle with a degree of international coordination and solidarity. Hence the need to organize "The International."

With Lenin and the Bolsheviks, the creation of a new type of long-term professional revolutionary, the strategy for the world revolution, and the construction of socialism became a bit more specific. The revolutionary center had moved from the core of the advanced capitalist countries to its margins—Russia and China—due to their position as "weak links" in the capitalist world system.

This development was a consequence of the polarizing effect created by the colonial expansion of capitalism, which dampened the revolutionary spirit in the advanced countries in the West, yet amplified the need for a revolution in the East.

This change of location within the world system also changed the model of transition from capitalism to socialism. In traditional Marxist thinking, the socialist mode of production does not develop *within* the old capitalist mode of production (as capitalism within feudalism), but rather replaces it when capitalism has exhausted its possibility to develop productive forces. However, in Russia and China, capitalism was underdeveloped: the revolutions occurred because their route to the development of productive forces within the world system was blocked by imperialism. The long transition from capitalism to socialism has therefore evolved not only through the class struggle between capital and labor on the national level, but also through struggles between states who wanted to promote capitalism and the post-revolutionary states who want to use elements of capitalism to develop their productive forces in order to build socialism.

On the one hand, we have a history of two hundred years of unsuccessful attempts to end capitalism and construct socialism. The term "socialism" in this process is discredited in many ways. On the other hand, it is obvious to more and more people that capitalism cannot continue, as its form of accumulation creates misery along with the destruction of the global environment. Capitalism is ripe for replacement by another mode of production, which can provide an equal, democratic world in balance with nature. But this leaves many questions: replacement by what, and how? Which way is China heading? Are new revolutions on the horizon as consequences of the capitalist crises? Will capitalism break down in chaos from which a "lifeboat socialism" will emerge?

The third part of this book draws some lessons on how to construct socialism. The socialist mode of production is not an ideal utopia—it is a solution to the problems caused by centuries of capitalism. The capitalist mode of production has turned from a dynamic system, leading to the huge development of the productive forces, to a system that blocks the solution to global problems and thereby the continuation of human development on Earth. The continued development of the productive forces demands a socialist mode of production. The task is to develop this mode of production as a realistic, rational praxis of how we manage society. How do we produce, divide, and consume the social products to solve global inequality and ecological problems?

In the final part of the book, I analyze the structural crises of capitalism and try to cast some light on possible roads toward socialism. I do not believe that capitalism will survive this century. Capitalism reached its zenith around 2000. It is still dominant, but is in decline, reflected in the turn from neoliberal economic globalization towards military defense of a US hegemony that is no longer economically based. The decline of US hegemony and the rise of China as a driver for a more multipolar world system can lead to a geopolitical balance, in which social movements and nations in the global South can move in the direction of socialism. The situation has some similarities with the "long sixties" (1955-1975) when the balance between the US and the socialist bloc, led by the Soviet Union, opened up space for decolonization with a socialist perspective. However, at that time Western capitalism was still virile. It was superior in technological terms, as it was leading in industrial production and it ruled the world market. The Third World couldn't turn national liberation into economic liberation from imperialism. The socialist bloc at the time did not have the technological and economic strength to support such a change. The Third World was not able to cut off the pipelines of imperialism. Instead, US imperialism wriggled free of the anti-imperialist offensive and launched neoliberal globalization as a counterattack, which gave it forty golden years under US hegemony. The situation is different today. The US is no longer the driving force in the development of the productive forces on a global scale. They do not have a monopoly on high-tech development, and they do not dominate global trade.

While the socialist bloc already was in a political and economic downturn in the late 1970s, China has a tailwind. It is the leading industrial producer and the biggest actor in the world market. It is the driving force behind the effort to establish a multipolar world-system. The intergovernmental organization BRICS has united the largest Global South economies of Brazil, Russia, India, China, and South Africa. In August 2023, it also added Saudi Arabia, Iran, Ethiopia, Egypt, Argentina, and the United Arab Emirates. As the membership indicates, it is not a socialist bloc, or even an anti-imperialist bloc. It includes very reactionary and conservative capitalist regimes. What unites them is that they no longer believe that the interests of the West are equivalent to their interests. They want to develop an alternative to the U.S. dollar-dominated trade and financial system. Many other countries in Asia, Africa, and Latin America are supporting this agenda. This is significant for shifts in the world balance, as it is now increasingly South-South after 500 years of uneven North-South economic relations. The decline of US hegemony and the emerging alternative financial world-system may give the Third World the possibility to accomplish the economic transformation it could not make in the 1970s.

Imperialism is crumbling. The ruling elite has calculated that the U.S. cannot compete with China economically, making China's rise an existential threat to the future of U.S.-led imperialism. This made the U.S. switch strategies from economic competition to geopolitical territorial rivalry. However, in this process of economic warfare—using boycotts, blockades, and economic punishment packets—the transnational institutions built under neoliberalism are eroding. The globalized market of neoliberalism is split apart. The U.S. is destroying the goose which, for the past few decades, was laying golden eggs.

The transformation towards socialism can be smooth as the Global South gradually delinks from imperialism, building socialism with different national characteristics and creating an alternative international economic world order. Or, the transformation can be traumatic, resulting in global wars, including the use of nuclear, biological, and chemical weapons. Then the transition will be, if not "the end," then starting from scratch. We must avoid this outcome; we must avoid revolutionary adventurism in our strategy. If capitalism is still dominant in the second part of the century, then catastrophic economic and social problems related to climate change will play a huge role. It is in these unstable and dramatic circumstances that the end-game of capitalism must be played out. The strategy for this struggle is discussed at the end of the book.

In my analyses and discussions, I hope to develop a form of applied thinking that does not reduce itself to pragmatic or cynical reformism, nor turn into a critique based on abstract or romantic ideals of communism, nor devolve into explanations based on conspiracy and personal treason. Much discussion related to the development of socialism has focused on the struggle between different political lines within communist parties operating first in the Soviet Union and later in China instead of the actual material conditions which these lines represent. My judgment of these struggles does not rest on some sacred socialist values but on being rational. When things go wrong, it is not necessarily because of mistakes or treason of subjective forces, nor because of communists betraying the "true" values of socialism. The history I want to review is not a history of morals. For a materialist approach, the questions of betrayal or rectitude have only minor relevance. The struggle for socialism is a collective project, created by the effort and support of millions over the past two hundred years. A specific economic and political constellation in the world system can make it impossible to move in the direction of socialism at any given point in history. A detour might be necessary. This does not mean that there are always excuses when things go wrong. Mistakes and treason do happen. However, we should be careful to not retreat to idealism and hand down a quick verdict, but rather conduct a dialectical historical materialist analysis of the facts so we might learn from history.

Marx and Engels were hesitant to describe communism in specific details because the development of the new mode of production would not be the result of ideal imagination. Marx and Engels "rigidly refused to paint pictures of future communist society," as Eric Hobsbawm says. Marx did not paint pictures with brush and oil: he took photographs of the world. That is to say, he sought the development of communism in the context of the *real movement*.[10] An analysis of the "real movement"

---

10   Hobsbawm, Eric. In Linebaugh, Peter. *Afterword to Karl Marx, Critique of the Gotha Program*. PM Press, 2021. https://www.counterpunch.org/2020/11/11/

is a necessary step toward developing a communist practice worthy of its name. The possibility of a successful and stable transition towards socialism will be limited if it only takes place in one country or region. There has not been one sole socialist country at any point in time. Not in the Soviet Union nor in China or elsewhere. Socialism in one country has obviously not been a success. A genuine and comprehensive transfer from capitalism to socialism has to involve the majority of the world. Capitalism is a global system, and the attempts to escape it from any nation-state have immediately been confronted by the surrounding dominant capitalist powers. However, the road towards global socialism passes necessarily through national struggles. The national state is still the primary political framework in the world system. Thus, any national struggle has to be fought with a clear understanding of the global perspective, prioritizing internationalism both in terms of economic and political cooperation.

There have been many attempts to build socialism in the past. Their failure does not necessarily mean that their strategies were wrong, that their attempts were fruitless, or that their mission is impossible. The transformation from capitalism toward socialism is a long ongoing historical process of effort, learning, and trials as the capitalist mode of production runs out of options and declines. As the capitalist mode of production is reaching its limits in economic, political, and ecological terms, the transition towards socialism becomes urgent if we are not to end up in a chaotic collapse of capitalism.

afterword-to-karl-marx-critique-of-the-gotha-program/

PART 1
Perspective, Methods, and Concepts

There are many reasons why people want socialism. Some people want socialism because they can hardly earn a living despite hard work. Others want socialism because capitalism is in the process of destroying the earth's ecosystem, or because it leads to war. Yet others want socialism because the current system causes alienation and stress, and they want more community, less inequality, more common property, and so on. Without anger and a burning desire to change the world, it is not possible to mobilize and organize the forces that will create radical change. It is these forces we call the subjective forces of revolution.

However, it is also a common experience that revolution and the establishment of socialism do not occur just because people want it. In the 1960s and 1970s, millions of people wanted to, and did, fight and die for socialism. They were in dozens of strong revolutionary movements with a socialist perspective from Southeast Asia across the Middle East to Africa and Latin America. Even in North America and Europe, the movements of 1968 put socialism on the agenda. However, this wave fizzled out. The possibility of radical change depends on not only the wish, will, and organizational strength of the subjective forces. It also depends on the contradiction within the mode of production: the objective conditions.

CHAPTER 1

My Method

Historical and dialectical materialism are very broad terms, covering many approaches and reaching very different conclusions. Therefore, I need to be more specific on my definition of historical and dialectical materialism. Dialectical materialism is not just a research method. It is the conscious capacity of seeing society as a process and of understanding the direction and the eventual goal of that process. The world is in constant transformation. Any phenomenon has a past and a future growing out of a synthesis of external and internal contradictions of this past; it presents itself to us in its current form. This is already due to the action of its own combination of contradictions, changing and giving rise to different future possibilities. The future world both preserves traces of the past and gives rise to new relationships, structures, activities, and ideas.

The meaning of seeing things as a whole lies in the ensuing capacity to act in line with reality thus understood. This future is dependent on the action of people, who under the influence of internal and external contradictions, change the present through transformative praxis. What distinguishes Marxist analysis is that it produces the theoretical insight that complements the kind of action that changes the world. My interpretation of dialectical materialism is not very philosophical: it is more a tool for analysis to develop strategy, and thereby practice.[1]

My method rests on three pillars. The first is the global perspective, which understands the world as a whole, as Marx writes in "Conclusions from the Materialist Conception of History."

> ...the more the original isolation of the separate nationalities is destroyed by

---

1   See Lauesen, Torkil. *The Principal Contradiction*. Kersplebedeb, 2020.

the developed mode of production and intercourse and the division of labour between various nations naturally brought forth by these, the more history becomes world history.[2]

The global perspective is grounded in both the history of capitalism as a world-system[3] and the development towards a global value of labor and goods within that system.[4] Taking the global perspective might seem obvious, but it is not so. Most political strategies take the starting point of the local perspective, and then add the international perspective as an afterthought.

The second pillar is the "driver" of this process, the contradiction between the development of the productive forces and the mode of production. This general contradiction has taken different forms in the history of capitalism as the system attempts to find a way to continue the development of the forces of production within the capitalist mode.

This leads us to the third pillar, "the principal contradiction."[5] If the development of global capitalism is one process, then this process has a principal contradiction. The principal contradiction determines the outcome of the local contradiction, but is at the same time modified by it. In this interaction, the principal contradiction changes over time. The concept of the principal contradiction takes us from the general level to the specific level. It is a tool for developing strategy and practice.

Let us look at these three assumptions in detail.

The Global Perspective

First, I want to emphasize the use of the *global perspective*, the understanding of the world-system, as a multiplicity of cultures and political systems integrated into an extensive division of labor within a single

---

2   Marx. *The German Ideology*. p. 56

3   Wallerstein, Immanuel. *The Modern World System: Capitalist Agriculture and the Origins of the European World Economy in the Sixteenth Century*. Academic Press, 1974.

4   Emmanuel, Arghiri. *Unequal Exchange: A Study of the Imperialism of Trade*. Monthly Review Press, 1972. p. 421; Amin, Samir. *The Law of Worldwide Value*. Monthly Review Press, 2010. p. 11.

5   Zedong, Mao. "On Contradiction." *Selected Works of Mao Zedong: Volume 1*. Foreign Languages Press, 1969. p. 332.

world economy. Capitalism was born in a long process of global colonization from 1500-1900, giving rise to the development of this particular economic system in Europe.[6] Wallerstein has described this process in detailed historical and political terms in his four-volume work: *The Modern World System*. Wallerstein argued that capitalism is a historical system that has gradually built northwestern Europe and North America as the *core*, a few other countries as the *semi-periphery*, and most of the world as the *periphery*.[7] The process of colonialism connected and polarized the world simultaneously into an imperial center and its exploited periphery. The arrangement was necessary for the continued accumulation of capital. The extra surplus value generated by the exploitation of low-wage labor in the periphery secured the rate of profit and funneled the spoils of this ever-expanding market toward the imperial core.

Wallerstein's theoretical framework originates from "dependency theory," which was a response to the "development theory" of the 1950s, according to which the underdeveloped countries in the Third World had to "progress" on a similar path as the U.S. and Europe. A group of scholars turned this paradigm around and claimed that Europe has developed due to the plunder and exploitation of the Third World. André Gunder Frank's *The Development of Underdevelopment* (1966), Giovanni Arrighi's *The Political Economy of Rhodesia* (1968), Arghiri Emmanuel's *Unequal Exchange* (1969), Samir Amin's *Accumulation on a World Scale*, (1970), Ruy Mauro Marini's *The Dialectics of Dependency* (1973) and Walter Rodney's *How Europe Underdeveloped Africa* (1974) are examples of discussions within and between radicals of Africa, the Caribbean, and Latin America in the 1960s and 1970s. Emmanuel and Amin underlined the "transfers of value" by unequal exchange between the so-called underdeveloped countries to so-called developed countries and that this is the essence of capitalist accumulation on a world scale. Amin argued that Marx's bourgeoisie and proletariat could be mapped to nations of the globe rather than merely as classes within nation-states. The current iteration of capitalism is not just enclosure. It is also the appropriation of wealth from the colonies.

Emmanuel and Amin were central in sparking world-systems

---

6   Lauesen. *The Global Perspective*. p. 29–94.
7   Wallerstein. *The Modern World System*.

analysis but they were also influential in extending this analysis into the realm of political economy by describing the creation of global value. The worldwide law of value operates through a truncated market that integrates goods and capital globally, but this is not applied to the labor force, and hence, not to the price of labor—the wage. In today's system of neoliberal capitalism, there is a global market for capital and commodities, with globalized production chains linking together labor-power in the North and South. Furthermore, with the increased industrialization of the Global South over the last several decades, the level of technology and management regimes are also becoming similar on a global level. The value of a commodity is no longer based on varied and isolated national conditions. The value is based on global conditions, and as such, labor-power has a globalized value. As Samir Amin explained:

> My major contribution concerns the passage from the law of value to the law of globalized value, based on the hierarchical structuring—itself globalized—of the price of labor-power around its value...this globalized value constitutes the basis for imperialist rent.[8]

The seaport worker who loads containers in Shanghai creates as much value as the port worker in Rotterdam who unloads them, assuming that the work is of the same intensity and uses the same technology. The price of labor-power—the wage—varies due to the different histories, social relations, and political conditions, and the limited mobility of labor, as Samir Amin noted:

> Capitalism is not the United States and Germany, with India and Ethiopia "only halfway" capitalist. Capitalism is the United States and India, Germany, and Ethiopia, taken together. This means that labor-power has but a single value, that which is associated with the level of development of the productive forces taken globally. In answer to the polemical argument that had been put against him—how can one compare the value of an hour of work in the Congo to that of a labor-hour in the United States? Arghiri Emmanuel wrote: "just as one compares the value of an hour's work by a New York hairdresser to that of an hour's labor by a worker in Detroit. You have to be consistent. You cannot invoke 'inescapable' globalization when it suits you and refuses to consider it when you find it troublesome! However, though there exists but one sole value of labor-power on the scale of globalized capitalism, that labor-power is nonetheless recompensed at very different rates."[9]

---

8   Amin. *The Law of Worldwide Value.* p. 11; Marini, Ruy Mauro. *Procesos y Tendencias de la Globalización Capitalista.* Prometeo, 1996. pp. 267–8.

9   Amin. *The Law of Worldwide Value.* p. 84.

The combination of globalized value and low wages in the South is the basis for the extraction of super-surplus-value, which generates super-profits for capital and relatively low commodity prices relative to Northern wage levels. The difference between the value of labor and its price, therefore, corresponds to a transfer of value from the South to both capital and labor in the North.[10] Therefore, my global perspective is founded on the historical development of the world-system and the prevalence of globalized value in capitalism.

Productive Forces and the Mode of Production

What is the driver of the development of capitalism? What is the contradiction that forces it to move ahead and constantly expand and change its appearance? The conventional Marxist answer is class struggle. However, change depends not only on the subjective conditions. It also depends on the objective conditions, as Marx explains it:

> In the social production of their existence, men inevitably enter into definite relations, which are independent of their will, namely relations of production appropriate to a given stage in the development of their material forces of production. The totality of these relations of production constitutes the economic structure of society, the real foundation, on which arises a legal and political superstructure and to which correspond definite forms of social consciousness.[11]

The prospects of revolution are determined by whether the existing relations of production promote or inhibit the development of productive forces. The status of that contradiction is what we call the material or objective conditions for revolution. Let me elaborate on this.

Marx and Engels write in *The Communist Manifesto*:

---

10   I am aware that elements of the cost of reproducing labor power are cheaper in the Global South than in the North—for instance, food and certain services. Others are more expensive, such as education and healthcare. Some elements are difficult to compare, such as housing. A simple flat in a slum is cheaper than an apartment in a European city. However, a flat that is up to European standards, with hot water, heating, or air conditioning, is often more expensive in the Global South than in the North. With respect to most consumer products, there is a tendency towards the formation of one global market price.

11   Marx, Karl. *A Contribution to the Critique of Political Economy*. Progress Publishers, 1977. p. 20.

The history of all hitherto existing society is the history of class struggle... Oppressor and oppressed, stood in constant opposition to one another, carried on an uninterrupted, now hidden, now open fight, a fight that each time ended, either in a revolutionary reconstitution of society at large or in the common ruin of the contending classes.[12]

Class struggle is a manifestation of an underlying contradiction. What Marx and Engels discovered was the foundation on which class struggle takes place: on the one hand, production maintains and develops society through a comprehensive division and organization of labor (the social character of production), but on the other hand, there exists the private ownership of the means of production, and thus the drive for private profit, regardless of the social needs or consequences. With this contradiction in mind, Marx and Engels laid the foundations of historical materialism. As Marx wrote in 1859:

> In studying such transformations, it is always necessary to distinguish between the material transformation of the economic conditions of production, which can be determined with the precision of natural science, and the legal, political, religious, artistic or philosophic—in short, ideological forms in which men become conscious of this conflict and fight it out. Just as one does not judge an individual by what he thinks about himself, so one cannot judge such a period of transformation by its consciousness, but, on the contrary, this consciousness must be explained from the contradictions of material life, from the conflict existing between the social forces of production and the relations of production.[13]

If we look at society as a whole, the fundamental contradiction is between the development of productive forces and the relations of production. The productive forces stand for technologies, practical and scientific knowledge, logistics, and management. The relations of production stand for the relations that humans enter into when using productive forces: first and foremost, they concern property relations. The contradiction between the productive forces and the relations of production exist in all societies. It defines societies and their classes. In capitalism, it takes the form of the contradiction between the social character of production and the private ownership of the means of production, or—as Engels puts it in *Socialism: Utopian and Scientific*—"the contradiction

---

12   Marx, Karl and Engels, Friedrich. "The Communist Manifesto." *Selected Works*. Vol 1. Progress Publishers, 1977. p. 33.

13   Marx. *A Contribution to the Critique of Political Economy*.

between social production and capitalist appropriation."[14] This refers to the fact that, on the one hand, production creates the basis of our lives, and develops society with the help of an extensive division of labor between workers as well as between corporations, while, on the other hand, this is done based on the means of production being privately owned.

Despite the damaged "brand" of socialism, in the past decades, this contradiction is expressed in common everyday considerations: Why not share and have more common wealth instead of individual consumption? Why are the financial capitalists so greedy and rich while there are so many poor people? Why do humans not live in balance with nature and instead destroy the living conditions of future generations? Because the conflict between capital and labor is the class expression of the basic contradiction of society; it is obvious that it ultimately determines when the class contradiction assumes the form of open antagonism and develops into revolution. When the property relations—that is, the way we produce and consume—conflicts with the development of the productive forces, then economic, political, and ecological crises develop, and revolution is around the corner. As Marx continues:

> At a certain stage of development, the material productive forces of society come into conflict with the existing relations of production or—this merely expresses the same thing in legal terms—with the property relations within the framework of which they have operated hitherto. From forms of development of the productive forces, these relations turn into their fetters. Then begins an era of social revolution. The changes in the economic foundation lead sooner or later to the transformation of the whole immense superstructure.[15]

It is worth noting the formulation "Then begins an era of social revolution." In such an era, different revolutionary processes develop, each of which can be explained only based on specific national contradictions and their interaction with the global principal contradiction at the time. In *The Communist Manifesto*, Marx and Engels apply this law to the bourgeois revolution, which breaks out when "feudal relations of property' come into contradiction with 'the already developed productive forces." Looking at the history of the transformation from feudalism to capitalism, we find that in no instance do we encounter a "pure" bourgeois revo-

---

14 Engels. "Socialism: Utopian and Scientific." pp. 95–151.
15 Marx. *A Contribution to the Critique of Political Economy*. p. 263.

lution.¹⁶ Similarly for the transition period from capitalism to socialism, there is no "pure" socialism.

It is also important to underline what Marx writes in the next sentence in *The Critique of Political Economy*:

> No social order is ever destroyed before all the productive forces for which it is sufficient have been developed, and new superior relations of production never replace older ones before the material conditions for their existence have matured within the framework of the old society.¹⁷

In addition, a positive—socialist—outcome is *not* given, and it is not mechanically determined by the contradiction between the productive forces and the relations of production. The outcome depends on how prepared the proletariat is ideologically, politically, and organizationally. Over the last two hundred years, there have been several severe crises in capitalism, creating multiple national attempts to develop socialism within the surrounding dominant capitalist world-system. However, capitalism has shown an extraordinary ability to roll back these attempts and assimilate its critiques, finding new escape routes from its problems. The capitalist mode of production has developed the productive forces at a speed and extent never seen before in history, creating growth in the earth's population from 0.9 billion in 1800 to 1.65 billion in 1900 to 7.8 billion in 2020. Fueled on fossil energy and constant innovations of new technology, capitalism has developed an enormous variety and volume of products for sale. However, it has also created hunger and misery for the majority of the world's population that cannot afford to buy the goods they need.

> Yet the scale of decent-living poverty is astonishing: 2.4 billion people lack food security; 3.2 billion cannot afford a healthy diet; 3.2 billion do not have a clean cooking stove; 3.6 billion do not have safely managed sanitation facilities; 3.8 to 5 billion people do not have access to essential health services. This is not because there is a deficit of productive capacity (on the contrary, these goods could be provided for everyone on the planet quite easily), but because production remains overwhelmingly organized around capital accumulation and profit maximization rather than around human needs and well-being.¹⁸

---

16 Losurdo, Domenico. *Class Struggle: A Political and Philosophical History*. Palgrave Macmillan, 2016. p. 169.

17 Marx. *A Contribution to the Critique of Political Economy*. p. 263.

18 Hickel, Jason and Sullivan, Dylan. "Capitalism, Global Poverty, and the Case for Democratic Socialism." *Monthly Review*. Vol. 75, no. 3, 2023, p. 104.

The historical development of capitalism is determined by the interaction between the economic laws of the accumulation of capital and class struggles, entailed by the consequences of these laws. Certain conditions must be fulfilled to secure the accumulation of capital. The laws of accumulation can even be expressed in mathematical formulas, such as the rate of profit. But "actually existing capitalism" is not a machine that functions exclusively through laws and rules of accumulation. Nor is it a system of balance and harmony. Quite the opposite: it is characterized by the constant struggle between the different aspects of its contradictions. For capitalism to function, it must constantly seek a specific historical form that allows it to secure profits and continue to accumulate capital. This historical form is determined by class struggle. The economic laws create class struggles that affect these laws by modifying the relations of production, creating new frameworks for a continued development of the productive forces. This happens not only on the national level but also in the world-system of nation-states. The class struggle on a national level shapes the economy and policy of the state, which is part of the world-system. The states interact and compete to secure their development based on their class character. The national class struggle affects the world system, which in turn affects the national class struggle. Thus, in the dialectic between economics and class struggle, we should avoid complete determinism and instead think in terms of conditioning.

The contradiction between the development of the productive forces and the mode of production had to find different historical forms of existence in which the accumulation of capital could continue. In the 19th century, wealth and raw materials were sucked from the colonial periphery into the center to develop industrial capitalism and the imperial mode of living. The development of "unequal exchange" became the historical solution to mediate the contradiction between capitalism's need to expand production on one hand, and the ability of consuming power to absorb the produced commodities on the other hand. To be more specific: The development of colonialism via super-exploitation in the periphery, generated the value transfer needed to raise the wage-level in the center—which was necessary to consume the growing production—and thereby realizing the profit of the sale. This was not a cunning plan by capital. It was the result of the development of colonialism and the struggle of the working class in Europe. In this specific way "history" found a way in which the contradiction in the capitalist mode of production could move ahead and continue in the development of its productive forces. It created a dynamic economic development in the center and a permanent crisis in the periphery. In the last quarter of the 20th century, new forms of imperialist relations had to be developed to maintain the profit rate, introducing massive outsourcing of industrial production to the periphery to take advantage of the low wages.

The dialectical process between the economic laws of capitalism, their political and social consequences, and the related class struggles, drives the development of capitalism—a development that takes winding roads and is characterized by ruptures. During certain periods, the economic and political system appears relatively stable. Even when revolutionary movements try hard to change it, the system keeps its balance. However, the system will always be affected by revolutionary efforts: it does not remain the same afterward. During other periods, the system finds itself in crisis: it is no longer able to keep its balance and thus becomes unstable, at which point revolutionary efforts take on special significance and revolutionaries turn into butterflies whose flapping wings can turn into a storm. The division of the world system into different political entities means that the transformation of capitalism into a new mode of production will require many revolutions and can be subject to reversal, as we have seen. The transitional state will continue to be characterized by class struggle on the national level and by the inter-state conflict between pro-capitalist and pro-socialist states. The transformation from one mode of production to another is a long process. Capitalism first took shape over several hundred years, from the Italian city-states of the fifteenth century to the industrial revolution in England 400 years later. The transformation from capitalism to socialism will be a long process as well. There have been devious roads and dead ends. However, at this point in history, it seems that capitalism is running out of both humans and nature to exploit. There is no spatial fix, as forecasted by Rosa Luxemburg in 1913:

> Once this is reached, Marx's model becomes valid: i.e. further expansion of capital becomes impossible. Capitalism comes to a dead end, it cannot function any more as the historical vehicle for the unfolding of the productive forces, it reaches its objective economic limit.[19]

---

19   Luxemburg, Rosa. *The Accumulation of Capital*. Monthly Review Press, 1972. pp. 145–6.

THE PRINCIPAL CONTRADICTION

If we have a capitalist world-system in the historical sense of Immanuel Wallerstein, and in the economic sense of Samir Amin, and if we consider the world-system as one process, then at any given point in time, this process has a principal contradiction emerging from the multiple contradictions in the capitalist mode of production, driving its development forward.

The principal contradiction affects all national, regional, and local contradictions decisively.[20] Like other contradictions, the principal contradiction changes during the course of history. The interaction between the principal contradiction and other contradictions is not one-sided. Particular national and local contradictions affect the principal contradiction. This feedback affects the struggle between the aspects of the principal contradiction, and can change the direction of its development.

Mao says this about the principal contradiction:

> If in any process there are a number of contradictions, one of them must be the principal contradiction playing the leading and decisive role, while the rest occupy a secondary and subordinate position. Therefore, in studying any complex process in which there are two or more contradictions, we must devote every effort to finding its principal contradiction. Once this principal contradiction is grasped, all problems can be readily solved.[21]

The expression "readily solved" should be taken with a grain of salt, not least when talking about social problems and the revolution in a country the size of China. What Mao means when he says "readily" is that you have a reliable guide for further analysis once you identify the principal contradiction. In other words, the critical problem of defining useful strategies, policies, means of propaganda, and military efforts are solved. Additionally, it is important to find the dominant aspect in the contradiction. As Mao states:

> It is a big mistake to look at the two aspects of any contradiction as though they are equal. Of the two aspects, one is inevitably the principal and the other the secondary aspect, and the former is the aspect, which plays the contradiction's so-called guiding role. In actuality which aspect is principal? It is necessary to observe the situation of the development of a process, and it will

---

20   Lauesen, *The Principal Contradiction*.
21   Zedong, Mao. *On Contradiction*. p. 332.

be determined under definite conditions.[22]

In defining the principal contradiction, we move from the abstract and general to the specific and concrete—to practice. When we act, we do it where we are situated. What else can we do? However, we should act locally from a global perspective and bear in mind the principal contradiction.

A determinate historical situation is characterized by a variegated multiplicity of conflicts; and every conflict involves the presence of a multiplicity of individuals and classes who express different, opposing interests and ideas. To analyze and get one's bearings in such a complex situation, it is necessary to examine not only the internal configuration of each contradiction, but also how they interact and are structured in a concrete totality. Mastering this is a challenge theoretically, as well as politically.[23]

To identify the principal contradiction at a certain point in history, we must consider more than the general, abstract contradictions. Contradictions such as "productive forces vs. relations of production," "proletariat vs. bourgeoisie," and "imperialism vs. anti-imperialism" usually do not cause much controversy among Marxists. Disagreements begin when we move from general to specific contradictions and when we need to identify the principal contradiction at a given time and place, the contradiction with the highest revolutionary potential. Note that Mao speaks of "finding" the principal contradiction in the quote above. This cannot be done by theoretical speculation. Contradictions are concrete phenomena: they reveal themselves in economic developments, in political action, and popular movements.

As I emphasize the global perspective and the principal contradiction, it is important to underline the dialectic. The world-level theory and universal trends consist of all the particularities. It is through the particular and local that we can act. We need to see how the principal contradiction is created and formed by the multitude of particularities and how the principal contradiction determines the outcome of partic-

---

22   Zedong, Mao. "Annotations, Lecture Notes on Dialectical Materialism." In Knight, Nick. *Mao Zedong on Dialectical Materialism: Writings on Philosophy, 1937.* M.E. Sharpe, 1990. p. 88.

23   Losurdo. *Class Struggle.* p. 121.

ular contradictions.

This is not only a theoretical issue. The grand theory of the global perspective without the dialectical understanding of the relation to the particular is of no practical use. It may give you pleasure in "understanding how the world works" and a platform from which to voice how unjust and unequal the world is and how it needs to be changed. However, "grand theory" alone offers no viable path toward an effective praxis. The meaning of seeing things as an interconnected whole lies in the ensuing capacity to act in line with reality thus understood. The purpose of identifying the principal contradiction is to intervene in it. It is the conscious capacity of seeing the world system as a process, and of understanding the direction and the eventual goal of that process. We cannot create contradictions, but we can influence the aspects of existing ones so that the contradictions move in a way that serves our interests. Identifying the principal contradiction tells us where to start.

To sum up: in the historical analysis in Part II, I will examine how the general contradiction—productive forces versus relation of production—manifests itself in the specific revolutionary process on the national level. Moreover, I will examine how these national and regional contradictions interact with the changing principal contradiction on the global level. Historical changes happen in qualitative leaps. The productive forces change constantly, and with them, power relations between classes. Eventually, this leads to tensions that shatter the framework of the old society and make way for a new one.

To then analyze the transition from capitalism to socialism, I have to specify the very concept of socialism.

CHAPTER 2

What is the Difference between Capitalism and Socialism?

A utopian and ideal definition of a socialist (communist) society is a classless, stateless system of direct democracy (participatory democracy) that has overcome the exploitation and alienation of humans and the devastating exploitation of nature. Production is based on the communal ownership of the means of production and is generated by the socialist (communist) mode of production, where you contribute according to ability and consume according to need. Critical arguments against attempts to build socialism have been made from such ideal definitions of how a socialist society ought to look, neglecting the historical, economic, and political circumstances under which these attempts were made.

When we look at the historical attempts to construct socialism in the last century, you may ask: if a planned economy should be better than capitalism, how is it that the living standards in the U.S. or Scandinavia are so much higher than in the old Soviet Union or contemporary China? Liberal economists and politicians often talk about the superior effectiveness of capitalism with reference to how the consumer market looks in capitalist and socialist states. In planned economies, there are queues in front of the stores, the selection of goods are limited and of lower quality than in the capitalist market economy, in which all kinds of goods are always available, etc. Why could the Soviet Union only produce an outdated copy of an old Fiat—the Lada—while customers in the West could choose between huge selections of stylish cars?

When actually existing socialism is compared to actually existing capitalism, you have to take into account that imperialism generated a polarized world system. Capitalism is not only the United States and Germany, but also Bolivia and Kenya. The shopping malls may look overwhelming, but that does not necessarily mean that the system fulfills the needs of the population. Abundance in the market is not always a sign of effectiveness in distribution and wealth. It can also be the result of an imbalance between the size of production and the power of consumption, which is generated by production. The capitalist market economy is an effective producer, but it has always been a problem to distribute the social product in accordance with the needs of the producers. There are all kinds of goods available to the consumer in both Copenhagen and Manila if the need is backed by purchasing power. This is, however, unequally distributed. Overproduction of food and hunger exist side by side within the system.

In comparing the two systems, one must take into consideration that the first attempt to develop actually existing socialism (Russia in 1917) took place in the least developed economy in Europe, and the rest of the Soviet Union was feudal or based on subsistence farming with no industrial development at all. If one wants to compare actually existing socialism and real existing capitalism, it would be fairer to compare the economic development of China with India, or Cuba with Haiti.

However, let us return to the fundamental difference between the capitalist and socialist modes of production. Humans are social beings. To appropriate nature and reproduce, we need to cooperate. In all historical modes of production, there is a certain division of labor inside each community. Some make bread, some make coats, others cut hair, etc. The division of labor implies rules of how to produce and divided production—that is, the exchange and distribution of the social product among the participants—based on class relations. However, it does not follow from these premises that the only way to make decisions on investment, the division of labor, and production should be the individual, or that the distribution of the goods should be determined by market forces, as in capitalism.

The basic problem in human production is the allocation of resources to a different kind of production. The solution to this question is determined by the social relations of production. In a socialist mode of production, the division of labor—and the rules of production and distribution—are the primary inseparable processes set up by a decision-making body tasked with planning the economy. The plan asks: what are the priority of needs? What are our human and natural resources and our technology? The plan then determines who is going to produce, what is necessary to fulfill these needs, and how.

The essence of a planned economy is that decisions on investment, production, and distribution are political, and determined *beforehand* ("upstreams") and not as a result of the capitalist market forces ("downstreams"). This means there exists the possibility for a democracy far more advanced and substantial than the bourgeois parliamentary democracy, in which the core economic decisions are in the hands of a minority, the owners of capital. Liberal political democracy can modify and regulate these private decisions to a certain degree, but the capitalist economy is the framework of society, and its laws set limits on the decisions of liberal democracy. Capital accumulation has to be secured.

The ownership of the means of production can take different collective forms to facilitate worker control and a fair distribution of income. However, collective ownership alone does not cancel the capitalist dynamic. Cooperatives and publicly owned companies within a market economy still function within the logic of capitalism. In an economy dominated by market relations, the producer's collective or privately organized production is inevitably motivated by competition to lower production costs and expand production to capture a bigger share of the market. Those who fail to do so will be threatened by a lower income or bankruptcy.

In an economy with a large-scale division of labor, there are only two types of institutional arrangements. The allocation of productive resources and the distribution of goods can be done either through market mechanisms or by planning. In a market economy, investment decisions are made on the prospect of profits, which is dependent on the realization of sales in the market. A planned economy is defined as an allocation of productive resources according to decisions made by a political institution. This presupposes the social ownership of the means of production.

In a capitalist economy, the relationship between production and consumption is turned upside down. The size of production, and the types of goods, are decided by market forces. Human needs are only valid if they are backed up by purchasing power. It is this private exchange that determines the future division of labor through independent decisions taken at the level of individual producers. Nothing is produced without an expectation of selling it, and anything will be produced if it can be sold. There may be idle hands and underutilized resources on the one hand, and an urgent need for food, clothing, and shelter on the other, and yet there will exist no possibility of these needs ever being met. In capitalism, the purchasing power is not just a matter of the distribution of the product: it is the very condition of its scale, and the nature of production. It is a common experience that you can get the goods you want if you have money. But, you cannot always get money for the goods you have. And so, capitalist crises occur when there is a lack of purchasing power to consume the produced goods.

We have become accustomed to this as the natural way of economics. But to make production dependent on consumption is to turn things upside down, and it has not always been that way. In most social formations before capitalism, the limiting factor for the fulfillment of needs was the ability to produce. Pre-capitalist societies produced what was possible according to the available natural resources, technology, management form, and the size of the workforce. Then production was distributed based on the prevailing social power relations and rules. There may be hunger or unfulfilled needs due to natural conditions, war, primitive technology, or labor shortages. However, it would be absurd to starve or stop the production of products in need because of some rules of consumption. As Hickel and Sullivan observe:

> It is not difficult to meet basic subsistence requirements, and historical data suggests that human communities are normally capable of doing so, even in pre-industrial contexts, with their own labor and with the resources available to them in their environment or through exchange. The main exceptions to this are in cases of natural disaster, or under conditions in which people are cut off from land and commons, or when their labor, resources, and productive capacities are appropriated by a ruling class or an imperial power. The historical data we review shows that it was the process of colonization and capitalist integration that mainly pushed people into extreme poverty and caused social indicators to deteriorate.[1]

---

1   Hickel and Sullivan. *Capitalism, Global Poverty, and the Case for Democratic Socialism*. p. 102.

The colonization of India, Africa, and Latin America, and the destruction of pre-capitalist production systems, caused extensive hunger and the death of millions.

In capitalism, the problem is marketing a saleable product. In socialism, the limiting factor for fulfilling needs is the ability to produce. The most advanced technology and effective governance enhances this ability: to transform human needs via a political process (and planning technologies) into priorities of production and rules for distribution.

In a planned economy, it is possible to decide the quantity and nature of the goods to be produced *beforehand through* an assessment of the capabilities of production and the priorities of the needs in society. The goods are produced according to the demands of society, so to speak. As soon as the goods are produced, they can be distributed by the rules adopted by society. All of this entails an enormous capacity to process information, which has been a historical problem for planned economies. However, with the development of new information and communications technology, this problem has been reduced.[2] The imbalance between the size of production and purchasing power, which haunts capitalism, does not need to exist in a planned economy. A planned economy does not have overproduction crises, as it can create its own market through political measures.

Therefore, the distribution of goods—the market—looks and works very differently in a planned economy as opposed to a capitalist system. The capitalist market is a buyer's market. The supply of goods is overwhelming and there is a variety in the designs of everything from clothing to cars. Huge sums are spent for branding and marketing to promote consumption. However, the "market" in a planned economy is the producer's "market." There is no pressure from advertising to buy more; on the contrary, the less unproductive consumption, the more there is for new productive investment to fulfill urgent needs in the future. In the transition-process towards socialism, it is possible to have a mixture of a planned economy—which decides major strategic investments—and a market economy, which allocates resources to the production of final

---

2   van der Pijl, Kees. "Democracy, Planning, and Big Data, A Socialism for the Twenty-First Century?" *Monthly Review*. Vol. 71, no. 11, 2020. https://monthlyreview.org/archives/2020/volume-71-issue-11-april/

consumer goods.

The planned economic system has the advantage of handling the relationship between investment in the production apparatus and the final consumption of goods in a rational way. The surplus generated by an economy—capitalist or planned—can be used in two ways: final consumption (food, clothes, furniture, consumer electronics, etc.) or investment in a new circle of extended production (development of new technology, etc.). The two parts are inversely proportional. The more that is used in final consumption, the less there is for investment, and vice versa. However, in capitalism, investment in production presupposes the consumption of final goods. Hence the need to treat final consumption and investment in production as directly proportional. The wish to invest in extended production is greatest when the available capital is lowest.

The different ways in which the market operates in a capitalist versus planned economy is also reflected in the labor market. Unemployment, which haunts the capitalist system, is not a problem in planned economies. A planned economy can use all the labor power they can get to fulfill the needs of society.

Conventionally, we think of the transition from capitalism to socialism within a national framework, although both Marx, and later Lenin, were aware that socialism could only be realized as a world system—or at least as a major part of the world. In the last five hundred years, the division of labor has taken an international form, which has polarized the world into rich and poor countries. However, one can very well conceive a socialist planned economy implementing the division of labor and the distribution of products on a planetary scale, one which promotes equality. In fact, it will be necessary for the solution to the planet's ecological and social problems.

On the one hand, two hundred years of industrial capitalism developed the productive forces to a level where there is no technological barrier to the solution of global social problems. Capitalism has paved the way for socialism. On the other hand, the capitalist imperative of growth has created a mode of production that has spawned social problems, and has threatened to destroy the global ecological balance. Marx's emphasis on the importance of the productive forces for the development of a society is very different from the capitalist preoccupation with the need for constant economic growth. In capitalism, the development of the productive forces are a double-edged sword. The development of productive forces make possible increasing emancipation from natural, as well as social, constraints. However, two hundred years ago, before today's climate problems, Marx wrote that capitalism can only develop the productive forces at the expense of the two ultimate sources of all wealth: nature and human beings.

> Capitalist production, therefore, develops technology, and the combining together of various processes into a social whole, only by sapping the original sources of all wealth—the soil and the labourer.[3]

Capitalism is—through its own logic of accumulation—forced to constantly develop technology, increasingly mechanize labor, and apply scientific knowledge to material production in order to force uninterrupted economic growth. By its very nature, it develops the productive forces—not as an end in itself, but as a way to increase profit. Through the development of the productive forces, capitalism in the end turns into a destructive force, blocking future progress.

> In the development of productive forces there comes a stage when productive forces and means of intercourse are brought into being, which, under the existing relationships, only cause mischief and are no longer productive but destructive forces.[4]

This prediction by Marx has taken on its full meaning in an era haunted by the possibility of atomic war, pandemics, pollution of soil and water, and climate crises. Nevertheless, the development of the productive forces under capitalism constitutes a favorable basis for the development of a future socialist mode of production. Assuming that the resources and technology available to humanity today are applied rationally—free from the demand of profit accumulation—the standard of living in the Global South would rise by leaps and bounds.

A social revolution will change the way we produce and consume goods from systems based on privatization to ones based on collectivization. It will not only change our choices and our ends, but will also rationalize and speed up the creation of the means of production themselves. For this, we must improve technology and increase the productivity of

---

3   Marx, Karl. *Capital: Volume I.* marxists.org/archive/marx/works/1867-c1
4   Marx. *The German Ideology.* p. 60.

living labor. Socialist production is not less advanced than capitalist production. *Au contraire*, a socialist mode of production desires to use the most advanced technology possible in order to produce higher quality sustainable goods with less labor power.[5] Robot industries are better than assembly line factories. Windmills and solar energy are better than power plants fueled with fossil energy.

Socialism is not only concerned with eliminating poverty within the national framework, but also creating a more equal world. Within the capitalist mode of production, it is not possible to raise the living standard of billions of poor people in the Global South to the level of the U.S. or Germany. There are simply not enough natural resources. To accommodate their needs, what is required is not only a change in the relations of production and the patterns of consumption, but also a continued development of, and implementation, of the most advanced technology. On this Emmanuel writes:

> Steel, aluminum and copper of which the masses of the center consume today such extravagant quantities, do not serve only to produce automobiles and gadgets. They produce doctors or books as well (It takes a tremendous amount of steel, cement or energy to produce a doctor or to school a village.)
>
> While no one up to now has laid out the model of this "anti-consumption" society, there exists at least one point on which everyone is in agreement. That is the absolute priority of the maximization of available leisure, time being the prerequisite for the quality of life. How then can we rid ourselves of "productivism," since for any given physical consumption, whatever its volume, leisure time is an increasing function of the return on time passed at work?
>
> Naturally, if it is shown that the "consumer society" is in any case a material impossibility on a world scale, the question of choice no longer presents itself for four-fifths of humanity. However, the idea that the remaining one-fifth, which has the privilege of this type of society, would profit from the change is not a statement so obvious that one could excuse oneself from demonstrating.[6]

The socialist mode of production is not only about economic ratio-

---

5   Emmanuel, Arghiri. *Appropriate or Underdeveloped Technology?* John Wiley & Sons, 1982.

6   Emmanuel, Arghiri. *Europe–Asia Colloquium. For Use by the Commission on International Relations. Some Guidelines for the "Problematiqe" of World Economy.* International Economic Relations Department at the Institute of Economics and Social Development Studies. [Manuscript found in Emmanuel's archive, dated October 6, 1976. Green portfolio marked "Imperialism"]. pp. 3–4.

nality and technology, but the means to fulfill needs. The definition of needs and the rules of distribution of social products is of a political nature. With advanced technology and changed consumption patterns, a raise in the quality of life and de-growth is possible.

The State in the Transition from Capitalism to Socialism

When you grow up in a capitalist society in the imperial core, its logic, norms, and values are internalized; it can be difficult to imagine that things can be organized differently. The American philosopher Frederic Jameson stated in 2003, that "someone once said that it is easier to imagine the end of the world than the end of capitalism. We can now revise that and witness the attempt to imagine capitalism by way of imagining the end of the world."[7] However, it is important to keep in mind that capitalism is like all other historical modes of production: it had a beginning and must have an end, and another world is possible.

One major factor of the transition is the role and character of the state. All revolutions with a socialist perspective, from the Paris Commune onwards, have organized a bureaucracy to run the economy and have established some kind of security to maintain the power of the proletariat against internal and external enemies. The form and role of this "bureaucracy" has constituted a problem for all new revolutionary states since.

In the first part of the transition period, from the moment the proletariat takes power to the moment when they reorganize the economy, the yield of the economy will fall. This happened in Russia and China. This was the experience of Cuba in the 1960s, of the Allende government in Chile in 1970, and in Venezuela today. To get through this difficult period, until the planned economy begins to function, the proletariat must organize itself for the direct exercise of political power.

The economic problem is not some supposed inefficiency of nationalized enterprises. The problem is that the capitalists will divest. They will salvage as much as can be salvaged from the economy while dilapidating the rest. This is not only a problem on the national level. The world mar-

---

7   Jameson, Frederic. "Future City." *New Left Review*. No. 21, 2003. https://newleftreview.org/issues/ii21/articles/fredric-jameson-future-city

ket has enormous power in terms of the movement of capital, exchange rates of currency, and determining the price of commodities. President Nixon ordered the CIA to "make the economy scream" in Chile to prevent Allende from building socialism.[8] Often, the pressure from the capitalist world system takes the form of outright economic sanctions and military intervention.

The attempt to defeat neocolonialism by transforming national liberation into economic liberation failed in many socialist-oriented states in the 1960s and 1970s in Asia, Africa, and Latin America. Their weak economies, often skewed by hundred years of colonialism, could not stand the weight of the internal and external pressures of capitalism. Despite the intention to build socialism, their economies slid back into capitalism under pressure from global neoliberalism.

Liberal ideology presents the difference between capitalist and socialist state management as respectively democratic and authoritarian political rule: the "free choice" in a market economy supplements the free choice between political parties in government, while a planned economy generates a bureaucratic authoritarian state. However, this connection is false. In 1970, the socialist Salvador Allende was elected president of Chile and began to nationalize industry and rural estates to transform Chile's economy from capitalism towards socialism. However, after a CIA-supported military coup in 1973, Chile became a testing ground for neoliberal economic ideas. The CIA, with the help of neoliberal economists from Milton Friedman's Chicago School of Economics, provided the economic policy that Chile's junta enacted immediately after seizing power.[9] It is ironic that Friedman, who wrote the book *Capitalism and Freedom*, driving home the argument that only economic liberalism could support political democracy, could so easily disentangle economics from politics, when the economic theories he advocated coincided with a fascist regime.[10] There is no fixed link between the capitalist or socialist mode of production and the political rule of the system.

---

8   Kornbluh, Peter. *The Pinochet File: A Declassified Dossier on Atrocity and Accountability*. New Press, 2004. p. 17.

9   Villaroel, Gilberto. "La Herencia de los 'Chicago boys.'" BBC Mundo, 2006. news.bbc.co.uk/hi/spanish/latin_america/newsid_3192000/3192145.stm

10   Friedman, Milton. *Capitalism and Freedom*. University of Chicago Press, 1962.

The Chinese political historian Zhang Weiwei has challenged Western liberal conceptions of "formal" market-based democracy. According to Zhang, China, while lacking in formal democracy in Western terms, has been successful in the development of a "substantive democracy." Western democracy means the election campaign is based on political marketing paid for by capital and lobby organizations. "Substantive" democracy, in Zhang's terms, means "good governance," relying on both meritocratic selection and elections, so as to generate a political system that draws on the full range of abilities of the wider population, while focusing on satisfying their real developmental needs, in line with popular opinion.[11]

So called "actually existing socialism" covers a variety of attempts to establish transitory economic and political systems within a dominant capitalist world system, using a mixture of planned economy, capitalist investment, and market forces. The former Soviet Union, China, Vietnam, and Cuba are examples of such states. For these states, situated in the periphery or semi-periphery of the world system, opening towards the surrounding capitalist world has been necessary to import technology, and thereby to develop their productive forces. The focus on advancing technological progress does not mean that social relations are irrelevant. The link between technology and social relations is flexible enough to enable the usage of the first to change the second, as Lenin, Mao, Ho Chi Minh, and Fidel Castro thought.[12] They all wanted to use the latest technology and methods developed by capitalism to fulfill social needs within a planned economy.

What has constituted a problem in the past (and certainly still does), both in theory and in practice, is the political form of the state, which corresponds to the period of transition to socialism—that is, between the proletariat seizing state power on the one hand and the substitution of cooperative production for all remaining capitalist forms of production and distribution on the other hand. Socialism is not established by a magic stroke, as when Fidel Castro and Che Guevara drove into Havana in 1959, or when Mao proclaimed the People's Republic of China

---

11   Weiwei, Zhang. In Ownby, David. "Zhang Weiwei on Telling China's Story." *Reading the China Dream*, 2021. https://www.readingthechinadream.com/zhang-weiwei-on-telling-chinas-story.html

12   Emmanuel, Arghiri. *Appropriate or Underdeveloped Technology?* p. 106.

in 1949. Taking state power can happen over a relatively short period, but the transition from capitalism to socialism is a long and complex transformative process. The transformation process is as complicated as the subsequent development of the socialist mode of production, which has to take place within a dominant capitalist world market. What kind of specific state is needed to keep the proletariat in power in relation to both internal national class struggles and the surrounding hostile capitalist world system? How should the economy and political system be organized to fulfill this task? A new revolutionary government must try to answer these kinds of questions.

Following lessons learned during the Paris Commune, Marx and Engels formulated their thesis concerning the role of the state in its transformation towards socialism in the preface of the new 1872 edition of *The Communist Manifesto*: The working class cannot simply lay hold of the ready-made machinery and wield it for its own purposes.[13]

The revolutionary forces have to establish their own, novel form of the state, as the old capitalist state is built to serve the interest of capital. They need to defend this state against counterrevolutionary forces. The proletariat needs to organize itself directly into a state apparatus. It is this exercise of power that constitutes what Marx labeled the "dictatorship of the proletariat."[14] This concept is often misunderstood because of Marx's polemic use of the word "dictatorship." It is actually an argument for democracy, as the rule of the working class, which establishes new institutions with which to dictate the will of the proletarian majority over the bourgeois minority. After the proletariat has established itself as the ruling class, it exercises its power as the class struggle continues both inside the state and between the new state and the surrounding capitalist world system.

The "dictatorship of the proletariat" is distinct from two other dominant perceptions of the state among socialists at the time: the reformist, represented by Ferdinand Lassalle, and the anarchists, represented by

---

13   Marx, Karl and Engels, Friedrich. "Preface to the 1872 Edition of the Communist Manifesto." 1872. https://www.marxists.org/archive/marx/works/1848/communist-manifesto/preface.htm

14   Marx, Karl. "Critique of the Gotha Program IV." 1875. https://www.marxists.org/archive/marx/works/1875/gotha/ch04.htm

Mikhail Bakunin. The reformer wanted to take over the bourgeois state and use its institution to introduce socialism, while the anarchists argued for the abolition of the state entirely. However, what the reformers failed to realize is that the state at hand is an expression of the economic and political logic of capitalism. It cannot be used as a tool for introducing socialism by the class that it exists to oppress.. And what the anarchists failed to realize is that as long as capitalism exists as a major force within the borders of the nation, and in the world-system, the proletariat needs a state to implement its policy, a dictatorship of class interests.

In all class societies, a coercive state ensures the existing order and preserves the social equilibrium. The bourgeois class set up an apparatus occupied by a permanent staff; the creation of its own hierarchy endowed with a degree of bureaucratic autonomy, in the sense that the office becomes its own end, making "efficiency" its ultimate goal. To accomplish this, it had to run the system according to the rules of the capitalist economy. Under the conditions of a dominating market economy, a so-called independent state apparatus cannot help but become an instrument of capitalist dynamics.[15]

This was the problem of the Allende government in Chile in 1970, both in terms of economic policy and state power. The old state machinery—the police and the military—could not serve the interest of the new socialist government, and so they turned against it. It is not enough to have power in the parliament; it takes "the dictatorship of the proletariat" to transform society.

However, this apparently necessary coercive apparatus has the potential to create a new ruling caste of bureaucrats. Within specific, unfavorable national and international relations of forces, the proletarian revolution thus has to face a dilemma: weakness and inefficiency or strength and bureaucracy.

To sum up the tasks of the state in the transition period, it must (a) develop the economic preconditions as well as the forces of production in terms of size, differentiation, and technological level in order to progress toward the socialist mode of production; and (b) to maintain the security of the state during the transition period from attacks from the

---

15   Emmanuel, Arghiri. "The State in the Transitional Period." *New Left Review*. No. 1/113–114, 1979, p. 123.

class enemy from within and by the surrounding capitalist world.

CHAPTER 3

Morals and Politics

Throughout history, humans have committed atrocities against their fellow human beings in pursuit of power and wealth; or for family, clan, class, or (in modern times) nation. However, love, compassion, and solidarity are also part of human history. Humans are biological creatures with certain biological needs and abilities, but humans are not by "nature" evil or good. Humans are social "animals" organized in societies to fulfill their needs and express their abilities. Violence is not inherent in certain trans-historical ideas or cultural values—nor are these related to certain ethnic groups. It is historically specific and related to the material basis of social reproduction.

Violence is endemic to class society. The wars and violent suppression of people in the Third World throughout the 20th century were necessary for capitalist accumulation. Without violence, there cannot be the super-exploitation of labor, which cheapens the costs of production and gives rise to unequal exchanges between the center and periphery in the world system.[1] In addition to being an essential precondition of the accumulation of capital in general, war is itself an industry. The weapons industry produces arms and reaps super-profits. War employs people to kill people. Violence intensely consumes labor at a high rate of exploitation. The productive life of a soldier is short.[2] War was also a method for primitive accumulation, the genesis of capitalism through colonial plunder and slavery, which costs millions of lives. The wars in Iraq have had a

---

1   Kadri, Ali. *China's Path to Development: Against Neoliberalism*. Springer Nature, 2021. p. 137.
2   *Ibid*. p. 138.

similar effect, handing over the nation's oil resources to U.S. companies. The major inter-imperialist wars in the first half of the twentieth century caused millions of deaths. The early quests for socialism were partly a reaction to these atrocities. Since World War II, there have been more than one hundred armed conflicts in the Third World, causing the deaths of more than twenty million people.

Politicians often take a moral stand and reject violence as a method for political means, even if their country's wealth is built upon violence. The global North possesses the vast majority of military hardware. U.S.-centered military alliances account for three-fifths of global military spending, and yet they are now looking to spend even more at an unprecedented rate.

In political practice, there is a dilemma between the means and the ends. What means are just and suitable to obtain the desired ends? The use of violence for political means has always been controversial. But in the historical quest for socialism, the ends are not petty issues: they are the end of exploitation and the suppression of millions, and to stop destruction of the ecological balance of the planet. Does this end justify any means? Alternatively, do the ends never justify the means? Do the wrong means compromise the ends? You will inevitably encounter these dilemmas as a political militant.

Machiavelli's Use of "The Ends Justifying the Means"

The reasoning that the ends justify the means is considered a cynical attitude in common mainstream thinking. It is often used as a critique of what is considered the use of excessive means to obtain a certain goal. The statement that "the ends justify the means" is often ascribed to Niccoló Machiavelli (1469-1527), the Italian philosopher of power and author of *The Prince*, a little book written in the early sixteenth century.[3]

Machiavelli was living in a tumultuous era in which wars were being waged against Italian city-states as France, Spain, and the Holy Roman Empire battled for power. Political and military alliances continually changed, and mercenary army leaders changed sides without warning, causing the rise and fall of many short-lived governments. Machiavelli

---

3   Machiavelli, Niccoló. *The Prince*. Penguin, 1961.

served as a civil servant and diplomat for different rulers of Florence. In 1513, the Medici rulers accused him of conspiracy and had him imprisoned. Despite being subjected to torture, he denied involvement and was released after three weeks. After that experience, Machiavelli retired to his farm estate, where he devoted himself to studying and writing political treatises.

The Prince was written in 1513, but only published after his death in 1532. It is a manual for the art of governing. It includes Machiavelli's justifications for violence as a means to secure power: "a prince wishing to keep his state is very often forced to do evil." His personal experience showed him that politics have always been played with deception and treachery. Machiavelli considered that violence might be necessary for the successful stabilization of power and the introduction of new political institutions.[4] Force may be used to eliminate political rivals, destroy resistant populations, and purge others who will inevitably attempt to replace the ruler.[5] Essentially, the book is a description of how power functions, regardless of ideological and moral considerations. One can read *The Prince* in various ways. To read it as a cynical manual for how to gain and defend power is one option. Machiavelli himself, however, suggests another reading:

> ...it being my intention to write a thing which shall be useful to him who apprehends it, it appears to me more appropriate to follow up the real truth of the matter than the imagination of it...[6]

Machiavelli is considered the first modern empirical political scientist, to draw generalizations from experience and historical facts. He was also one of the Renaissance's first secular thinkers. He wrote about separating religion (the dominant form of morality at the time) and politics. He refused to analyze political realities based on religious dogma. He was, in contrast to many of his contemporaries, a realist. He could not avoid noticing how far removed the theological idealizations were from the real and harsh world of politics.

Not all interpretations of Machiavelli are cynical. Antonio Francesco Gramsci (1891– 1937), founding member and former leader of the

---

4   *Ibid.* Ch. 18.
5   *Ibid.* Ch. 3; 5; 8.
6   *Ibid.* Ch. 15.

Communist Party of Italy, until he was imprisoned by Benito Mussolini's Fascist regime, argued that Machiavelli's audience was not the ruling class, but rather the common people, because rulers already knew of these methods by way of their education. Gramsci was inspired by Machiavelli's writings on morals and how they related to state-building and revolution. Popular notions of morality and ethics could be manipulated as part of establishing a hegemony to control society.[7] It is also said that Stalin carefully read *The Prince* and annotated his own copy.[8] However, *The Prince* is far from the first text to discuss the relationship between ends and means. In the tragedy *Electra*, the Greek dramatist Sophocles asked in 400 BC whether "the end excuses any evil," while, in 10 BC, the Roman poet Ovid concluded in his lyrical collection *Heroides* that "the result justifies the deed." The dilemma is as old as humanity.

Let us—for a moment, in line with Machiavelli—consider political reality rather than noble rhetoric. Towards the end of the Second World War, the U.S. government was ready to use excessive power to achieve a quick end to the war. The Air Force dropped two nuclear weapons over the Japanese cities of Hiroshima and Nagasaki on August 6 and 9, 1945, killing 226,000 people, mostly civilians. The minutes of the "target committee" who selected these means were declassified years ago, and it was revealed that the committee settled on two objectives:

> It was agreed that psychological factors in the target selection were of great importance. Two aspects of this are (1) obtaining the greatest psychological effect against Japan and (2) making the initial use sufficiently spectacular for the importance of the weapon to be internationally recognized when publicity on it is released.[9]

A more recent example of balancing means and ends in U.S. policy is from the war in Iraq. On December 5, 1996, shortly after being appointed U.S. Secretary of State, Madeleine Albright was interviewed by Lesley Stahl for the TV program "60 Minutes":

> Lesley Stahl: "We have heard that a half million children have died. I mean,

---

7   Landy, Marcia. "Culture and Politics in the Work of Antonio Gramsci." In Gramsci, Antonio. *Intellectuals, Culture, and the Party*. Routledge, 2002.

8   Service, Robert. *Stalin: A Biography*. Macmillan, 2004. p. 10.

9   Wellerstein, Alex. "A 'purely military' target? Truman's changing language about Hiroshima." *Restricted Data*. http://blog.nuclearsecrecy.com/2018/01/19/purely-military-target/

that's more children than died in Hiroshima. And—and you know, is the price worth it?" Madeleine Albright: "I think this is a very hard choice, but the price—we think the price is worth it."[10]

Apparently, when it came to the war in Iraq, the end, to get rid of Saddam Hussein, justified a high price in terms of Iraqi civilians' lives.

If the motto of the ends justifying the means implies that you can use any means you want (without any consideration for the consequences for others) in order to achieve any end you have decided to pursue, it means that you have lost your moral compass. The same goes for the motto that the ends *never* justify the means. After all, there is a third option, which—in fact—is much more realistic than the other two: not *all* ends justify *all* means, but, depending on the circumstances, *some* ends justify *some* means. It is a position, of course, that implies challenges. One has to consider and balance three factors: ends, means, and circumstances. It is not always easy to draw the right conclusions.

I do not claim that Albright would argue that all means are justified once you have decided to pursue a certain goal—although half-a-million dead children, 700,000 casualties, and four million displaced Iraqis are evidently justifiable to her. With stakes like these, political actors have to be very clear about both their ends and their means. Morality plays an important role in this discussion, but a reference to moral principles alone is not enough. In the eighteenth century, Immanuel Kant argued that the ends alone can never justify the means, and that means need to be justifiable in and of themselves. This is a reminder that the means we employ need to be carefully examined. But Kant's argument does not rid us of the responsibility to go through a political discussion that clearly lays out the ends and means and how to balance them. For example, the threat of the use of nuclear weapons, and the climate crises, make the balancing of means and ends an existential question in the endgame of capitalism.

Violence as a Political Means

The role of the state is to defend the existing order, in the last instance by the use of violence. The state claims a monopoly on the use of violence,

---

10   *60 Minutes*, May 12, 1996.

both internally and internationally. States build an enormous capacity to utilize this monopoly of violence. This shows no signs of abating: the "peace dividend" promised after the collapse of the Soviet Union never came. In the past decade military spending has boomed.

The state reserves "legitimate violence" for itself, so non-state actors' use of violence is usually deemed criminal through charges of terrorism. But other states might think differently and label such a group freedom fighters. However, most people find non-state actors' violence acceptable only if the end is worthy enough, and the situation urgent. For example, few people would—politically or morally—question the use of violence in the context of the resistance against the Nazis in occupied Europe. Even if the resistance movement was labeled "terrorist" by the state (like in Denmark by the Danish government up until October 1943), the overall opinion remains that under the given circumstances, the use of violence was justified. The right to resist occupation has even been enshrined in international law. Resolution 2625 of the United Nations 1970 General Assembly explicitly endorsed a right to resist "subjection of peoples to alien subjugation, domination and exploitation."[11] However, in practice this has not made much difference. Time will tell if these rights will be equally applied to, for instance, the Palestinian liberation struggle.

Whether they were legitimated or not, anti-colonial and anti-imperialist struggles seem to always turn violent. This is no surprise: the violence of European colonialism in the 19th century was extreme. The colonial attitude was summarized by the former British Prime Minister Lord Salisbury in his 1898 speech at Albert Hall:

> You may roughly divide the nations of the world as the living and the dying [...] the living nations will gradually encroach on the territory of the dying..."[12]

The imperialism of the twentieth century has been equally brutal. The U.S. killed one million people during the war in Vietnam. France's attempt to save the French settler regime in Algeria also cost one million lives. It was against the background of the Algerian struggle that Frantz Fanon,

---

11 Viñuales, Jorge. *The UN Friendly Relations Declaration at 50: An Assessment of the Fundamental Principles of International Law*. Cambridge University Press, 2020.

12 Gascoyne-Cecil, Robert Arthur Talbot. In Roberts, Andrew. "Salisbury, the Empire Builder who Never Was." *History Today*. Vol. 49, no. 10. https://www.historytoday.com/archive/salisbury-empire-builder-who-never-was

who was active in the liberation movement, concluded in his book *Wretched of the Earth*, that the people of the Third World—held down by violence, exploitation, and oppression—must rise and gain self-consciousness by violently resisting colonialism under the leadership of liberation movements. The liberation struggles in the Third World were an act of self-defense. In his preface to *Wretched of the Earth*, Jean-Paul Sartre wrote:

> Try to understand this at any rate: if violence began this very evening and if exploitation and oppression had never existed on the earth, perhaps the slogans of nonviolence might end the quarrel. But if the whole regime, even your nonviolent ideas, are conditioned by a thousand-year-old oppression, your passivity serves only to place you in the ranks of the oppressors.[13]

Many liberation movements had originally been founded as legal political movements. South Africa's African National Congress (ANC) is one example. It advocated a nonviolent struggle until the late 1950s. Only after the Sharpeville massacre in 1960,[14] and the subsequent criminalization of the ANC, did the organization turn to armed struggle. The ANC was considered a terrorist organization right up until the fall of the apartheid regime. It was not until 2008 that Nelson Mandela was removed from terrorist watchlists and celebrated as a great statesman.

The Use of Violence in the Struggle for Socialism

How do we judge the use of violence in the quest for socialism? Besides evaluating social and economic facts, we must perceive political-moral choices. The struggle against exploitation and oppression has often taken a violent turn and caused immense human suffering. As Mao stated after the Shanghai Kuomintang massacre of communists in 1927, where thousands of people were killed:

> A revolution is not a dinner party, or writing an essay, or painting a picture, or doing embroidery; it cannot be so refined, so leisurely and gentle, so temperate, kind, courteous, restrained and magnanimous. A revolution is an in-

---

13   Jean-Paul, Satre. *"Preface to Frantz Fanon's 'Wretched of the Earth.'"* 1961. https://www.marxists.org/reference/archive/sartre/1961/preface.htm

14   On March 21, 1960, sixty-nine people were killed when the South African police opened fire during a protest outside the police station of the township of Sharpeville, south of Johannesburg.

surrection, an act of violence by which one class overthrows another.[15]

The efforts to defend the revolution and build socialism in poor countries, surrounded by a hostile capitalist world system, have also resulted in forms of violence and suffering—conditions that are in stark contrast with socialist ideals. To evaluate such cases often seems cynical, but these dilemmas cannot be avoided if one is part of the struggle, and not merely an observer.

The Hungarian philosopher György Lukács (1885–1971), originally a neo-Kantian, was drawn towards communism by the Russian Revolution. The change is evident between his two essays, "Bolshevism as an Ethical Problem" from 1918, in which he rejected Bolshevism on ethical grounds, as a part of "the endless, senseless chain of struggle"[16] and "Tactics and Ethics" (1919), in which he publicly declared his commitment to the revolutionary cause after joining the Hungarian Communist Party in December 1918.[17] In "Tactics and Ethics" Lukács transcended his previous neo-Kantian position, and commitment to nonviolence, and accepted the need for the moral "sacrifice" of the use of violence in revolutionary action.[18]

> The individual's conscience and sense of responsibility are confronted with the postulate that he must act as if on his action or inaction depended on the changing of the world's destiny.[19]

Lukács reintroduced a classic dilemma formulated by Sophocles in the tragedy *Antigone* (441 BC).[20] The theme in *Antigone* is the right of the individual to reject society's infringement on her freedom to perform a personal obligation. Antigone upholds the idea that state law is not absolute and that it can be broken in civil disobedience in extreme cases,

---

15   Zedong, Mao. "Report on an Investigation of the Peasant Movement in Hunan." *Selected Works: Vol. I.* p. 28.

16   Lukács, Georg. "Bolshevism as an Ethical Problem." Kadarkay, Arpad. *The Lukács Reader*. Wiley–Blackwell, 1995. pp. 216–21.

17   Lukács, Georg. *Tactics and Ethics*. New Left Books, 1972; Foster, John Bellamy. "Lukács and the Tragedy of Revolution: Reflections on 'Tactics and Ethics.'" *Monthly Review*. Vol. 73, no. 9, 2022.

18   Lukács. *Tactics and Ethics*. p. 10.

19   *Ibid*. p. 8.

20   Sophocles. *The Three Theban Plays: Antigone, Oedipus the King, Oedipus at Colonus*. Trans. Fagles, Robert. Penguin, 1986.

such as one's obligations toward the Gods. To this Lukács adds that, in the case of the revolutionary, if the "soul" is to be saved, the "soul" must be sacrificed. The revolutionary is forced to become a "realpolitiker" and to violate the absolute commandment "Thou shalt not kill," and thus maintains no obligations to any institution, state or religion.[21]

Lukács ends his essay "Tactics and Ethics" by referring to Friedrich Hebbel's interpretation of the myth of Judith, from the Old Testament.[22] Judith beheaded the brutal general Holofernes who had placed a siege on the Jewish city of Bethulia. Hebbel's play, entitled *Judith*, written in 1840, focuses on the dilemma between the sin of killing and the struggle to save the freedom of her city.

A short while after he wrote "Tactics and Ethics," Lukács was appointed People's Commissar of Education and Culture during the Hungarian Soviet Republic in 1919. As such, he discussed the ethical dilemma of the revolution. As a fellow communist, József Lengyel indicated in his memoirs, it was determined in the discussions that:

> ...we communists should take the sins of the world upon ourselves, so that we may be capable of saving the world...Just as God could order Judith to kill Holophernes—that is, to commit a sin—so may he order the communists to destroy the bourgeoisie, both metaphorically and physically.[23]

For Lukács, ethics relate to the individual, but are mediated by class, giving rise to a historically generated totality.[24]

Similar sentiments were captured by an acquaintance of mine, the late Patrick Mac Manus, an Irish-Danish political activist, who wrote an article called "Angels no longer exist" as a response to the Danish left-wing party *Enhedslisten's* (Unity List) critique of the use of violence by the Popular Front for the Liberation of Palestine (PFLP) and the Revolutionary Armed Forces of Colombia (FARC).

> A struggle for liberation or resistance stems in itself from profound violations of human rights, and in many cases will invariably lead to a continued

---

21 Lukács. *Tactics and Ethics*, p. 10.

22 Hebbel, Friedrich. *Judith: A Tragedy in Five Acts*. Trans. Van Doren, Carl. R.G. Badger, 1914.

23 López, Daniel Andrés. *Lukács: Praxis and the Absolute*. Haymarket, 2019. p. 5.

24 Lukács. *Tactics and Ethics*. p. 8.

violation of these rights. War is in itself a violation of the most fundamental human right, the right to life. That's how it is in the real world. And in all its imperfection, that is the world that exists...Any resistance must seek to maintain ethical standards of its own conduct, regardless of state terror, regardless of the bitterness that every civil war brings with it. Every legitimate resistance is animated by love for the country and for the population for which it is fought. Terror is destructive, it is nihilistic. Liberation struggle is, also regardless of its pain, fundamentally creative...While Enhedslisten may be waiting for the true liberation movement, a movement of angels with arms adorned with nacre, we must point to the world and say: here it is, here are the young women and men fighting in the world, here is the pain and suffering, here are the mistakes that belong to an imperfect world, here is the world, and here it must be changed.[25]

From my own praxis of committing robbery to finance revolutionary activities, and coming from a well-behaved middle-class background, I can, on my small scale, relate to the problems of "sinning" for a greater purpose.[26] We witnessed the liberation struggle in the Third World during the 1960s on the one hand and lived privileged lives in a Scandinavian country on the other. We concluded that we had to act. We felt that there existed an incredible injustice in the world, and we wanted to contribute to a profound change. We also felt that we were in a position that allowed us to act and that it would have been inexcusable if we did not. If you want to act politically, you cannot escape such reflections. In the eyes of the Danish state and most people, we were criminals, pure and simple. From our perspective, transferring value from the rich countries to the poor, particularly if they were received by liberation movements, was justified.

This is not a free pass. The choice to use violence as a means of action should never be taken lightly. However, when you have seen and understood exploitation and oppression, you cannot turn a blind eye. Doing nothing becomes as much of a political act as resistance. You cannot claim to be an innocent bystander, because you know what is going on.

The quest for a better and more just world does not begin with a cost-benefit or philosophical analysis. It begins with a simple statement: "Enough!" Reflections about what you can achieve, and at what price,

---

25 Mac Manus, Patrick. "Engle Findes Ikke Mere: Åbent Brev til Enhedslisten." *Kommunistisk Politik*. No. 6, 2006. p. 4.

26 See Kuhn, Gabriel. *Turning Money into Revolution*. Kerrsplebedeb, 2014.

come later. Bear these thoughts on means and ends when you read the historical evaluation in Part II, which, taken in isolation, can seem rather cynical.

PART II
THE HISTORY OF REVOLUTIONS

CHAPTER 4

THE COMMUNIST SPECTER OF 1848

In the first decades of the 19th century—an era marked by the English monopoly on industrial capitalism—the principal contradiction was between the enormous growth of production and the corresponding lack of consumption power, leading to recurring overproduction/under-consumption crises.

In November 1847, Marx and Engels were given the task to write the program of The Communist League (at the time a secret organization): *The Communist Manifesto*. At the time when *The Communist Manifesto* was published in 1848, Marx and Engels believed that capitalism would be a rather short episode in history, to be swiftly replaced by some kind of socialism in the advanced countries of Europe, as Engels wrote in 1847:

> Wherever we look, the bourgeoisie are making stupendous progress...They intend to shape the whole world according to their standard; and, on a considerable portion of the earth's surface, they will succeed...They are so short-sighted as to fancy that through their triumph the world will assume its final configuration. Yet nothing is more clear than that they are everywhere preparing the way for us, for the democrats and the Communists; than that they will at most win a few years of troubled enjoyment, only to be then immediately overthrown. Behind them stands everywhere the proletariat...So just fight bravely on, most gracious masters of capital!...You have to clear the vestiges of the Middle Ages and of absolute monarchy out of our path; you have to annihilate patriarchalism; you have to carry out centralisation; you have to convert the more or less propertyless classes into genuine proletarians, into recruits for us; by your factories and your commercial relationships you must create for us the basis of the material means which the proletariat needs for the attainment of freedom. In recompense whereof you shall be allowed to rule for a short time...but do not forget that "The hangman stands

at the door!" (Heinrich Heine in *Ritter Olaf*).[1]

The *Manifesto* marked a turning point in the history of socialism because it pointed away from utopian idealism and towards an analytical framework from which the struggle for socialism could take place. In bitter polemics, debates, and organizational battles, Marx and Engels struggled to shift the socialist movement to a materialist perspective of class struggle.

In the same year *The Communist Manifesto* was published, a wave of social unrest swept over Europe. The causes of the uprisings were a mess of actors and ideas. There were democratic aspirations of middle-class liberals who wanted to get rid of various monarchs' reactionary regimes and get a share of the political power. Nationalism was another component of the revolutionary hot pot. Today's Germany and Italy were fragmented into petty states, and there was a demand for more unified democratic states. However, most prominently, the late 1840s were characterized by an economic slump, creating massive unemployment and social misery in the overcrowded new industrial cities of Europe. On top of this, bad harvests and high food prices created what was called "the hungry forties."

The first of the revolts of 1848 was a bourgeois nationalist uprising in Sicily in January; however, the revolt in Paris soon overshadowed it. The bourgeoisie had not forgotten the French Revolution of 1789-92, which saw the royal family guillotined and noble privileges abolished. They thought the revolution had gone too far and feared their heads were the next to go. Socialist thinkers like Gracchus Babeuf declared that the problem was not just feudal property but private property in general. Conditions in Europe had long been building up for such an outburst. In France, the liberal politician Alexis de Tocqueville, speaking in the Chamber of Deputies to his colleagues just before the outbreak of the 1848 revolutions in Europe, said that:

> Do you not hear them repeating unceasingly that all that is above them is incapable and unworthy of governing them; that the present distribution of goods throughout the world is unjust; that property rests on a foundation, which is not an equitable foundation? And do you not realize that when such opinions take root, when they spread in an almost universal manner, when they sink deeply into the masses, they are bound to bring with them soon-

---

1   Engels, Friedrich. *The Movements of 1847*. Marx, Karl and Engels, Friedrich. *Collected Works*. Vol. 6. Progress Publishers, 1978. p. 529.

er or later, I know not when nor how, a most formidable revolution? This, gentlemen, is my profound conviction: I believe that we are at this moment sleeping on a volcano.[2]

The insurrection in France began on February 22, 1848, when a demonstration outside the Ministry of Foreign Affairs in Paris was fired upon, killing 52 protestors. After that, street fighting erupted all over the city. The National Guard was called out to restore order, but they refused to fire upon the citizens. King Louis Phillipe's fate was sealed, and he fled the country. Tocqueville describes the situation in Paris on February 25:

> Although the working classes had often played the leading part in the events of the First Revolution, they had never been the sole leaders and masters of the State, either de facto or de jure; it is doubtful whether the Convention contained a single man of the people; it was composed of bourgeois and men of letters...The Revolution of February, on the contrary, seemed to be made entirely outside the bourgeoisie and against it...Throughout this day, I did not see in Paris a single one of the former agents of the public authority. The people alone bore arms, guarded the public buildings, watched, gave orders, punished; it was an extraordinary and terrible thing to see in the sole hands of those who possessed nothing all this immense town, so full of riches...
>
> I found in the capital a hundred-thousand-armed workmen formed into regiments, out of work, dying of hunger, but with their minds crammed with vain theories and visionary hopes. I saw society cut into two: those who possessed nothing, united in a common greed; those who possessed something, united in a common terror. There were no bonds, no sympathy between these two great sections; everywhere the idea of an inevitable and immediate struggle seemed at hand.[3]

Out of the 300,000 proletarians living in Paris at the time, more than 10,000 participated actively in the revolt. The monarchy was gone, but it was not clear what would replace it. Paris's cafés and public squares buzzed with political excitement. Revolutionaries from all over the continent poured into Paris. Marx, who was expelled from Brussels, arrived in Paris in early March at the invitation of the revolutionary government. However, conservative forces reorganized and managed to form a new

---

2   de Tocqueville, Alexis. *The Recollections of Alexis de Tocqueville*. Trans. de Mattos, Alexander Teixeira. MacMillan, 1896. https://oll.libertyfund.org/title/de-mattos-the-recollections-of-alexis-de-tocqueville-1896. p. 14. Tocqueville (1805–1859) was a Member of the Chamber of Deputies and a supporter of the "Party of Order" against the socialists.

3   *Ibid.* pp. 92-132.

government in April. In an effort to discipline the rebellious working class in Paris, they conscripted all workers between the age of 18 and 25 to the army; others would be sent to the province to clear land for the peasants. It provoked a new outburst of anger in Paris in June. For three days, the proletariat fought against the forces of the French regular army. Rapidly, over 1,000 barricades were built to defend working-class neighborhoods. Artillery hammered at the barricades. Parts of the city were laid in ruins. The disorganized insurgent army was defeated piecemeal. In the end, thousands of soldiers outgunned the more or less spontaneous uprising, with its barricades and primitive weapons. The June uprising was drowned in blood. After killing tens of thousands, thousands more were sentenced to forced labor or deported to the colonies.

Revolutionary events happened across Europe, in Rome, Milan, Munich, Brussels, Vienna, Berlin, Budapest, and Stockholm. Mostly students and the middle classes participated in revolts in these cities, as the working class was smaller than in Paris. Besides social questions, which were predominant in the Paris uprising, demands were made to put an end to monarchy, to establish republics, expand suffrage, and implement freedom of speech.

From Paris, in April 1848, Marx and Engels issued a statement on behalf of the Communist League. They demanded that Germany be proclaimed a republic and that royal and feudal estates, together with the mining industry and transport sector, were to be nationalized. They also demanded the establishment of publicly owned workshops, and that the state should provide education for all children. In June, Marx moved from Paris to Cologne and founded the *Neue Rheinische Zeitung (New Rhenish Newspaper)*. Its support for revolution caused the Prussian regime to deport Marx from Germany. He returned to Paris in May 1849, but the political climate had changed, and he was denied permission to stay in the capital. Forced into a difficult situation, Marx decided to leave France for England. Engels took part in the armed struggle in the southwestern part of Germany, but he was also forced to return to England via Italy.

By the end of 1849, it was clear that reaction had triumphed throughout Europe. The revolutions of 1848 never really had a chance. Despite the anger and revolutionary spirit, the working class was too disorganized and did not have the necessary strength in terms of military force and strategy to counter the regular army of the state. The bourgeoisie was of the opinion that the democratic reforms would be a threat to the order of the existing system, so the uprisings had to be crushed—and they were. In the following decades, the forces of reaction were in firm control throughout most of Europe, from France to Sweden.

Despite the meager result of the 1848 uprisings, the events were important for the development of Marx and Engels' theory of social transformation. In the article "Address of the Central Committee to the Communist League," written in 1850, they concluded that the liberal wing of the bourgeoisie betrayed the interests of the working class and popular masses:

> We told you already in 1848, brothers, that the German liberal bourgeoisie would soon come to power and would immediately turn its newly won power against the workers. You have seen how this forecast came true. It was indeed the bourgeoisie which took possession of the state authority in the wake of the March movement of 1848 and used this power to drive the workers, its allies in the struggle, back into their former oppressed position.[4]

The mass movements of 1848 were largely proletarian. However, they relied on liberal politicians to transmit their demands via the parliament to the state. The liberal parliamentary projection of the political movement attests to its political incapacity to rule the state. Hence the recurrent theme of the politicians in power betraying the political movement. The crucial question was the power of the state. The lesson for future struggles was that the bourgeoisie and the middle classes could not be trusted in the struggle, the proletariat had to take the lead themselves. As Marx summed up in the Address:

> ...they themselves must contribute most to their final victory, by informing themselves of their own class interests, by taking up their independent political position as soon as possible, by not allowing themselves to be misled by the hypocritical phrases of the democratic petty bourgeoisie into doubting for one minute the necessity of an independently organized party of the proletariat. Their battle-cry must be: The Permanent Revolution.[5]

---

4   Marx, Karl and Engels, Friedrich. *Address of the Central Committee to the Communist League*. 1850. https://www.marxists.org/archive/marx/works/1847/communist-league/1850-ad1.htm

5   *Ibid.*

Another lesson learned was that the working class must gain and maintain its own arms to be able to match the armed forces of the bourgeois state:

> To be able forcefully and threateningly to oppose this party, whose betrayal of the workers will begin with the very first hour of victory... The workers must try to organize themselves independently as a proletarian guard... Under no pretext should arms and ammunition be surrendered; any attempt to disarm the workers must be frustrated, by force if necessary.[6]

The lessons from the Paris rebellion of June 1848 was of great importance for the strategy for future struggles for socialism:

> Thus only the June defeat has created all the conditions under which France can seize the initiative of the European revolution. Only after being dipped in the blood of the June insurgents did the tricolor become the flag of the European revolution—the red flag! And we exclaim: The revolution is dead! Long live the revolution![7]

Major historical crises were characterized by the conjunction of multiple, contradictory class struggles. Rather than presenting themselves in a direct economic guise, the class struggle assumed varied political forms: social struggles, popular revolts, national insurrections—all repressed using force. There was a need in theory and practice to put in order the different forms of class struggle—that is, to identify the principal contradiction—to develop a strategy with which victory would be achieved, a capacity that the movements did not have at the time. The results of the uprisings of 1848-9 were primarily bourgeois reforms: getting rid of remaining feudal institutions and establishing parliamentary rule. Modern state administration was to be the framework for renewed development of the productive forces after the capitalist crises in the mid-nineteenth century. But it was also the first step for the anti-capitalist forces in terms of organizing and developing strategies for the long transition from capitalism toward socialism.

---

6 *Ibid.*

7 Marx, Karl. "The Class Struggles in France, 1848 to 1850." Marx, Karl and Engels, Friedrich. *Selected Works*. Vol. 1. Progress Publishers, 1969. https://www.marxists.org/archive/marx/works/subject/hist-mat/class-sf/ch01.htm

The Foundation of the International

After the 1848 uprising, Marx became a refugee in London, his base for the rest of his life. The Communist League had been dissolved in 1852 after the arrest of the leadership of the German section. As the revolutionary spirit of 1848 petered out in Europe, Marx shifted his perspective from the immediate social revolution to the building of an international movement of workers aimed at overthrowing the capitalist system. In the 1850s, the capitalist mode of production only covered a small part of the planet: England, the Netherlands, Belgium, the northern parts of France, and the Westphalian part of Germany. One would think that capitalism then still had a vast potential for expansion. This was foreseen by Marx, who in 1858 wrote in a letter to Engels:

> The proper task of bourgeois society is the creation of the world market, at least in outline, and of production based on that market. Since the world is round, the colonisation of California and Australia and the opening up of China and Japan would seem to have completed this process. For us, however, the difficult question is this: on the [European] Continent revolution is imminent and will, moreover, instantly assume a socialist character. Will it not necessarily be crushed in this little corner of the earth, since the movement of bourgeois society is still in the ascendant over a far greater terrain?[8]

It was precisely this colonial expansion, both in terms of economics and migration of European settlers to "the New World," that eased the pressure on the social kettle in Europe. Raw materials for industrial production—sugar, tea, coffee and food products—became cheaper, new markets opened, and the industrial output of cotton material and iron doubled in the 1850s. Migration reduced unemployment and wages grew rapidly.

The attempts to construct socialism in Europe failed primarily because capitalism still had options for growth, both in terms of terrain and in terms of developing productive forces. The inclusion of the non-European world into a center-periphery structure postponed the world revolution.

Nevertheless, Marx and Engels predicted that social revolution would occur within a few decades in Europe. They ruled out Britain to

---

8   Marx, Karl. "Letter to Engels, 8 October 1858." Marx, Karl and Engels, Friedrich. *Collected Works*. Vol. 40. Progress Publishers, 1987. p. 347.

be the first, even though it was the most advanced capitalist country and therefore ripe for a transition to socialism. Tributes from Ireland and overseas colonies to the British economy smoothed out the political contradictions in the country. Engels wrote in 1858:

> [T]he English proletariat is actually becoming more and more bourgeois, so that this most bourgeois of all nations is apparently aiming ultimately at the possession of a bourgeois aristocracy and a bourgeois proletariat alongside the bourgeoisie. For a nation which exploits the whole world this is of course to a certain extent justifiable.[9]

After a short break in 1857, the economic boom continued in the 1860s and 1870s. In England, liberal trade union laws were passed in 1867, and in the following years, revolutionary politics diffused into a liberal scramble for the proletarian vote. However, on the European continent, particularly in France, the revolutionary socialist movement advanced.

The recognition that capitalism was an expanding international system led to the argument that the working class had to organize internationally as well. On the 28th of September 1864, Marx finally saw his idea of The International Working Men's Association (The First International) realized, an organization he proposes in *The Communist Manifesto*.

The First International had its historical roots in the general strike of London workers in 1859 and their radical trade union. Marx attended a mass meeting of The London Trades Council in March 1863, in which the members proclaimed their support for the war against slavery and their opposition to British intervention on the side of the Confederacy in the American Civil War. Another incident that played a role in the founding of the International was the efforts of European workers to support Italian and Polish workers' liberation struggles. The final push, which led to the establishment of the International, was an effort to counter the threat from leading capitalists to bring workers from France, Belgium, and Germany to act as strikebreakers in their struggle against British trade unionism.[10]

---

9   Engels, Friedrich. "Letter to Marx, October 7th, 1858." Marx, Karl and Engels, Friedrich. *Selected Correspondence*. Progress Publishers, 1965. p. 110; Cope, Zak and Lauesen, Torkil. *Marx & Engels: On Colonies, Industrial Monopoly, and the Working Class Movement*. Kersplebebedeb, 2016. pp. 5–52.

10   Collins, Henry and Abramsky, Chimen. *Karl Marx and the British Labour*

Marx was one of the German delegates at the founding meeting and was elected to write the inaugural address. In the text, he linked economic and political struggles, and made internationalism an essential part of the struggle. Marx was also elected to the General Council and became a leading figure in the organization. He drafted all its main resolutions and prepared all its congress reports. Yet, the maintenance of unity was difficult at times. Marx's clear anti-capitalism clashed with a majority reformist opinion. Marx managed to reconcile the seemingly irreconcilable, and formulated a non-exclusionary, yet firmly class-based, political program that changed the initial moderate political strategy of the organization into a coherent anti-capitalist platform.

The majority of the French and German Social Democrats were initially against the strike as a weapon of struggle. However, from late 1866 onward, strikes intensified in many European countries, and their positive results convinced all the tendencies in the International that strikes were a fundamental weapon of labor struggle.

It was also a dominant trend in the early years of the International that workers should only fight for socioeconomic improvements through trade union struggle and not to organize for political power. Marx tried to argue for political struggle; however, it was the experience of the Paris Commune that convinced the International, and the labor movement more generally, that they had to establish proper political organizations to fight capitalism. The International also created awareness among workers that the emancipation of labor could not be won in a single country, but was an international objective.

From the beginning, the International was persecuted by nervous governments on the European continent. At the time of the Basel Congress of the International in 1869, it had around fifty thousand affiliated trade union members. The International was successful in increasing the efficiency of strikes, with workers across Europe helping each other financially in times of action. However, the organization was soon wracked by political differences. At the Brussels Congress in 1868, there were disputes between Marxists and Proudhonists, who rejected state ownership of the means of production in favor of production co-operatives. The Basel Congress in 1869 was characterized by harsh debates between

---

Movement: Years of the First International. St. Martin's Press, 1965.

followers of the anarchist Bakunin and Marx.

Adding to this fracturing of the working class, the Italian and German unification, and the strengthening of the nation-state in general throughout Europe, caused nationalism to grow within the labor movement, reflected in labor's support of each European nation's colonialism. The proletariat in the colonies were not at all represented in the First International. The repression of the organization following the defeat of the Paris Commune in 1871 was yet another blow. All these factors weakened the First International more and more until it was finally dissolved in 1876.

CHAPTER 5

THE FRANCO–PRUSSIAN WAR AND THE PARIS COMMUNE

The outbreak of the Franco-Prussian War in 1870 opened the stage for the Paris Commune. France and Germany had long competed to be the dominant power in continental Europe. In a dispute on the succession of the Spanish throne, Otto von Bismarck maneuvered an overconfident Napoleon III into a declaration of war in July 1870 and then whipped up German nationalist fervor against the French, even managing to get the Lasallian faction of the German socialist movement to support the war effort.

The outbreak of the Franco-Prussian War in 1870 caused problems for the International. Marx wrote a statement on behalf of the International in which he called for class solidarity with the workers of both France and Prussia against the "fratricidal feud" concocted by the ruling classes.[1] At a meeting of the International in Chemnitz, Germany, delegates representing 50,000 Saxon workmen unanimously adopted a resolution to this effect:

> We declare the present war to be exclusively dynastic... We are happy to grasp the fraternal hand stretched out to us by the workmen of France... Mindful of the watchword of the International Working Men's Association: Proletarians of all countries, unite, we shall never forget that the workmen of all countries are our friends and the despots of all countries our enemies.[2]

---

 1 International Working Men's Association. "The First Address: The Beginning of the Franco-Prussian War, July 23, 1870." https://www.marxists.org/archive/marx/works/1871/civil-war-france/ch01.htm

 2 *Ibid.*

However, the International was faced with the fact that the working class in Germany would respond to a war of national defense against the French army. On the other side of the border, the French workers would fight against an invasion by the Prussian army in spite of their resistance against the regime of Napoleon III. The International had the difficult task of curbing the nationalism and anti-French hysteria in the German working class. At the same time, Marx hoped that the Germans would prevent the reactionary Napoleon III from triumphing. The International proved powerless to stop the slaughter despite their call for cross-border solidarity. It was an early warning of the catastrophic result of national chauvinism in the working class that would erupt in 1914.

The French army soon collapsed, and Napoleon III himself was captured. When the news reached Paris, crowds poured onto the streets, and the Third Republic was proclaimed in Paris on September 4, 1870. The International called on Prussia to make peace, but the Prussian army headed for Paris. However, the French National Guard in Paris refused to hand over the city to the Prussian army, directly disobeying the French government. Social tensions grew due to hunger, unemployment, and overall misery under the siege of the Prussian Army. French troops in Paris loyal to the government tried to disarm the National Guard, but people poured into the street and attacked the soldiers, and two generals were lynched. The response of the National Guard was to hold an election on the 26th of March and set up a civil administration of the city: the Paris Commune. The assembly included members of the International, workers, artisans, shopkeepers, and radical intellectuals. Similar communes were set up in Lyon, Marseilles, and Toulouse, but they were quickly suppressed.

The establishment of the Paris Commune proved that a war between capitalist states could be a "window of opportunity" to bring the national class struggle to a head. The Communards rose and seized the opportunity. Napoleon III's ousted government, which escaped from Paris to Versailles, regarded the Commune as a threat to bourgeois society and called for the remaining French army to attack. On April 2, 1871, the Germans retreated in order to give French troops the possibility to turn their attention to the communist rebels. The Germans also released prisoners of war to help strengthen the French Army. Germany did not want a socialist Commune at its doorstep to serve as an inspiration for the socialist movement in Germany. The French Army moved into Paris and faced the Commune in a nearly two month street-to-street battle. Around twenty thousand communards lost their lives and the subsequent executions. Around 50,000 were taken prisoner, many of whom were later put in prison or deported to French colonies in Africa and New Caledonia. The rise and fall of the Paris Commune were determined by the French-German inter-capitalist struggle over dominance of the European continent. We will see this pattern of inter-state rivalry and the opportunity for revolution repeated up through the 20th century.

The French government accused the International of being the mastermind behind the establishment of the Paris Commune. In February 1871, Marx was practically unknown outside of a dozen small circles of left-wing revolutionaries; by the end of the year, Marx was infamous. The Paris Commune generated a "red scare" across Europe. The French government and the bourgeois press managed to organize a crusade against the International throughout Europe. Britain and Switzerland were among the few states where the organization was not banned.

In this atmosphere of growing nationalism in Europe, and repression from state power, the political struggle between the Marxist and anarchist lines inside the International intensified. The influence of anarchism was growing in Italy, Spain, France, and Switzerland. In 1872, the Marxist faction of the International held a congress in New York. The anarchist-dominated faction held their congress in Saint-Imier in Switzerland, where they declared themselves to be the true and legitimate International. Consequently, they were expelled by the New York Congress. This was the end of the first attempt to organize the proletariat across frontiers. The International was formally dissolved in 1876.

Despite *The Communist Manifesto*'s call for internationalism and its claim that the proletariat has no motherland, the history of the socialist movement is a history of national movements operating within the boundaries of the modern world system of nation-states. Consequently, the idea of revolution has mainly revolved around seizing state power and controlling national governmental institutions. On the one hand, this focus enabled national revolutions. On the other hand, it stood in the way of socialism because the socialist mode of production, and its political system, cannot be fully realized in an isolated national context, particularly in a world system where economics and politics are becoming more and more transnational, a lesson that would be repeated again and again in the history of socialist revolutions.

The Paris Commune is the first case in which the proletariat assumed the task of transforming society. Based on the experience of the Commune, Marx came to the conclusion, in his pamphlet *The Civil War in France*, that the bourgeois state machine must not only be "conquered" but broken, giving way to a new kind of state. Marx praised the Commune's abolition of a professional army in favor of directly arming the people, as well as the election of new civil servants. However, state-building was a difficult task for the first Commune. Marx deplored its statist incapacities: its lack of military expertise, its inability to define financial priorities, and its shortcomings in spreading the idea of the Commune to the provincial masses—the peasants.

The solution to these deficiencies became the establishment of a Communist *Party*, not only as the organizer of a centralized, disciplined capacity to struggle for state power, but also to govern the new state, "the dictatorship of the proletariat." The party *realizes* the ambiguity of Marx's account of the Commune and gives it a body. The French Philosopher Alain Badiou writes:

> It becomes the political site of a fundamental tension between the non-state, even anti-state, character of a politics of emancipation and the statist character of the victory and duration of that politic...The party-state is endowed with capacities designed to resolve problems the Commune left unresolved: a centralization of the police and of military defense; the complete destruction of bourgeois economic decisions; the rallying and submission of the peasants to workers' hegemony; the creation of a powerful international, etc. It is not for nothing that, as legend has it, V.I. Lenin danced in the snow the day Bolshevik power reached and surpassed the seventy-two days in which the Paris Commune's entire destiny was brought to a close.[3]

The party-state may solve the problem that the Commune was unable to resolve—of how the proletariat could achieve and execute state power—but, as we will see, the party-state raised other problems.

Marx wrote his pamphlet *The Civil War in France* as an obituary for the Commune, which contained political lessons for the future of

---

3   Badiou, Alain. "The Paris Commune: Marx, Mao, Tomorrow." *Monthly Review*. Vol. 73, no. 1, 2021. pp. 61–62.

communism, concerning the organization and the use of armed struggle. Marx and Engels nevertheless saw the uprisings of 1848 across continental Europe, and the Paris Commune, as the prelude to new proletarian revolutions. In France, the repression which followed the defeat of the Commune turned mere membership in the International into a criminal offense. It took years for the socialist movement in France to reorganize. However, the situation in Germany was quite different: here Engels had high expectations for the revolutionary movement.

CHAPTER 6

From Revolutionary France to German Reformism

Europe after the 1848 rebellions and the Paris Commune was different from the world in which Marx and Engels formulated *The Communist Manifesto*. Unification transformed Germany: rapid industrialization in the 1860s created a large urban proletariat. Thus, the center of gravity of the socialist movement moved from England and France toward Germany. The German socialist movement grew rapidly in the form of trade unions and political parties. One of the first was Ferdinand Lassalle's *Allgemeiner Deutscher Arbeiter-Verein* (German General Workers' Association) founded in May 1863. Though a former member of the Communist League, Lasalle believed in reformist tactics to achieve socialism within a bourgeois political framework. To this end, he was prepared to cooperate with Prime Minister Bismarck in exchange for labor reforms. Marx regarded this approach as a betrayal. Matters came to a head when Lassalle launched the Workers Association in May 1863 with a program consisting of universal suffrage and state support for producer's co-operatives. Marx declared that there was no possibility of a peaceful transition to socialism in Prussia. When Lassalle died a year later in 1864, in a duel over a love affair, Marx was invited to take over the leadership of the party, but he declined due to fundamental disagreements.

In 1869, the *Sozialdemokratische Arbeiterpartei Deutschlands* (Social Democratic Workers' Party of Germany) was founded by Wilhelm Liebknecht and August Bebel. In the first years of its existence, the social democrats were on par with Marx's revolutionary line. However, as the growing strength of the working class resulted in higher living standards, matters changed. In a move to consolidate their reformist position, the General Workers' Association and the Social Democratic Workers' Party held a meeting in Gotha in 1875, where they merged into the *Sozialistische Arbeiterpartei Deutschlands* (Socialist Workers' Party of Germany). The "Gotha Program" adopted by the nascent party called for universal suffrage, progressive income tax, free elementary education, freedom of association, limits on the length of the working day, and other laws protecting the rights and health of workers.[1] The aim of the Gotha Program was still socialism, but a socialism developed by peaceful means within the capitalist system:

> ...the socialist labor party of Germany endeavors by every lawful means to bring about a free state and a socialistic society, to effect the destruction of the iron law of wages by doing away with the system of wage labor, to abolish exploitation of every kind, and to extinguish all social and political inequality.[2]

The leading ideologue of the German Social Democratic Movement, Eduard Bernstein, believed that Marx was wrong on several points. In his book *The Prerequisites of Socialism and the Tasks of Social Democracy*, Bernstein explained that Marx's thesis on capitalism's polarization of poverty on one pole and wealth on the other was wrong.[3] Bernstein argued that the standard of living of the German working class was in fact rising. Furthermore, Bernstein criticized Marx's statement in *The Communist Manifesto* that: "The working men have no country." According to Bernstein, the working class had gained rights by social democratic struggle and had become citizens in the nation. The struggle of social democrats was therefore to reconcile the interests of the working class and the nation. Thus, the Social Democrats were in favor of German colonialism. Bernstein argued in the section "On the Military Question, Foreign Policy, and the Colonial Question" that Germany had the right to conquer new colonies to process extracted tropical raw materials. Moreover, Bernstein concluded that it is possible for the working class to achieve improvements in wages, and thus living standards, and to conquer ever-increas-

---

1   Hanover Historical Texts Project. *The Gotha and Erfurt Programs (1875)*. https://history.hanover.edu/courses/excerpts/111gotha.html
2   *Ibid*.
3   Bernstein, Eduard. *Die Voraussetzungen des Sozialismus und die Aufgaben der Sozialdemokratie*. Rowoht, 1969.

ing rights within capitalism. Using parliamentarian struggle, the working class—which, after all, constitutes the majority of the population—can, without revolution, gain the power of the state and quietly and incrementally introduce socialism. Bernstein's revision of Marx became the backbone of social democracy, which, in future historical situations, caused social democrats to choose the side of capital and the nation-state instead of class-based internationalism. However, the German Social Democrats' nationalist strategy was successful in drawing voters. Led by Karl Kautsky, it became Europe's strongest social democratic party. The Gotha Program became the model for social democrats across Europe.[4]

The rising wage levels and expanded political rights strengthened the belief in the possibilities of reforms within the system, which again made it less risky for the capitalists to make compromises that softened the class struggle. The change of strategy of the socialist movement in Germany mirrored a changed response from the state towards reforms. In the 1880s, German Chancellor Otto von Bismarck introduced a series of social reforms and welfare measures. These were intended to ensure internal class peace while the state intensified an aggressive foreign policy of colonialism and foreign market penetration, which more than compensated the bourgeoisie for its social welfare expenses. Furthermore, in order to finance investment in weapons manufacturing and shipbuilding, Bismarck introduced a state tobacco monopoly in 1882 and the nationalization of the railways.

At the same time that the social reforms were implemented, repressive laws were adopted to weaken the ability of the radical wing of socialists to organize. The laws outlawed social democratic organizations and trade unions but allowed social democrats as individuals to participate in elections. This left the party in the odd position of being illegal as an organization, even while its representatives operated openly in parliament. This also left the political line of the party in the hands of the parliamentarians, which reinforced their pragmatic reformist line. In the 1912 elections, the Social Democrats became the largest party, with 34.8% of the votes. Like other socialist parties in Europe, the Social Democratic

---

4   Lauesen, Torkil. *Riding the Wave, Sweden's Integration into the Imperialist World System*. Kersplebedeb,

2021. pp. 54–58.

Party of Germany (SPD) voted for war grants in 1914. Thus, the SPD allied itself with capital in Germany's conflict with France and England over the imperialist division of the world. The social democrats in Germany were drawn into the system, their representatives became members of parliament, entered into governments, and became administrators of a capitalist society. Their integration was complete when, as a social democratic government, under the leadership of Friedrich Ebert and defense minister Gustav Noske, they used the army and paramilitary forces to suppress the communist uprisings of 1919.

Marx and Engels' Critique of Reformism

As early as 1847 in *The Poverty of Philosophy*, Marx drew attention to a reality ignored by bourgeois economists, when they claimed capitalism's capacity to improve the conditions of the working class:

> ...in speaking of improvement, the economists were thinking of the millions of workers who had to perish in the East Indies so as to procure for the million and a half workers employed in England in the same industry three years' prosperity out of ten.[5]

Likewise, Marx wrote a harsh criticism of the Gotha Program in 1875 admonishing its reformism and lack of internationalism:

> It is altogether self-evident that, to be able to fight at all, the working class must organize itself at home as a class and that its own country is the immediate arena of its struggle—insofar as its class struggle is national, not in substance, but, as the Communist Manifesto says, "in form." But the "framework of the present-day national state," for instance, the German Empire, is itself economically "within the framework" of the world market, politically "within the framework" of the system of states. Every businessman knows that German trade is at the same time foreign trade, and the greatness of Herr Bismarck consists, to be sure, precisely in his pursuing a kind of international policy.
>
> And to what does the German Workers' party reduce its internationalism? To the consciousness that the result of its efforts will be "the international brotherhood of peoples"—a phrase borrowed from the bourgeois League of Peace and Freedom, which is intended to pass as equivalent to the international brotherhood of working classes in the joint struggle against the ruling classes and their governments. Not a word, therefore, about the international

---

5   Marx, Karl. "The Poverty of Philosophy." Marx, Karl and Engels, Friedrich. *Collected Works*. Vol. 6. Progress Publishers, 1976. p. 160.

functions of the German working class! And it is thus that it is to challenge its own bourgeoisie—which is already linked up in brotherhood against it with the bourgeois of all other countries—and Herr Bismarck's international policy of conspiracy...

The international activity of the working classes does not in any way depend on the existence of the International Working Men's Association. This was only the first attempt to create a central organ for the activity; an attempt which was a lasting success on account of the impulse which it gave but which was no longer realizable in its historical form after the fall of the Paris Commune.

Bismarck's *Norddeutsche*[6] was absolutely right when it announced, to the satisfaction of its master, that the German Workers' party had sworn off internationalism in the new program.[7]

Internationalism also had to include the struggles of people in the colonies. Capitalist relations penetrated these societies and generated forces of national resistance. Engels defined the Chinese resistance at the time of the Second Opium War in 1856 as "a popular war for the maintenance of Chinese nationality," and Abd el-Kader's struggle in Algeria as national resistance against the French.[8]

Resistance against slavery in the U.S., and resistance against colonialism, was to grow in frequency and scale as an integrated part of the struggle for world socialism, affecting the development of the working-class movement both nationally and internationally. The English working class could not liberate themselves on the backs of the Irish working class, and "Labour in a white skin," as Marx wrote in *Capital* regarding the U.S. Civil War, "cannot emancipate itself where it is branded in black skin."[9]

Marx was critical of the abstract "universal brotherhood of peoples" expressed in the Gotha Program. Internationalism had to have a concrete form, connecting it dialectically to national struggles. It had to take on the same global dimensions as capitalism itself.

Marx sent his critique as an internal letter to the Social Democratic

---

6 *Norddeutsche* was a daily newspaper and the official organ of Bismark's government.

7 Marx. *Critique of the Gotha* Program. pp. 13–30.

8 See Marx, Karl and Engels, Friedrich. *On Colonialism*. International Publishers, 1972. pp. 124, 160.

9 Marx. *Capital*. Vol. 1. Ch. 10, sect. 7.

Workers' Party of Germany with whom Marx and Engels were in close association. As Engels explains in a letter to SPD leader August Bebel, considering the importance of the program, they believed it was necessary to step in:

> People imagine that we run the whole show from here, whereas you know as well as I do that we have hardly ever interfered in the least with internal party affairs, and then only in an attempt to make good, as far as possible, what we considered to have been blunders—and only theoretical blunders at that. But, as you yourself will realise, this programme marks a turning-point which may very well force us to renounce any kind of responsibility in regard to the party that adopts it.[10]

Marx's critique did not affect the program. Marx and Engels refrained from criticizing the SPD's theoretical shortcomings in public, but it remained a constant concern. In the late 1870s, the ideas of Eugen Dühring were gaining influence in the SPD, including among the leaders Bebel and Bernstein. Dühring criticized what he considered Marx's economic determinism and revolutionary strategy. Engels took up the task of refuting Dühring's ideas by publishing *Anti-Dühring* in 1878.[11] Engels' work aimed at demolishing Dühring's influence inside the SPD, but he also wished to popularize the point that a revolutionary movement requires a revolutionary philosophy and strategy.

When Bismarck passed the Anti-Socialist Laws, outlawing the organization of the SPD but not the legality of its members of parliament, the SPD parliamentary faction, including the leader Wilhelm Liebknecht, signaled its willingness to compromise with the German government by remaining within the law and by voting for tariffs and the state budget. In September 1879, Engels responded to the policy of SPD parliamentarians:

> For almost 40 years we have emphasized that the class struggle is the immediate motive force of history and, in particular, that the class struggle between bourgeoisie and proletariat is the great lever of modern social revolution; hence we cannot possibly co-operate with men who seek to eliminate that class struggle from the movement. At the founding of the International we

---

10   Engels, Friedrich. "Letter to August Bebel. 18–28 March 1875." Marx, Karl and Engels, Friedrich. *Collected Works*. Vol. 45. Progress Publishers, 1985. p. 65.

11   Engels, Friedrich. *Anti-Dühring: Herr Eugen Dühring's Revolution in Science*. Progress Publishers, 1947. https://www.marxists.org/archive/marx/works/1877/anti-duhring/

expressly formulated the battle cry: The emancipation of the working class must be achieved by the working class itself. Hence, we cannot co-operate with men who say openly that the workers are too uneducated to emancipate themselves and must first be emancipated from above by philanthropic members of the upper and lower middle classes. If the new party organ is to adopt a policy that corresponds to the opinions of these gentlemen, if it is bourgeois and not proletarian, then all we could do—much though we might regret it—would be publicly to declare ourselves opposed to it and abandon the solidarity with which we have hitherto represented the German party abroad.[12]

Engels demanded that the SPD oppose the capitalist state outright and reject collaboration with all bourgeois parties, as well as advocate the primacy of class struggle and working-class emancipation.

At its 1891 Congress in Erfurt, the SPD decided to adopt a new program written by Karl Kautsky and Eduard Bernstein. The rhetoric was still revolutionary, but the practical demands were deeply reformist. As a response to the Erfurt Program, Engels decided to go public with a critique. His first move was the publication of Marx's *Critique of the Gotha Programme*. In particular, he highlighted its emphasis on the importance of the "dictatorship of the proletariat" and how this was a problem for the SPD leadership. In the Reichstag, SPD deputy Karl Grillenberger publicly repudiated Marx and declared that "for us, there was never any question of a revolutionary dictatorship of the proletariat."[13] Engels answered back by releasing a new introduction to Marx's *Civil War in France*. In the final paragraph of the introduction, Engels states:

> Of late, the Social Democratic philistine has once more been filled with wholesome terror at the words: Dictatorship of the proletariat. Well and good, gentlemen, do you want to know what this dictatorship looks like? Look at the Paris Commune. That was the dictatorship of the proletariat.[14]

Engels was worried that the party's parliamentary successes and their focus on opportunism threatened its class character and wrote to Lafargue in 1894 that:

---

12   Marx, Karl and Engels, Friedrich. "Circular Letter to August Bebel, Wilhelm Liebknecht, Wilhelm Bracke and Others, September 1879." Marx, Karl and Engels, Friedrich. *Collected Works*. Vol. 24. Progress Publishers, 1985. p. 269.

13   Draper, Hal. *Karl Marx's Theory of Revolution, Vol. III: The Dictatorship of the Proletariat*. Monthly Review Press, 1986. p. 313.

14   Engels, Friedrich. "Introduction to Karl Marx's Civil War in France." Marx, Karl and Engels, Friedrich. *Collected Works*. Vol. 27. Progress Publishers, 1985. p. 191.

[Bebel] complains with reason that the party is going bourgeois. That is the misfortune of all extreme parties when the time approaches for them to become "possible."[15]

Imperial Socialism and Settlerism

Drawing attention to the national liberation struggle and colonial question was necessary because colonialist ideology was making inroads into working-class parties. Marx noted in 1870, that far from being in solidarity with the Irish worker, the English worker:

> ...feels himself to be a member of the ruling nation...His attitude towards him (Irish worker) is roughly that of poor whites to the "niggers" in the former slave states of the American Union.[16]

The British working class was simultaneously sliding into chauvinism, racism, and reformism. However, it was not only the profit from colonial investments, which allowed capital to raise wages and promote reformism. Settler-colonialism also played a significant role in the rise of *imperial socialism* both in the country the emigrants left and in the settler colonies. Followers of the utopian socialists Charles Fourier and Henri de Saint-Simon tried to construct enclaves of "socialist" communities from North America to Algeria on land that was taken in brutal colonial wars.[17]

Settlerism was partly a consequence of the poverty and distress that resulted from the rise of industrial capitalism in Europe, and partly a result of the possibilities created by colonialism and a new means of transport, which enabled millions of Europeans to settle in the "New World." Approximately 70 million people emigrated from Europe throughout the nineteenth century. They were often "surplus" laborers in the countryside who could not find work in the cities. Poverty and famine, as in

---

15   Engels, Friedrich. "Letter to Paul Lafargue 22 November 1894." Marx, Karl and Engels, Friedrich. *Collected Works*. Vol. 50. Progress Publishers, 1985. p. 369.

16   Marx, Karl. "Letter from Marx to Meyer and Vogt, April 9, 1870." Marx, Karl and Engels, Friedrich. *Collected Works*. Vol. 43. Progress Publishers, 1982. pp. 473–74

17   Zouache, Abdallah. "Socialism, Liberalism and Inequality: The Colonial Economics of the Saint-Simonians in 19th-century Algeria." *Review of Social Economy*. Vol. 67, no. 4, 2009. pp. 431–56.

Ireland and Sweden, drove the emigrants across the globe: 36 million to the United States, 6.6 million to Canada, 5.7 million to Argentina, 5.6 million to Brazil, and others to Australia, New Zealand, Rhodesia, South Africa, and Algeria. A significant number of the emigrants settled and claimed land, often displacing and dispossessing the original population in bloody conflicts. Overall, the proportion of emigrants accounted for more than 17 percent of the 408 million people living in Europe in 1900. This settler colonialism was different from ordinary colonialism. The settler did not want to just pass on the values from colonial exploration to the mother country. They wanted to become the new mother country. Hence, the American War of Independence in 1776. The settler colonies, which were successful in eliminating most of the Indigenous population, became clones of the center. The U.S. even overtook the British Empire by the turn of the century.

By acquiring land or work in the New World, emigrants helped to reduce the "reserve army of labor" in their old homelands, thus securing the remaining workers a better starting point in the struggle for higher wages. Emigration was a safety valve alleviating social unrest in Europe. In *Imperialism, the Highest Stage of Capitalism*, Lenin quotes the businessman and later Prime Minister of the Cape Colony in South Africa, Cecil Rhodes:

> I was in the East End of London yesterday and attended a meeting of the unemployed. I listened to the wild speeches, which were just a cry for "bread! bread!" and on my way home I wondered over the scene and I became more than ever convinced of the importance of imperialism…My cherished idea is a solution for the social problem, i.e., in order to save the 40,000,000 inhabitants of the United Kingdom from a bloody civil war, we colonial statesmen must acquire new lands to settle the surplus population, to provide new markets for the goods produced in the factories and mines. The Empire, as I have always said, is a bread and butter question. If you want to avoid civil war, you must become imperialists.[18]

In the United States, impoverished European workers and peasants turned into settlers, in a nation that was on the verge of replacing England as the leading global power. The success of the settler state was based on the dispossession of the Indigenous population and the exploitation of enslaved Africans. Imperialist profits from Latin America, along with

---

18   Lenin, Vladimir Ilyich. "Imperialism, the Highest Stage of Capitalism." *Collected Works*. Vol. 22. Progress Publishers, 1972. pp. 256–57.

land speculations and the practice of slavery, generated the capital necessary for the fast-growing U.S. economy.

This racist hierarchy, embedded in the foundations of the American state, positioned immigrants from Northwestern Europe as an upper part of the working class. Between 1830 and 1860, 4.5 million immigrants from Europe arrived in the United States. These new Irish, German, Scandinavian, Italian, and Polish workers supplemented the former generations of European immigrants. The original settlers, the first generations of Anglo-Saxon origin, retained their privileged positions in skilled jobs or as foremen in charge of teams of workers. At the time, they received the highest wages of any worker in the world, approximately double the wages in Britain. The result was that, by 1900, the American working class was divided by national origin into three main groups: at the top, the Euro-American labor aristocracy, a privileged layer of "born in the U.S.A." workers who constituted approximately 25 percent of the industrial working class. They got the best-paid skilled jobs and were protected by the American Federation of Labor (AFL). Below them were a layer of workers made up of the new immigrants from Europe, which comprised between 50 and 75 percent of the industrialized working class in the northern states. They were mostly unorganized and were systematically excluded from the AFL, and thus from the better-paid jobs. However, their wage levels were significantly above salaries in Northwestern Europe at the time. At the bottom were the "colonial proletariat" of African, Latin American, and Asian origin. They did the hardest work for the lowest wages—on the railways, in construction, in mining, as well as on the plantations of the southern states.[19]

Gerald Horne describes how European settlers were able to climb up "the class ladder with sugar stalks and Africans as the rungs" by acquiring a share of the profits from land privatization and speculation, and the benefits from slavery.[20] A racist ideology of white supremacy was gradually shaped as "pan-Europeanism: an invented solidarity between Europeans that transcended class, ethnic, and religious lines." Through

---

19   Sakai, J. *Settlers, The Mythology of the White Proletariat from Mayflower to Modern*. Kersblebedeb, 2014. p. 123.

20   Horne, Gerald. *The Apocalypse of Settler Colonialism: The Roots of Slavery, White Supremacy, and Capitalism in Seventeenth-Century North America and the Caribbean*. Monthly Review Press, 2018. p. 91.

the journey across the Atlantic and the confrontation with the Indigenous population, as well as slavery, an identification of belonging to the white race was strengthened. Racism against Black and Indigenous people, Latin Americans, Indian, and Chinese immigrants, combined with an identity as Anglo-Saxon Protestants of Northwest European origin, lent a particular quality to American nationalism. The United States was "God's own land," ruled by the white man. Racism and nationalism blocked the development of solidarity based on class consciousness. The trade unions, along with the socialist and communist movements never succeeded in establishing as strong a foothold as they did in Europe. Not even social democracy developed in the United States. But racism and, as a consequence, the anti-racist struggle, has been prominently recurring features of U.S. history, and white supremacy has characterized U.S. domestic and foreign policy right up to the present day.

These effects of colonialism confirm that class struggle seldom presents itself in the pure state—workers versus capitalists. In Britain, the bourgeoisie could consolidate their rule thanks to the colonial subjugation of Ireland. In Ireland itself, colonialism made the social class struggle take the form of a national liberation struggle. In the U.S., as Engels wrote in 1850:

> There, (in North America) the class contradictions are but incompletely developed; every clash between the classes is concealed by the outflow of the surplus proletarian population to the west.[21]

Class struggle was defused via the expropriation and deportation of the natives, as the settlers moved to the West. Later, during the American Civil War, Marx observed that whites of "modest means" espoused the cause of the slave owners and often formed the mass base for attempts to export slavery to Central America:

> Only by acquisition and the prospect of acquisition of new territories, as well as by filibustering expeditions [like that which saw William Walker conquer Nicaragua in the mid-nineteenth century and reintroduce slavery], is it possible to square the interests of "poor whites" with those of the slaveholders, to give their restless thirst for action a harmless direction and tame them with

---

21 Engels, Friedrich. "On the Slogan of the Abolition of the State and the German 'Friends of Anarchy' Draft intended for Neue Rheinische Zeitung Revue No. 5." Marx, Karl and Engels, Friedrich. *Collected Works*. Vol. 10. p. 486.

the prospect of one day becoming slaveholders themselves.[22]

Thus, class struggle within the white community was also diffused through the enslavement of African Americans. Although supporting the Irish people against British colonialism, Marx did not shy away from mentioning the reactionary, anti-abolitionist role played by immigrants of Irish origin before and during the Civil War in the U.S. As they crossed the Atlantic Ocean, emigrants changed from poor proletarians to settlers, finding their place in the class hierarchy. As Marx writes: "The Irishman sees the Negro as a dangerous competitor."[23]

As the communist specter haunted Europe, theories emerged demanding that the annexation of land in the colonies should be assigned to the property-less class in the capitalist metropolis. In 1868, in France, Ernest Renan attacked the French Revolution of 1789 for having prevented: "the development of colonies…thereby obstructing the only route by which modern states can escape the problems of socialism," a thesis he repeated three years later, following the Paris Commune: "Large-scale colonization is a political necessity of the first order. A nation that does not colonize is irrevocably condemned to socialism, to war between rich and poor." It was necessary to put "inferior races' to work for the benefit of the conquering race." It was clear that "the Europeans are a race of masters and soldiers. Reduce this noble race to work for life like Negroes and Chinese, and it will revolt."[24]

Some decades later, Theodor Herzl, the founder of Zionism, recommended the colonization of Palestine as an antidote to the ascendant revolutionary movement in Europe. A "proletariat that instills fear" should be diverted towards a territory that "requires men to cultivate it." Freeing itself of "a surplus of proletarians and desperate men," the European metropolis could at the same time export civilization to the colonial world:

> Hand in hand with this increase in civilization and order would go the emasculation of revolutionary parties. In this connection, it must be recalled that we are everywhere at grips with revolutionaries and will detach young Jewish intellectuals and workers from socialism and nihilism to the extent that we

---

22   Marx, Karl. "The Civil War in the United States." Marx, Karl and Engels, Friedrich. *Collected Works*. Vol. 19. Progress Publishers, 1984. p. 41.

23   Marx, "The election results in the Northern States. Article in Die Presse No. 321 November 23, 1862." *Collected Works*. Vol. 19. p. 264.

24   Renan, Ernest. In Losurdo. *Class Struggle*. pp. 153–54.

hold out a purer popular ideal.²⁵

Indeed, socialists and anarchists of Jewish descent were "converting to Zionism," or the Zionist form of settler-colonial socialism, in the form of the kibbutz movement. The first Kibbutz, "Degania Alef," was established in 1910 in northern Palestine. The kibbutz's attracted thousands of young volunteers from North America and Western Europe to work in these settler colonial projects, regarding them as socialist. European antisemitism and the Nazi Holocaust added to the Zionist colonization of Palestine and the establishment of the State of Israel. A "garrison state" that, from the start, was supported by the U.S. as its "battleship," controlling its interests in the region.

The late Italian philosopher Domenico Losurdo (1941–2018) notes that on the eve of the First World War, the nationalist political leader Enrico Corradini called on Italian socialists to support their own country's colonial expansion, taking to heart the British example:

> The British worker knows that in the massive British Empire, spread over five continents, an activity occurs on a daily basis of which he is part, and which has a far from negligible impact on his household budget: this is Britain's immense trade, which is strictly dependent on British imperialism. The London worker knows that Egypt and the Cape and India and Canada and Australia contribute and compete to increase his welfare and, above all, to disseminate it to an ever-greater number of British workers and British citizens.²⁶

Five years after Engels' death, writing in the *Sozialistische Monatshefte (Socialist Monthly Bulletins)*, the German Social Democratic Party leader Eduard Bernstein noted:

> [I]f, in England and elsewhere, many nutritious and flavorsome tropical products have become staple items of popular consumption; and if the great American and Australian ranges and fields supply cheap meat and bread to millions of European workers, we must thank the colonial enterprise…Without the colonial expansion of our economy, the poverty that still exists in Europe today, which we are trying to eradicate, would be much worse and we would have much less hope of eliminating it. Even when counter-balanced by the crimes of colonialism, the benefits derived from colonies always weigh much more heavily in the scales.²⁷

---

25   Herzl, Theodor. In Losurdo. *Class Struggle*. p. 154.

26   Corradini, Enrico. In Losurdo. *Class Struggle*. p. 155.

27   Bernstein, Eduard. "Der Sozialismus und die Kolonialfrage." *Sozialistische Monatshefte*. 1900. https://www.marxists.org/deutsch/referenz/bernstein/1900. p. 559.

Concurrent to Bernstein's writing, Germany committed genocide against the Herero people in Namibia, expropriating their land for settler farmers and cattle breeders. In the preparatory materials for his writing on imperialism, Lenin transcribed passages from a German historian on the matter, with the comment: "'...rob the land and become landowners!'—this was how the imperialist powers proposed to resolve the social question."[28]

Like the British Labour Party, Bernstein's Social Democrats resolved that promoting colonial expansion to obtain social reforms was the right strategy. "Imperial socialism" was progressing in the most authoritative socialist party of the time, spreading to the Netherlands and Scandinavia.

The advance of "imperial socialism" made the connection between reformism and imperialism explicit, drawing attention to the revolutionary potential of colonial peoples. The anti-reformist communist movement needed to develop an analysis of the totality of political and social relations, national and international, as a precondition for the formation of revolutionary strategy. Along with the colonial question, inter-imperialist contradictions in the prelude to the First World War demonstrated the need for a global perspective on class struggle.

---

28 Lenin, Vladimir Ilyich. "Notebooks on Imperialism." *Collected Works*. Vol. 39, p. 682.

CHAPTER 7

THE ESTABLISHMENT OF THE SECOND INTERNATIONAL

After the repression of the Commune, the situation for French socialists only improved at the end of the 1870s. A new socialist party, *Parti Ouvrier* (Workers' Party), was founded in Marseilles in 1879. The Party's leading figure, Jules Guesde, asked Marx to assist him in writing the new program in 1880. In the preamble, Marx got the chance to present his position in a concentrated form.

> Considering: That the emancipation of the productive class is that of all human beings without distinction of sex or race. That the producers can be free only when they are in possession of the means of production. That this collective appropriation can arise only from the revolutionary action of the productive class—or proletariat—organized in a distinct political party. That such an organization must be pursued by all the means the proletariat has at its disposal including universal suffrage which will thus be transformed from the instrument of deception that it has been until now into an instrument of emancipation.[1]

However, after just three years, the party experienced a large breakaway led by Paul Brousse. He founded the *Fédération des Travailleurs Socialistes de France (The Federation of the Socialist Workers of France)* as a protest against Marx's revolutionary thrust of the *Parti Ouvrier*. Brousse preferred a more accommodating approach that worked within the framework of the parliamentary system.

In 1889, Brousse and Guesde's factions convened in Paris to estab-

---

1   Marx, Karl and Guesde, Jules. *The Programme of the Parti Ouvrier*. https://www.marxists.org/archive/marx/works/1880/05/parti-ouvrier.htm

lish an organization to succeed the dissolved International. The rivalry between the two was intense, with delegates wandering back and forth between them. Though Guesde's Marxist faction would triumph, with four hundred delegates from twenty countries, the establishment of the Second International was ravaged by conflicts between the reformist and revolutionary lines from the start.

Nationalism Engulfs the Left

The assumption in the *Communist Manifesto* that proletarians have no "fatherland" did not match reality. The basis for such a proclamation was that all proletarians were exploited by capital and that this common relation would transcend their citizenship. This was not an unlikely assumption in 1848. Proletarians worldwide shared more or less the same living conditions and they did not owe anything to the national state. However, this situation changed. Colonialism—the globalization of capitalism—was a polarizing process, dividing the world into a system of center, semi-periphery, and periphery. Exploitation was not only confined to the relationship between the worker and capital, but it was also a relation between nation-states. The gains from imperialism trickled down to the citizens of the imperialist countries, including the working class, increasing their nationalist feelings.

In 1904, Lenin noted a correlation between the absence of a militant English communist movement, the political strength of the organized trade unions, and the growing foreign investment of English capital.[2] Despite this, he continued to advocate for proletarian internationalism while arguing against reformism and national chauvinism in the Second International. The strength of nationalism became clear in 1914, when rows of people lined the streets in England, France, and Germany, hailing their troops as they marched to war. The German SPD, as the leading power of the Second International, had, as late as July 25, 1914, spoken out against militarism. However, the SPD had only one foot in the pacifist camp. The party guidelines issued in 1891 by August Bebel nourished patriotic sentiment:

> The soil of Germany, the German fatherland, belongs to us the masses, as

---

2   Lenin, Vladimir Ilyich. "Review: J.A Hobson: The Evolution of Modern Capitalism." *Collected Works*. Vol. 4. p. 102.

much as and more than to the others. If Russia, the champion of terror and barbarism, went to attack Germany...we should be as much concerned as those who stand at the head of Germany.[3]

After Germany declared war on Russia on August 1, 1914, the majority of the SPD newspapers shared their enthusiasm for the war—the so-called "Spirit of 1914." Because of the general enthusiasm for the war among the population, many SPD deputies worried that they might lose their voters if they followed the pacifist line expressed by the congress of the Second International.

On August 4th, 96 SPD deputies, including Friedrich Ebert, approved war bonds, arguing that hostilities had been forced on Germany. This decision made the full mobilization of the German Army possible. The Kaiser welcomed the so-called political "truce" in the Reichstag, declaring: "I no longer see parties, I see only Germans!"[4]

The SPD decision had fatal consequences for the Second International. The immediate reaction of the other parties was disgust, but with the desertion of the antiwar position by the best-organized social democratic voice in the setup, other parties soon fell into line behind their respective governments. After August 4, 1914, the parliamentarian social democrats and radical socialists took very different paths. Lenin urged all true socialists to leave the Second International.

When information of the deaths of millions in the trenches reached Paris, Berlin, and London, despite suffocating censorship, some social democrats regretted their first flush of patriotism. However, the SPD leadership expelled members of parliament who were against the war effort and continued to support their government and the Kaiser, a sign of what the social democratic government's role in post-war Germany would be.

An evaluation of the strategy to obtain socialism in the second half of the nineteenth century might conclude that the revolutionary approach of 1848, and the Paris Commune of 1871, led to a massive loss of human lives, while the reformist strategy successfully gave the working class a better living standard. But what was the cost of the lives of colonial

---

3   Joll, James. *The Second International. 1889-1917*. Praeger, 1966. p. 112.

4   Haffner, Sebastian. *Die Verratene Revolution: Deutschland 1918/19*. Stern Buch, 1969. p. 12.

projects and the inter-imperialist wars, which were supported by social democratic policy?

The Architect of Revolution

By the end of his life, Marx turned his hope towards Russia as the site for a possible socialist revolution, despite its less developed capitalism and hence, smaller working class. However, there were other factors at play. The polarizing dynamics of capitalism had trapped a semi-peripheral country like Russia in a deadlock, which made it impossible for it to develop its productive forces and catch up with the more advanced center countries in Europe and North America. The destruction of pre-capitalist modes of production, and the ruthless exploitation at the margins of the world system, caused social upheaval. By the turn of the century, the revolutionary spirit had moved from Northern and Western Europe to the weak links of capitalism in the semi-periphery (Russia) and to the periphery (China and Mexico). Russia had a revolutionary upheaval in 1905 and China a huge peasant revolt in 1911, which overthrew the Qing Dynasty. Moreover, Latin America gave the world its first peasant revolution in 1910, the Zapatista Revolution.

With the outbreak of the war in 1914, the contradiction between the leading capitalist powers in Europe became the principal contradiction in the world system: this created a window of opportunity for a new revolution in Russia.

Lenin became the main architect of the Russian revolution. In the first half of the 1890s, he had already begun to develop his ideas concerning how to revolutionize Russia. Marx had not left much advice on how to build socialism, apart from some remarks in his critique of the Gotha Programme. The young Lenin was forced to develop an alternative to capitalism himself. First, he rejected utopian socialism. In his book, *What the "Friends of the People" Are and How They Fight the Social-Democrats*, written in 1894, he criticized the dreamy visions of socialism espoused by the Narodniks.[5] Lenin argued instead that socialism becomes a historical possibility when the existing mode of production becomes a

---

5   Lenin, Vladimir Ilyich. "What the 'Friends of the People' Are and How They Fight the Social-Democrats." *Collected Works*. Vol. 1. pp. 129–332.

fetter upon the development of the productive forces. This was the situation created by the tsarist regime in Russia. However, the construction of socialism had to take as its starting point the productive forces developed by capitalism.[6] Lenin reflected in 1914 on how capitalism prepared for socialism:

> The Taylorist system—without its initiators knowing or wishing it—is preparing for the time when the proletariat will take over all social production and appoint its own workers' committees for the purpose of properly distributing and rationalizing all social labor. Large-scale production, machinery, railways, and telephony all provide thousands of opportunities to cut by three-fourths the working time of the organized workers and make them four times better off than they are today. And these workers' committees, assisted by workers' unions, will be able to apply these principles of the rational distribution of social labor when the latter is freed from its enslavement by capital.[7]

The problem was that Russia was not a developed capitalist society ripe for socialism in terms of the development of its productive forces. It was Russia's position on the margins of capitalism that blocked its development. The construction of socialism in Russia necessitated catching up technologically as well as changing its mode of production to unblock the development of its productive forces. But the first step for the Bolsheviks was to take state power—the revolution.

In January 1917, Lenin was based in Switzerland. At that time, he publicly stated that his generation may not live to see the triumph of the revolution in Russia. He had been in exile since 1900, following his banishment to Siberia for three years on charges of revolutionary activities. In Switzerland, he built—together with other exiled Russians—a vanguard party of professional revolutionaries: the Bolsheviks. His argument for that organization is set out in the essay *What is to be Done?*, written in 1902.[8] Lenin argued that to execute a revolution, it is necessary to have an organization that could act fast, decisively, and in unison—hence the principle of *democratic centralism*, that is, a practice of democratic elections that elevates members into a position of hierarchical responsibility. Policy decisions are then freely debated by these members until a deci-

---

6   Ibid. p. 172.

7   Lenin. "The Taylor System: Man's Enslavement by the Machine." *Collected Works*. Vol. 20. p. 154.

8   Lenin. "What is to Be Done?" *Collected Works*. Vol 5. pp. 347–530.

sion is reached, after which all dissent has to cease for unity in action. The organization should then have the capability to coordinate various kinds of political activities: parliamentary struggles, influencing the workers in self-elected councils (Soviets), and organizing party cells within army units. This last task was important, as it was necessary for a secret, armed Red Guard to assist in seizing the power of government when the time was right. All this demanded a high degree of organizational strength: a *vanguard party* to lead the working class. In his preparation for founding this organization, Lenin had studied Marx and Engels' evaluations of the Paris Commune and the civil war in France carefully, hence the emphasis on an independent, disciplined working class party to struggle for state power, and the subsequent rule of the dictatorship of the proletariat.

Lenin was shocked by the behavior of the leaders of the Second International in 1914 and he branded them as "traitors to socialism." Contrary to the social democrats, Lenin was calling on socialists to "transform the present imperialist war into a civil war."[9]

---

9   Lenin. "Socialism and War." *Collected Works*. Vol. 41. p. 337.

CHAPTER 8

THE RUSSIAN REVOLUTION OF 1917

At the beginning of the 20th century, Russia was a semi-feudal society under a tsarist regime in the semi-periphery of capitalist Europe, with its development blocked by imperialism. The Dutch Marxist theorist Anton Pannekoek also noted an ideological difference between the Western European and Russian bourgeoisie:

> During the Middle Ages, England, France, Holland, Italy, Germany, and Scandinavia, had a strong bourgeoisie with petty-bourgeois and primitive capitalist production methods; when feudalism was defeated, a strong, independent class of farmers emerged, who were also masters in their own little economies. Upon this foundation, bourgeois spiritual life developed a definite national culture.[1]

The situation in Russia was different: there was no strong bourgeois culture to dominate intellectual life. In the East, the masses were less engulfed in bourgeois liberal politics and so might be more receptive to leaping over capitalism and into the idea of socialism. Simultaneously, the First World War created the external conditions for the Russian Revolution. The inter-imperialist contradictions amplified Russia's national contradictions and opened up a "window of opportunity" for revolutionary change in a weak link within the capitalist world system. In 1917, this crisis became acute in the final phase of the war. Lenin defined the revolutionary situation as follows:

> We shall certainly not be mistaken if we indicate the following three major symptoms: (1) When it is impossible for the ruling class to main-

---

1 Pannekoek, Anton. *Pannekoek and Gorter's Marxism.* Trans. Smart, D.A. Pluto, 1978. p. 12.

tain their rule without any change; when there is a crisis in one form or another, among the "upper classes," a crisis in the policy of the ruling class, leading to a fissure through which the discontent and indignation of the oppressed classes burst forth. For a revolution to take place, it is usually insufficient for "the lower classes not to want" to live in the old way; it is also necessary that "the upper classes should be unable" to live in the old way. (2) When the suffering and want of the oppressed classes have grown more acute than usual. (3) When, as a consequence of the above causes, there is a considerable increase in the activity of the masses, who uncomplainingly allow themselves to be robbed in "peace time," but, in turbulent times, are drawn both by all the circumstances of the crisis and by the upper classes themselves into independent historical action. Without these objective changes, which are independent of the will, not only of individual groups and parties but even of individual classes, a revolution, as a general rule, is impossible. The totality of all these objective changes is called a revolutionary situation.[2]

Without these preconditions, there is *no* revolution, but even with them, there may not necessarily be revolution. It is not mechanical, therefore, as Lenin goes on to say:

> Such a situation existed in 1905 in Russia, and in all revolutionary periods in the West; it also existed in Germany in the sixties of the last century, and in Russia in 1859-61 and 1879-80, although no revolution occurred in these instances. Why was that? It was because it is not every revolutionary situation "that gives rise to a revolution"; revolution arises only out of a situation in which the above-mentioned objective changes are accompanied by a subjective change, namely, the ability of the revolutionary class to take revolutionary mass action strong enough to break (or dislocate) the old government, which never, not even in a period of crisis "falls," if it is not toppled over.[3]

A successful revolution is a combination of objective conditions and subjective forces. The Bolsheviks managed to seize the opportunity of the revolutionary situation. The tsarist regime was overthrown. The Russian working class and poor peasants were forced by the intransigence of the ruling class to rise up in desperate self-defense, demanding three things: peace, land, and bread. Taking into consideration the actual situation in Russia and the world of 1917, the Bolsheviks were the only force that

---

2   Lenin. "The Collapse of the Second International." *Collected Works*. Vol. 21. pp. 213–14.

3   *Ibid*.

could end the war and make the wheels of the economy turn again, making possible the development of the forces of production.

Taking state power was, however, only the first step: how, then, to proceed? Lenin wrote *State and Revolution* as late as August and September 1917, which deals with the problems of constructing socialism. Following Marx, Lenin's interpretation of socialism was the establishment of communal ownership of the means of production and direct control over the workplace through the soviets of workers. However, the theorizations in *State and Revolution* conflicted with the practicalities of the times after the revolution.

The Bolsheviks had to face a very difficult situation: after a bloody civil war and a Western military intervention, the Soviet Union had to navigate under unfavorable "objective" circumstances. The Bolsheviks were confronted with the task of developing methods to govern a state transitioning to socialism in a hostile surrounding world. And last, but not least, the "Russian backwardness," which in some sense facilitated the revolution, made the *realization* of socialism difficult. Lenin hoped that revolutions in Western Europe would create a socialist bloc, assisting the development of productive forces in the Soviet Union. However, the Bolsheviks had to change their views faced with the defeat of the German revolution. As a result, the desired plan to develop socialism had to be modified, and history moved toward building what became so-called "actually existing socialism" in its peculiar Russian form, something Lenin had wanted to avoid.

CHAPTER 9

THE ATTEMPT TO BUILD SOCIALISM UNDER LENIN

The new Soviet state had to develop their productive forces rapidly to meet the most urgent needs of the population while also struggling to stay in power. The attempt to build socialism became a devious road, determined by interactions between national contradictions and the changing global principal contradiction. We can periodize the post-October Revolution into (1) a short attempt to establish a "mixed economy," (2) "war communism" from May 1918 until Spring 1921, (3) "state capitalism" of the New Economic Policy (NEP), and (4) collectivization during the first years of Stalin.

From 1917 to 1921, the situation in the Soviet Union was unstable in every respect. The establishment of the Soviet Union cut off a part of the world market from the capitalist center, and the existence of the Soviet Union inspired revolutionary uprisings in Germany, Hungary, and Finland. From the point of view of capital, the Soviet Union had to be destroyed. This led to foreign interventions during the Russian Civil War. France, England, the U.S., Canada, and Japan supported the counterrevolutionaries. In 1920, there were about 250,000 foreign troops on Russian soil. Winston Churchill stressed the importance of "strangling Bolshevism in its cradle."[1]

---

1   In Washington on June 28, 1954, Churchill stated: "If I had been properly supported in 1919, I think we might have strangled Bolshevism in its cradle, but everybody turned up their hands and said, 'How shocking!'" See Churchill, Winston Spencer and Langworth, Richard. *Churchill in His Own Words*. Ebury, 2012.

Lenin had believed that the Russian Revolution was the beginning of a socialist world revolution. He emphasized repeatedly that an understanding of the roots of opportunism—primarily the benefits from imperialism—and the fight against social chauvinism was the main task of Western European revolutionaries.[2] His political strategy for Western Europe was to bypass the highest-paid layers of the working class (the labor aristocracy) and to mobilize the proletariat properly for the revolution. This strategy was applied not least in Germany, which had lost the war, been stripped of its colonies, and made to pay war reparations. Lenin saw the revolution in Germany as essential for the survival of the Russian Revolution, and for the further advance of the world revolution. In a political report to the Central Committee on March 7, 1918, Lenin wrote:

> Regarded from the world-historical point of view, there would doubtlessly be no hope of the ultimate victory of our revolution if it were to remain alone, if there were no revolutionary movements in other countries…I repeat, our salvation from all these difficulties is an all Europe revolution.[3]

However, the German revolution did not transpire, and this placed the Soviet Union in a difficult position. The Bolsheviks had to prioritize defending their own revolution while awaiting future progress in the world revolution.

THE MIXED ECONOMY IN THE WAKE OF THE REVOLUTION

The priority of the Bolsheviks' policy just after the revolution was to preserve state power and to develop the economy so they could provide the essential needs of the population. It was a day-to-day battle for survival. At the congress of the Communist Party on March 6-8, 1918, Lenin stated that it was an illusion that socialism could be introduced by decrees, considering the fact that 80% of the population was illiterate. Lenin concluded that capitalism, as a sector, would have to remain as part of the economy for some time:

> If we decided to continue to expropriate capital at the same rate at which we

---

2 Lenin, Vladimir Ilyich. *On Imperialism and Opportunism*. Kersplebedeb, 2019. p. 133.

3 Lenin, Vladimir Ilyich. *Extraordinary Seventh Congress of the R.C.P.(B.), March 6-8, 1918*. Political Report of the Central Committee. https://www.marxists.org/archive/lenin/works/1918/7thcong/01.htm

have been doing up to now, we should certainly suffer defeat...[instead we must be] utilizing bourgeois specialists for proletarian state power.[4]

Yet Lenin was aware of a possible corruption of the system:

> The corrupting influence of high salaries—both upon the Soviet authorities and upon the mass of the workers—is indisputable...We have introduced workers' control as a law, but this law...is only just beginning to penetrate the minds of broad sections of the proletariat.[5]

Lenin thought that the development of socialism depended on "combining the Soviet organization of administration with the up-to-date achievements of capitalism."[6]

War Communism

The civil war left the economy in ruins. The plan to establish a mixed economy under proletarian supervision became impossible in the spring of 1918. Famine ravaged the cities. In May 1918, the state-supervised mixed market economy was transformed into a state subsistence economy called "War Communism." It included forced requisitioning of foodstuffs, redistribution of land, nationalization of industry, state management of production, centralization of resource allocation, state monopolization of trade, partial suspension of money transactions, and the introduction of strict labor discipline. During War Communism, housing and meals at work were free and wages were paid in kind, at low subsistence levels. The time of War Communism is also associated with the institutionalization of the one-party state and increased party discipline.

The state, primarily as a military force of authority, acted as the director of the economy. Property rights were reduced. War Communism was the collectivization of poverty. Some Bolsheviks regarded poverty as a condition of purity and moral excellence, an attitude criticized in *The Communist Manifesto*:

> Nothing is easier than to give Christian asceticism a Socialist tinge. Has not Christianity declaimed against private property, against marriage, against

---

4 Lenin. "The Immediate Tasks of the Soviet Government." *Collected Works*. Vol. 27. p. 246.

5 *Ibid*. p. 248.

6 *Ibid*. p. 259.

the State? Has it not preached in the place of these, charity and poverty?[7]

By focusing on the distribution of wealth, one tends to neglect the development of productive forces. *The Communist Manifesto* again criticized this attitude: "...the 'first movements of the proletariat' are often characterized by demands stamped by 'universal asceticism and social leveling' in its crudest form."[8]

To be certain, Lenin did not identify War Communism with socialism: it was an emergency economy. The Soviet government implemented War Communism under the pressure of concrete circumstances, without foreseeing its internal effects. The forced requisitioning of foodstuffs was unpopular with the peasants, who responded by sowing less grain and hiding food. As a result, the food shortage became even more acute. The industrial output fell and aggravated the economic crisis, which was topped by a trade blockade initiated by the capitalist West. The masses grew tired of the hardship and sacrifices. For Lenin, a sailors' uprising at Kronstadt in March 1921, along with frequent peasant revolts, signified that War Communism was a dead end and the thumbscrews on the economy had to be eased. The response to the economic crisis was the New Economic Policy (NEP).

THE NEW ECONOMIC POLICY (NEP)

To overcome mass poverty, it was necessary to restart the economy and develop the Soviet Union's productive forces. When the chaotic years of War Communism had passed, the Bolsheviks realized that they had to develop the economy to fulfill the basic needs of the population and broaden support for revolutionary power. It was also necessary not to lag in economic development compared to the capitalist countries. It was necessary that the Soviet Union be prepared for defense, as the threat of foreign intervention continued to loom.

Lenin believed that the Soviet Union was far from the level of development which would make socialism possible. For Lenin, NEP was a necessary step backward in the transition to socialism. In a speech in 1921, Lenin posed the alternatives for Russia:

---

7   Marx and Engels. *The Communist Manifesto.* p. 508.
8   *Ibid.* p. 514.

> We must face this issue squarely—who will come out on top? Either the capitalists succeed in organising first—in which case they will drive out the Communists and that will be the end of it. Or the proletarian state power, with the support of the peasantry, will prove capable of keeping a proper rein on those gentlemen, the capitalists, so as to direct capitalism along state channels and to create a capitalism that will be subordinate to the state and serve the state...You will have capitalists beside you, including foreign capitalists, concessionaires and leaseholders. They will squeeze profits out of you amounting to hundreds per cent; they will enrich themselves, operating alongside of you. Let them. Meanwhile you will learn from them the business of running the economy, and only when you do that will you be able to build up a communist republic.[9]

The Bolsheviks needed investment and new technology. Already on November 23, 1920, Lenin introduced a law giving concessions and advantages to foreign investors. In 1921, the NEP was formally adopted, instituting market conditions over War Communism's militarized production, strict state distribution, and the compulsory appropriation of grain.

The Soviet state gave preferential treatment to organized large-scale capital. The Bolsheviks used the technology and management associated with capitalism to boost production. Under NEP, a return to capitalism was permitted in trade, agriculture, and small-scale manufacturing. The requisitioning of food was replaced by a graduated tax. Moreover, the peasants were allowed to sell their surplus on the market, rent land, and employ labor. Other policies included monetary reform in 1922, and a docket of laws meant to attract foreign capital.

However, the "commanding heights" of the economy, such as finance, infrastructure, large industry, and mining remained in the hands of the state.[10]

The Russian working class had seized power before the preconditions for socialism were present. Lenin's strategy was to maintain the dictatorship of the proletariat while developing the material conditions. Lenin criticized those who interpreted Marx as arguing that the working class should never seize power until capitalism had developed large-scale

---

9   Lenin. "The New Economic Policy and the Tasks of the Political Education Departments Report to the Second All-Russia Congress of Political Education Departments October 17, 1921." *Collected Works*. Vol. 33. pp. 60–79.

10   Lenin. "The Role and Functions of the Trade Unions Under the New Economic Policy." *Collected Works*. Vol. 33. p. 188.

industry and had made it the dominant factor in society. Lenin knew that the revolution, and victory in the civil war, had not made the Soviet Union socialist. He wrote in 1921:

> Socialism is inconceivable without large-scale capitalist engineering based on the latest discoveries of modern science. It is inconceivable without planned state organization, which keeps tens of millions of people to the strictest observance of a unified standard in production and distribution. At the same time, socialism is inconceivable unless the proletariat is the ruler of the state.[11]

The Soviet state had survived the first years, but there was a lack of skilled cadres for the administration of the state. There were internal party splits and outright revolts, such as the rebellion at Kronstadt. Although Lenin was surrounded by a disparity of comrades, he faced this reality in the article "Better Fewer, But Better":

> [A]t the present time we are confronted with the question—shall we be able to hold on with our small peasant production, and in our present state of ruin, until the West-European capitalist countries consummate their development towards socialism?... They are not consummating it through the gradual "maturing" of socialism, but through the exploitation of some countries by others, through the exploitation of the first of the countries vanquished in the imperialist war combined with the exploitation of the whole of the East. On the other hand, precisely as a result of the first imperialist war, the East has been definitely drawn into the revolutionary movement, has been definitely drawn into the general maelstrom of the world revolutionary movement...
>
> We must display extreme caution so as to preserve our workers' government and to retain our small and very small peasantry under its leadership and authority. We have the advantage that the whole world is now passing to a movement that must give rise to a world socialist revolution...Can we save ourselves from the impending conflict with these imperialist countries?...In the last analysis, the outcome of the struggle will be determined by the fact that Russia, India, China, etc., account for the overwhelming majority of the population of the globe. And during the past few years it is this majority that has been drawn into the struggle for emancipation with extraordinary rapidity, so that in this respect there cannot be the slightest doubt what the final outcome of the world struggle will be. In this sense, the complete victory of socialism is fully and absolutely assured.[12]

There was no giving up in Lenin's mind. He sought a longer, more devious path, but one that would enable him to reach the summit. He de-

---

11 Lenin. "The Tax in Kind." *Collected Works*. Vol. 32. p. 334.
12 Lenin. "Better Fewer, But Better." *Collected Works*. Vol. 33. pp. 498–500.

scribes this procedure in his article "On Ascending A High Mountain."

> Let us picture to ourselves a man ascending a very high, steep and hitherto unexplored mountain. Let us assume that he has overcome unprecedented difficulties and dangers and has succeeded in reaching a much higher point than any of his predecessors, but still has not reached the summit. He finds himself in a position where it is not only difficult and dangerous to proceed in the direction and along the path he has chosen, but positively impossible. He is forced to turn back, descend, seek another path, longer, perhaps, but one that will enable him to reach the summit. The descent from the height that no one before him has reached proves, perhaps, to be more dangerous and difficult for our imaginary traveler than the ascent—it is easier to slip; it is not so easy to choose a foothold; there is not that exhilaration that one feels in going upwards, straight to the goal, etc...Russia's proletariat rose to a gigantic height in its revolution, not only when it is compared with 1789 and 1793, but also when compared with 1871...We accomplished the task of getting out of the most reactionary imperialist war in a revolutionary way...We have created a Soviet type of state and by that we have ushered in a new era in world history, the era of the political rule of the proletariat, which is to supersede the era of bourgeois rule. Nobody can deprive us of this, either, although the Soviet type of state will have the finishing touches put to it only with the aid of the practical experience of the working class of several countries. But we have not finished building even the foundations of socialist economy and the hostile powers of moribund capitalism can still deprive us of that. We must clearly appreciate this and frankly admit it; for there is nothing more dangerous than illusions (and vertigo, particularly at high altitudes). And there is absolutely nothing terrible, nothing that should give legitimate grounds for the slightest despondency, in admitting this bitter truth; for we have always urged and reiterated the elementary truth of Marxism—that the joint efforts of the workers of several advanced countries are needed for the victory of socialism.
>
> We are still alone and in a backward country, a country that was ruined more than others, but we have accomplished a great deal. More than that—we have preserved intact the army of the revolutionary proletarian forces; we have preserved its maneuvering ability; we have kept clear heads and can soberly calculate where, when and how far to retreat (in order to leap further forward); where, when and how to set to work to alter what has remained unfinished.
>
> Those Communists are doomed who imagine that it is possible to finish such an epoch-making undertaking as completing the foundations of socialist economy (particularly in a small-peasant country) without making mistakes, without retreats, without numerous alterations to what is unfinished or wrongly done. Communists who have no illusions, who do not give way to despondency, and who preserve their strength and flexibility "to begin from

the beginning" over and over again in approaching an extremely difficult task, are not doomed (and in all probability will not perish).[13]

It is worth pointing out that Lenin was completely open about the consequences of NEP—it was introducing elements of capitalism. There was no beating around the bush or paraphrasing. The NEP was a descent—to find another path toward the summit of socialism. The use of capitalist elements had been used before, however now they came into play in a much more structured manner. A special form of capitalism had come into being in Russia, one previously unknown to history: capitalism under the control of a state committed to developing socialism. In 1922, Lenin suggested the term "state capitalism" for the relations of the transitional period:

> State capitalism would be for us, and for Russia, a more favorable form than the existing one…We did not overrate either the rudiments or the principles of socialist economy, although we had already accomplished the social revolution. On the contrary, at that time in 1918 we already realized to a certain extent that it would be better if we first arrived at state capitalism and only after that at socialism.[14]

Lenin's speech at the Eleventh Party Congress in 1922 stressed that during the NEP, various forms of economies compete and therefore mobilize different social forces. Small proprietors, the state capitalist, the state socialist, and self-governing cooperative sectors, together formed a system of market economies, which meant that the direct realization of socialism as a system was taken off the political agenda for the time being.[15] However, this was a transition period, in which the possibilities to develop socialism could mature both in terms of the development of productive forces and in the mode of production.

During the 1920s, direct communal production was established either in the form of voluntary associations or by way of state mediation, though only in a small fraction in agricultural and industrial production.

---

13   Lenin. "On Ascending a High Mountain." *Collected Works.* Vol. 33. pp. 204–211.

14   Lenin. "Fourth Congress of the Communist International, November 5, 1922." *Collected Works.* Vol. 33. p. 420.

15   Krausz, Tamas. "Lenin's Socialism—From the Perspective of the Future: Some Considerations." *LeftEast.* 2022. https://mronline.org/2022/01/21/lenins-socialism-from-the-perspective-of-the-future-some-considerations/

Lenin called them "islands of socialism" and imagined that this model could be the way to establish socialism in the longer run. In the article "On Cooperation," written in January 1923, he argued that cooperatives are part of the road toward socialism:

> All we actually need under NEP is to organize the population of Russia in cooperative societies on a sufficiently large-scale, for we have now found the degree of combination of private interest, with state supervision and control of this interest, that degree of its subordination to the common interests, which was formerly the stumbling block for very many socialists...It is this very circumstance that is underestimated by many of our practical workers. They look down upon cooperative societies, failing to appreciate their exceptional importance, first, from the standpoint of principle (the means of production are owned by the state), and second, from the standpoint of transition to the new system by means that are the simplest, easiest and most acceptable to the peasant...It is one thing to draw out fantastic plans for building socialism through all sorts of workers associations, and quite another to learn to build socialism in practice in such a way that every small peasant could take part in it. We went too far when we reintroduced NEP, but not because we attached too much importance to the principal of free enterprise and trade—we went too far because we lost sight of the cooperatives, because we now underrate cooperatives, because we are already beginning to forget the vast importance of the cooperatives from the above two points of view... In conclusion: a number of economic, financial and banking privileges must be granted to the cooperatives—this is the way our socialist state must promote the new principle on which the population must be organized.[16]

Though the NEP was meant to be functional for a longer period, Lenin did not remove socialism from his agenda. Incorporating the whole population into voluntary cooperatives of production and consumption would take a longer period to realize. The cooperatives, as Lenin wrote about in "On Cooperation," are the products of capitalism; they are "collective capitalist institutions" in which the future of socialism can be glimpsed. He spoke about the possibility of coexisting state socialist and cooperative socialist enterprises, though a differentiation between the two forms of cooperative, state and self-governed, would soon come.[17] By the mid-1920s, nearly 10 million people worked in state-organized and state-subsidized consumer cooperatives. Lenin explicitly stressed that a shift must be made from the interpretation of socialism previously reached (war communist, state powered, and politicized) to the position

---

16 Lenin. "On Cooperation." *Collected Works*. Vol. 33. pp. 467–75.
17 *Ibid*. pp. 472–73.

of "cooperative socialism."[18] As Lenin states at the end of "On Cooperation":

> Now we are entitled to say that for us the mere growth of cooperation…is identical with the growth of socialism, and at the same time we have to admit that there has been a radical modification in our whole outlook on socialism…the emphasis is changing and shifting to peaceful, organizational, "cultural" work. I should say that emphasis is shifting to educational work, were it not for our international relations, were it not for the fact that we have to fight for our position on a world scale.[19]

The development of the Soviet Union's productive forces had to enable the fulfillment of the needs of the people. This required the transfer of technology and knowledge from the advanced European states, combined with the development of the ability of the population in the new state to command these productive forces. The fact that 80% of the population were illiterate constituted a barrier. There was a lack of skilled workers and engineers.

The Soviet Union was the first genuine attempt in history to build socialism, and which survived its traumatic birth. It represents historical experience, which remains relevant when we evaluate current attempts to overcome capitalism. What kind of socialism would be viable in replacing capitalism in our current situation? Is it an updated edition of state socialism taking advantage of new information technologies for effective and democratic planning? Does it take the direction of self-governing socialism of workers' councils and different forms of cooperatives? Certainly, socialism will take different forms from country to country in the world system depending on the specific history and culture of each nation.

Under NEP there was still no centrally planned economy. Economic organizational forms, such as collectivized farming, and five-year plans, which came to define "actually existing socialism" in the 1930s and onwards, were still unknown. No one had a clear idea of what socialist economics and political governance might look like in praxis by the time the revolution was firmly consolidated.

---

18   Krausz. "Lenin's Socialism."
19   Lenin. "On Cooperation." *Collected Works*. Vol. 33. p. 474

The Debate About the NEP

The NEP worked to some extent—development of the productive forces began to take place. The living conditions of the masses improved because social wealth increased, and desperate hunger disappeared, yet social inequalities increased. These inequalities provoked a feeling of betrayal of the original ideals of socialism. Domenico Losurdo writes:

> Literally tens of thousands of Bolshevik workers tore up their party cards in disgust at the NEP, which they re-named the New Extortion from the Proletariat…A rank-and-file militant very effectively described the spiritual atmosphere prevailing in the immediate aftermath of the October Revolution—the atmosphere arose from the horror of war caused by imperialist competition in plundering the colonies in order to conquer markets and acquire raw materials, as well as by capitalists searching for profit and super-profit: "We young Communists had all grown up in the belief that money was done away with once and for all…If money was reappearing, wouldn't rich people reappear too? Weren't we on the slippery slope that led back to capitalism?"[20]

The idealist attitude toward the construction of socialism was not confined to devoted Bolsheviks in the Soviet Union. When the young German Marxist philosopher Ernst Bloch (1885-1977) published the first edition of *Spirit of Utopia in 1918*, he called on the Soviets to implement the "transformation of power into love" and to put an end not only to "every private economy," but also to any "money economy" and with it the "mercantile values that consecrate whatever is most evil in man."[21] When the second edition of *Spirit of Utopia* was published in 1923, Bloch had deleted the passages. However, these idealist attitudes towards the construction of socialism did not vanish in either the Soviet Union or elsewhere. The transition to NEP found passionate critics among the militant Bolsheviks as well as among Western communist leaders. At the 11th Congress of the Communist Party in 1922, Lenin said:

> …at the last extended Plenary Meeting of the Executive Committee of the Communist International, moved by the best communist sentiments and communist aspirations, several of the comrades burst into tears because—oh

---

20   Losurdo, Domenico. "Has China Turned to Capitalism? Reflections of the Transition from Capitalism to Socialism." *International Critical Thought*. Vol. 7, no. 1, 2017. pp. 15–31. (The quote from the young communist stems from Figes, Orlando. *A People's Tragedy: The Russian Revolution 1891–1924*. Pimlico Random House, 1996. p. 771).

21   Bloch, Ernst. In Losurdo. "Has China Turned to Capitalism?" pp. 15–31.

horror!—the good Russian Communists were retreating...At every step you find a certain mood of depression. We even had poets who wrote that people were cold and starving in Moscow, that "everything before was bright and beautiful, but now trade and profiteering abound." We have had quite a number of poetic effusions of this sort.[22]

Yet Antonio Gramsci had a very different evaluation of War Communism:

> Collectivism of poverty and suffering will be the principle. But those very conditions of poverty and suffering would be inherited from a bourgeois regime...The suffering that will come after peace will be tolerated only because the workers feel that it is their will and their determination to work to suppress it as quickly as possible.[23]

The "collectivism of poverty and suffering" is justified by the specific situation in the Soviet Union in the immediate post-revolutionary period. However, it had to be overcome as quickly as possible. Therefore, Gramsci had no objections to NEP as he made clear in a letter from the Politburo of the Italian Communist Party to the Central Committee of the Soviet Communist Party:

> The reality of the Soviet Union put us in the presence of a phenomenon "never before seen in history." A politically "dominant" class "as a whole" finds itself "in living conditions inferior to certain elements and strata of the [politically] dominated and dependent class." The masses of people who continued to suffer a life of hardship were confused by the spectacle of "the NEP-man dressed in fur who has at his disposal all the goods of the earth." And yet this should not constitute grounds for a scandal or feelings of repugnance, because the proletariat, as it cannot gain power, also cannot even keep power if it is not capable of sacrificing individual and immediate interests to the "general and permanent interests of the class."[24]

NEP was not the return of capitalism in the Soviet Union. It was introduced as an instrument to resolve the problem of mass poverty. The return of an economically privileged class does not necessarily mean that they are the politically dominant class in charge of the state.

The debate in Western Europe on the development in the Soviet Union focused on whether the October Revolution had been bourgeois

---

22   Lenin. *Extraordinary Seventh Congress of the R.C.P.(B.).*
23   Gramsci, Antonio. In Losurdo. "Has China Turned to Capitalism?" pp. 15–31.
24   *Ibid.*

or socialist, or whether a potentially proletarian revolution was degenerating into a bourgeois one, due to the absence of a Western European revolution, or due to political mistakes made by the Bolshevik leaders. The idea that the transition from capitalism to socialism would be a long historical process, in which different social and economic transitional forms of states might occur, was not within the mindset at that time. From 1918, Karl Kautsky (1854–1938), the leader of the German Social Democrats, carried on a persistent criticism against Bolshevism. The revolution was in the wrong place and premature. Socialism could only be established in a highly developed capitalist society like Germany. Therefore, the Bolshevik attempt to force the establishment of socialism through a *coup d'état,* promulgated as a revolution, could only result in a historically impossible deformity. Since bourgeois social relations persisted, either an old or a new exploiting class held power in Russia.[25]

Lenin responded in an article published in *Pravda* on November 7, 1919, stressing that the transition from capitalism to communism:

> ...must combine the features and properties of both forms of social economy (and encompassed) a historical era...crying scandal because of the co-presence of heterogeneous social relations during the transition meant bemoaning the fact that the conquest of power did not betoken the cessation of class struggle...petty-bourgeois democrats are distinguished by an aversion to class struggle, by their dreams of avoiding it, by their efforts to smooth over, to reconcile, to remove sharp corners. Such democrats...avoid recognizing any necessity for a whole historical period of transition from capitalism to communism.[26]

On the left wing in Germany, the communist Rosa Luxemburg argued against Kautsky's interpretation that Russia, due to its economic backwardness, was not "ripe" for a socialist revolution. Kautsky's position would write off the idea of the world revolution, as Luxemburg writes in 1918:

> It is not Russia's un-ripeness which has been proved by the events of the war and the Russian Revolution, but the un-ripeness of the German proletariat for the fulfillment of its historic tasks. And to make this fully clear is the first

---

25 Salvadori, Massimo. *Karl Kautsky and the Socialist Revolution, 1880–1938.* New Left Books, 1978. pp. 218–25.

26 Lenin. "Economics and Politics in the Era of the Dictatorship of the Proletariat." *Collected Works.* Vol. 30. pp. 107–8.

task of a critical examination of the Russian Revolution.[27]

Luxemburg's position was that any criticism had to be based on fundamental solidarity with the new Soviet state. This does not mean that she did not have critical points. First, she was concerned about the rural policy of the Bolsheviks immediately after the revolution. By redistributing land and allowing the peasants to divide the large feudal estates, a more communal approach to property had not been strengthened; instead, a new form of private property had been created. The new class of property-owning peasants would defend their land and obstruct the future socialization of agriculture.

Her second point of criticism concerned the national question. After the revolution, Lenin fought against Russian nationalism and granted the different nationalities a certain degree of autonomy with the Soviet Union. Luxemburg agitated against the demand for the self-determination of nations inside the Soviet Union. If the workers have no country, as proclaimed by *The Communist Manifesto*, nationalities did not exist. The "fatherland of the workers," she wrote once, was the socialist international.[28] Luxemburg feared that the Bolshevik policy on the national question would lead to the disintegration of the Soviet Union. One nationality after the other would use its new autonomy to make connections with imperialism and promote counter-revolution. Through their rural and their national policy, the Bolsheviks had created powerful opponents for themselves, which would crumble their attempts to construct socialism.[29]

Luxemburg's critique of the Russian Revolution was not directed at the Bolsheviks taking power—at this point she was in full agreement with Lenin. She criticized German Social Democrats like Ebert and Kautsky and exposed their hypocrisy and defended the revolution in the following terms:

> Let the German Government Socialists cry that the rule of the Bolsheviks in Russia is a distorted expression of the dictatorship of the proletariat. If it was or is such, that is only because it is a product of the behavior of the German proletariat, in itself a distorted expression of the socialist class struggle...The

---

27   Luxemburg, Rosa. In Waters, Mary-Alice. *Rosa Luxemburg Speaks*. Pathfinder Press, 1970. p. 368.

28   van der Linden, Marcel. *Western Marxism and the Soviet Union A Survey of Critical Theories and Debates Since 1917*. Brill, 2007. p. 27.

29   *Ibid*. pp. 28–30.

Bolsheviks have shown that they are capable of everything that a genuine revolutionary party can contribute within the limits of historical possibilities. They are not supposed to perform miracles. For a model and faultless proletarian revolution in an isolated land, exhausted by world war, strangled by imperialism, betrayed by the international proletariat, would be a miracle. What is in order is to distinguish the essential from the non-essential, the kernel from the accidental excrescences in the politics of the Bolsheviks.[30]

Luxemburg's critique of the October Revolution is from the perspective of the future, when the seeds laid by the Bolsheviks in 1917 *could* lead to a betrayal. In this way, Luxemburg's critique opened, from the perspective of a participant in the revolutionary project, the possibility of reexamining the revolution itself.[31]

György Lukács responded in 1923 to Luxemburg's criticism.[32] He claimed that Luxemburg failed to see that the process of bourgeois and proletarian revolutions was qualitatively different. It was characteristic of a bourgeois revolution that capitalism could develop within the feudal order. The revolution was just the political and juridical adjustment on the level of the state to economic changes, which had already occurred. That was the reason why bourgeois revolutions proceeded relatively smoothly.[33] The proletarian revolution was a completely different process. A socialist economy could only be built *after* the proletariat had seized political power, which explained why proletarian revolutions were much more complicated than bourgeois revolutions. This process had to be guided by a conscious political strategy, in which the revolutionary vanguard party played an important role. Consequently, it was imperative for "the proletariat to use all the means at its disposal to keep the power of the state in its own hands."[34] No playbook of the correct method to implement socialism could be written in advance. The state in the

---

30 Luxemburg, Rosa. *The Russian Revolution*. 1922. https://www.marxists.org/archive/luxemburg/1918/russian-revolution/index.htm

31 Hui, Wang. "The Prophecy and Crisis of October: How to Think about Revolution after the Revolution." *The South Atlantic Quarterly*, October 2017. p. 673.

32 Georg Lukács describes Lenin's revolutionary practices and ideology in his book *History and Class Consciousness: Studies in Marxist Dialectics* and coined the term 'Leninism', which Zinoviev and later Stalin adopted.

33 van der Linden. *Western Marxism and the Soviet Union*. p. 32.

34 Lukács, Georg. *History and Class Consciousness. Studies in Marxist Dialectics*. Merlin Press, 1971. p. 292.

hands of the proletariat must have a free hand to maneuver in the difficult national and international context. Lukács considered that no other course of action than the one followed by the Bolsheviks had been possible. Luxemburg had not recognized this, because she had presented the process of the proletarian revolution too simplistically: "She constantly opposes to the exigencies of the moment the principles of future stages of the revolution."[35]

The Bolsheviks themselves were not silent in this debate. In his pamphlet *The Proletarian Revolution and the Renegade Kautsky*, Lenin replied to the various arguments by Kautsky that the Bolsheviks had gone too far, and socialism had no future in Russia. According to Lenin, there had been no other possibility:

> Yes, our revolution is a bourgeois revolution, as long as we march with the peasantry as a whole. This has been as clear as clear can be to us, we have said it hundreds and thousands of times since 1905, and we have never attempted to skip this necessary stage of the historical process or abolish it by decrees... But beginning with April 1917, long before the October Revolution, that is, long before we assumed power, we publicly declared and explained to the people: the revolution cannot now stop at this stage, for the country has marched forward, capitalism has advanced, ruin has reached unprecedented dimensions, which (whether one likes it or not) will demand steps forward, to socialism.[36]

In 1923, a few months before his death, Lenin criticized people who concluded that the October Revolution had been in vain. The situation in Russia, and the world as a whole, had made the revolution possible. Lenin wrote about the common allegation that the development of the productive forces in Russia had not attained the level that makes socialism possible:

> All the heroes of the Second International...keep harping on this incontrovertible proposition in a thousand different keys, and think it is the decisive criterion of our revolution... What if the complete hopelessness of the situation, by stimulating the efforts of the workers and peasants tenfold, offered us the opportunity to create the fundamental requisites of civilization in a different way from that of the West- European countries? Has that altered the general line of development of world history? Has that altered the basic relations between the basic classes of all the countries that are being, or have

---

35   *Ibid.* pp. 276-77.

36   Lenin. "The Proletarian Revolution and the Renegade Kautsky." *Collected Works.* Vol. 28. p. 299.

been, drawn into the general course of world history?

If a definite level of culture is required for the building of socialism (although nobody can say just what that definite "level of culture" is for it differs in every West-European country), why cannot we begin by first achieving the prerequisites for that definite level of culture in a revolutionary way, and then, with the aid of the workers' and peasants government and the Soviet system, proceed to overtake the other nations?[37]

However, the debate about whether the West or the East was ripe for socialist revolutions was answered by historical events.

---

37   Lenin. "Our Revolution." *Collected Works*. Vol. 33. p. 477.

CHAPTER 10

EUROPE—THE REVOLUTIONS THAT FAILED

The establishment of the Soviet Union inspired revolutionary attempts in many parts of Europe. "Actually existing socialism" had immense importance. Socialism was no longer a utopian dream, but a possibility. In neighboring Finland, a civil war occurred between January and May 1918. On one side stood the "reds," socialists and communists, which consisted of urban and rural workers in the south of Finland. On the other side stood the "whites," the Swedish-speaking middle and upper class and the farmers in the north. The "whites" were receiving support from the German government, which was concerned by socialism spreading from the east, but they also received support from the social democratic government in Sweden, which harbored the same fears. After the "white" victory in Finland in May 1918, suspected "reds" were interned in concentration camps where thousands died. 37,000 people perished in connection with the civil war in Finland.[1] Again, we see how foreign intervention from a hostile surrounding capitalist world interfered in a possible transition towards socialism.

In Hungary in 1919, the communist leader Béla Kun proclaimed the Soviet Republic of Hungary. However, its lifespan was short. Only 133 days later, the revolution ended with the entry of the "white" Rumanian army into Budapest. There were also communist uprisings in Warsaw and Vienna in 1919, and in Belgrade, Montenegro, Kosovo, South Serbia, and Macedonia in 1920. In Bulgaria, there were worker unrest, strikes, and a communist uprising from 1919-1920. But the most important and

---

1   Hämäläinen, Pekka. "Revolution, Civil War, and Ethnic Relations: The Case of Finland." *Journal of Baltic Studies*. Vol. 5, no. 2, pp. 117–25.

decisive event in the future development of socialism in Europe was the revolutionary attempt in Germany.

At the end of the First World War, conflicts began to sharpen in Europe. The war was exhausting both civilians and soldiers. The stress of confronting the realities of the war emphasized the differences among German Social Democrats. By 1917, they had split into factions. On the left was a small revolutionary faction called the Spartacists, led by Karl Liebknecht and Rosa Luxemburg. The rump was the biggest part of the SPD, which Lenin called "social patriots." Now that the left wing had decamped, the remaining SPD's desire for respectability could flourish without being reminded of its revolutionary past. In SPD's congress, towards the end of the war in October 1917, a delegate from Hamburg and leader of the National Construction Workers Association, August Winning, expressed the mood in the party:

> It was our historical error to believe before the war... that we should achieve something through a revolutionary ideology. A working class whose progress is guaranteed by organizational and parliamentary work will never let itself be persuaded to the risk of revolution.[2]

However, the revolutionary events in Russia were electric. Strikes broke out in Germany in April 1917 involving hundreds of thousands of workers. Workers' councils were formed, inspired by Petrograd. The SPD and the trade unions saw these actions as a threat to the German war effort. Philipp Scheidemann, co-chairman of the SPD and future Prime Minister, called them "a serious danger to peace."[3]

In 1918, the German people wanted an end to war. In November, marines in Kiel and Wilhelmshaven, who did not want to die in a losing war, rebelled against their officers and refused to go into battle. Troops sent to suppress the trouble went over to the rebels, who formed councils and hoisted the red flag on their battleships. The SPD saw its opportunity to prove how useful it could be to the establishment. It dispatched one

---

2   Stern, Geoffrey. *Communism*. Amazon Publishing Ltd.,1991. p. 66. August Winning was *Reichskommissar* for East and West Prussia from 1917-18. However, he was expelled from the SPD in 1920 and became more involved in Nazism later. He initially welcomed the Nazis in 1933 as providing the "salvation of the State" from Marxism. In his various autobiographies, Winning states that he went from being a Nazi to a Christian conservative during the Nazi rule over Germany.

3   *Ibid.*

of its leaders, Gustav Norske, to calm down the marines, but instead the rebellion spread. On the 6th of November, workers' and soldiers' councils controlled the ports of Bremen and Hamburg. In cities all over Germany, people took to the streets in huge demonstrations. On the 9th of November, the Kaiser abdicated. Friedrich Ebert, the leader of the SPD, formed a new government. Liebknecht was offered a place, but refused to give a left cover to an SPD government. Friedrich Ebert appointed Gustav Noske as Minister of National Defense. Noske, who was a butcher by trade, had worked his way up in the SPD. On his appointment as minister, he stated that: "someone must be the bloodhound."[4] Scheidemann proclaimed the establishment of the republic from the balcony of the Reichstag in the afternoon. Karl Liebknecht raised the red flag two hours later on the roof of the royal palace.

The task facing the German revolutionaries was difficult. Except for the Spartacists, which were a rather small organization, the radical elements had no united organization of their own. While strikes and street fighting were enough to bring down the old regime, they were not sufficient in creating a new order. Lacking leadership and strategy, and in the absence of a clearly formulated alternative, workers were inclined to look to their traditional leaders. Many were taken by the seemingly radical rhetoric of the SPD leaders. The SPD government was welcomed by a large meeting of workers' and soldiers' representatives. They elected fourteen workers and fourteen soldiers to an "Executive Committee of the Revolution" to participate in the government's work. The councils might have possessed the trappings of a revolution, but beneath the surface the old framework survived. The parliamentary road did not lead SPD to change the system, but to *become* the system.

Rosa Luxemburg took the initiative to build an organization able to lead the revolutionary struggle. The Communist Party of Germany (KPD) was founded at the end of December 1918, consisting of approximately 3,000 members. The KPD's program focused on the self-activity of the working class themselves:

> In my view and in that of my most intimate associates in the Party, the economic struggle will be carried on by the workers' councils. The direction of the economic struggle and the continued expansion of the area of this strug-

---

4   Shirer, William. *Rise and Fall of The Third Reich: A History of Nazi Germany.* Simon Schuster, 2011. p. 55.

gle must be in the hands of the workers' councils. The councils must have all power in the state.[5]

Luxemburg insisted that the revolution was still in its early stages:

> We must not...repeat the illusion of the first phase of the revolution...thinking that it is sufficient to overthrow the capitalist government and set up another to bring about the socialist revolution...The conquest of power will not be seized with one blow. It is a question of fighting step by step in order to take and transfer all the powers of the state bit by bit from the bourgeoisie to the workers' and soldiers' councils. But before these steps can be taken, the members of our own Party and the proletarians in general must be educated... We must make the masses understand that the workers' and soldiers' council is in all senses the lever of the machinery of state, that it must take over all power and must unify the power in one stream—the socialist revolution. The masses of workers who are already organized in workers' and soldiers' councils are still miles away from having adopted such an outlook, and only isolated proletarian minorities are clearly conscious of their tasks.[6]

However, the majority of the delegates did not share Luxemburg's strategy of a long-term struggle for power. She was also unable to prevent the Party from breaking with the unions and labeling them "reformist" institutions. Revolutionary shop stewards had been expected to join the Party, but as a consequence of the positions adopted by the KPD Congress, the Party lost the possibility to include some of the most influential workers' leaders in its ranks.

The impatience of the majority of the Party was not surprising considering the political developments at the beginning of 1919. The army was falling apart, and a strike wave was bringing more and more workers into struggle. Yet, in the Party paper *Die Rote Fahne (The Red Flag)* on January 7th, Luxemburg stressed the difference between the fighting mood of the masses and the fatal indecision of the leaders, and warned that the government was preparing to destroy the revolution:

> The Ebert-Scheidemann clique are not wasting their time in endless discussion. Behind the scenes they are preparing to act with the usual cunning and energy of counterrevolutionaries; they are loading their weapons for the final surprise attack to destroy the revolution...Disarm the counter-revolution.

---

5   Luxemburg, Rosa. "Our Program and the Political Situation." *Selected Political Writings of Rosa Luxemburg*. Monthly Review Press,1971. https://www.marxists.org/archive/luxemburg/1918/12/31.htm

6   *Ibid.*

Arm the masses. Occupy all positions of power. Act quickly!⁷

Luxemburg was right; the SPD government began to destroy the revolutionary movement. Norske used a volunteer group of right-wing ex-officers called "Freikorps," together with regular troops, to wipe out disorganized left-wingers in Berlin. The Social Democrat paper *Vorwärts (Forward)* openly called for the death of the Spartacist leaders. On January 15, 1919, Luxemburg and Liebknecht were found and murdered, and their bodies were thrown in the river. The murder of the Spartacist leaders created an outrage in Berlin. On March 2nd, a general strike was called on and street fighting broke out on a large scale. Again, the government used the Freikorps to crush the opposition with brutal force. This was the end of the German revolutionary attempt.

In an article written on January 14, 1919, and published shortly after she was murdered, Luxemburg recognized the defeat of the revolution:

"Order prevails in Berlin!" So proclaims the bourgeois press triumphantly, so proclaim Ebert and Noske, and the officers of the "victorious troops," who are being cheered by the petty-bourgeois mob in Berlin waving handkerchiefs and shouting "Hurrah!"...Was the ultimate victory of the revolutionary proletariat to be expected in this conflict? Could we have expected the overthrow of Ebert-Scheidemann and the establishment of a socialist dictatorship? Certainly not, if we carefully consider all the variables that weigh upon the question. The weak link in the revolutionary cause is the political immaturity of the masses of soldiers, who still allow their officers to misuse them, against the people, for counterrevolutionary ends...

Because of the contradiction in the early stages of the revolutionary process between the task being sharply posed and the absence of any preconditions to resolve it, individual battles of the revolution end in formal defeat. But revolution is the only form of "war"—and this is another peculiar law of history—in which the ultimate victory can be prepared only by a series of "defeats"...The whole road of socialism—so far as revolutionary struggles are concerned—is paved with nothing but thunderous defeats. Yet, at the same time, history marches inexorably, step by step, toward final victory! Where would we be today without those "defeats," from which we draw historical experience, understanding, power and idealism? Today, as we advance into the final battle of the proletarian class war, we stand on the foundation of those very defeats; and we cannot do without any of them, because each one contributes to our strength and understanding... There is but one condition. The question of why each defeat occurred must

---

7   Luxemburg, Rosa. In Harman, Chris. *The Lost Revolution: Germany 1918 to 1923*. Aakar Books, 1982. pp. 83–84

be answered. Did it occur because the forward-storming combative energy of the masses collided with the barrier of unripe historical conditions, or was it that indecision, vacillation, and internal frailty crippled the revolutionary impulse itself?

Both! The crisis had a dual nature. The contradiction between the powerful, decisive, aggressive offensive of the Berlin masses on the one hand and the indecisive, half-hearted vacillation of the Berlin leadership on the other is the mark of this latest episode. The leadership failed. But a new leadership can and must be created by the masses and from the masses. The masses are the crucial factor. They are the rock on which the ultimate victory of the revolution will be built.[8]

What are the lessons from the European uprising in the wake of the First World War? We are again presented with dilemmas on how to organize the revolutionary forces. A vanguard party and centralized command like the Bolsheviks, or Workers' Councils and "people in arms"?

Lenin held out great hopes for the German revolution, both to ease the pressure on the Soviet Union and to continue the world revolutionary process. However, the defeat of the German revolution confirmed Lenin's belief—much in line with the above evaluation by Luxemburg—that a disciplined organization backed by a well-organized "red armed force" was necessary to win a revolution, and most of all to sustain it.

The idea of a vanguard party has been criticized by the contention that only the masses can "liberate themselves." However, to do so, the masses have to organize themselves. The ability to act in unity, quickly, and coordinated at the right moment does not flow spontaneously from the depths of the mass movement. It takes an organization in close contact with the masses to be able to concentrate and formulate the demands and plan the strategy to reach them.

Taking the global perspective on the German Revolution, we have to remember that unlike the Russian Revolution, which happened in the semi-periphery, the German revolutionary attempt took place in the imperialist center of the world-system. Germany was an imperialist power striving to be a dominant world power. The main reason for the defeat was the split in the socialist movement (and the working class) between revolutionaries and social democrats—a split caused by imperialism—which

---

8 Luxemburg, Rosa. "Order prevails in Berlin!" *Gesammelte Werke*. Vol. 4. https://www.marxists.org/archive/luxemburg/1919/01/14.htm

became apparent in the struggle in the Second International leading up to the First World War. The social democrats abandoned the international class position and turned against the revolutionaries to defend the capitalist state. Social democracy arrives at this end through an emphasis on sharing the results of capitalism in the sphere of circulation. Capital pays, and pits one section of the working class against another to secure itself. And yet, the communist movement, in line with Luxemburg, did not consider the failed revolutions in Europe the end of the transition to socialism. The world revolution, including new attempts in Europe, was still high on the agenda in 1919.

CHAPTER 11

THE THIRD INTERNATIONAL: COMINTERN

When judging the legacy of the Soviet Union, its significance was not solely that it was the world's first experience constructing "actually existing socialism." The Soviet Union was the major architect of the Communist International (COMINTERN), the third attempt to organize the proletariat on a world scale and promote the idea of the unification of anti-imperialist struggle and socialist revolution. The COMINTERN could not have been established without the prestige of Lenin and the success of the Russian Revolution. It had a unifying impact on the communist movement worldwide.

When 44 delegations assembled on March 2, 1919 at the founding congress, they thought the world revolution was underway. Their hosts were the world's first state founded by a proletarian revolution and a wave of revolutionary uprisings was engulfing central Europe. Lenin assured the delegates that they would one day "see the founding of the World Federative Republic of Soviets."[1] The driving force behind the founding of the COMINTERN was the division of the Second International between the social democrats who supported nationalism and imperialism, and the communist faction, who decided to establish a Third International dedicated to promoting and coordinating world revolution. The COMINTERN would provide assistance and disciplined leadership, serving as the Political Bureau (Politburo) of world communism. The COMINTERN defined its aims in the "Manifesto of the Communist International to the Proletariat of the Entire World":

---

1   Stavrianos, Leften Stavros. *Global Rift: The Third World Come of Age*. William Morrow & Co., 1981. p. 492.

If the First International predicted the future course of development and indicated the roads it would take, if the Second International rallied and organized millions of proletarians, then the Third International is the International of open mass struggle, the International of revolutionary realization, the International of action.[2]

In contrast to the Second International, the COMINTERN's position on anti-imperialism was clear cut. A resolution passed at the congress in 1919 read:

> At the expense of the plundered colonial people, capital corrupted its wage slaves, created a community of interest between the exploited and the exploiters against the oppressed colonies—the yellow, black and red colonial people—and chained the European and American working class to the imperialist "fatherland."[3]

The COMINTERN still assumed that the decisive battles for world revolution would be fought in Europe. The aforementioned Manifesto read:

> The workers and peasants not only of Annam, Algiers and Bengal, but also of Persia and Armenia, will gain their opportunity of independent existence only in that hour when the workers of Britain and France, having overthrown Lloyd George and Clemenceau, have taken state power into their own hands…Colonial slaves of Africa and Asia: the hour of proletarian dictatorship in Europe will also be the hour of your liberation![4]

Their strategy was to prioritize the mobilization of the European proletariat below the top tier of the unionized workers, but it failed. Revolutionaries within the workers' movement and most trade unions were not able to challenge the reformist leadership. In Germany, their influence remained strong, even after the revolution's defeat in 1919, but subsequent communist uprisings were crushed with brute force by the SPD government. The situation was the same in Vienna and in the Balkans. In Hungary, the Soviet Republic was defeated and Belá Kun managed to escape and join the COMINTERN. In England and Scandinavia, social

---

2   Trotsky, Leon. *Manifesto of the Communist International to the Proletariat of the Entire World*. 1919. http://soviethistory.msu.edu/1921-2/COMINTERN/texts/manifesto-of-the-communist-international. p. 1019.

3   Degras, Jane. In Cope, Zak. *Divided World, Divided Class: Global Political Economy and the Stratification of Labour Under Capitalism*. Kersplebedeb, 2015. p. 77.

4   Trotsky. *Manifesto of the Communist International to the Workers of the World*. p. 32.

democrats benefited from the post-war economic crises, forming governments backed by the working-class majority. In Europe, reforms seemed safer than revolution.

THE 1920 SECOND CONGRESS OF THE COMINTERN: EAST OR WEST?

In July 1920, one hundred and sixty seven delegates, now including sections from Asia, Africa, and Latin America, met at the COMINTERN's Second Congress. The response to the defeats in Europe was to increase discipline so as to eliminate reformist and nationalist tendencies. "Twenty-one Conditions for Admission to the Communist International" were adopted and all affiliates of the COMINTERN had to accept its decisions as binding. The congress undertook to create a link between the struggle for socialism in Europe and the anti-colonial struggle. Lenin labeled the British working class stance toward the struggle of oppressed nations "treachery":

> ...the rank-and-file British worker would consider it treasonable to help the enslaved nations in their uprisings against British rule...the jingoist and chauvinist-minded labour aristocrats of Britain and America present a very great danger to socialism and are a bulwark of the Second International...We must proclaim this publicly for all to hear, and it is irrefutable. We shall see if any attempt is made to deny it.[5]

Even among Europe's communists, support for anti-colonial struggles was often half-hearted and it was widely believed that communist movements in the imperial core were more important than those in the periphery.

Communists from Asia criticized these attitudes. Pak Din Shoon, the Korean delegate at the 1920 COMINTERN congress, attempted to point attention "to the East, where the fate of the world revolution may very well be decided."[6] The Indian delegate Manabendra Nath Roy, head of the COMINTERN's Far Eastern Bureau, declared the exploitation of the colonies to be the limitation for European revolution:

> Super-profits gained in the colonies are the mainstay of modern capitalism,

---

5   Lenin. "Report of the Commission on the National and Colonial Questions." *Collected Works*. Vol.31. p. 245.

6   Bashear, Suliman. *Communism in the Arab East, 1918–28*. Ithaca Press, London 1980. p. 13.

and as long as these exist, it will be difficult for the European working class to overthrow the capitalist order...By exploiting the masses in the colonies, European imperialism is in a position to make concession after concession to the labor aristocracy at home.[7]

One of the previously mentioned "Twenty-One Conditions" adopted at the 1920 congress, was the demand of every member party "...to denounce without any reserve all the methods of 'its own' imperialists in the colonies," complemented by the demand to work for the "expulsion of its own imperialists from such colonies."[8]

However, the European communist parties had great difficulty abiding by these demands. A few months after the congress, Lenin met with a delegation of English workers and discussed the issue with them. He reported the following:

> They made faces...They simply could not get into their heads the truth that in the interests of the world revolution, workers must wish the defeat of their government.[9]

At the 1920 congress, there was an intense debate between Nath Roy and Lenin concerning communist strategy in the colonies. Due to the relative weakness of communist parties there, Lenin suggested that they should forge alliances with bourgeois democratic movements. Roy, however, opposed any collaboration with the Indian National Congress, which he considered to be a "debating society." Lenin pointed out that there was no functional communist party in India, and that, under these circumstances, the idea of communists acting alone was doomed to fail.[10] He added that there was "not the slightest doubt that every national movement can only be a bourgeois-democratic movement."[11] The COMINTERN adopted a series of positions on the "national and

---

7 *Ibid.* p. 14.

8 Daniels, Robert Vincent. *A Documentary History of Communism and the World: From Revolution to Collapse.* University Press of New England, 1994. p. 33.

9 Pipes, Richard. *The Unknown Lenin, From the Secret Archives.* Yale University Press, 1996. p. 99.

10 Petersson, Frederik. *"We Are Neither Visionaries nor Utopian Dreamers:" Willi Münzenberg, the League Against Imperialism, and the COMINTERN, 1925–1933.* [Ph.D. thesis]. Queenston Press, 2013. p. 28.

11 Lenin. "Report of the Commission on the National and Colonial Questions." *Collected Works.* Vol. 31. pp. 213–263.

colonial question." Communists in Asia were directed to immerse themselves in the struggle for national independence and to form alliances with other movements for colonial freedom. The revolutions in the colonial world were seen as a two-stage process: first, a national bourgeois revolution against colonial rule, and then a socialist revolution.

In China, at the time a semi-colonial country, the May Fourth Movement sparked an uprising in 1919. The movement also resulted in the founding of the Communist Party of China in 1921, and this provided a testing ground for the COMINTERN's strategy. By the mid-1920s the Communist Party of China had, under the COMINTERN's direction, established an alliance with the Kuomintang, China's nationalist party, in an attempt to create a bourgeois revolution. The communists had allowed the Kuomintang to take military leadership in the struggle against the warlords; however, the Kuomintang turned against their partners. This led to the Shanghai massacre of communists in 1927. It took years to rebuild the movement. While Mao Zedong—who would soon be appointed commander-in-chief of the Chinese Red Army—concurred with the COMINTERN that the Chinese revolution first had to be a national revolution, he also stressed the importance of communist leadership in the struggle.

The Baku Conference

In September 1920, the COMINTERN organized a "Congress of the Peoples of the East" in Baku, Azerbaijan. Nineteen hundred delegates attended, a mix of communists, anarchists, and radical nationalists. The congress was the first forum where anti-colonial militants met to discuss the future of the peoples of the East. The goal was to establish a common understanding of the fight against imperialist domination and capitalist exploitation, and to form an alliance between the COMINTERN and the anticolonial liberation movements in Asia, with the ultimate objective being to win them fully to communism.[12]

Two documents were adopted, a "Manifesto of the Peoples of the East" and an "Appeal to the Workers of Europe, America, and Japan," a

---

12   Weiner, Michael. "COMINTERN in East Asia, 1919–1939." McDermott, Kevin and Agnew, Jeremy. *The COMINTERN: A History of International Communism from Lenin to Stalin*. Macmillan, 1996. p. 162.

call to workers in the imperialist countries to support the anti-imperialist struggle. Both ended with a new slogan: "Workers of All Lands and Oppressed Peoples of the Whole World, Unite!" "Oppressed peoples" had now emerged alongside "workers" as fully-fledged revolutionary subjects. This formulation represented an innovation *vis-à-vis* Marx and Engels—not to abandon the perspective of class struggle and internationalism, but an attempt to grasp the peculiar configuration assumed by each of them in a world system characterized by increasing international colonial inequality.

An executive body was elected to carry out the COMINTERN's work in the East. At a time when the Soviet Union was close to bankruptcy and facing severe famine, Moscow allotted 750,000 gold rubles to establish two radio stations with a range of 20,000 kilometers—among the farthest-reaching in the world—to broadcast anti-imperialist propaganda to the colonized nations of Asia.[13]

The Third Congress of 1921

At the third congress in the summer of 1921, the COMINTERN developed a structure of a central institution with regional bureaus, local agents, and various political, cultural, and trade union front organizations. The COMINTERN had imbued trust with the leaders of every national Communist Party, and relied on them to willingly accept orders directly from the COMINTERN. This process was accompanied by a merging of the COMINTERN and Soviet foreign policy, as it moved from an emphasis on the continuation of world revolution to the defense of socialism-in-one-country. This was reflected in article 15 of the 21 conditions for membership in the COMINTERN:

> 15. It is the duty of any party wishing to join the Communist International selflessly to help any Soviet republic in its struggle against counter-revolutionary forces. Communist parties must conduct incessant propaganda urging the workers to refuse to transport war materials destined for the enemies of the Soviet republics; they must conduct legal or illegal propaganda in the

---

13 Brown, Anthony Cave and Macdonald, Charles. *On a Field of Red: The Communist International and the Coming of World War II*. G.P. Putnam's Sons, 1981. p. 189.

armed forces dispatched to strangle the workers' republics, etc.[14]

THE FIFTH CONGRESS OF THE COMINTERN AND THE LEAGUE AGAINST IMPERIALISM

In late 1923, after Lenin's death, Ho Chi Minh traveled from Paris to Moscow and began to work for the COMINTERN. He met with Bolshevik leaders such as Leon Trotsky, Nikolai Bukharin, Karl Radek, and Joseph Stalin. He also participated in the Fifth Congress of the COMINTERN in 1924, where he criticized the communists of Europe for ignoring the colonial question:

> You must excuse my frankness, but I cannot help but observe that the speeches by comrades from the mother countries give me the impression that they wish to kill a snake by stepping on its tail. You all know today the poison and life energy of the capitalist snake is concentrated more in the colonies than in the mother countries...Yet in our discussion of the revolution you neglect to talk about the colonies...Why do you neglect the colonies, while capitalism uses them to support itself, defend itself, and fight you?[15]

He went on to lay out his critique in detail:

> So long as the French and British Communist Parties have not brought out a really progressive policy with regard to the colonies, have not come into contact with the colonial peoples, their programme as a whole is and will be ineffective because it goes counter to Leninism...According to Lenin, the victory of the revolution in Western Europe depends on its close contact with the liberation movement against imperialism in enslaved colonies and with the national question, both of which form a part of the common problem of the proletarian revolution and dictatorship...As for our Communist Parties in Great Britain, Holland, Belgium and other countries—what have they done to cope with the colonial invasions perpetrated by the bourgeois class of their countries? What our Parties have done in this domain is almost worthless. As for me, I was born in a French colony, and am a member of the French Communist Party, and I am very sorry to say that our Communist Party has done hardly anything for the colonies.[16]

---

14   Lenin. "Terms of Admission into Communist International." *Collected Works*. Vol. 31. pp. 206–11.

15   Lacouture, Jean. *Ho Chi Minh: A Political Biography*. Vintage, 1968. p. 41.

16   Minh, Hồ Chí. "The Path Which Led Me to Leninism." *Selected Works of Ho Chí Minh*. Vol. 4. Foreign Languages Publishing House, 1962. Originally published in the Soviet review *Problems of the East*, on the occasion of the 90th anniversary of Lenin's birthday (April 1960). https://www.marxists.org/reference/archive/ho-chi-minh/

The communist parties of Europe never took Ho's criticism to heart. In 1925, Ho moved to Canton to deepen contacts with the newly formed Communist Party of China on behalf of the COMINTERN. He also visited Siam (present day Thailand) and other Asian countries to coordinate COMINTERN activities.

The COMINTERN had not given up trying to forge an alliance between the communists of the West and the East. In the mid-1920s, its leadership employed the help of German communist Willi Münzenberg to establish a broad-based front organization for the struggle against imperialism, The League Against Imperialism (LAI). An "Anti-Imperialist Commission" was established in Moscow to oversee the process of launching the LAI. It was important to mobilize the workers in the imperialist countries for the anti-imperialist struggle, first of all denouncing the social democratic position as "direct support of imperialism."[17]

Berlin was chosen as the base of LAI's work. Germany had lost its colonies in World War I and as a result, the government wasn't much concerned by anti-colonial movements. In 1927, the LAI was launched at a congress in Brussels, attended by 174 delegates representing 134 organizations from 34 countries.[18] Albert Einstein, appointed honorary president, proclaimed in the opening speech: "In your congress, the solidly united endeavor of the oppressed to achieve independence takes bodily shape."[19]

For many militants from the colonies, the LAI congress was an opportunity to meet militants from other colonies. They exchanged experiences and discussed future strategies. This explains the historical significance of the event. When Sukarno, as Indonesia's president, opened the Bandung Conference in 1955, he explicitly mentioned the 1927 LAI congress as a crucial stepping stone in the development of the anti-imperialist struggle.

While its headquarters remained in Berlin, the LAI also established bureaus in Paris, London, Amsterdam, and Boston, which were sup-

---

works/1960/04/x01.htm

17   Petersson, Frederik. "Imperialism and the COMINTERN." *Journal of Labor and Society*. Vol. 20, no. 1, March 2017. p. 34.

18   Petersson. *"We Are Neither Visionaries nor Utopian Dreamers."* p. 136.

19   Ibid. p. 137.

posed to advance anti-imperialist politics in collaboration with the various communist parties. The results were modest. European communists simply did not prioritize anti-imperialist work. They knew that it wasn't a burning issue for the European working class and certain factions even deemed it unpatriotic.

The LAI never lived up to the expectations of the COMINTERN. In 1933, when the Nazis took power in Germany, its headquarters moved to Paris. When Germany occupied France in 1940, the LAI ceased to exist. Ho Chi Minh's doubts concerning the mobilization of European workers for anti-imperialist politics was justified. However, LAI had been an important factor in the embrace of Marxism-Leninism by many national liberation movements. Communists became leading figures in the struggle for the colonies' freedom.

The Sixth Congress of the COMINTERN

In 1928, COMINTERN again adopted a new mode of confrontation with the reformist West and the social democrats, who, in June 1928, had formed a new government in Germany. The COMINTERN's Sixth Congress in 1928 was also meant to reorganize activities in the East after the Shanghai massacre of communists by the Kuomintang.[20]

Palmiro Togliatti, leader of the Italian Communist Party, summed up the attitudes of Europe's social democrats:

> The Social Democrats have become colonial politicians. They recognise the possession of colonies as something which their countries could never renounce and that, when their country has no colony, it is up to them to demand a colony in a more or less open manner.[21]

Togliatti pointed out that Social Democracy had always had a co-

---

20 Degras, Jane. *The Communist International, 1919–1943: Documents. Volume 2: 1923–1928*. Oxford University Press, 1960. p. 247.

21 Togliatti, Palmiro (1928) Social Democracy and the Colonial Question. In *International Press Correspondence*, no. 68, October 4, 1928, page 1234–1243. When Togliatti later became attorney general in 1946, he insisted that Eritrea, Libya, and Somalia should remain Italian colonies. He argued that the Italian post-war coalition government was no longer imperialist but a "people's government," and that the Italian proletariat would lead the colonies to independence. See Jaffe, Hosea. *Progress and Nationality*. Jaca Books, 1990. p. 55.

lonial policy, "one which consisted in allying itself with or directly participating in the colonial enterprises of the bourgeoisie."[22] The Italian social democrats had always voted in support of the colonial agenda. At a 1927 congress for Italian social democrats, it was declared that the "postwar problems" could not be solved without colonies. The French social democrats supported military intervention in Syria to crush the nationalist movement there. In the Netherlands, the Socialist Party did not even discuss whether there should be colonies or not: the only question was how to govern them. They condemned the communist-led mass rebellions in Western Sumatra and Java in 1926 as being orchestrated by "Moscow or Canton." In Germany, the SPD repeatedly bemoaned the fact that Germany had lost its colonies and demanded their return. In England, the Labour Party made it very clear that it did not support decolonization. Rather, it was ready to "defend the rights of British citizens who have overseas interests," concluding that "as for this community of races and peoples of different colors, religions and different stages of civilization which is called the British Empire, the Labour Party is in favor of its maintenance."[23] The 1929–1931 Labour government under Prime Minister Ramsay MacDonald rejected all demands made by the Egyptian government to withdraw British troops, constrain British capital, and cede control over the Suez Canal.

The harsh critique leveled at the social democrats during the 1928 Congress reflected the COMINTERN's new strategy of "Class against Class." Yet problems remained concerning anti-imperialist politics in the communist movement itself. The COMINTERN secretary Otto Kuusinen, who had left Finland for the Soviet Union after the defeat of the Reds in the Finnish Civil War, presented a document entitled "Theses on the Revolutionary Movement in Colonial and Semi-Colonial Countries." It addressed the lackluster approach to anti-imperialist politics by Europe's communist parties:

> It must be admitted that, up until now, not all the parties in the Communist International have fully grasped the decisive importance which the establishment of close, regular and unbroken relations with the national revolution-

---

22   Edwards, H.W. *Labour aristocracy: Mass Base of Social Democracy*. Aurora, 1978. p. 39.

23   Togliatti, Palmiro. "Social Democracy and the Colonial Question." *International Press Correspondence*. No. 68, October 4, 1928, pp. 1234–43.

ary movements in the colonies has in affording these movements active and practical help.[24]

For Kuusinen, engaging in anticolonial politics was "one of the weakest sides of COMINTERN's activity." In his opinion, since the COMINTERN's inception in 1919, communist parties had either ignored anti-colonialism or regarded it as a waste of time.[25] All efforts by COMINTERN leaders to rectify this had been in vain. Kuusinen suggested the creation of a commission, headed by the British communist Robin Page Arnot, to visit the communist parties of Western Europe to discuss anticolonial politics and prepare a "Colonial Conference" to be held in 1929. Arnot first went to London where he attended the Communist Party's 1929 congress. He reported that the anti-colonial question was raised, but only in passing, and on the final day. The British communists had simply disregarded the directives of the COMINTERN.[26] Arnot's next stop was Paris. If anything, the French communists' interest in the anti-colonial question was even lower than that of the British. Arnot saw all aspects of Ho's critique confirmed.[27] His experiences in Belgium and the Netherlands were similar. In short, the anticolonial work of the European communists was close to nonexistent. Even the simplest tasks, such as establishing contact with militants in the colonies, had not been carried out. Arnot summed up his impressions in the "Report on the Parties," in which he dryly concluded that "at the moment not much is being done."[28]

The Colonial Conference of 1929

After receiving Arnot's report, the commissioners of the Colonial Conference deemed it necessary to rewrite the position paper on the colonial

---

24   Degras. *The Communist International.* pp. 526–48.

25   *Ibid.* p. 526, 537–47.

26   According to Arnot, the Communist Party of Great Britain should carry out the "ideological strengthening of the Party," a process that "will...take some time and much vigilance to weed out the right-wing tendencies." The CPGB was at the time "plagued by internal conflict and...political stupefaction." See Worley, Matthew. *Class Against Class: The Communist Party in Britain between the Wars.* I.B. Tauris, 2002. p. 116; Petersson. *We Are Neither Visionaries Nor Utopian Dreamers.* p. 257.

27   Duiker, Walter. *Ho Chí Minh: A Life.* Hyperion, 2000. pp. 148–150.

28   Petersson. *"We Are Neither Visionaries Nor Utopian Dreamers."* p. 258.

question. This task was assigned to the Hungarian operative Lajos Magyar. In his paper titled "The Organisation of the Colonial Work of the European Communist Parties," he reached the following conclusion:

> The most important task of the Communist Parties of the imperialist countries with regard to the colonial question is...the establishment of a direct contact between the Communist Parties and the revolutionary trade union organisations...The relationships existing up to now between the Communist Parties and the revolutionary movement in the respective colonial countries cannot be considered...satisfactory...Not all of the Parties have so far grasped the great significance of regular close connections with the revolutionary movements in the colonies for the practical support of these movements. Only to the extent that the Communist Parties in the imperialist countries actually support the revolutionary movement [and] assist the struggle of [the] colonial countries against imperialism, can their position with regard to the colonial question be accepted as truly Bolshevik.[29]

Magyar identified five tasks for the parties to focus on: producing political literature to be distributed effectively in the colonies; sending out members to the colonies as regular workers—that is, not as representatives of the COMINTERN—to find employment and organize on a grassroots level; establishing contacts with sailors, workers, soldiers, and students from the colonies living in Europe; and, finally, penetrating the communities of people from the colonies living in Europe to exert "communist influence" among them.[30] Entirely absent from Magyar's paper were any recommendations on how to mobilize the working classes in the metropolis to act against imperialist war and racism.

The Seventh Congress of the COMINTERN: From Anti-Imperialism to the Popular Front

The repeated efforts of the COMINTERN to get the communist parties of Europe to make the anticolonial question a priority were largely in vain. Many Europeans were convinced that the main purpose of the colonies was to serve their colonizers and this was in their own best interest, since it would bestow civilization upon them. The undeniable suffering that this process entailed was seen as "collateral damage."

The German Marxist Fritz Steinberg criticized Lenin and the COM-

---

29 *Ibid.* pp. 264–265.
30 *Ibid.* p. 265.

INTERN for having unrealistic expectations. In 1935 he wrote:

> As Lenin misjudged the real strength of Reformism so did his epigones even more. He never gave a systematic analysis of the sociological prerequisites which formed the basis of Reformism, and which prevented it from being shaken during the period up to the victory of Fascism. The Comintern has contented itself with slogans. It has never made it clear that the differentiation in the pre-war years within the working class took place based on the increasing wages of the entire class. The Comintern has not corrected Lenin's mistake as to the question of the labor aristocracy and thus the evaluation of the real strength of Reformism. On the contrary: it has made it even deeper.[31]

Sternberg's critique must be read against the background of German politics in the 1930s. In 1933, the Nazis had risen to power with significant working-class support. When Adolf Hitler was appointed chancellor by President Paul von Hindenburg, social democratic party leaders had advised against mass protests.[32] After much internal debate, the majority of SPD Reichstag delegates (48 out of 65) even endorsed Hitler's "commitment to peace," made at a Reichstag speech in May 1933. In her 1993 book *German Social Democracy and the Rise of Nazism*, historian Donna Harsch writes about the vote in the Reichstag:

> When the Social Democratic deputies rose as a body to vote with the bourgeois parties, the chamber, including Hitler, broke into a storm of applause. The German Nationalists burst into *Deutschland, Deutschland, über alles*, and many Social Democrats joined in. Bavarian member of parliament Wilhelm Hoegner later reflected, "It was as if we Social Democrats, ever cursed as the prodigal sons of the fatherland, for one eternal moment clasped Mother Germany to our hearts."[33]

A few months later, the SPD was declared illegal, and its leaders were forced into exile. The social imperialist policies they had pursued now helped cement Nazi power.

The ruling class in Europe was horrified by the destruction of the old order in Russia. In order to stay in power, they were prepared to form alliances with anyone who would keep the communists at bay. This helped to pave the way for fascism, first in Italy in 1922 and then in Germany in 1933. One of the first things Hitler did after becoming chancellor was to

---

31 Sternberg, Fritz. *Der Faschismus an der Macht*. Contact, 1935. p. 91.

32 Harsch, Donna. *German Social Democracy and the Rise of Nazism*. University of North Carolina Press, 1993. p. 225.

33 *Ibid.* p. 236.

suppress the Communist Party.

This made the COMINTERN change one more policy. Due to the danger of fascism, it abandoned its revolutionary "Class against Class" strategy. The new COMINTERN leader Georgi Dimitrov was a key figure in this policy change. Dimitrov argued that the rise of fascism demonstrated the danger of a divisive conflict on the left. It had to be replaced by a "popular front" approach that sought cooperation with social democrats and others now opposed to fascism. France was the only country where the popular front became a success. In the general election in April 1936, the popular front of Communist, Socialist, and Liberal Radicals gained an absolute majority in the parliament, 378 seats out of 618. Seventy-two of the seats were communist. In Britain, the Communist Party's attempt to affiliate with Labour was rebuffed. In Germany, it was too late. However, the relevance of this strategy was confirmed by the Anti-COMINTERN pact signed by Japan and Germany in 1936. Fascism was an immediate threat against communism.

The COMINTERN's central concern was now the defense of the Soviet Union. At the Seventh Congress of the COMINTERN, it became clear that the pursuit of world revolution, and the focus on the countries of the East, were no longer priorities. The sense was, once again, that the future of the Soviet Union would be decided in Western Europe. Stalin had no illusions about the working classes there. In communication with Dimitrov, Stalin wrote:

> Without their colonies they [the imperialist powers] could not exist. The workers know this and fear the loss of the colonies. And in this connection, they are inclined to go with their own bourgeoisie. Internally, they are not in agreement with our anti-imperialist policy. They are even afraid of this policy. And for just this reason it is necessary to explain and approach these workers correctly...We can't immediately and so easily win millions of workers in Europe.[34]

During the Seventh, and last, Congress of the COMINTERN in 1935, the anti-colonial struggle was hardly mentioned. After listing various groups that could aid in the struggle against fascism—social democrats, Catholics, anarchists, unorganized workers, peasants, the petty bourgeoisie, and the intelligentsia—Dimitrov now called the peoples'

---

34   Redfern, Niel. "The COMINTERN and Imperialism." *Journal of Labor and Society*. Vol. 20, no. 1, March 2017, p. 13.

struggles in the colonies an "important reserve for the world proletariat."³⁵ Dimitrov made it clear that the priority of the communist parties was "the struggle for peace and the defense of the USSR." Communists, he declared, were "irreconcilable opponents, on principle, of bourgeois nationalism…but we are not supporters of national nihilism and should never act as such." He insisted that communist organizations must persist in educating the working classes in the "spirit of proletarian internationalism," but must not "sneer at all the national sentiments of the wide masses of working people."³⁶

The COMINTERN's revised position on nationalism in the imperialist countries was confirmed in the May Day statement one year later in 1936. The declaration asserted that the Bolsheviks had been correct in insisting that the proletariat had to defeat the national bourgeoisie in the Russian Revolution, but that "today the situation is not what it was in 1914."³⁷ In a statement on the 1938 Nazi annexation of Czechoslovakia, the reversal of the COMINTERN's stance on nationalism was even more pronounced. The paper proclaimed that the working class had "begun to revise its relationship with the nation" and had "won a place" in it. Essentially, this meant that the COMINTERN accepted the power-sharing agreement between the capitalists and the working class in the imperialist countries. The leaders of the COMINTERN even went so far as to accuse the bourgeoisie of "betraying the national interests," declaring that: "it is the working class and its Communist Party which takes over the legacies of the bourgeois revolution, maintains them against the traitors and develops them to a richer and fuller life."³⁸

The COMINTERN's Popular Front strategy came to an abrupt end with the signing of the Treaty of Non-Aggression between Germany and the Union of Soviet Socialist Republics in August 1939. Stalin signed the pact because he feared that the Western powers would sit back and clap their hands while Germany destroyed the Soviet Union. Within weeks, the COMINTERN's strategy of antifascist unity had been abandoned

---

35   Dimitrov, Georgi. *Report to the 7th Congress Communist International 1935: For the Unity of the Working Class against Fascism.* Red Star Press, 1973. p. 59.

36   Dimitrov, Georgi. *The United Front.* Proletarian Publishers, 1975. pp. 11, 36, 79, 82.

37   Redfern. "The COMINTERN and Imperialism." p. 50.

38   *Ibid.* p. 51.

in favor of peace at all costs. The Soviets' efforts to avoid a military confrontation with Nazi Germany were in vain. Germany invaded the USSR in June 1941 and the Soviets entered into an alliance with the Allies. This caused the COMINTERN to revive the Popular Front tactic.

This approach meant that anti-colonial struggles were no longer a priority. In fact, Soviet leaders feared that they might distract the imperialist powers from confronting the Nazis in Europe. The COMINTERN urged the working classes of Britain and France to stand with their governments in defense of the colonies in Asia, which were "menaced by Japanese imperialism."[39]

This completed the transformation of the COMINTERN from an organization to enhance world revolution to one defending the national interests of the Soviet Union. The consequences for the colonies were disastrous. The opportunism of the Communist Party of India (CPI) serves as an example. Before 1941, the CPI had always tried to take advantage of Britain's difficulties. At the outbreak of World War II, its leaders cheered: "Never again shall we get an opportunity like this. The Empire is cracking. It cannot survive this crisis."[40] But by the summer of 1942, when social unrest engulfed India, the CPI had accepted the COMINTERN's position, that national liberation had to be delayed until the Soviet Union's survival was secure. The Party helped prevent the uprising of the masses and urged people to support the British in their war efforts. Shortly after, the CPI was declared legal by the British authorities for the first time.[41]

In 1943, the Soviet government decided to dissolve the COMINTERN. Stalin explained the decision by pointing to the fact that communist parties outside of the Soviet Union were constantly accused of being "agents of a foreign state."[42] But many felt that the dissolution of the COMINTERN was mainly a concession to the Soviet Union's imperialist allies. The demise of COMINTERN was not met by resistance from its

---

39   Degras. *The Communist International, 1919–1943: Documents. Volume 3: 1929–43*. p. 390.

40   Redfern. "The COMINTERN and Imperialism." p. 53.

41   *Ibid.*

42   Banac, Ivo. *The Diary of Georgi Dimitrov, 1933–1949*. Yale University Press, 2003. p. 13.

member sections. The change of the COMINTERN into an instrument of Soviet foreign policy had laid the roots of the post-war disintegration of the communist movement as a unified international political force. Instead, a variety of different national roads to a transition toward socialism developed.

In an assessment of why the international communist movement turned from a force with worldwide revolutionary ambitions into the servant of the Soviet Union, historian Neil Redfern writes:

> It is one of the great ironies of history that the Comintern, founded in a rupture with the "social-patriots" of 1914-1918 itself became primarily an organisation of "social-patriots," even if this was perceived as an internationalist defense of the Soviet Union. How can we explain this? For the present writer, the fundamental reason was a materialist reason—the strength of bourgeois ideology, in the imperialist countries, including in the communist movement.[43]

I would like to add that the "strength of bourgeois ideology" was rooted in imperialism, that is, in the fact that the majority of the working class of the imperialist countries benefited from imperialist profits.

During the 1920s, the COMINTERN genuinely tried to establish a worldwide, class-based, and revolutionary communist movement. It failed. The division of the global working class proved too big an obstacle. In the imperialist countries, "social patriotism" reigned. Workers identified first and foremost as citizens of their respective nation-states. They were integrated into the nation-state's political system and the political parties representing them were often included in government—sometimes even leading it. The stratification between the working class in the imperialist center, and the exploited in the periphery, was a fact during the history of the COMINTERN.

In retrospect, one of the important effects of the Russian Revolution was the establishment of COMINTERN. It was the first—and until now, the only—well-organized and serious attempt backed by a state to enhance a communist world revolution. It did not succeed. But the COMINTERN was a crucial factor in bringing the revolutionary torch from the West to the East and South. In this sense, the Russian Revolution opened up the anti-colonial struggle from the end of the First World War

---

43   Redfern. "The COMINTERN and Imperialism." p. 56.

until the mid-1970s. The revolutions of China and Vietnam—along with the processes of decolonization—would have moved more slowly, if not for the establishment of COMINTERN.

Since the dissolution of COMINTERN, there has not been an effective International. After his expulsion from the Soviet Union, Trotsky established a Fourth International in 1938. However, the Fourth International never gained much influence, except in narrow Trotskyist circles, and has since been haunted by splits. Today the Fourth International exerts no major influence.

The communist movement never achieved unity in ideology and action as during the time of Lenin. Instead of the main road towards a coordinated socialist World Revolution, the transition was to move on national roads, developing socialism with different national characteristics.

But let us return to socialist development in the Soviet Union itself, as it may shed some light on the changing policies of COMINTERN.

CHAPTER 12

STALIN: FROM THE WORLD REVOLUTION TO SOCIALISM IN ONE COUNTRY

The revolution, the civil war, and the economic policy in the first years of the Soviet Union did not produce the governance which Lenin envisioned in his *State and Revolution*, written just before the Bolshevik revolution. In the book, Lenin described the proletarian dictatorship as a state without professional army or police, a state constituted by "a people in arms," before progressively "withering away." This was a great concern of Lenin towards the end of his life. Out of the thirty years in which Lenin was active in politics, he exercised state power in only six, from 1917-23. During this period, his theoretical positions were tested by experience: he had to revise and admit errors. The Soviet state he created, with *a* powerful army and political police, was unlike the ideal model in *State and Revolution*. For sure, the Bolshevik vanguard party had been effective in carrying out the revolution; however, it was not the ideal organizational form to rule the state and develop socialism.

Lenin felt he had to retreat from his ideals under the pressure of circumstances. A "people in arms" could not defend the revolution against the professional armies of reactionary powers—a lesson learned from the Paris Commune. A centralized army was needed. Moreover, the political police were indispensable in suppressing internal counterrevolution. The chaos of revolution had to be handled by a strong state, particularly through the transitional period of unpredictable duration. This conviction gave Lenin self-confidence in his course of action. The single-party state began to take shape.

Under NEP, the economy reached a pre-war level, and the food market began to function; however, it did not produce the industrialization necessary for economic development. Left-wing Bolsheviks criticized NEP for favoring the peasants over the workers. Inequalities re-emerged. The partial reinstatement of capitalist conditions entailed a restructuring of social classes and a change in their relationships. Lenin had hoped that the NEP would be a decade-long transition period, before returning to a more communal form of economic development. However, history went in another direction.

The state apparatus also transformed. During the civil war, the competing Menshevik and Socialist Revolutionary parties ceased to exist, but instead of achieving unity, different factions inside the Bolshevik party proliferated. At the Tenth Party Congress in 1921, the formation of factions were banned on pain of expulsion, as divisions demonstrated weaknesses, which could be exploited by enemies inside and outside of the Soviet Union.

When Lenin died, the question of whether the NEP should continue became part of the struggle for succession. Stalin, who was one of five members of the Politburo, used Lenin's ban on factions to eliminate his rivals. Stalin was elected as General Secretary of the Central Committee on April 3rd, 1922. From this position, he controlled the agenda of the Politburo and the appointment and demotion of the high-level party functionaries. This enabled Stalin to fill posts with his supporters, and thereby secure his position.

Nearing his death, Lenin realized that centralizing power had gone too far. During his last Party Congress, in March-April 1922, he surveyed the factors of the situation: the isolation of the Russian revolution; the poverty and the backwardness of Russia; the individualism of the peasantry; the weakness and demoralization of the working class. But another problem now struck him: state power had been concentrated in the hands of a few Bolshevik leaders.

In May 1922, a stroke left Lenin partially paralyzed. In his last weeks, Lenin dictated a series of letters to his wife Krupskaya, addressed to the Central Committee. In the letters, later called "Lenin's testament", he proposed changes to the structure of the Soviet governing bodies and gave his evaluation of the different Bolshevik leaders: Zinoviev, Kamenev, Trotsky, Bukharin, and Stalin. He warned of the possibility of a damaging split in the party leadership between Trotsky and Stalin:

> Comrade Stalin, having become Secretary-General, has unlimited authority concentrated in his hands, and I am not sure whether he will always be capable of using that authority with sufficient caution. Comrade Trotsky, on the other hand, as his struggle against the C.C. on the question of the People's Commissariat of Communications has already proved, is distinguished not only by outstanding ability. He is personally perhaps the most capable man in the present C.C., but he has displayed excessive self-assurance and shown excessive preoccupation with the purely administrative side of the work. These two qualities of the two outstanding leaders of the present C.C. can inadvertently lead to a split, and if our Party does not take steps to avert this, the split may come unexpectedly.[1]

In a post-script, Lenin wrote:

> Stalin is too coarse and this defect...becomes intolerable in a Secretary-General. That is why I suggest that the comrades think about a way of removing Stalin from that post and appointing another man in his stead who in all other respects differs from Comrade Stalin in having only one advantage, namely, that of being more tolerant, more loyal, more polite and more considerate to the comrades, less capricious, etc. This circumstance may appear to be a negligible detail. But I think that from the standpoint of safeguards against a split and from the standpoint of what I wrote above about the relationship between Stalin and Trotsky it is not a [minor] detail, but a detail which can assume decisive importance.[2]

It was only after Lenin's death, on January 21, 1924, that Krupskaya turned the documents over to the Central Committee Secretariat. The letters were read to the delegates of the Thirteenth Party Congress in May 1924 under the condition that they should be kept secret.[3] Because of Lenin's words, Stalin offered to withdraw as General Secretary. However, he was asked to remain in his post by the Central Committee.[4]

In 1923, Stalin had already formed a coalition against Trotsky. The first issue which divided the two sides was whether socialism could be

---

1 Lenin, Vladimir Ilyich. *Letter to the Congress.* 1922. https://www.marxists.org/archive/lenin/works/1922/dec/testamnt/congress.htm

2 *Ibid.*

3 Lih, Lars T. "Political Testament of Lenin and Bukharin and the Meaning of NEP." *Slavic Review.* Vol. 50, no. 2, Summer 1991, pp. 241–52.

4 Kotkin, Stephen. *Stalin: Paradoxes of Power, 1878–1928.* Allen Lane, 2014. p. 473.

built in one country or whether, as both Lenin and Trotsky had believed, the revolution had to be spread to the most advanced countries in Europe. This was the dividing line, far more than any difference in internal outlook. Trotsky was no different in perspective on the Party than any other Bolshevik. At the Thirteenth Party Congress, in May 1924, he stated:

> None of us desires or is able to dispute the will of the Party. Clearly, the Party is always right...We can only be right with and by the Party, for history has provided no other way of being in the right. The English have a saying, "My country, right or wrong"...We have much better historical justification in saying whether it is right or wrong in certain individual concrete cases, it is my party...And if the Party adopts a decision which one or other of us thinks unjust, he will say, just or unjust, it is my party, and I shall support the consequences of the decision to the end.[5]

Trotsky also agreed on the need for purges, "of a police character," to "review the whole Soviet system and cleanse it ruthlessly from all the accumulated filth."[6] Taking Trotsky's record as the leader of the Red Army in the Civil War in mind, I think it is incorrect to assume that a party led by Trotsky would not have used repression in "the cause of revolution."

In 1924, Stalin published *Problems of Leninism*, which claimed that a proletarian revolution could build socialism in one country.[7] In 1925, the Fourteenth Party Conference accepted this strategy. The construction and defense of socialism in one country had top priority. Trotsky became isolated, and Zinoviev and Kamenev began to criticize the NEP from a left position. The three formed an "united opposition" against Stalin. As a consequence, they were accused of forming a faction and thereby violating the decree on Party unity. All three lost their seats in the Politburo, and in 1927 were expelled from the Party. Trotsky was exiled to Kazakhstan, and then later deported from the Soviet Union in 1929.

In his campaign against the "united opposition," Stalin was allied

---

5   Trotsky, Leon. "Speech to the Thirteenth Party Congress on May 26, 1924." Trotsky, Leon. *The Challenge of the Left Opposition: 1923–1925*. Pathfinder Press, 1975. pp. 161–62.

6   Twiss, Thomas. *Trotsky and the Problem of Soviet Bureaucracy*. Brill, 2014. p. 303.

7   Stalin, Joseph. *Problems of Leninism*. International Publishers, 1934. http://www.marx2mao.com/Stalin/POLtc.html

with the "right-wing" of the party: Bukharin, Rykov, and Tomsky, who supported a continuation of the NEP. However, once the "united opposition" had been defeated, Stalin decided to terminate the NEP and swept away both capitalist production and market and communal forms of production—a switch from "state capitalism" to so-called "state socialism." The reasons for the shift were motivated by problems in food production and the desire for rapid industrialization so the USSR could effectively resist the eventuality of an invasion. A precondition for increased industrialization was to control food production so the industrial workers could be fed. If War Communism and the NEP were difficult for the people of the Soviet Union, still harder times awaited.

Collectivization

The Bolsheviks formed an alliance between workers and peasants during the revolution by redistributing feudal land. However, this had not increased agricultural production, as many small farmers had reverted to subsistence cultivation during the chaos of the civil war. With the NEP, agricultural production increased, but often the peasants hoarded grain to force the price up. To enforce rapid industrialization, Stalin had to secure delivery of food for the cities. Part of the new industrial labor force came from rural areas, so those that remained had to supply more food to the cities than before. Rapid collectivization became the answer. The number of collective farms rose from 4 percent in 1929 to 58 percent in March 1930. Farmers were forced to pool their resources and work as a collective. The state purchased most of the production at fixed prices, although the collective farms were allowed a small plot and some livestock for private consumption. As a response, many peasants slaughtered their livestock, burned their grain, and destroyed their farming tools. Fearing that the peasants would refuse to sow summer crops, the collectivization campaign came to a temporary halt in the spring of 1930. Many peasants used this opportunity to leave the collectives. The collectivization was resumed in the summer of 1930, creating around 250,000 collective farms. The process was opposed by the majority of peasants, especially the kulaks—the richer farmers. Stalin wanted to "liquidate the kulaks as a class." Their property was appropriated, and they were deported to remote areas. Thousands died in the process. The opposition to collectivization and acquisition of grain for the cities—combined with unusually severe cold and drought—caused famine in rural areas of the Soviet Union in 1932-33, costing millions of lives and ending the forced transition to collective farming.

Industrialization

The Bolshevik party under Stalin was convinced that rapid industrialization was necessary to develop socialism and repel Western aggression. At the Sixteenth Party Congress in June 1930, Stalin stated: "We are on the eve of transformation from an agrarian into an industrial country."[8] The ambition for such a transformation was not new; it had been an objective since the revolution. To facilitate this process, the Soviet Union imported advanced technology from the West to accelerate the development of their productive forces. However, in 1929, Stalin shifted from the NEP to a new form of management—the centrally planned economy, implemented through Five Year Plans. The first was launched in April 1929. In 1925-26, under the NEP, the state sector constituted 46 percent of the economy; by 1932, this had risen to 91 percent.[9] Instead of market forces, political decisions were to decide what should be produced. Production targets set by economic planners dominated life, eliminating remnants of pluralism in the political sphere. Simultaneously, harsh discipline was introduced in the labor force. Even arts, sciences, and philosophy were subordinated to support reaching the goals set by the planned economy.

The priority of the first Five Year Plan was the production of capital goods, with a focus on heavy industry, machinery, and energy supply. The total production of any society can be divided into two inversely proportional sectors: capital goods and goods for final consumption. The fewer goods produced for final consumers, the more goods can be produced for expanded production. The second Five Year Plan from 1933-37 followed the same lines. The results were astonishing. The industrial workforce increased from 4.3 million in 1928 to 11.6 million in 1937. After less than a decade of industrialization, the Soviet Union's industrial output was

---

8   Deutscher, Isaac. *Stalin, A Political Biography*. Oxford University Press, 1949. https://archive.org/stream/in.ernet.dli.2015.463015/2015.463015.Stalin--_djvu.txt

9   Nove, Alec. *An Economic History of the U.S.S.R.* Penguin, 1990. p. 137.

greater than Germany and England. It was only surpassed by the United States. The Moscow metro was constructed, and a vital defense industry was established. But only a portion of the fruits of industrialization became available to Soviet citizens. The majority was appropriated by the state for military expenditure and further industrialization. In the first Five Year Plan, defense was 5.4% of total expenditures, but by January 1941, it had reached 43.4%. In 1931, Stalin stated: "We are 50-100 years behind the advanced countries. We have to traverse this distance in ten years. We will either accomplish it or else we will be crushed."[10]

By the time of Hitler's invasion in June 1941, "'the industry had produced 2,700 modern aircraft and 4,300 tanks.' Judging by these figures, it cannot be said that the USSR arrived unprepared for its tragic appointment with war."[11] The Soviet Union achieved industrial development in a decade—an achievement which had taken Europe a hundred years—all during a time when the rest of the world was in an economic depression.

Though Stalin's priority was "socialism in one country," the Soviet Union still managed to support revolution internationally. Leading up to the Second World War, the Soviet Union supported the anti-fascist forces in the Spanish Civil War.[12] In total, the Soviet Union provided Republican Spain with 806 planes, 362 tanks, and 1,555 artillery pieces. The Soviet Union was the Republic's far most important source of weapons, without which the Republic would not have lasted long. In 1936, the USSR dispatched 50% of its precious annual production of military aircraft to Republican Spain.[13] The Soviet government provided credit to the Republic, knowing it had no chance of remuneration. Besides that, the COMINTERN urged communists all over Europe to support Republican Spain. Thousands of Communist Party members around the world joined the International Brigades as volunteers.

---

10   Stalin, Joseph. "Speech to Industrial Managers, February 1931." *Problems of Leninism*. Foreign Languages Publishing House, 1953. pp. 454–458.

11   Losurdo, Domenico. *Stalin: History and Critique of a Black Legend*. Iskra Books, 2023. p. 15.

12   Haslam, Jonathan. *The Soviet Union and the Struggle for Collective Security in Europe, 1933–1939*. Macmillan, 1984. p. 115.

13   Graham, Helen. *The Spanish Republic at War, 1936–1939*. Cambridge University Press, 2002. p. 153.

The Purges

Besides the economic transformations, there were also political changes in the state and the Party. Stalin conducted purges of opponents against his political line. This method of resolving political differences was egregious and damaging to the development of socialism. Besides the sheer brutality, it hindered the development of policy inside the party and weakened popular support. It damaged the reputation of socialism as a liberating project inside and outside the Soviet Union and has had negative consequences for the communist movement to this day.

This is not to say that purges are always wrong. Class struggles are sometimes transmitted to political struggles inside the Party, and they can take an antagonistic form in which exclusion of members is a method to enforce a political line. However, political differences in a communist party should not be solved by criminalization or the physical elimination of opponents.

Inside the Bolshevik party, there had been fierce political struggles since the revolution. Lenin's call to storm the Winter Palace was considered a deviation from Marxism by Kamenev and Zinoviev. They alerted the Mensheviks of Lenin's plans, risking the revolution and inviting the accusation of betrayal from other Bolsheviks.[14] Long before Trotsky made the accusation that the revolution had been betrayed, such allegations loomed like shadows over the party.

However, during the early history of the Soviet Union, it was Trotsky, as commander of the Red Army, who was labeled a brutal dictator and a traitor of socialist ideals. During the civil war, he had to secure the very existence of the newborn state.

In 1918-21, elements of the peasantry were quite indifferent to the needs of the cities for supplies of food. Instead, they were inclined to establish spontaneous "peasant republics" centered on subsistence production. Deserters from the Red Army also claimed to represent "authentic" socialism, creating the "Free Republic of Deserters" in the district of Bessarabia. They appealed to Lenin to support them against state administration. The situation was the same in Kronstadt, where Soviet marines revolted.

---

14   Losurdo, Domenico. *Stalin.* p. 40.

Trotsky was in charge of ending these revolts and was considered the "defender of a bureaucratic organization." Trotsky, for his part, suspected Zinoviev of having encouraged the Kronstadt revolt by wielding the banner of "worker democracy."[15]

The accusation of betrayal has occurred in many revolutions when ideals meet reality, and these accusations are often linked to personal ambitions and power struggles. It is important to differentiate between political struggle and personal ambition.

In December 1934, Politburo member Sergei Kirov was assassinated. This led to a paranoiac purge. Most of the Bolshevik Old Guard from the revolution were arrested and sentenced to death or imprisoned in labor camps. The result was that 70% of the Central Committee, and over 90% of the delegates of the Seventeenth Party Congress in 1934, were no longer able to attend the Eighteenth Congress in 1939. Their replacements were people with a more technocratic outlook, and were also more loyal to Stalin. In the end, one of the central figures in the execution of the purges, the chief of the secret police (the NKVD) N.I. Ezhov was purged, and Lavrentiy Beria took charge of NKVD. At the Eighteenth Congress Stalin declared that:

> It cannot be said that the purge was not accompanied by grave mistakes. There were unfortunately more mistakes than might have been expected. Undoubtedly, we shall have no further need of resorting to the method of mass purges. Nevertheless, the purge of 1933-36 was unavoidable and its results, on the whole, were beneficial.[16]

Stalin's method "to solve" disagreement was a disaster, as it created a political atmosphere that could not lead to innovations in the development of socialism. The leading Bolsheviks developed into a new privileged layer in society. While Lenin was still alive, no party member was allowed to earn more than a skilled worker. This principle was formally abolished in 1932.[17] Of importance for the development of this privi-

---

15   Losurdo, Domenico. *Stalin*. p. 41.

16   Stalin, Joseph. "Report on the Work of the Central Committee to the Eighteenth Congress of the C.P.S.U.(B.), March 10, 1939." *J.V. Stalin, Works*. Vol. 14. Red Star Press, 1978. https://www.marxists.org/reference/archive/stalin/works/1939/03/10.htm

17   Tucker, Robert. *Stalin in Power: The Revolution from Above, 1928-1941*. W.W. Norton & Company, 1990. pp. 111–12.

leged class were also several perks and special treatments. Party leaders, and so-called "apparatchiks"—leading bureaucrats, administrators, and "comrades in responsible positions"—lived a different life than the general population. They were provided with special apartments with modern amenities, free cars with drivers, access to shops with food and luxury goods, free holiday stays, etc.[18] The Bolshevik party lost legitimacy as the people's party. Rather than regulating the "general production" to the benefit of the people, the bureaucracy alienated themselves from society.

From 1924 to 1934, the political climate in the Soviet Union radically changed. However, this was seldom criticized by European communists (except in Trotskyist circles). The contrast between economic depression and the spread of fascism in the West—and the rapid modernization in the Soviet Union—led many Western Marxists to tone down their criticism of Stalin's authoritarian tendency. One example of this attitude can be seen in the Austro-Marxist Otto Bauer. He had initially been critical of the Soviet Union, but he revised his opinion. In his 1936 book *Between Two World Wars?* he defends Stalin's policy as a historical necessity:

> Yet just as terrible the sacrifices which the great industrialisation and collectivisation process incurred, just so intoxicating are its consequences.[19]

The Ideology of "Actually Existing Socialism"

One mistake made by Stalin was his statement that socialism had been realized in the Soviet Union. In his report to the Eighth Extraordinary Soviet Congress in November 1936, he declared that "socialist construction" had been successfully completed:

> As a result of all these changes in the sphere of the national economy of the U.S.S.R., we now have a new Socialist economy, which knows neither crises nor unemployment, which knows neither poverty nor ruin, and which provides our citizens with every opportunity to lead a prosperous and cultured life. Such, in the main, are the changes which have taken place in the sphere of our economy during the period from 1924 to 1936. This means that the proletariat of the U.S.S.R. has been transformed into an entirely new class, into the working class of the U.S.S.R., which has abolished

---

18   *Ibid.* pp. 112–14.
19   Bauer, Otto. In van der Linden. *Western Marxism and the Soviet Union.* p. 47.

the capitalist economic system, which has established the Socialist ownership of the instruments and means of production and is directing Soviet society along the road to Communism.[20]

On the same occasion, Stalin proclaimed that the Soviet Union was "the most developed democracy" in the world—indeed the only consistent democracy.

> In a few days' time the Soviet Union will have a new, Socialist Constitution, built on the principles of fully developed Socialist democratism. It will be an historical document dealing in simple and concise terms with the facts of the victory of Socialism in the U.S.S.R., with the facts of the emancipation of the working people of the U.S.S.R. from capitalist slavery, with the facts of the victory in the U.S.S.R. of full and thoroughly consistent democracy.[21]

All this was an illusion. The Soviet Union was not socialist. While it was the first attempt to develop a socialist economy and state within a dominating capitalist world system, it was on the wrong track.

In Marx and Engels' definitions of socialism in the *Communist Manifesto*, they write about a society where the free development of the individual is the condition for the free development of all. In *The Civil War in France*, Marx wrote about "the despicable state machinery" and the necessity to "shatter the state." This was hardly the situation in the Soviet Union in 1936. The Soviet Union had eradicated illiteracy and managed to provide free healthcare; it had overcome famine and developed its productive force to a level comparable with states in the West. But socialism? No. It was a state-centered economy run by a party-state bureaucracy.

However, there are pragmatic reasons why Stalin proclaimed "the realization of socialism" in 1936. One reason was the mobilizing effect. The idea of the Soviet Union as a "first mover" in a global transition towards socialism could generate enthusiasm and help drive the modernization process forward. Through media, literature, film, theater, painting, and the educational system, this "image" of the Soviet Union as the "existing utopia" was spread.

It was a tale about the first country of the world where workers and peasants had taken power. It was the story of the abolition of poverty.

---

20 Stalin, Joseph. "On the Draft Constitution of the U.S.S.R. Report Delivered at the Extraordinary Eighth Congress of Soviets of the U.S.S.R., 25 November 1936." *Stalin, J.V. Works*. Vol. 14.

21 *Ibid.*

It was an ideology about international solidarity between the oppressed and exploited. However, it was not "the whole truth and nothing but the truth." The story of "socialism in one country" had elements of truth. Children received an education, and the health system was effective. When Stalin died in 1953, millions of Soviet citizens mourned him—the largest demonstration of public mourning in Soviet history. This fact has caused problems for anti-Stalinist academic research, which emphasize the psychological "fascination of Stalin" to explain the phenomena, instead of using a balanced historical materialist analysis.[22]

In the latter part of the 1930s, and during World War II, the ideology of "actually existing socialism" moved in a more nationalistic and conservative direction. "The great retreat" from the revolutionary policies of 1920.[23] An example of this could be seen in criminal law. In the 1920s, punishment was inspired by Anton Makarenko's principles of upbringing and resocialization of children and young people. New institutions had been established to bring child gangs and juvenile delinquents "back to a normal life." However, in 1935, the death penalty was reintroduced starting from the age of 12.[24] In the 1920s, the Bolsheviks supported Evgeny Pashukanis' philosophy of law, in which it was argued that criminal law would gradually vanish with the economic change from capitalism to socialism.[25] However, in 1936 the criminal system was strengthened in order to serve the state.[26] Family law was also moved in a conservative direction; abortion bans were reintroduced, and divorce laws tightened.

On the cultural front, the Proletarian Writers' Association (RAPP), was dissolved in 1932 and replaced with a "Writers' Union," which praised the industrialization, collectivization, and glorified Russian history—all in the form of "social realism." Alexei Tolstoy wrote an ode to

---

22   Cohen, Stephen. *Rethinking the Soviet Experience: Politics & History Since 1917*. Oxford University Press, 1986. pp. 101–103.

23   Timashieff, Nicholas. *The Great Retreat: The Growth and Decline of Communism in Russia*. E.P. Dutton & Co., 1946.

24   Makarenko, Anton Semenovich. *The Road to Life*. University Press of the Pacific, 2001.

25   Pashukanis, Evgeny. "The General Theory of Law and Marxism." *Selected Writings on Marxism and Law*. 1924. https://www.marxists.org/archive/pashukanis/1924/law/index.htm

26   Ward, Chris. *Stalin's Russia*. Bloomsbury Academic, 1999. pp. 233–35.

Peter the Great. The director Sergei Eisenstein—who, in his 1926 film *Battleship Potemkin*, had depicted a heroic mutiny during the 1905 revolution—now paid tribute to the despots of the past in his films *Alexander Nevsky* and *Ivan the Terrible*.[27]

There was a parallel development in historiography. The leading Soviet historian of the early 1930s, Mikhail Pokrovsky, emphasized the ruthlessness of Ivan the Terrible and Peter the Great.[28] Pokrovsky's heroes were the leaders of the great uprisings in Russia's history: Kondraty Bulavin, Stenka Razin, and Yemelyan Pugachov, all of whom were portrayed as forerunners of the "proletarian revolution." However, after Pokrovsky's death to cancer in 1932, scholars were given the task by the Politburo to write a new history textbook. Pokrovsky's attack on the old tsarist regime as a "prison of peoples" was deemed to be anti-patriotic. To eliminate this "national nihilism," a new Russian nationalist historical orthodoxy was established in which rebels were portrayed as "bandits" with no political significance.[29]

Leading Marxist theorists of the late 1920s, such as Abram Deborin, David Ryazanov, and Isaak Rubin, were purged and replaced by theorists like Mark Mitin and Vladimir Adoratsky—with Stalin being the final authority in all theoretical-philosophical questions. Even in architecture, the idea of grandiose nationalism had its influence in what was to be called "Stalin Baroque." In Moscow, central districts were demolished, and streets widened to accommodate processions and parades.

Conservative tendencies and strong nationalism were introduced in the Red Army as well. New uniforms, with the old-time epaulets for officers' uniforms, were reintroduced. There were special officers' clubs, and military academies were established according to the tsarist model. Any recruit for the Red Army had hitherto sworn that he would: "devote all (his) deeds and (his) thoughts to the great goal, to liberate the workers and to fight for the Soviet Union and for socialism and brotherhood between the peoples." Now, it was changed to: "I will for my last breath

---

27   Ibid. p. 235.

28   Mikhail Nikolayevich Pokrovsky (1868–1932) is regarded as the most influential Soviet historian of the 1920s and was known as "the head of the Marxist historical school" in the USSR.

29   Tucker. *Stalin in Power*. p. 114.

serve my fatherland and my government." The political commissars in the army were abolished in 1943 and World War II was later referred to in Soviet history as "The Great Patriotic War."[30]

In Stalin's speech from atop Lenin's Mausoleum on November 7, 1941—while soldiers marched from Red Square directly to the frontlines, just outside Moscow—he gave the troops some examples of historical figures to emulate:

> The war you are waging is a war of liberation, a just war. Let the manly images of our great ancestors—Alexander Nevsky, Dimitry Donskoy, Kuzma Minin, Dimitry Pozharsky, Alexander Suvorov and Mikhail Kutuzov—inspire you in this war! May the victorious banner of the great Lenin be your North star![31]

Among these 7 figures were four despotic rulers and one saint.

In 1943, the COMINTERN was disbanded, and in 1944, "The Internationale" was replaced with "The Soviet Anthem." The ideology of "actually existing socialism" legitimized state institutions and leaders, mobilized the population, and strengthened their labor efforts. For European communists, the myth of a "real existing socialist state" translated to hope in an era marked by economic crisis and the rise of fascist movements.

Today, the postulate that "actually existing socialism" *is* socialism has been persistently cultivated by liberals, as well the right-wing, with success. The political function is obvious: use Stalin's myth of a socialist Soviet Union to damage the entire "brand" of socialism.

THE GREAT PATRIOTIC WAR

The development of Soviet military capacity was enhanced by the delay of the German invasion, secured by the Nazi-Soviet Non-Aggression Pact, which Stalin agreed to in 1939 following his failure to secure an alliance with Britain and France. Between 1939 and 1941, the Soviet Union used this postponement to expand its number of military personnel by

---

30   Ibid.
31   Stalin, Jospeh. "Speech at the Red Army Parade on the Red Square, Moscow. November 7, 1941." https://www.marxists.org/reference/archive/stalin/works/1941/11/07.htm

132.4%; guns and mortars by 110.7%; tanks by 21.8%; and aircraft by 142.8%.[32]

On June 22, 1941, Germany broke the pact and invaded. By July, German forces had penetrated Soviet territory from Odessa in the South to a hundred miles short of Leningrad in the North. However, pockets of resistance left behind by this rapid advance did not capitulate as the Germans had experienced in Poland, Belgium, and France. Fierce and unpredictable counter attacks impeded Germany. The resistance of Soviet forces was unbroken. This gave the Soviet Union time to transfer resources and industry eastwards and thereby keep up their defense production. Nazi Germany was never able to conquer Moscow, Leningrad, or Stalingrad, and by 1943 the tide had turned.

The contributions made by the Soviet Union against Nazi Germany were decisive for the result of the Second World War as a whole. The Third Reich suffered its heaviest losses on the eastern front: more than 75% of its soldiers, tanks, aircraft, and artillery.[33] In the winter of 1944-45, the Red Army advanced through Eastern Europe and ended the Holocaust. In October 1944, Red Army soldiers uncovered the horrors of the concentration camps in central Poland and, after fierce fighting, liberated the prisoners of Auschwitz-Birkenau on January 27, 1945. It is often forgotten that in addition to the six million Jewish victims of the Nazi genocide, at least 20 million Soviet civilians were deliberately exterminated in two hundred prison camps across occupied Eastern Europe. The Soviet Union suffered the most casualties of the war—between 24-26 million. The losses suffered by Western European and the U.S. were significantly lower.

THE SOVIET UNION AS A WORLD POWER

In April 1945, the Red Army conquered Berlin. The British and French empires were weakened by the war. The U.S. emerged as the leading imperialist power. The Soviet Union, however, was also triumphant. Its military strength proved powerful enough to overcome the German war ma-

---

32   Harrison, Mark. *Accounting for War: Soviet Production, Employment, and the Defense Burden, 1940–1945.* Cambridge University Press, 1996. pp. 68, 284.

33   Zhilin, Pavel. *Recalling the Past for the Sake of our Future: The Causes, Results and Lessons of World War Two.* Novosti, 1985. p. 4.

chine. Despite the war's immense costs, the Soviet Union had established itself as an important political player in the world system.

The communist resistance across Europe strengthened the position of the Soviet Union. But the split within anti-Nazi movements between "Western-oriented" and communist forces intensified, such as in Poland, where bloody infighting started during the occupation and continued years after the war had ended. The U.S. and Britain attempted to contain Soviet influence in Europe. The primary objective of the Soviet Union immediately after 1945 was to avoid war with its former allies. The United States' willingness to use nuclear weapons on Hiroshima and Nagasaki suggested that any military confrontation with imperialism would end in catastrophe.

The Soviets also enjoyed diplomatic influence, as at the Yalta Conference in 1945, where Roosevelt, Churchill, and Stalin divided Europe into spheres of influence so as to avoid armed confrontation—at least in Europe. East Germany, Poland, Hungary, Czechoslovakia, Bulgaria, and Romania had been wrested from German control by the Red Army and declared peoples' republics under Communist Party leadership in the late 1940s. The communist led National Liberation Movement in Yugoslavia and Albania liberated themselves from Italians, Germans, and local fascists.

Even in Western Europe, communist often led resistance struggles. Many of the communist partisans got their first military experience as volunteers in Spain. Italy and France—both with strong communist movements—were liberated by U.S. and English forces and ended up in the Western camp. The Italian communist leader Palmiro Togliatti, a former hardliner in the fight against the social democrats, declared that the task of the Italian workers was not revolution but to rebuild the nation. This required loyalty to the Allied forces. His position did not change, even when the Allies disarmed communist partisans who, in April 1945, had seized power in several towns in northern Italy.[34] The Italian Communist Party helped impose the rule of capital and was included in the country's first postwar government. The situation was similar in France, where the French Communist Party participated in the coalition government that ordered the brutal suppression of anticolonial revolts in Alge-

---

34 Redfern. "The COMINTERN and Imperialism." p. 54.

ria and Indochina.[35]

This flirtation between the bourgeoisie and the communists in Italy and France didn't last long. By 1947, collaboration with communists was unacceptable. Delegates across Europe established the Communist Information Bureau (Cominform) as a new alliance of communist organizations. Soviet delegate Andrei Zhdanov declared that the world was now divided into an "imperialist camp" headed by the U.S., and an "anti-imperialist camp" headed by the Soviet Union. The Yugoslav delegate Edvard Kardelj criticized the Italian and French communists for adopting "Social-Democratism."[36] For the Yugoslav communists, the formation of the Cominform signaled an offensive against imperialism. For Stalin, the foundation of the Cominform was a defensive measure against the Marshall Plan. These different interpretations between the Soviet Union and the communists in the Balkans led to a conflict within the international communist movement.

The Communist Party of Greece maintained its armed forces after the German occupation had ended. The British liberation of Greece from Nazi Germany meant the restoration of a bourgeois regime and the suppression of the communist forces that had led the liberation struggle. Albania rejected British "aid" and instead received support from the Soviet Union.[37] While the Yugoslav communists demanded aid to be given to the Greek communists, Stalin deemed any challenge to the postwar arrangement too risky. In a meeting with Churchill in 1944, Stalin agreed that Greece would remain in the British sphere of influence. In 1948, he told Milovan Djilas, a Yugoslav partisan and politician, that the uprising of the Greek communists had "no prospect of success" and had to be stopped "as quickly as possible."[38] Diplomatic relations were broken off between the Soviet Union and Yugoslavia, and the Cominform denounced the latter as revisionist.

The principal contradiction in the world during World War II was between the Axis powers and the Allies. Toward the end of the war, an-

---

35 *Ibid.*

36 *Ibid.* p. 55.

37 Walters, Robert. *American and Soviet Aid: A Comparative Analysis.* University of Pittsburgh, 1970. p. 91.

38 Milovan, Djilas. *Conversations with Stalin.* Penguin, 1963. p. 141.

other contradiction rose in importance between the U.S. and the Soviet Union. Churchill desperately wanted Western Allied forces to reach Berlin before Soviet troops to limit Soviet influence in Germany. The establishment of peoples' republics in Eastern Europe created a socialist bloc in the world system. The principal contradiction was written along the "Iron Curtain" declared by Churchill, later the Berlin Wall, and the frontiers of NATO and the Warsaw Pact.

The Soviet Union and Post-War Anti-Imperialism

The situation in Asia was different from Europe. Here there was no agreed balance of power, and the communist parties did not abide Moscow. Communists had withstood Japan and used the post-war confusion to take the offensive. In 1946, the Communist Party of Vietnam launched a campaign against French colonialism. China's communists fought Japan and the Kuomintang, and in 1949 proclaimed the People's Republic.

The Soviet Union offered assistance to the anticolonial armed struggle. In the Korean peninsula, the communists fought Japanese colonialism. At the Cairo Conference of 1943, the U.S., Britain, and China agreed that Korea should become independent once the country was freed from Japan.

After the surrender of Japan, on September 6, 1945, the People's Republic of Korea (PRK) was proclaimed based on a system of People's Committees. But Korea was divided into two occupation zones, with the Soviet Union occupying the north, and the U.S. occupying the south. In the south, the U.S. military government outlawed the PRK on December 12, 1945. In the north, the Soviet authorities merged the People's Committees into the Democratic People's Republic of Korea (DPRK). Along with arming the DPRK, the Soviet Union provided technical personnel and equipment.[39] Only the strength of the Soviet Union could prevent the wholesale U.S. takeover of Korea in the aftermath of the Second World War. Yet Stalin warned Kim Il-Sung against pursuing a war of national liberation in U.S.-occupied Korea.

---

39   Wilson Centre Digital Archive. "Notes of the Conversation between Comrade I.V. Stalin and a Governmental Delegation from the Democratic People's Republic of Korea headed by Kim Il Sung, March 5, 1949." https://digitalarchive.wilsoncenter.org/document/112127

However, Stalin's position would change after the liberation of China in 1949, and Kim Il-Sung then proceeded with his attempt to unify Korea.[40] The result was a war in Korea from June 1950 to July 1953. To prevent communist forces from uniting the country, more than 428,000 bombs were dropped on Pyongyang—the capital of the DPRK—roughly one bomb for each resident at that time. In all, 600,000 tons of bombs were dropped on North Korea, 3.7 times the amount of ordnance dropped on Japan during World War II. The U.S. killed 1,231,540 civilians in northern Korea during the three-year war.[41] Blaine Harden quotes American officers and political leaders:

> "Over a period of three years or so, we killed off—what—20 percent of the population," Air Force Gen. Curtis LeMay, head of the Strategic Air Command during the Korean War, told the Office of Air Force History in 1984. Dean Rusk, a supporter of the war and later secretary of state, said the United States bombed "everything that moved in North Korea, every brick standing on top of another." After running low on urban targets, U.S. bombers destroyed hydroelectric and irrigation dams in the later stages of the war, flooding farmland and destroying crops.[42]

The U.S. bombing was, in per capita terms, the deadliest in history:

> The war was endorsed by the newly established United Nations under the control of the US, UK, and France. The Soviet delegation was boycotting the Security Council and Chiang Kai-shek, who had fled to Taiwan, held China's seat.[43]

The Korean war has to be situated within the wider geopolitical framework of the time, which includes the anticolonial movement and the U.S effort to "contain" the Soviet Union and China. As U.S. forces invaded North Korea in October 1950 and drove north, China entered the war and forced them back to the thirty-eighth parallel. In February

---

40   Wilson Centre Digital Archive. "Telegram Shtykov to Vyshinsky on a Luncheon at the Ministry of Foreign Affairs of the DPRK, January 19, 1950." https://digitalarchive.wilsoncenter.org/document/112135

41   Korean Committee for Solidarity with the World People Societies for Friendship with the Asia-Pacific People. "67th Anniversary of Outbreak of Korean War." https://www.timbeal.net.nz/geopolitics/67_Korean_War.pdf

42   Harden, Blaine. In Beal, Tim. "The Continuing Korean War in the Murderous History of Bombing." *Monthly Review*. Vol. 72, no. 8, January 2021.

43   Armstrong, Charles King. "The Destruction and Reconstruction of North Korea, 1950-1960." *Asia-Pacific Journal*. Vol. 7, 2009.

1950, the Soviet Union and China entered the Sino-Soviet Treaty, committing to defend one another, just as Douglas MacArthur, commander of the U.S. army in the Far East, agitated for nuclear war on China. In April 1951, the Joint Chiefs of Staff drafted orders authorizing nuclear attacks on Manchuria and the Shandong Peninsula in East China, but were uncomfortable about giving them to MacArthur, for fear that he might prematurely carry out his orders.

> In the end, President Truman considered a war with China too dangerous. However, MacArthur's belligerence enjoyed support in anti-communist circles which viewed the wars in Korea and Vietnam as ways to contain China. The confrontation with North Korea was, in geopolitical terms, about China.[44]

All this shows the complicated and dangerous position Stalin had to navigate in the immediate post-war period. The assistance provided to Eastern Europe, China, and Korea are demonstrative examples that even in the context of postwar devastation, the Soviet Union under Stalin was willing to provide significant assistance to countries in the name of anti-imperialism.

An Evaluation of the Stalin Era

The Stalin era is a prime example of the difficulties of evaluating socialist history. Due to the "Cold War" and its intense anti-Soviet rhetoric, there is pressure to denounce Stalin completely. You cannot say anything positive about Stalin and still remain in good company. This problem extends to the left in the West. Here it is difficult to have a balanced discussion of the Stalin era. If you say something positive or negative, depending on the company, feelings grow and anger bursts. However, I think it is necessary "to face the music" and commit to a balanced evaluation, because the Stalin era had an enormous impact on the quest for socialism—and we must learn from it. In my historical account, I have tried to be pragmatic. I have tried to take into consideration the historical context and possible choices of action that existed at the time.

We have to evaluate the Stalin era from the perspective of the long transition from capitalism to socialism. The loss of human life in the

---

44 James, Dorris Clayton. *Triumph and Disaster 1945–1964: The Years of MacArthur.* Vol 3. Houghton Mifflin, 1985. p. 591.

Soviet Union during the 1920s and 1930s cannot only be explained by mistakes and malice of Stalin. An assessment must also be based on the modernization processes and concrete historical circumstances under which they took place.

In the years 1927-1938, it is estimated by Alec Nove that 10 million people lost their lives.[45] Richard Overy claims a total number of 6-7 million.[46] Approximately 5 million of these deaths were caused by the famine of 1931-33—a combination of cold, drought, and the consequences of the collectivization process.[47]

The transition from a peasant society to industrial capitalism in Europe and North America was no less violent, but a significant part of the violence was "exported" to Latin America, Africa, and Asia in the form of colonialism. On the two American continents, the indigenous population was between 60 and 100 million, of which more than half died during the European induced genocides.[48] In the United States, the native population was estimated to have been between 4 and 9 million at the time of colonization. By the year 1900, it was 237,000—95% of the indigenous population had been exterminated.[49] "We shall destroy all of them," declared the third President of the United States, Thomas Jefferson.[50] The capture, transportation, and enslavement of millions of humans ruined societies in Africa and cost uncountable lives. Under Belgian King Leopold II's regime of terror in the Congo alone, 8 million Congolese died.[51] In Australia, white settlers exterminated approximate-

---

45   Nove, Alec. *The Stalin Phenomenon*. Weidenfeld & Nicolson, 1993. p. 30.

46   Overy, Richard. *The Dictators: Hitler's Germany, Stalin's Russia*. Penguin, 2005. pp. 42, 194, 556.

47   Davies, R.W., Harrison, Mark and Wheatcroft, Stephen George. *The Economic Transformation of the Soviet Union, 1933–1945*. Cambridge University Press, 1994. p. 77.

48   Ponting, Clive. *World History: A New Perspective*. Pimlico, 2001. pp. 490–94.

49   Mann, Michael. *The Dark Side of Democracy*. Cambridge University Press, 2005. p. 76.

50   *Ibid.* p. 70.

51   Hochschild, Adam. *King Leopold's Ghost: A Story of Greed, Terror and Heroism in Colonial Africa*. Mariner Books, 1999.

ly 80% of the indigenous population.⁵²

Liberal "democratic" institutions were no obstacle to mass murder. Theodore Roosevelt, an admired social liberal U.S. President declared:

> I do not go so far as to think that the only good Indians are dead Indians, but I believe nine out of ten are, and I shouldn't like to inquire too closely into the case of the tenth.⁵³

The U.S. and Australia were democratic states for the white population, and fascist states for colonized peoples. On several occasions, Hitler referred to the U.S. genocide of indigenous peoples as an example to follow.⁵⁴

The emphasis on communist-induced starvation in the Soviet Union elides the imperialists' same atrocities. Historian Mike Davis writes in *Late Victorian Holocausts* about colonial famines in northeastern Brazil, India, and China in the late nineteenth century. Cases of famine were the result of ruthless colonial exploitation, which cost between 31 and 61 million lives.⁵⁵ Concerning British colonialism in India, Hickel and Sullivan write:

> If we estimate excess mortality from 1891 to 1920...we find 165 million excess deaths in India between 1880 and 1920. This figure is larger than the combined number of deaths from both World Wars, including the Nazi holocaust.⁵⁶

In 1943-44, there was yet another widespread famine in Bengal, India. The famine was not caused by war action, but by English policy. In 1943, food prices suddenly rose by 300%, causing three million civilians in the poorest rural classes to starve to death. The English government had just printed rupees to cover the huge expenditures of Indian foodstuffs provided to the Allied forces in the east, causing inflation. The measures leading to the price rise were introduced by the advice of none other

---

52 Mann. *The Dark Side of Democracy*. p. 76.

53 *Ibid*. p. 94.

54 *Ibid*. p. 98.

55 Davis, Mike. *Late Victorian Holocausts: El Niño Famines and the Making of the Third World*. Verso, 2001. p. 183.

56 Sullivan, Dylan and Hickel, Jason. "Capitalism and Extreme Poverty: A Global Analysis of Real Wages, Human Height, and Mortality since the Long 16th Century." *World Development*. Vol. 161, January 2023. p. 12.

than Maynard Keynes, the top adviser for the English finance minister at the time.[57] Widespread hunger is still a recurring phenomenon in the capitalist world system today. This is not to diminish the millions who died during Stalin's rule, but one must put the numbers in historical perspective.

As the intensity of the "Cold War" grew, anti-Stalin rhetoric hardened. The criticism of Stalin from the 20th Communist Party Congress in 1956 was a gift to the anti-communist ideologues in the West. Intellectuals and liberal politicians could forget the sympathy they had for Stalin during the war and castigate him as an evil communist dictator who was single handedly responsible for the 1932-33 famine, the purges, and the gulags. This critique disconnected historical-structural preconditions from the actor's choices and actions. It became common to put Stalin in line with Hitler, and the Soviet Union with Nazi Germany. Hannah Arendt put forward the idea of "totalitarianism" as a distinct political movement.[58] In Arendt's view, although many totalitarian movements existed in Europe in the 1920s and 1930s, only the governments of Stalin and Hitler successfully implemented totalitarian aims. Arendt's criticism of Stalin was absurd for the German author Thomas Mann, who fled Nazism in 1933:

> To place communism and Nazi-fascism on the same moral place, in the measure that both are totalitarian, is superficial at best, fascism at worst. Anyone who insists on this comparison could very well be considered a democrat, but deep in their heart a fascist is already there, and naturally they will only fight fascism in a superficial and hypocritical way, while they save all their hatred for communism.[59]

It is sometimes claimed that Stalinism emerged from Lenin's mistakes. The NEP chose the goal of catching up with the West over constructing an alternative social formation. The consequence was the centralization of state power and the formation of a class of bureaucrats, which allowed for the state's unrestrained power, and hence, its misuse.

---

57 Patnaik, Utsa and Patnaik, Prabhat. *Capital and Imperialism: Theory, History and the Present.* Monthly Review Press, 2021. pp. 205–7.

58 Arendt, Hannah. *The Origins of Totalitarianism.* Meridian Books, 1958. p. 310.

59 Mann, Thomas. *Essays: Volume II, 1914-1926.* Fischer Verlag, 2002. pp. 311–12.

Collectivization was the price. The severing of the worker-peasant alliance engendered by collectivization was the abandonment of revolutionary democracy and the autocratic turn of the Soviet state.

However, if the country had neglected rapid industrialization, with all its costs, it would probably have brought an end to the Soviet Union in 1943 and the consequences of that would have created a completely different world. The Soviet Red Army was *the* decisive element in the defeat of Nazi Germany.

While the vanguard party was able to execute the revolution, it was less adequate for the development of a socialist state. The two tasks are very different. The day before the revolution, you sabotage infrastructure; the day after, you rebuild it. Secrecy in preparation and unity in action are important characteristics for a revolutionary process, but not necessarily for developing democratic structures. For Stalin, the preservation of the first socialist state meant that any opposition had to be crushed, at any cost. This political line was the only bulwark that could protect the fragile revolution from its many enemies. Yet after Stalin, the Communist Party was never able to regain its popular legitimacy. The Party became a bureaucratic elite apart from the people. This is one reason that there was apathy towards the Party when the Soviet Union was dissolved by Yeltsin in 1990.

Stalin was the first to promote the idea of building "socialism in one country" instead of giving priority to the world revolution as a necessary condition for developing socialism on the national level, but he was certainly not the last. All the revolutions that followed gave priority to the national development of socialism at the expense of the world revolution—except, perhaps, for Cuba. One reason for this was that all subsequent revolutions took place in a colonial or semi-colonial context, and therefore had a substantial element of *national* liberation. Communist organizations were able to take the lead in revolutions which were nationalist as much as they were socialist.

Throughout the 20th century, it seemed that the national road towards socialism was the only viable way, particularly in a world-system still dominated by economic, political, and military capitalism. However, this strategy had implications on how far the transition toward socialism was possible—especially in a world system which became more and more globalized. Nationalism, just as it had done in the 19th century, hindered socialists from the realization of Marx and Engels' vision of a strong internationalist trend in the building of socialism.

Stalin's change of strategy coincided with the defeat of revolutionary attempts in Western Europe and looming fascism. This might have been a wise decision with socialism on the backfoot, but it was not "the realization of socialism," as proclaimed by Stalin in 1936. The Soviet Union was only the first attempt to construct socialism. An acknowledgment of this would create better opportunities for the future development of socialism.

The Soviet Union came out of the Second World War as a major world power. It recovered remarkably fast from the destruction of the war. It acquired nuclear weapons in 1949, which created a "balance of deterrence" in the "Cold War," important for the progressive forces in the decolonization of the Third World. However, it acted more and more as a superpower in the world system, with its own national interest rather than as a promoter of the socialist world revolution. Its construction of "actually existing socialism" started to fade and lost its inspirational power.

Mao's Critique of Stalin

While Khrushchev ruthlessly criticized Stalin at the 20th Congress in 1956, Mao and the Communist Party of China assessed Stalin in a more balanced way. The Chinese evaluation did not suffer from an inherent Eurocentrism, and it was made by a party that had experienced similar dilemmas as that of the Stalin era.

Mao's main critique rested on the fact that Stalin failed to recognize—following collectivization, nationalization, and the introduction of a planned economy—that the class struggle continued, and this struggle was then reflected within the Communist Party as different political lines.

> For a long time, Stalin refused to recognize that under the socialist system contradictions between the relations of production and the forces of production and contradictions between the superstructure and the economic base [continue to exist]... Since the Second World War, the Communist Party of the Soviet Union and the parties in some countries in East Europe have no

longer concerned themselves with the fundamental principles of Marxism. They are no longer concerned about class struggle, the dictatorship of the proletariat, the leadership of the Party, democratic centralism, and the connection between the Party and the masses.[60]

According to Mao, the Bolshevik party under Stalin never developed proper relations with the masses. The Party wanted to change society *for* the masses *from* above, instead of using the mass line of mobilizing the masses to change society for themselves. As a specific example of this failure, Mao mentioned the political struggle within the Party leading up to the purges. In Party conflicts, Stalin relied entirely on security agencies instead of the masses to resolve the conflict. Stalin confused contradictions *among* the people with contradictions *between* the people and the enemy. This led him to unjustly imprison and execute a great number of people. Mao writes:

> We must distinguish clearly between the two categories of contradictions. The first category of contradictions between the enemy and ourselves, cannot be confused with the second category of contradictions among the people. On the subject of the socialist society, [we must recognize that] it does have contradictions, and contradictions do exist [in it]. Stalin—in the period immediately after Lenin's death—[allowed for] a relative liveliness and activity in the domestic life in the Soviet Union... They had all sorts of [political] parties and factions, even some well-known people like Trotsky... There were also some other people in the society who were allowed to say all sorts of things, including criticizing the government. Then later, things became very dictatorial. [Stalin] would not allow for criticism. He was afraid of people who wanted to criticize, to let a hundred flowers bloom. He would only allow for the blooming of fragrant flowers. He was afraid also of letting a hundred schools contend. At the slightest hint of suspicion, he would say that it was a counterrevolutionary [incident] and would have people arrested or executed.[61]

Mao continues in his "On the Correct Handling of Contradictions among the People":

> There were two sides to him (Stalin). One side was the elimination of true counterrevolutionaries; that was the correct side. The other side was the incorrect killing of numerous people, important people. On the question of

---

60   Zedong, Mao. "Speech at the Conference of Provincial, Municipal, and Autonomous Region Party Secretaries (Jan. 27, 1957)." *The Writings of Mao Zedong 1949-1976: Vol. II*. Armonk, 1992. pp. 261–62.

61   Zedong, Mao. "On the Problem of Ideological Work (March 20, 1957)." *The Writings of Mao Zedong 1949-1976: Vol. II*. pp. 439–40.

heavy industry, light industry, and agriculture, the Soviet Union did not lay enough emphasis on the latter two and had losses as a result. In addition, they did not do a good job of combing the immediate and the long-term interests of the people. In the main they walked on one leg...Another point: Stalin emphasized only technology, technical cadre. He wanted nothing but technology, nothing but cadre; no politics, no masses. This too is walking on one leg![62]

More generally, after the pre-war transformations of industry and agriculture, Stalin seemed to resign himself to the continuation of the existing relations of production. Mao writes:

> Stalin's book [*Economic Problems of Socialism in the USSR*] from first to last says nothing about the superstructure. It is not concerned with people; it considers things, not people... The basic error is mistrust of the peasants... Essentially Stalin did not discover a way to make the transition from collective to public ownership... Communism cannot be reached unless there is a communist movement.[63]

Mao's evaluation of the COMINTERN is also mixed:

> When Lenin was alive, the Third International was well led. After Lenin's death, the leaders of the Third International were dogmatic leaders (for instance, leaders [like] Stalin, Bukharin were not that good...Of course, the Third International had [its] merits as well, for instance, helping various countries to establish a [communist] party. Later on, [however] the dogmatists paid no attention to the special features of various countries [and] blindly transplanted everything from Russia. China [for one] suffered great losses.[64]

After the Second World War, according to Mao, Stalin tended to be too frightened of the imperialist powers, and attempted to prevent revolutions in other countries because he feared they might lead to the involvement of the Soviet Union in yet another world war. On August 22, 1945, Stalin sent a telegram to Mao saying that the Communist Party of China must hold onto the road of peaceful development. He believed the Nationalists and the Communists should reach a peace accord because a civil war would destroy the Chinese nation. He insisted that Zhou Enlai

---

62   Zedong, Mao. In Mac Farquhar, Roderick, Cheek, Timothy and Wu, Eugene Wu. *The Secret Speeches of Chairman Mao: From the Hundred Flowers to the Great Leap Forward*. Harvard University Press, 1989. pp. 141–42.

63   Zedong, Mao. "Critique of Stalin's Economic Problems of Socialism in the USSR." *A Critique of Soviet Economics*. Monthly Review Press, 1977. pp. 135–36.

64   Zedong, Mao. In Mac Farquhar, Cheek, and Wu. *The Secret Speeches of Chairman Mao*. p. 255.

and Mao go to Chongqing for negotiations with Chiang Kai-shek. After receiving Stalin's cable, an angry Mao remarked:

> I simply don't believe that the nation will perish if the people stand up and struggle [against the Kuomintang].[65]

According to Mao, the Soviet distrust of the Chinese communists continued:

> Stalin wanted to prevent China from making a revolution, saying that we should not have a civil war and should cooperate with Chiang Kai-shek, otherwise the Chinese nation would perish. But we did not do what he said. The revolution was victorious. After the victory of the revolution, he next suspected China of being a Yugoslavia, and that I would become a second Tito. Later, when I went to Moscow to sign the Sino-Soviet Treaty of Alliance and Mutual Assistance, we had to go through another struggle. He was not willing to sign a treaty. After two months of negotiations, he at last signed. When did Stalin begin to have confidence in us? It was the time of the "Resist America, Aid Korea" campaign, from the winter of 1950. He then came to believe that we were not Tito, not Yugoslavia.[66]

Despite Mao's criticisms of Stalin, he regularly repeated that "Stalin was 30 percent bourgeois, 70 percent Marxist," a bluntly quantitative way of evaluating a political line.[67] Let us now turn to Mao's home country to investigate the next major revolutionary process from its beginning.

---

65 Goncharov, Sergei, Lewis, John, and Litai, Xue. *Uncertain Partners: Stalin, Mao, and the Korean War.* Stanford University Press, 1993. p. 7.

66 Zedong, Mao. "Speech at the Tenth Plenum of the Eighth Central Committee of the CPC (September 24, 1962)." *Chairman Mao Talks to the People: Talks and Letters: 1956-1971.* Pantheon, 1974. p. 191.

67 Mac Farquhar, Cheek, and Wu. *The Secret Speeches of Chairman Mao.* p. 173.

CHAPTER 13

THE CHINESE REVOLUTION

IMPERIAL CHINA

If Russia was the semi-periphery of the European capitalist center in 1917, then China was the periphery; or rather, it had been turned into the periphery by nineteenth-century imperialism. In the preceding eight centuries, China was actually more developed than Europe. During the Song dynasty (960-1279), China developed commercial capitalism, managed within the framework of an imperial state. In the following centuries, a market economy proliferated across China and long-distance trade linked China with other parts of the world-system.[1] All the key features of capitalism, as defined by Marx, were present: commodity production for exchange on the market, money as the universal commodity, and accumulation of capital based on the exploitation of labor power. China's manufacturing ranged from silk and cotton textile factories to ceramic, porcelain, prints, and furniture production.[2] This early form of manufacturing and mercantile capitalism also influenced agricultural production. China developed a system of buying and selling real estate property by deeds, enforced through the imperial judicial system. Tenant farming and agricultural day labor grew in importance. Farming became

---

1   Liu, William Guanglin. *The Chinese Market Economy, 1000–1500.* SUNY Press, 2015. pp. 17–21.

2   Hammond, Ken. "Beyond the Sprouts of Capitalism: Toward an Understanding of China's Historical Political Economy and Its Relationship to Contemporary China." *Monthly Review Essays*. March 3, 2021. https://mronline.org/2021/03/03/beyond-the-sprouts-of-capitalism

commercialized by producing for market distribution.³

The attributes of capitalism developed in their own historically specific forms throughout the Yuan and Ming dynasties. In the fifteenth and sixteenth centuries, China's commercial capitalism flourished, as the international demand for Chinese goods such as tea, porcelain, silk, and cotton textiles drew increasing amounts of silver—first from Japan, and then from the mines of the New World via European galleon trade. Foreigners were allowed to trade with China in a regulated system at the port of Guangzhou, known to Westerners as Canton. The trade had mainly been one way—Chinese goods for gold and silver. However, with the industrial revolution, Britain prioritized "free" trade, desiring to open more ports in China and have a permanent diplomatic presence in Beijing. The Qianlong emperor declined these requests and reminded the British, in a letter in 1793 to King George III, that:

> Our celestial empire possesses all things in prolific abundance and lacks no product within its borders. There is, therefore, no need to import the manufactures of outside barbarians in exchange for our own produce.⁴

As late as 1820, China was the world's largest economy, accounting for 33 percent of the world's economic output. However, contradictions within the existing mode of production in China were intensifying, and the rise of England's industrial revolution brought both goods to compete with China's domestic products and the military capacity to force the Qing government to open the empire to Western imperialism.

Chinese manufacturing capitalism generated a stratum of urban-based merchants and rural-based landowning elite that, through their domination of the civil service, controlled the operations of the imperial government. In ancient Confucian thought, there was a tradition of aversion to commercial wealth; however, with the emergence of the commercial elite, these ideas began to erode.

Members of the rural elite invested some of their wealth into the businesses of merchants and manufacturers, resulting in a convergence of interests rather than a relationship of antagonism. This is in contrast

---

3   Zelin, Madeleine, Ocko, Jonathan, and Gardella, Robert. *Contract and Property in Early Modern China*. Stanford University Press, 2004.

4   Internet Modern History Sourcebook. "Emperor Qian Long: Letter to George III, 1793." https://sourcebooks.fordham.edu/mod/1793qianlong.asp

with the history of class conflict between the rising bourgeoisie and the feudal aristocracy in Europe, but not entirely. In the German industrial revolution, there was a similar fusing of interest between the landowning Junkers and the upcoming bourgeoisie.[5]

The convergence of the urban-rural elite in China was reflected in the policy and administration of the imperial state. The state-sponsored construction and maintenance of roads and canals facilitated long-distance trade. State intervention in the grain market served to stabilize prices and buffer extreme market fluctuations. Fundamental to the imperial political culture was the idea that the state's primary purpose was to create and maintain stability and security.[6]

The Breakdown of the Imperial Order

The Industrial Revolution in Europe reconfigured the global economic and political order. It was in this context that China was subordinated to Western imperialism. China's commercial capitalism, already under pressure from internal contradictions, had to give in to foreign competition. China assumed a subordinate role as a source of raw materials and as a market for European manufactured products.

China was never properly colonized, but it became a semi-colonial country in which foreign powers established enclaves around Shanghai and other big cities and enjoyed extraterritorial privileges, such as their own administration, courts, and police. To reverse the flow of silver from Europe to China, Britain decided to flood China with opium. When China resisted this poisoning of its people, the British initiated the first Opium War (1839-42), which ended with the "Treaty of Nanjing" in which Britain took possession of Hong Kong and imposed upon the Chinese the rule of opium. British officials reported in 1844 that:

> ... almost every person possessed of capital who is not connected with government employment, is employed in the opium trade... opium is in general traded along the whole coast.[7]

---

5   Lauesen, Torkil. *Riding the Wave: Sweden's Integration into the Imperialist World System*. Kersplebedeb, 2021. p. 52.

6   Hammond. "Beyond the Sprouts of Capitalism."

7   Derks, Hans. *History of the Opium Problem: The Assault on the East, ca. 1600-1950*. Brill, 2012. p. 74.

The decline of the imperial order continued during the Taiping Rebellion from 1851-64. The peasant revolt was one of the bloodiest civil wars in world history, with an estimated 20 to 30 million dead. However, it was not just an internal class conflict; it also had a nationalist dimension. This surge of nationalism was a consequence of the humiliation, financial drain, and breakdown of the whole nation caused by the first Opium War. The rebels struggled to put an end to a dynasty that had capitulated to the aggression of British narco-traffickers.[8] In the areas controlled by the rebels, the consumption of opium was prohibited—a direct challenge to the London government, which had propped up the eroding dynasty.

After China lost the second Opium War (1856-60), British and American traders continued to flood the country with opiates. Britain's East India Company, and the British firm Jardine, Matheson & Company, led the way—followed by Americans entrepreneurs like Samuel Russel, Warren Delano, and Robert Forbes. Millions of Chinese people became addicted to opium and foreign powers continued to extract China's silver. The British and French also imposed war indemnities on China to the amount of 32 million ounces of silver, which China had to then borrow from European banks.[9]

The weakening of the Chinese Empire caused resentment against Western influence. The response was yet another huge peasant revolt, the Boxer Rebellion (1898-1900). Foreign powers like the U.S., Great Britain, France, Germany, and Japan sent troops to crush the uprising. This time, they imposed war indemnities on China to the tune of 450 million ounces of silver. The formerly mighty empire had been brought to its knees.

In 1904-05, the Russo-Japanese War, which affected northeast China, triggered a nationalist revolutionary movement under the leadership of Sun Yat-sen. This eventually led to the republican Xinhai Revolution of 1911, which ended the Qing dynasty and four thousand years of monarchic rule. But the revolution failed to create national unity. China be-

---

8   Davis. *Late Victorian Holocausts.* pp. 6, 12.

9   Han, Dongping. "The Socialist Legacy Underlies the Rise of Today's China in the World." *Aspects of India's Economy.* No. 59–60, October 2014. https://rupe-india.org/old-site/59/han.html

came more and more fragmented. The following years were characterized by peasant uprisings and feuds between different warlords.

The effect of western capitalist penetration into China in the late nineteenth century was described by Mao as:

> the collusion of imperialism with the Chinese feudal forces to arrest the development of Chinese capitalism...their purpose is to transform China into their own semi-colony or colony.[10]

The western powers divided up the largest Chinese towns and cities and made them into foreign concessions. They took control of customs and communication networks and dominated China's exports and imports. At the same time, the imperialist forces kept feudalism alive—and later, propped up the warlord regime and Chiang Kai-shek. In the absence of the former coherence of imperial state regulation, the extraction of surplus from agricultural production by rural elites intensified and was exacerbated by warlord taxation and the corrupt practices of the Chiang Kai-shek regime. The consequence was the underdevelopment of productive forces in China, which led to a hitherto unprecedented impoverishment of the population. This historical background set the scene for the establishment of the Communist Party of China.

THE FORMATION OF THE COMMUNIST PARTY OF CHINA

After the defeat of the German Revolution, the COMINTERN and the Soviet Union turned their focus to the east in their hopes of continuing the world revolution. In East Asia, colonialism created a prime environment for the development of revolutionary socialism, inspired by the Leninist theory of imperialism. Yet because of underdevelopment, Lenin proposed that the small communist parties in the colonies should enter into alliances with bourgeois democratic movements in order to secure national liberation. In China, the "May Fourth Movement"—a nationalist uprising led by students in 1919—became a touchstone of the COMINTERN's strategy. The movement led to a reorganization of the bourgeois nationalist party, the Kuomintang, later led by Chiang Kai-shek. The COMINTERN advised the small numbers of Communists to ally themselves with the Kuomintang while basing themselves within the

---

10 Zedong, Mao. "The Chinese Revolution and the Communist Party of China." *Selected Works. Vol. II.* p. 310.

urban working class.

According to Party documents, The Communist Party of China was founded July 23-24, 1921, at secret meetings, the first of which, in Shanghai's French Concession, was disturbed by security forces, leading to the delegates leaving for nearby Zhejiang province, with the proceedings being completed on a houseboat on a lake to avoid further disruption. These meetings were attended by at most 13 people, including Mao Zedong. They represented just 53 members. In addition, two representatives of the COMINTERN were present as advisers.

The COMINTERN strategy for China was contentious. Part of the new Party was pushing for a socialist revolution, while others questioned its feasibility. The different positions were represented by the two founding members of the Party—Li Dazhao and Chen Duxiu. In January 1920, Li Dazhao had already put forward the concept of a "proletarian nation." According to Li, there was a difference in position between the proletariat in the colonies and in the imperialist center. In Europe, the proletariat was only oppressed by the national capitalist class, but in China, the imperialist powers oppressed the entirety of the Chinese people. China as a whole was a proletarian nation. Li's conception of the Chinese nation being proletarian meant that he included the peasants as a revolutionary force. In a letter dated March 20, 1921, Li wrote:

> ...If one asks whether or not the economic conditions of present-day China are prepared for the realization of socialism, it is first necessary to ask whether or not present-day world economic conditions are tending toward the realization of socialism, because the Chinese economic situation really cannot be considered apart from the international economy. The contemporary world economy is already moving from capitalism to socialism, and although China itself has not yet undergone a process of capitalist economic development such as occurred in Europe, America, and Japan, the common people [of China] still indirectly suffer from capitalist economic oppression in a way that is even more bitter than the direct capitalist oppression suffered by the working classes of the various [capitalist] nations...Therefore, if we want to develop industry in China, we must organize a government made up purely of producers in order to eliminate the exploiting classes within the country, to resist world capitalism, and to follow [the path of] industrialization organized upon a socialist basis.[11]

---

11   Dazhao, Li. In Meisner, Maurice. *Li Ta-Chao and the Origins of Chinese Marxism*. Harvard University Press, 1967. pp. 150–53.

According to Li, although it lacked developed industrial capitalism and a well-defined proletariat as preconditions for building socialism, China was ready for a socialist revolution because China as a nation suffered under the yoke of imperialism.

The strength of the Communist Party at the beginning of the 1920s was limited. Party membership developed slowly, reaching only a thousand by 1924. Heeding the advice of the COMINTERN, the Party thus allowed the Kuomintang to take the lead in the national liberation struggle. In January 1923, the Soviet Union signed a pact with Sun Yat-sen and the Kuomintang to wage a campaign against the other warlords in China. The Communists and Kuomintang established a joint military academy—with Kai-shek in charge and the communist Zhou Enlai as second in command. Another key figure in the new military cooperation was Mao; in fact, he was so successful that he was elected to the Central Executive Committee of Kuomintang. However, in March 1925, Sun Yat-sen died and Chiang Kai-shek, representing the right wing, seized the party. The joint military campaign of the Kuomintang and the Communists was successful. In the spring of 1925, the Communists led a successful strike in Shanghai, and within a few months, their membership reached 30,000. As the Kuomintang army approached Shanghai in March 1927, the workers, under Zhou Enlai's leadership, seized the city.

From the beginning of his takeover of the Kuomintang, Chiang Kai-shek had tried to undermine the influence of the Communists, and now he sought to eliminate them. He used criminal gangs in the city to attack workers of Shanghai while the Kuomintang army laid siege. On April 12, 1927, a massacre ensued. Thousands of Communists and unionists were killed. Zhou, with a bounty of 80,000 dollars on his head, managed to escape. The "Shanghai Massacre" initiated the nationwide destruction of the urban communist movement. Uprisings in Guangzhou, Changsha, and Nanchang were crushed. In the space of twenty days, more than 10,000 communists across China's southern provinces were arrested and executed. By 1928, it is estimated that as many as 300,000 people died in the Kuomintang's anti-communist extermination.[12] This was a turning point in the Communist Party of China's strategy in terms of alliances and the class basis of the Party.

---

12 *Zhongguo gongchangdang lishi, 1919–1949* [History of the Communist Party of China, 1919–1949]. Vol. 1. People's Press, 1991. p. 216.

The Development of Chinese Marxism

As the cities became unsafe for the Communists, many members transferred to the countryside, where they began to develop relationships with the peasants. Mao retreated to the isolated hills on the border of Jiangxi province, which became a communist base. It was here that Mao developed the skills of guerrilla warfare, learning much from local bandits—the lumpenproletariat.

A mainstream interpretation within Marxism posits that class position is determined by a people's ability to function in the sphere of production and distribution. But that is not the only way classes are formed in real existing capitalism.[13] Capitalism can give birth to class-positions by criminalizing people out of their old socio-economic roles, or by destroying their basis of existence through war and expulsion. The lumpenproletariat consist of people without a steady relation to the labor market—unemployed people who live on casual work and are often supported by friends, family, and clan relations. It can include homeless people, beggars, petty criminals, gang members in organized crime, and sex workers. In general, traditional Marxism has a negative attitude towards the lumpenproletariat.[14] The claim is that they lack a clear class position towards capitalism and are more likely to be mobilized by reactionary forces, as was the case in the Shanghai Massacre. However, if you look carefully into the history of uprisings, you will see that the lumpenproletariat has been an important factor in the revolutionary process. This was the case in the Paris Commune; however, one of the major examples of this mobilization is the Chinese Revolution. Mao wrote in his class analysis of Chinese society in 1926:

> ...there is the fairly large lumpenproletariat, made up of peasants who have lost their land and handicraftsmen who cannot get work. They lead the most precarious existence of all...One of China's problems is how to handle these people. Brave fighters but apt to be destructive, they can become a revolutionary force if given proper guidance.[15]

---

13   Sakai, J. *The "Dangerous Class" and Revolutionary Theory: Thoughts on the Making of the Lumpen/Proletariat*. Kersplebedeb, 2017. p. 2.

14   *Ibid*. p. 22.

15   Zedong, Mao. "Analysis of the Classes in Chinese Society". *Selected Works: Vol I*. p. 19.

Mao knew the lumpenproletariat very well. In 1929, he stated that "the lumpenproletariat constitutes the majority of the Red Army," which was scornfully called the "vagabond army" by the Kuomintang. The lumpen brought to the Red Army combat experience and tactical knowledge from gang activity, as well as an extreme toughness. Here they were met with acceptance instead of prejudice. When Edgar Snow asked the soldiers of the Red Army about the reasons for their adhesion to the armed struggle undertaken by the Communist Party they responded:

> ...the Red Army has taught me to read and write...Here I have learned to operate a radio, and how to aim a rifle straight. The Red Army helps the poor... Here everybody is the same. It's not like the White districts, where poor people are slaves of the landlords and the Kuomintang.[16]

The Communist Party promoted social mobility in its own ranks, in the army, and in the liberated zones. In May 1928 Mao welcomed Zhu De, an ex-bandit who had joined the Party and was to become a famous general in the Red Army. Together they created a strategy for guerrilla warfare. Mao was influenced by the Chinese philosopher and general Sun-Tzu (500 BC). Together with Zhu's practical experience, they formulated their plan of action:

> The enemy advances, we retreat; the enemy camps, we harass; the enemy tires, we attack; the enemy retreats, we pursue.[17]

The Communists distributed to the peasants land seized from rich landowners and recruited thousands of members. Mao stressed Party discipline to the troops:

> Political power grows out of the barrel of a gun. Our principle is that the Party commands the gun, and the gun must never be allowed to command the Party.[18]

Mao also issued "Eight Points for Attention" to the Red Army when they were in contact with civilians:

1. Be polite when speaking
2. Be honest when buying and selling
3. Return all borrowed articles

---

16 Snow, Edgar. *Red Star Over China*. Grove Press, 1994. p. 83.

17 Zedong, Mao. "A Single Spark Can Start a Prairie Fire." *Selected Works: Vol. I*. p. 124.

18 Zedong, Mao. "Problems of War and Strategy (November 6, 1938)." *Selected Works: Vol. II*. p. 224.

4. Pay compensation for everything damaged
5. Do not hit or swear at others
6. Do not damage crops
7. Do not harass women
8. Do not mistreat prisoners[19]

By 1930, the Red Army had established the Chinese Soviet Republic in the provinces of Jiangxi and Fujian, comprising 3 million people. In the areas controlled by the Communists, they began to organize the economy as a coexistence of different forms of property. Edgar Snow described the economy in the "liberated" areas:

> Soviet economy in the Northwest was a curious mixture of private capitalism, state capitalism, and primitive socialism. Private enterprise and industry were permitted and encouraged, and private transactions dealing in the land and its products were allowed with restrictions. At the same time the state owned and exploited enterprises such as oil wells, salt wells, and coal mines, and it traded in cattle, hides, salt, wool, cotton, paper, and other raw materials. But it did not establish a monopoly in these articles and in all of them private enterprises could, and to some extent did, compete. A third kind of economy was created by the establishment of cooperatives, in which the government and the masses participated as partners, competing not only with private capitalism but also with state capitalism![20]

As the focus of the Chinese revolution shifted from the industrial proletariat to the peasant class, Mao continued Li's adaptation of Marxism to China's specific conditions, rather than the more Eurocentric COMINTERN edition of Marxism. Li was quickly won over to the new strategy, which fit well with his views of the multi-class nature of the Chinese Revolution. But the focus on the peasant class brought Mao into conflict with core members of the Party, including Chen Duxiu. Chen's priority was a revolution like that of Russia in 1917, led by the working class. Chen saw the defeat of this strategy as demonstrating the futility of working toward a socialist revolution in China. Instead, he opted for a Bourgeois-democratic revolution led by the capitalist class. Chen denied that a radical land policy and the vigorous organization of the rural areas

---

19 Zedong, Mao. In Uhalley, Stephen. *Mao Zedong: A Critical Biography*. New Viewpoints Publishing, 1975.

20 Snow. *Red Star Over China*. p. 262.

under the Communist Party was the way forward. Chen also opposed Mao's rejection of the major role of the national bourgeoisie in the revolution. This division within the Party came to a head after Chen and many of the elder Party members refused to publish one of Mao's essays, "An Analysis of Classes in Chinese Society," in the central executive organ.[21] However, the masses did not care about these disputes within the Party, as Mao observed in reference to the seminal peasant movement in Hunan Province:

> In a very short time, in China's central, southern and northern provinces, several hundred million peasants will rise like a mighty storm, like a hurricane, a force so swift and violent that no power, however great, will be able to hold it back. They will smash all the trammels that bind them and rush forward along the road to liberation. They will sweep all the imperialists, warlords, corrupt officials, local tyrants and evil gentry into their graves. Every revolutionary party and every revolutionary comrade will be put to the test, to be accepted or rejected as they decide. There are three alternatives. To march at their head and lead them? To trail behind them, gesticulating and criticizing? Or to stand in their way and oppose them? Every Chinese is free to choose, but events will force you to make the choice quickly.[22]

The difference in strategy concerning alliances led Mao to campaign against his opponents, accusing them of being de facto agents of the Kuomintang. In December 1931, when the campaign turned violent, the Party replaced Mao with Zhou Enlai as Secretary of the First Front Army and political commissar of the Red Army.

The conflict was discussed at the Party Conference in Ningdu in 1932.[23] Liu Bocheng, Lin Biao, Zhu De, and Peng Dehuai all criticized Mao's tactics. Mao received support from Zhou Enlai, but it was not enough. Mao was demoted to figurehead status.

The COMINTERN placed two political commissars, Bo Gu and Otto Braun, alias Li De, a German communist, in Jiangxi. As emissaries of the COMINTERN, they had the authority to dictate policy. Because

---

21   Mouret, Sébastien and Wang, Kevin. "The Manchurian Crisis and Chinese Civil War." *PIMUN*. 2018. http://pimun.fr/wp-content/uploads/2017/12/historical-crisis-topic-guide.pdf

22   . Zedong, Mao. "Report on an Investigation of the Peasant Movement in Hunan." *Selected Works: Vol. I*. Foreign Languages Press, 1969.

23   Whitson, William and Huang, Chen-hsia. *The Chinese High Command: A History of Communist Military Politics 1927–71*. Praeger, 1973. pp. 57–8.

they disagreed with Mao's guerrilla strategy, they used their power to exclude him from the Central Committee. In the autumn of 1934, Braun assumed command of the Red Army, together with Bo and Zhou Enlai. Braun and Bo enforced a conventional strategy. Braun advocated a direct attack on the larger, better-equipped Kuomintang. This strategy played into the hands of Chiang Kai-shek, and the communist army suffered great casualties. Slowly, the Kuomintang army encircled Jiangxi. Within a year, the Communists lost sixty thousand soldiers and half of their territory. They had no alternative but to retreat to a more secure remote area.

THE LONG MARCH

On October 16th, 1934, the remaining Red Army soldiers and party cadres, led by Bo Gu and Otto Braun, began the "Long March." The conditions of the Red Army's forced withdrawal demoralized some leaders, but Zhou Enlai remained calm and retained his command.[24] After escaping encirclement, it was obvious that the Kuomintang Army intended to pursue what remained of the Red Army. There were disputes between Bo/Braun and Mao on both route and military tactics.[25] In these confrontations, Zhou supported Mao's proposals and encouraged other leaders to overrule the objections of Bo and Braun. It was decided that all military plans had to be submitted to the Politburo for approval, depriving Braun of the right to direct military affairs. On January 15, 1935, the Red Army captured Zunyi, the second-largest city in Guizhou. Zhou used the opportunity to call an enlarged Politburo meeting.[26] In the meeting, Mao again opposed Braun and Bo's military tactics. Their direct attacks were costing too many lives of the Red Army. Instead, Mao suggested that their smaller, poorer equipped forces should retreat when under pressure and make surprise pinprick attacks, using the guerrilla tactics for which Mao was to become famous. Many military leaders agreed with Mao. Braun and Bo were removed as commanders and Mao became Zhou's assistant leader of the Long March.[27] After this conference, the COMINTERN

---

24   Barnouin, Barbara and Yu, Changgen. *Zhou Enlai: A Political Life*. Chinese University of Hong Kong, 2006. p. 58.
25   *Ibid*. p. 58.
26   *Ibid*. pp. 60-61.
27   *Ibid*. p. 60.

was pushed aside as an influential force in the Communist Party.

The March was long both spatially and temporally. The retreat to Yan'an traversed over 9,000 kilometers, 18 mountains, and 24 rivers in 370 days. The route passed through some of the most difficult terrain in western China. During the Long March, the Communist Army confiscated property and weapons from warlords and landlords and recruited new members from the peasants and lumpenproletariat. Nonetheless, only 8,000 troops out of the 86,000 who tried to escape from the Kuomintang Army ultimately survived. The Long March gave the Communists a secure base needed to recuperate and rebuild. The Communists used the base in Yan'an for planning, experimenting, and building a new society. In November 1935, Mao became the Chairman of the Military Commission, with Zhou and Deng Xiaoping as Vice-Chairmen.

The Long March had a profound impact on the Communist Party of China. All the major figures in the following decades were participants: Mao, Zhou, Deng, Lin Biao, Wang Jiaxiang, and Liu Shaoqi. The Long March was vital to the Chinese Communists in translating their Marxism from an urban workers' perspective into a rural, peasant perspective. It not only created a physical distance between the Communists and the Kuomintang, but also a political distance between the COMINTERN's Eurocentric interpretation of Marxism and the Chinese interpretation of Marxism.

To make his analysis, Mao used the philosophical method of Marxism: dialectical materialism. Mao wrote his philosophical writings "On Practice" and "On Contradiction" in the guerrilla camp in Yan'an, based on notes from many lectures he gave for cadres in the camp. The style is accessible, for the content had to be understandable by people without an academic background. For Mao, dialectics is not just an interesting philosophy, but a practical tool with which to develop strategy, particularly during dramatic times in which the conditions were rapidly changing. Based on the concept of contradiction, Mao analyzed Chinese history as a constant struggle of opposites: workers vs. capitalists, peasants vs. landlords, imperialists vs. nationalists, and the old vs. the new. Contradictions were seen as absolute, harmony as temporary, and revolution as frequent.

Mao's understanding of revolution is also more complex than the traditional Leninist one, in which seizing state power is the key to transformation. In Mao's understanding, the transition from capitalism to socialism is a long process consisting of several stages—many revolutions. The process was characterized by waves; setbacks on the long road to socialism were followed by steps forward, taking us ever closer to our final destination. As Daniel Frost formulates it:

> The process of the "long revolution" is neither a triumphant and linear climb to a peak, nor a leisurely stroll along the slopes of history. It is trudging out with a sense of our destination in mind, never forgetting the importance of placing one foot in front of the other, of knowing where our next step must fall, fully cognizant of our surroundings and of the sacrifices involved in coming this far. And it is doing so together.[28]

What Mao did during the Long March and in Yan'an was to adapt Marxism and the experience of the Soviet Union to the specific Chinese situation. The term "Sinification" of Marxism was coined by Mao in 1938 for the re-issue of the *Selected Works of Mao Zedong*, where he used the term instead of his original phrase of "concretion of Marxism in China." The term "Sinification" seemed more apt since the basic principles of Marxism belong to the world, not only to China. Each revolution has to apply Marxism to its specific time and place. "Copy and paste" does not work. The concept of "socialism with Chinese characteristics" is not a post-Mao development. In his report to the Central Committee of the Party in 1938 Mao said:

> A Communist is a Marxist internationalist, but Marxism must take on a national form before it can be put into practice. There is no such thing as abstract Marxism, but only concrete Marxism. What we call concrete Marxism is Marxism that has taken on a national form, that is, Marxism applied to the concrete struggle in the concrete conditions prevailing in China, and not Marxism abstractly used. If a Chinese Communist…talks of Marxism apart from Chinese peculiarities, this Marxism is merely an empty abstraction. Consequently, the sinification of Marxism—that is to say, making certain that in all its manifestations it is imbued with Chinese characteristics, using it according to Chinese peculiarities—becomes a problem that must be understood and solved by the whole Party without delay.[29]

---

28 Frost, Daniel. "Long Marches, Long Revolutions." *Red Pepper*. April 22, 2022. https://www.redpepper.org.uk/long-marches-long-revolutions/

29 Zedong, Mao. "The Role of the Communist Party of China in the National War, October 1938." *Selected Works: Vol. II*. https://www.marxists.org/reference/archive/mao/selected-works/volume-2/mswv2_10.htm

National Liberation Struggle

In July 1937, a new factor entered the equation of the Chinese revolution—the Japanese invasion from Manchuria overran the majority of China's largest cities within two years. Amidst a complex civil war and Japanese invasion, Mao used the concept of the principal contradiction to develop a strategy. The revolutionary class struggle now consisted of resistance to Japanese imperialism—a national struggle. In a 1938 article Mao wrote:

> ...to subordinate the class struggle to the present national struggle against Japan—such is the fundamental principle of the united front...In a struggle that is national in character, the class struggle takes the form of national struggle, which demonstrates the identity between the two. On the one hand, for a given historical period the political and economic demands of the various classes must not be such as to disrupt co-operation; on the other hand, the demands of the national struggle (the need to resist Japan) should be the point of departure for all class struggles. Thus, there is identity in the united front between the national struggle and the class struggle.[30]

The Japanese invasion had forced the Communists to ally with the Kuomintang. This was not an easy step after two decades of life and death struggle with the Kuomintang army. However, the United Front strategy—based upon the principal contradiction of the time, between the axis powers and the Allied forces—only lasted until 1941, when hostilities resumed between the Communists and the Kuomintang. The Japanese atrocities during World War II made the Chinese population turn to the Communists. Party membership rose to 800,000 and the Red Army swelled to half-a-million dedicated fighters. This mass influx of membership underwent intensive political schooling. With the Japanese now defeated, the civil war between the Communists and the Kuomintang resumed. Unlike prior to the war, the Red Army now dominated. This was partially due to assistance from the communist intelligence service. Chiang Kai-shek's Assistant Chief of Staff, General Fei, was a communist spy, and all Kuomintang military plans were sent to the Red Army in advance. Demoralized, the Kuomintang sent a delegation to negotiate a ceasefire, with assistance from the U.S.

In October 1949, Mao proclaimed the People's Republic of China

---

30 Zedong, Mao. "The Question of Independence and Initiative Within the United Front." *Selected Works: Vol. II.* p. 215.

from the Gate of Heavenly Peace in Peking. Nearly 100 million Chinese lost their lives in the years between 1840 and 1949 as a result of foreign intervention, civil wars, and famine. Mao's first words in the proclamation were: "The Chinese People Have Stood Up!" a reflection of not only the humiliations of a century, but also of the mobilization of human power under the leadership of the Communist Party.

On December 10th, 1949, Communist troops laid siege to Chengdu, the last Kuomintang-controlled city in China. Chiang Kai-shek was evacuated to Taiwan. Two million people—consisting mainly of soldiers, members of the ruling class, intellectuals, and business elites—were also evacuated from mainland China to Taiwan, adding to a population of approximately six million on the island. The U.S. Navy patrolled the waters between mainland China and Taiwan, preventing the Communist forces from pursuing the remnants of the Kuomintang army and liberating Taiwan.

In 1949, the U.S. did not have the capacity to roll back communist forces in China and block the Soviet Union in Europe at the same time. In the first years after the Second World War, Europe was the U.S. priority. Mao described the situation as follows:

> The US policy of aggression has several targets. The three main targets are Europe, Asia and the Americas. China, the centre of gravity in Asia, is a large country with a population of 475 million; by seizing China, the United States would possess all of Asia...But in the first place, the American people and the peoples of the world do not want war. Secondly, the attention of the United States has largely been absorbed by the awakening of the peoples of Europe, by the rise of the People's Democracies in Eastern Europe, and particularly by the towering presence of the Soviet Union, this unprecedentedly powerful bulwark of peace bestriding Europe and Asia, and by its strong resistance to the US policy of aggression. Thirdly, and this is most important, the Chinese people have awakened, and the armed forces and the organized strength of the people under the leadership of the Communist Party of China have become more powerful than ever before.[31]

---

31   Zedong, Mao. "Farewell, Leighton Stuart." *Selected Works: Volume IV*. Foreign Languages Press, 1969. p. 433–34. John Leighton Stuart, who was born in China in 1876, started working as a missionary in the country in 1905. He was appointed US ambassador to China in 1946. On August 2, 1949, after all US efforts to obstruct the victory of the Chinese revolution had failed, Leighton Stuart was forced to quietly leave the country.

The Chinese Revolution forced the U.S. to abandon its plans of including China in its sphere of influence. As early as 1945, Douglas MacArthur argued for U.S. military intervention in China on the side of Chiang Kai-shek, but the U.S. government limited itself to sending money and weapons. The contradiction between the Communists and the Kuomintang in China was resolved nationally, without direct foreign intervention, because other contradictions took precedence: the U.S. versus the Soviet Union and the U.S. versus the old colonial powers in Europe.

To sum up the Chinese Revolution: it came about for similar reasons as those in Russia. There was a need to break the restrictive fetters which hampered the development of the forces of production. In China, as in Russia, the power of the workers and poor peasants—mobilized through the Communist Party—was a necessary condition in order to set the wheels of industry turning again. The effect of western capitalist penetration into China was the disintegration of the old feudal economy, but imperialist intervention also converted China into a semi-colony. The Chinese people rose up spontaneously with two basic demands: foreigners must leave and the wheels of the economy must turn again. To fulfill these demands, the Communist Party led a people's war. Since China lacked a developed working class to lead the struggle, the peasants had to be looked upon as an effective force of proletarian revolution. If the preconditions for socialism were absent in China, then the reorganization of Chinese society under the proletariat, represented by the Communist Party, was even more necessary to achieve these preconditions. Taking into consideration the situation that existed in China and the world in the 1920s-40s, only the power of the working class and the poor peasants, under the leadership of the Communist Party, was able to force through the necessary policies for the development of the forces of production in China. All other forces in society—the landlords, the great capitalists, and the petty bourgeoisie—either resisted because of their own narrow economic interests, or were too weak when faced with imperialism. There was no other road open to the development of the forces of production other than the forced removal of the old rulers of the country and the dismantling of imperialism. That is why the revolution occurred—and because the Communist Party was able to fulfill this mission, it won.

CHINA 1949 – 1965: CONSTRUCTING THE "IRON RICE BOWL"

The attempt to construct socialism in China had its own peculiarities, which distinguished it from the Soviet attempts. Compared to the Russian Revolution, the Chinese Revolution was a long process that took more than twenty years to complete. Mao was aware of the tensions between nationalism and socialism. He tried to ensure that the Communist Party did not lose sight of the ultimate goal: a socialist society. Even during the conflict with Chiang Kai-shek, and during the war against the Japanese, the commitment to the production and development of the economy with a socialist profile in the liberated areas became a priority of the Communist Party. The People's Liberation Army made land reforms in areas under its control. Coming to power in 1949, revolutionary China was in quite a different situation than the Soviet Union in 1917. While China was under pressure from U.S. imperialism, it was also not alone in the world as the new born Soviet state had been. The Soviet Union's position in the post-war period provided some security for the new People's Republic. The Soviet Union also provided technological and economic assistance, despite its own heavy losses in the Second World War. Instead of proclaiming a "dictatorship of the proletariat," as in the Soviet Union, Mao called for a "people's democratic dictatorship" as the first step on the long road toward socialism:

> All the experience the Chinese people have accumulated through several decades teaches us to enforce the people's democratic dictatorship...Who are the people? At the present stage in China, they are the working class, the peasantry, the urban petty bourgeoisie and the national bourgeoisie. These classes, led by the working class and the Communist Party, unite to form their own state and elect their own government; they enforce their dictatorship over the running dogs of imperialism—the landlord class and bureaucrat-bourgeoisie, as well as the representatives of those classes, the Kuomintang reactionaries and their accomplices—and suppress them...Democracy is practiced within the ranks of the people...The combination of these two aspects, democracy for the people and dictatorship over the reactionaries, is the people's democratic dictatorship.[32]

In 1820, China was the world's largest economy, accounting for 33

---

32 Zedong, Mao. "On the People's Democratic Dictatorship. In Commemoration of the Twenty-eighth Anniversary of the Communist Party of China (June 30, 1949)." https://www.marxists.org/reference/archive/mao/selected-works/volume-4/mswv4_65.htm

percent of global economic output. By 1949, China's share of the global economic output was reduced to less than 5 percent.[33] After one hundred years of colonialism, imperialism, and civil war, China had become one of the poorest countries in the world—even poorer than India. In 1949, 90% of the Chinese population was illiterate, and life expectancy dipped to 38 years. The new republic was in a state of destitution.

In addition, China was soon embroiled in the Korean War and was completely blockaded by the West.[34] The Korean War was a test of the new state's capacity, as the Chinese army came to the aid of the Koreans and fought the U.S. military to a standstill. China's half-starved army of illiterate peasants was able to hold off the most advanced military power in the world.

A national economy was gradually sewn together out of separate economic sub-regions. Yet the most fundamental characteristic of China's national economy was the cross-country division between city and countryside. The development of the economy had to link the two together. A precondition for industrialization was the channeling of resources from the countryside to the city. Yet how could this task be accomplished while at the same time increasing the country's total social wealth? How could it be possible to implement an agrarian revolution—allowing for equality and not just distributing poverty—without also undermining the basis of that egalitarian project? Could this task be accomplished while not privileging geographically concentrated industrial zones and generating new hierarchies through urbanization?

To put this task in perspective, we need only to remember that compared to China in 1943, Russia in 1913 had already manufactured three times as many tons of steel, twice the tonnage of iron, had double the kilometers of railways, and produced thirty times the amount of petroleum. And this does not even take into consideration the much larger

---

33 Maddison, Angus. *Chinese Economic Performance in the Long Run, 960-2030 AD, Second Edition, Revised and Updated*. OECD Development Centre, 2007. p. 213.

34 At the Cairo Conference of 1943, the U.S., Britain, and China had agreed that Korea should become independent once the country was freed from Japanese occupation. Korean communists were an important force in the resistance against the Japanese. In order to prevent them from seizing power after independence, the U.S. army pushed them to the north. China entered the war and drove the U.S. forces back to the thirty-eighth parallel. Korea remains divided to this day.

Chinese population.[35]

After taking power in 1949, the Communists inherited the hyperinflation that had plagued the Chinese economy for decades—yet they solved it in one year. They accomplished this by putting an end to the speculative economy and establishing an economy related to the real production of goods. The stability and credibility of the new currency, the renminbi (RMB, the people's currency), was consolidated, linking its value to the price of essential supplies used in daily life, such as rice, cotton, oil, and coal. The state took control of finance, and the nationalization of the banking system was completed by 1952. This was combined with a political campaign called *San Fan Wu Fan*, meaning "against corruption, bureaucratization, theft of state property, tax evasion, and shoddiness." The campaign was a self-cleansing movement to solve economic problems by political means.

The land reform, which had already begun in liberated areas during the civil war, stabilized the rural sector.[36] After the revolution, a comprehensive land reform was implemented nationally; 300 million peasants were given land, sweeping away the last vestiges of the old landowning class in the countryside, while collectivizing property and giving small farmers the right to use the land, thereby building a new agricultural system based on collective ownership and planned development.[37]

The new government emphasized the expansion of agricultural production. In just three years, from 1950-1952, 420,000 kilometers of embankments along rivers in China were repaired and reinforced. Twenty million people participated in irrigation infrastructure construction. The earthworks were estimated to be over 1.7 billion cubic meters, the equivalent of 23 Suez Canals.[38] Dams and irrigation facilities were constructed on rivers that used to be plagued by floods. This opened up thousands of

---

35 Cheng, Chu-yuan. *Communist China's Economy, 1949-1962: Structural Changes and Crisis*. Seton Hall University Press, 1963. Table 1, p. 14.

36 Tiejun, Wen. *Ten Crises: The Political Economy of China's Development (1949–2020)*. Macmillan, 2021. p. x.

37 Riskin, Carl. *China's Political Economy: The Quest for Development Since 1949*. Oxford University Press, 1987. p. 50.

38 Tiejun. *Ten Crises*. p. 91.

acres of land for crop production. Between 1949-1952, total arable land area increased by 10.25% and grain production increased by 46.1%.[39] The significance of land reform cannot be overstated. By handing over land, the Party had handed the people a reason to support the communist state. Agrarian reform could also be seen as the extension of a revolutionary tactic (the strategy of encircling cities from villages) to an economic dimension. It brought a divided nation together. The distribution of land to the tillers mobilized the nation for the construction of a socialist economy. Internal mobilization, thus achieved, became a tool for economic liberation. It was the ability to delink from imperial dependency and to realize sovereignty.

In 1950, the peasants were 80% of the workforce and the urban proletariat represented less than 7%. The Chinese Revolution was a peasant revolution. But while the Party concentrated on rural land reform, the task in the city became the revival of production. If the Chinese state could not get the factories running again, agricultural production could not be modernized, leaving the peasantry to suffer from recurrent floods and famine. In the cities, the workers and unemployed were literally living in the rubble left by twenty years of war. As the West's blockade of the People's Republic began, the country was starved of necessary imports. If China was to rebuild its cities, it would need to produce its own concrete, steel, electricity, and, most importantly, grain to feed the workers at every stage of this process. In June 1949, on the eve of the conquest of power, Mao clarified the Communist Party's position towards the remaining capitalist elements in the economy:

> The national bourgeoisie at the present stage is of great importance. Imperialism, a most ferocious enemy, is still standing alongside us. China's modern industry still forms a very small proportion of the national economy... only about 10 per cent of the total value of output of the national economy. To counter imperialist oppression and to raise her backward economy to a higher level, China must utilize all the factors of urban and rural capitalism that are beneficial and not harmful to the national economy and the people's livelihood, and we must unite with the national bourgeoisie in common struggle. Our present policy is to regulate capitalism, not to destroy it. But the national bourgeoisie cannot be the leader of the revolution, nor should it have the chief role in state power.[40]

---

39   *Ibid.* p. 53.
40   Zedong, Mao. "On the People's Democratic Dictatorship." *Selected Works:*

This distinction between the political expropriation of the bourgeoisie and the bourgeoisie's propensity toward economic expropriation, which had emerged during the Soviet NEP, was repeated. In the summer of 1958, Mao reiterated his point: "There are still capitalists in China, but the State is under the leadership of the Communist Party."[41]

In early 1950, China and the Soviet Union signed the Sino-Soviet Friendship, Alliance and Mutual Assistance Treaty. The Soviet Union was a vital ally, given the U.S. embargo and the complete absence of any overland routes between China and other industrial nations. Of equal importance was the fact that the Soviet Union was the world's only nuclear power besides the U.S., in an era when General MacArthur was threatening China and Korea with nuclear attacks.

Both the Soviet Union and the Communist Party of China agreed that China should develop national capitalism, as opposed to domination by foreign capital. Only after establishing mass industrial production could China be transformed into a socialist country. The Communist Party aimed to complete the "bourgeois revolution" in the cities. This was effectively appeasement of the remaining urban capitalists, who would be gradually bought out of their own industries by the state in exchange for offering their technical expertise to the project of recovery and development.[42]

As the state pushed for industrialization, it had to rely on extracting surplus from the rural sector. By restoring the peasant economy through agrarian reform, a "land reform dividend" was gained, colloquially expressed as "nine peasants are capable of supporting one urban citizen."[43]

Compared to Europe, which accomplished primitive accumulation and industrialization partly through revenues from colonization, China had to industrialize through an internal accumulation process. The basic policies were to advance gradual industrialization under national capitalism and enhance commodity circulation between the light textile industry in cities and the rural sector. The industrial base would be expanded

---

Vol. IV. p. 421–23.

41   Zedong, Mao. *On Diplomacy*. Foreign Languages Press, 1998. p. 251.

42   "Sorghum and Steel." *Chuang*. No. 1. https://chuangcn.org/journal/one/sorghum-and-steel/

43   Tiejun. *Ten Crises*. p. 18.

to facilitate the development of large industries. Mao emphasized that he opposed "peasant socialism" and stressed that only after the completion of industrialization and socialized production would the Communist Party push for socialism with the consensus of the people.[44] In the early 1950s, small and medium-sized private production was maintained in the cities within limits, preserving at the same time the absolute control of the State over key sectors such as banking, foreign trade, and wholesale trade. Thus, in the mid-1950s, China had a mixed economy made up of the State-owned sector, the cooperative sector, the private and individual sectors (artisans), and the peasant sector (small farmers).

The first Five-Year Plan, from 1953 to 1957, intentionally focused on industry at the expense of agriculture. Between 1952 and 1958, 51.1 percent of capital went to industry, while only 8.6 percent to agriculture.[45] During this period, China was completely delinked from the capitalist world market, a decision that was not necessarily voluntary, as the U.S. and Western Europe tried to isolate the racialized enemy. The "Yellow Peril" was now considered more dangerous than the "Red Scare." However, the Korean War changed China's international situation. China received strategic aid from the Soviet Union—military and heavy industry was rendered as state capital. Within a short period of time, state capitalism became dominant. The Soviet Union gave China blueprints, technical assistance and turn-key ready factories on a massive scale. "The most extensive transfer of techniques in the whole history of humanity," wrote Leo Orléans in an OECD report.[46] China's industrialization in the 1950s was dominated by Soviet strategic investment made possible by the Cold War alignment.

Oriented toward the Soviet Union, China developed a state capitalist industrial sector located mainly in large and medium cities. During China's first Five-Year Plan, the Soviet Union provided know-how and investment to China, while the latter set up institutions complying with Soviet management models. The superstructure had to be brought into conformity with the economic base. Soviet experts coming to China not

---

44 Tiejun. *Ten Crises.* p. 8.
45 Cheng. *Communist China's Economy.* p. 115.
46 OECD. *La Science et la Technologie en République Populaire de Chine.* 1977. p. 106.

only worked as managers in factories and enterprises, but also helped to overhaul the entire superstructure of China. Chinese governmental and university systems were copied from the Soviet Union.

The tension between state capital and private capital soon became aggravated. Facing internal and external contradictions, China pushed for more state ownership, beginning in 1953. The New Democracy strategy of promoting private capital through a traditional market economy became obsolete. Private capital was banned in 1956 and the state acquired the three essential factors of the economy: land, labor, and capital. Zheng Zhenqing writes:

> From 1952 to 1956, state ownership rose from 19.1 percent to 32.2 percent of the economy; cooperatives increased from 1.5 percent to 53.4 percent, and joint state-private ownership increased from 0.7 percent to 7.3 percent. Meanwhile, the individual economy fell from 71.8 percent to 7.1 percent, and the capitalist economy fell from 6.9 percent to zero. State ownership, cooperatives, and joint state-private ownership together accounted for 92.9 percent of the economy.[47]

In purely economic terms, the overall result was one of the most extensive industrializations ever seen in human history. National income doubled between 1949 and 1954, and more than tripled by 1958.[48] Every year between 1952 and 1957 saw industrial production expand by an astounding 17%, and the groundwork for sustained future growth was laid through massive investments in education and worker training. This allowed for rapid social mobility, as farmers moved into the city and young people entered college. For decades after, this period would be remembered nostalgically as a golden age for urbanites, marked by peace, progress, and prosperity.[49]

Despite this performance, some of the Chinese leadership remained critical of the economic and institutional transition according to the Soviet model, known as "Sovietization."[50] It was seen as fostering bureaucratization, dogmatism, and formalism. The industrial economy led by

---

47 Zheng, Zhenqing. "An Interactive Evolution Between Capitalism and Statism in Modern China." *Chinese Studies in History*, No. 47, 2013, pp. 21–39.

48 Cheng. *Communist China's Economy*. p.109-12.

49 Naughton, Barry. *The Chinese Economy: Transitions and Growth*. MIT Press, 2007. p. 68.

50 Tiejun. *Ten Crises*. pp. xi-xii.

state capital in the cities stood in opposition to the traditional peasant economy rehabilitated in rural China after the agrarian reform. A labor force of 100 million was mobilized to abandon agricultural production and move into the cities to assist in industrialization. This drastic cut in the labor force had a great impact on peasant agricultural production. It was only with the formation of rural cooperatives that the government was able to extract surplus value from the countryside to purchase staple foods, build agricultural infrastructure, and provide pensions for the families of soldiers killed in Korea. The burden on cooperatives, however, became heavy. Some peasant households chose to withdraw from the cooperatives rather than deliver their product at a low fixed price to the state.[51]

To aggravate matters, at the end of the 1950s, the Soviet Union began to withdraw investment from China because of growing political disagreements on economic development and foreign policy. The Chinese communists felt that the Soviet Union was acting like a paternalistic big brother, knowing what was best for China, as the Soviets claimed to lead the world communist movement. The relationship with the Soviet Union soon became a question of Chinese sovereignty—an issue on which China was uncompromising.

"The Great Leap Forward"

When the Soviet Union began to withdraw its investment and support in autumn 1957, China began to change its industrialization strategy. Without foreign aid, heavy-industry development, relying on external investment, became unsustainable. The Second Five-Year Plan (1957-61), prepared with assistance by Soviet experts, was aborted. In 1958, the government instead proposed to localize formerly centralized industrial construction to substitute for the disrupted foreign capital input. The mobilization of local public funds was barely able to support a heavy-industry oriented economy. In addition, mass mobilization became a relatively effective means to extract surplus from the labor force and to substitute for capital. Not only workers and peasants, but also soldiers, officials, and intellectuals were mobilized to contribute their labor to infrastructure building essential to industrialization. China emphasized "self-reliance"

---

51   *Ibid.* p. 181.

instead of Soviet aid.

Mao was part of the faction, which was critical of Sovietization, primarily because it compromised Chinese sovereignty, but also because the agricultural sector was squeezed too much to create surplus for industry. Additionally, the Soviet model created a bureaucratic administration. Mao insisted on a Chinese version of socialism, in which the modernization of industry and the collectivization of agriculture would go hand in hand. This was the aim of the policy called the "Great Leap Forward" of 1958–1961, but it was easier said than done. Lacking road, rails, electricity, and access to petroleum products, much of the Chinese countryside required enormous investment just to make technologies such as tractors and electrified food-processing or fertilizer plants functional. This presented central planners with a catch: in order to invest in this sort of infrastructure, urban industry needed to be built up; but in order to build up urban industry, agriculture needed to be modernized to feed the growing industrial workforce, largely composed of new migrants from the countryside. The central planners' solution to this dilemma was not to slow the process and implement modernization piecemeal—a politically unfeasible option when the possibility of renewed global war was still a salient fear—but instead to intensify extraction of surplus from the peasantry and introduce "intermediate" technologies to agricultural production that required less infrastructural support and less technical prowess.[52]

In an effort to develop agriculture without modern technology, rural labor was collectivized. The process had begun in the 1950s with the formation of collectives, allowing the smallholding economy to be "economically viable" by sharing scarce resources, but now it was intensified.[53] Supply and marketing cooperatives were also integrated into a purchasing system as private merchants were forced out of the agricultural market.[54] While only 2% of rural households were members of cooperatives in 1954, by the end of 1956, 98% had joined.[55] But the production of the

---

52 "Sorghum and Steel." *Chuang*. No. 1, p. 50. https://chuangcn.org/journal/one/sorghum-and-steel/

53 Unger, Jonathan. *The Transformation of Rural China*. Routledge, 2002. p. 8.

54 Doak, Barnett. "China's Road to Collectivization." *Journal of Farm Economics*. Vol. 35, 1953, p. 195.

55 Naughton. *The Chinese Economy*. p. 67.

agricultural surplus was growing slower than expected and, due to this, disagreements within the Communist Party began to emerge concerning the speed of rural transformation. Mao and others pushed for a more rapid shift, despite the lack of an industrial base that could provide for the mechanization of agriculture, since they regarded the slowing growth of agricultural production as a roadblock to rapid industrialization.

From 1956 to 1957, in a new stage of collectivization, the former producers' cooperatives were turned into collectives, called "higher agricultural producers cooperatives," in which individual households gave up their ownership of land, livestock, and agricultural implements to collectives of between 40 and 200 households.[56] The larger size of these collectives made it easier for the state to collect the agricultural surplus it needed to feed the cities.

In 1958, the "Great Leap Forward" began with the emergence of even larger collectives called communes—the final stage of collectivization. These rural communes consisted of, for the most part, a small marketing town and its surrounding villages, with tens of thousands of members. The commune was formed to mobilize a larger labor force for infrastructure works. As a critique of Sovietization's emphasis on heavy industry, Mao proclaimed the need to "walk on two legs," meaning that large-scale, capital-intensive urban industries should develop alongside labor-intensive, low-capital rural ones.[57] Agriculture was to be technologically modernized not by the import of industrial inputs, but instead by low-tech local industrial production—a process of self-reliance. The countryside had to mobilize its own labor for its own development, all while much of its surplus was being deployed for urban industries. This meant mobilizing and diverting part of the rural labor into non-agricultural production. Seven and a half million new small low tech factories were set up in rural areas in less than a year at the beginning of the Great Leap Forward.[58] In the winter of 1957-1958, as many as 100 million peasants worked in irrigation and water conservancy projects.[59] Most famously, backyard iron and steel factories sprang up all over rural China. Farm

---

56   Unger. *The Transformation of Rural China*. p. 8.
57   Riskin. *China's Political Economy*. p. 116.
58   *Ibid*. p. 125–26.
59   *Ibid*. p. 119.

labor declined as a share of total rural employment during the Great Leap Forward, and output soon followed. With the diversion of workers out of agriculture, harvests were neglected, and food rotted. Grain production dropped, with the 1962 output at just 79% of that of 1957. Though the Great Leap Forward was meant to sustain economic development, as the Soviet Union pulled out, it ended by disrupting production and transferring surplus grain from the countryside to the city. This caused widespread famine.

The conversion of the strategy for modernization during the Great Leap Forward, and the fact that China had to pay its $5.4 billion debt to the Soviet Union in agricultural and pasture products—all during severe floods and bad weather—led to a shortage of agricultural products, which had disastrous consequences. The estimation of China's population changes during 1960-1962, known as the "three years of natural disaster," has been controversial. According to the data published by the Chinese government in 1982, the population growth curve turned downwards during these three years, failing to reach estimated projections of 20 million. Most of this was caused by declining fertility and infant mortality due to malnutrition. Part of the rising adult mortality could be attributed to starvation.[60]

Western scholars have painted a dire picture of the Great Leap Forward, claiming that it caused a famine the likes of which was unprecedented in Chinese history. They also portray the Mao era as one of ceaseless suffering. The Indian economist Utsa Patnaik has refuted these claims and considers them ideologically motivated.[61] Historian Dongping Han, who grew up in rural China during the Great Leap Forward and has done extensive research on the subject, also doubts the numbers. Few deny that people in the countryside suffered during the Great Leap Forward, but China experienced natural disasters during this period, and the suffering was not *only* the consequence of economic policies. Local officials shared the hardships of the people.[62] William H. Hinton, an American farmer who spent several years in China and authored the influential book *Fan-*

---

60 Tiejun. *Ten Crises*. p. 182–83.

61 Patnaik, Utsa. "Revisiting Alleged 30 million Famine Deaths During China's Great Leap." *Monthly Review Online*, June 26, 2011.

62 Xiuling, Han, Liyun, Zhang and Xiulian, Fan. In Han, Dongping. "The Socialist Legacy Underlies the Rise of Today's China in the World."

shen: A Documentary of Revolution in a Chinese Village, observed:

> Isn't it indeed strange that this famine was not discovered at the time but only extrapolated backward from censuses taken 20 years later, then spinning the figures to put the worst interpretation on very dubious records.[63]

A case study carried out by historian Mobo Gao confirms that there was widespread famine in China in 1959-1960, but that there is uncertainty about the causes and the role played by the Great Leap Forward.[64] It must not be forgotten that natural disasters and famine were by no means new phenomena in China. They had haunted the population for centuries, claiming millions of lives. In fact, the famine of 1959-1960 was the first and only famine during Mao's thirty-year rule and during the entire history of the People's Republic. Dreze and Sen point out:

> ...despite the gigantic size of excess mortality in the Chinese famine, the extra mortality in India from regular deprivation in normal times vastly overshadows the former...[E]very eight years or so more people die in India because of its higher regular death rate than died in China in the gigantic famine of 1958-61.[65]

In general, the health of the Chinese population improved markedly after the establishment of the People's Republic of China, with the death rate dropping to 6 per 1,000 by 1978. India and many other low-income capitalist states did not approach this level until the 2010s.[66] Since the end of the Great Leap Forward, China's rural sector has succeeded in feeding 22% of the world's population with only 6% of the world's arable land.[67] It is a result of an agricultural policy prioritizing self-sufficiency of food, with massive

---

63 Hinton, William. "On the Role of Mao Zedong." *Monthly Review*. Vol. 56, no. 4, September 2004; Hinton, William. *Through a Glass Darkly: U.S. Views of the Chinese Revolution*. Monthly Review Press, 2006.

64 Gao, Mobo. *Gao Village: A Portrait of Modern Life in Rural China*. University of Hawaii Press, 1999.

65 Drèze, Jean and Sen, Martya. *Hunger and Public Action*. Clarendon Press, 1989. pp. 214–15.

66 Sullivan and Hickel. "Capitalism and Extreme Poverty." p. 14.

67 Amin, Samir. *The Long Revolution of the Global South*. Monthly Review Press, 2019. p. 341.

infrastructure projects controlling the rivers and irrigation systems.[68] The recovery of the economy in 1962-1963 was due to changes in the rural policy. Traditional peasant economy based on village communities was again prioritized. Rural industries were shuttered, and the remuneration and distribution systems were continually reformed to raise production. This meant restructuring control over production decisions and labor management from the huge communes to a much smaller scale. Villages within the commune were split into production teams of 10 to 50 households, which were given control over land and production decisions. Because of it, agricultural production gradually recovered.[69]

The key problem was how to increase work incentives for agricultural labor—that is, how to improve economic output and raise quality, on the one hand, while not increasing inequality and destroying the collective system, on the other. The post-1962 new smaller type of commune became a flexible system for organizing rural production both to sustain the peasants and for the extraction of agricultural surplus to the cities. The collective system led to a spreading of risk across the collective, reducing the risks to individual farmers. Meanwhile, rural living standards increased in terms of health and education.[70] Basic medical care came to the countryside, which cut child death rates dramatically and raised life expectancy. Rural school enrollment doubled from the 1960s into the 1970s.[71] In addition, the rural commune was efficient at accumulating collective welfare funds that ensured a minimum of survival during normal times for disadvantaged families.[72]

Another factor that contributed to the rise in agricultural production was that the unemployed labor force from the cities was transferred to the rural sector through ideological mobilization to assist the peasants and learn from them. The countryside has often functioned as a sponge to absorb economic and political problems and provide a soft landing for

---

68   Gao, Mobo. "Why Is the Battle for China's Past Relevant to Us Today?" *Aspects of India's Economy*. No. 59–60, October 2014. https://rupe-india.org/old-site/59/gao.html

69   Tiejun. *Ten Crises*. p. 183.

70   Nolan, Peter. *The Political Economy Of Collective Farms: An Analysis Of China's Post-Mao Rural Reforms*. Routledge, 1988. p. 67.

71   *Ibid*. p. 67-68.

72   Naughton. *The Chinese Economy*. p. 236-68.

crises in China.⁷³ An example was the "Up to the Mountains and Down to the Villages" movement in 1960, which involved the transfer of a large-scale surplus of urban labor to people's communes and state-owned collective farms.

By 1964, conditions had improved such that a new investment push was initiated. But international conditions had changed significantly since the first industrialization campaign in the 1950s. The United States, which still had tens of thousands of soldiers stationed in Korea, intensified its wars against Third World countries pursuing a socialist development, staging a failed invasion of Cuba and intensifying its military intervention in Vietnam. Meanwhile, Sino-Soviet relations had completely broken. China had lost its primary trading partner and source of international aid. At the beginning of the 1960s, China found itself increasingly isolated. Not surprisingly, the logic of self-sufficiency and national security became important components of economic policy. In 1964, China developed its nuclear bomb and initiated an industrial expansion called the "Third Front," which focused investment on China's interior. The tense international situation forced China to use huge amounts of its resources to secure its safety. As Mao said, "Even a beggar must have a stick to drive off dogs."⁷⁴ The goal was to create an entire industrial base that would provide China with strategic independence by building factories in "remote and mountainous" inland regions.⁷⁵ The new industrial expansion had to be undertaken without the Soviet aid and technical support offered in the 1950s, signaling a period in which "self-sufficiency" would become one of the most important watchwords of Chinese socialism.

The economic problems triggered by the cut of Soviet support and the changing economic policies of the central state led to resistance against government measures in both rural areas and the cities. This was reflected in the political struggles in the Communist Party on how to respond. The Communist Party of China is not a monolith. Different political lines have existed since its foundation in 1921. Nor is it a Lenin-style vanguard party. The party stressed the "mass line," a policy de-

---

73   Tiejun. *Ten Crises.* p. 155.
74   *Ibid.* p. 186.
75   Naughton. *The Chinese Economy.* p. 73-74.

veloped during the revolutionary period. The essential element is investigating the conditions of people, learning about and participating in their struggles, gathering ideas from them, and creating a plan of action based on the concerns of the people. In short: from the masses to the masses. With millions of members, the Party has always consisted of different factions reflecting the class struggle in China and changes in global contradictions. These dynamic political struggles within the Party are often expressed in campaigns and slogans simplifying the different political positions and have caused constant shifts in the political line. One of the recurrent divergent issues has been how to handle the relationship between rural development and urban industrialization, and on the use of voluntarist methods or more economic incentives in the development towards socialism.

The economic crises and the famine in the early 1960s weakened Mao's socialist voluntarist line within the Communist Party and strengthened a line that wanted to use more economic incentives as a means to develop the economy, at that time represented by Liu Shaoqi. Mao's response was to launch the Great Proletarian Cultural Revolution in 1965, to which we will return, after placing it in the developments of the global contradiction in the 1960s.

CHAPTER 14

THE THIRD WORLD ON THE RISE

China was not the only revolution to come out of the Second World War. The war had determined who was to become the new hegemon after the British Empire. This struggle created a "window of opportunity" for liberation movements in what became called the Third World.

The old colonial powers in Europe were weakened by the destruction of the war. The new hegemon, the U.S., pushed for decolonization to open the former European colonies for U.S. investment and trade—the transformation from colonialism to neo-colonialism. But the counter-hegemon, the Soviet Union, balanced the U.S. and viewed new states opposed to colonialism as possible new allies against Western capitalism.

The 1955 Bandung Conference in Indonesia convened the Asian and African countries from the first wave of decolonization. They stressed the importance of independence from both East and West and the development of their national economies. The Bandung conference was not a new Communist International that strived for the socialist world revolution like the COMINTERN in 1919, but the expression of the national liberation struggle against colonialism, in which communists sometimes took precedence.

Sukarno, leader of the nationalist movement in Indonesia, declared the country independent in 1945. Iran nationalized its oil industry in 1951; Egypt took control of the Suez Canal in 1956; Iraq experienced a nationalist revolution and the nationalization of its oil industry in 1958. At the same time, liberation movements from Vietnam, Thailand, and the Philippines in the East to Algiers, Angola and Kenya in Africa to Guatemala and Cuba in the West went on the offensive. If they were victorious, imperialism's reach would shrink even further than the third of the globe it had already lost to the socialist bloc. In other words, from the perspective of the U.S., they had to be fought.

In 1928, Mao wrote an article titled "Why Is It that Red Political Power Can Exist in China?" When it was published in 1951, Mao added a note explaining the Communist Party's position on decolonization after World War II:

> During World War II, many colonial countries in the East formerly under imperialist rule were occupied by the Japanese imperialists. Led by their Communist Parties, the masses of workers, peasants and urban petty bourgeoisie and members of the national bourgeoisie in these countries took advantage of the contradictions between the Western imperialists on the one hand and the Japanese imperialists on the other, organized a broad united front against fascist aggression, built anti-Japanese base areas and waged bitter guerrilla warfare against the Japanese. Thus the political situation existing prior to World War II began to change. When the Japanese imperialists were driven out of these countries at the end of World War II, the Western imperialists attempted to restore their colonial rule, but, having built up armed forces of considerable strength during the anti-Japanese war, these colonial peoples refused to return to the old way of life. Moreover, the imperialist system all over the world was profoundly shaken because the Soviet Union had become strong, because all the imperialist powers, except the United States, had either been overthrown or weakened in the war, and finally because the imperialist front was breached in China by the Chinese revolution. Thus, much as in China, it has become possible for the peoples of the colonial countries in the East to maintain big and small revolutionary base areas and revolutionary regimes over a long period of time, and to carry on long term revolutionary wars in which to surround the cities from the countryside, and then gradually to advance to take the cities and win nation-wide victory.[1]

In the late 1940s and 1950s, communists across East Asia followed this strategy. As a response the U.S.'s position on decolonization was characterized by: (1) The demand for decolonization in the context of the U.S.'s position towards the old European colonial powers; and (2) The governments of the newly independent countries had to support the U.S.'s confrontation with the "socialist bloc." Therefore, the British, who fought a barbaric colonial war against Malaya, got full U.S. support because the Malayan liberation movement was led by communists. The same applied to the French fighting anti-colonial movements in Indochi-

---

1   Zedong, Mao. "Why is it that Red Political Power can Exist in China?" *Selected Works: Vol. I.* Note 7, p. 71.

na. On the other hand, the Netherlands was forced by the U.S. to grant Indonesia independence because Sukarno's vision for the country had become acceptable to U.S. interests. The U.S. also made it clear to the French that the countries of Indochina should become independent once the communists were defeated. The U.S. eventually intervened in Indochina when the French were humiliated at Dien Bien Phu in 1954.

In the late 1950s and early 1960s, decolonization advanced, but not primarily as a result of successful liberation struggles. Not many national liberation movements, whether communist or of a different kind, formed governments during this period. In various colonies, Madagascar and Malaya among them, communist liberation movements were brutally repressed before they could get to that point. Instead, U.S.-friendly regimes were installed. In Africa, decolonization happened either without any liberation movements or with liberation movements whose influence on independence was very limited. Africa's destiny was, once again, decided without Africans. The decisive factors were economic developments in capitalism's center and the contradictions between imperialist powers, first and foremost between the U.S. and the old colonial powers of Europe. Most of the newly independent countries in Asia and Africa were under petty-bourgeois leadership and tried to position themselves as the Third World between the West and the East. This was the message of the 1955 Bandung Conference. But there were exceptions: in Algeria, the National Liberation Front seized power in 1962 after many years of fighting against France and European settlers, at the cost of one million lives. The Cuban Revolution of 1959 took the U.S. entirely by surprise and the attempt to correct this misjudgment through the Bay of Pigs invasion in 1959 failed miserably.

THE "COLD WAR" WAS HOT IN THE SOUTH

The "Cold War" period was not only defined by the threat of a nuclear war between the U.S. and the Soviet Union. The term "Cold War" is Eurocentric; the confrontation between the U.S. and communism was boiling hot in the Global South.

The Korean War, the historical zenith of bombing as an instrument of war, exemplified the dangers of picking the wrong analogy.

The war and continued hostility from the West motivated North Korea to delink totally from the surrounding capitalist system. However, this isolation has caused severe economic problems, and led to the ideological affirmation of full self-reliance (the "Juche" ideology), and idiosyncratic forms of Party structure, and leadership. Another hot war was in Indochina, focused primarily on Vietnam, but spreading into Laos and Cambodia. In 2008, the British Medical Journal estimated that more than 3 million lives were lost during the American phase of the Indochina wars.[2]

From 1965 to 1973, the U.S. Air Force dropped more bombs on North Vietnam than all those dropped during the Second World War. Landmines have stolen 40,000 Vietnamese lives since 1973. American anti-communist warfare brought on another wave of bloodletting in Indonesia. From 1965 to 1966, the Indonesian Army, and paramilitary bands supported by the U.S., murdered as many as 500,000 suspected *Partai Komunis Indonesia* (PKI) supporters and overthrew Sukarno, the founder of the world's fourth most populous country, and leader of the Afro-Asian movement.[3]

THE REVOLUTIONARY SPIRIT OF THE LONG SIXTIES

In 1956, the 20th Congress the Communist Party of the Soviet Union lost its revolutionary spirit in the opinion of many communists, especially in the Third World. By introducing peaceful coexistence, the Soviet Union chose to compete with the capitalist system on capitalist terms instead of pursuing a qualitatively different road. The Soviet Union and the U.S. competed in armament, space programs, and on producing consumer goods. The Soviet Union tried to provide the same standard and form of living as in the developed capitalist world. But in the end, Lada, GUM, and Trabant lost to Ford, Hollywood, and McDonald's. Without an im-

---

2   Obermeyer, Ziad, Murray, Christopher and Gakidou, Emmanuela. "Fifty years of violent war deaths from Vietnam to Bosnia: analysis of data from the world health survey program." *BMJ*, 2008. https://www.bmj.com/content/336/7659/1482

3   National Security Archive. "Declassified U.S. Embassy Jakarta Files Detail Army Killings, U.S. Support for Quashing Leftist Labor Movement." October 17, 2017. https://nsarchive.gwu.edu/briefing-book/indonesia/2017-10-17/indonesia-mass-murder-1965-us-embassy-files

perialist contribution to its economy, "Actually Existing Socialism" could not compete with Western capitalism in providing consumer goods.

The consequence of a full-scale nuclear war during the "Cold War" would have been a catastrophe of proportions not yet seen in human history, and such an event was a real possibility, as the historical documentation has proven. In that sense, the Soviet policy of peaceful coexistence may have saved the world from nuclear winter. But nevertheless, the world revolutionary spirit moved to the Third World, where imperialist exploitation made rebellion an imperative. Through the 1960s and beginning of the 1970s, with its climax in the 1968 uprisings, a revolutionary wave washed over the world. On September 23, 1960, the Soviet Union put forward a resolution for decolonization. This resolution was opposed by the entire Western bloc, led by the United States. Less than three months later, forty-three countries from Africa and Asia affirmed the Bandung principles and put forward their own resolution with the same content as the Soviet resolution. On December 14, 1960, the UN General Assembly adopted the resolution: Declaration on the Granting of Independence to Colonial Countries and Peoples.[4] Eighty-nine countries—including the Soviet Union—voted for it, and no one voted against, but nine countries abstained: Australia, Belgium, France, Portugal, Spain, the Dominican Republic, the Union of South Africa, the United Kingdom, and the United States.

In Cuba and Algeria, the revolutionary spirit continued in the mid-sixties. They were involved in support for revolutionary movements in Africa, Asia, and Latin America—the tricontinental movement. The wave of revolutionary socialist movements surged in Vietnam, Palestine, Angola, Mozambique, South Africa, Chile and more.

China took the idea of a continuous world revolution seriously, thus supplanting the Soviet Union in providing a revolutionary spirit. China's inspiration for world revolutionaries relied on both the Cultural Revolution from 1965-69, which promoted radical egalitarianism at home, and

---

4   Office of the United Nations High Commissioner for Human Rights. "General Assembly Resolution 1514 (XV), 14 December 1960: Declaration on the Granting of Independence to Colonial Countries and Peoples." https://www.ohchr.org/en/instruments-mechanisms/instruments/declaration-granting-independence-colonial-countries-and-peoples

confrontation with imperialism internationally.[5] In Southeast Asia, Chinese influence on communist parties and their anti-imperialist armed struggles was huge. The Communist Party of Vietnam had been under the influence of China since its foundation. Ho Chi Minh worked for the COMINTERN and moved to Canton in 1925 to deepen contact with the Communist Party of China. The Vietnamese people's war against France and the U.S. was inspired by Mao's military strategy of a people's war. In India, the Communist Party fractured during the Sino-Soviet split, creating a large pro-China faction called the Communist Party of India (Marxist) in 1964. However, the CPI(M) saw armed struggle as peasant self-defense, rather than a struggle for a full-scale communist revolution.[6] This led to a new split when the Naxalbari peasant uprising broke out in 1967, founding the Communist Party of India (Marxist-Leninist). The leading figure, Charu Majumdar, declared "China's Chairman is Our Chairman."[7] Naxalbari, together with Nepal and the Philippines, remain areas where Maoist parties still play a prominent role.

Chinese influence in Africa was not only ideological. Insurgents from Algeria, Angola, Botswana, Cameroon, both Republics of Congo, Guinea, Kenya, Malawi, Zimbabwe, Mozambique, and South Africa all received training from China in the 1960s.[8]

Maoist China also exercised influence on revolutionary nationalists and communists who pursued armed struggle in Latin America. For nationalists, China provided a model for independent economic development in a semi-colonial context. To communist revolutionaries who waged armed struggle, the Chinese people's war and Maoist guerrilla tactics were an inspiration. The Cuban Revolution of 1959 was an example of an armed struggle that could lead the way to socialism, but the Cubans

---

5   Rothwell, Matthew. "The Road Is Tortuous: The Chinese Revolution and the End of the Global Sixties." *Revista Izquierdas*. No. 49, April 2020. https://peopleshistoryofideas.com/wp-content/uploads/2020/04/The_Road_Is_Tortuous-The_Chinese_Revolution_and_the_End_of_the_Global_Sixties.pdf

6   Banerjee, Sumanta. *India's Simmering Revolution: The Naxalite Uprising*. Zed Press, 1984. pp. 20–21.

7   Mazumdar, Charu. "China's Chairman is Our Chairman: China's Path is Our Path." *Liberation*. Vol. 3, no. 1, November 1969, pp. 6–13.

8   Brady, Anne-Marie. *Making the Foreign Serve China: Managing Foreigners in the People's Republic*. Rowman & Littlefield, 2003. p. 127.

developed their own variant of guerilla struggle—the "*foco*" strategy.[9] The Cuban example fueled the emergence of guerrilla struggles across Latin America in contrast to the line of peaceful coexistence.

In Western Europe, Maoism was an inspiration for the student revolt in Paris. The Maoist newspaper *La Cause du peuple* was a major organ for the movement. In Germany, it influenced the student leader Rudi Dutschke.[10] My own organization, the Communist Working Circle, was founded in 1964 by people who left the Danish Communist Party, which was loyal to the Soviet Union. It was precisely the compromising attitude of Moscow and the revolutionary spirit of China that led to the formation of the organization, which I joined.

In the United States, Maoist China's most important influence was on radical African American movements. Malcolm X directed the movement to study the Chinese experience with his 1963 "Message to the Grassroots."[11] The Revolutionary Action Movement (RAM), which followed Malcolm X's position in situating the Black liberation struggle in the context of Third World liberation, served as a milieu in which many activists adopted Maoist ideas. Among them were Huey Newton and Bobby Seale, founders of the Black Panther Party. The Black Panthers adopted many Maoist ideas and popularized the idea that domestic armed struggle against the U.S. government was possible, which was then practiced by the Black Panthers and later the Weathermen and Black Liberation Army.[12]

Inspired by the anti-imperialist victories in Cuba and Algeria, and the successful resistance in Vietnam, strong revolutionary movements appeared in numerous countries: Laos, Cambodia, India, Nepal, Indonesia, Thailand, the Philippines, Palestine, Lebanon, South Yemen, Oman, Angola, Mozambique, Guinea-Bissau, Zimbabwe, South Africa,

---

9 The central principle of *foco* is that a small group fast-moving guerrilla group can provide a focus (in Spanish *foco*) for popular discontent against a sitting regime and thereby lead a general rebellion.

10 Suri, Jeremi. *Power and Protest: Global Revolution and the Rise of Détente*. Harvard University Press, 2003. pp. 179–180.

11 X, Malcom. "Message to the Grassroots." *Malcolm X Speaks*. Grove Weidenfeld, 1965. pp. 4–18.

12 Bloom, Joshua and Marin Jr, Waldo. *Black Against Empire: The History and Politics of the Black Panther Party*. University of California Press, 2013.

Namibia, Guatemala, El Salvador, Nicaragua, Brazil, Chile, Uruguay and Mexico. In some of these countries, socialist movements came to power. In the decade from 1965-75, the principal contradiction on the world level was between imperialism, led by the U.S., and the numerous anti-imperialist movements and progressive Third World states, which tried to build socialism. The guerrilla fighter was the new revolutionary subject. From revolutionary practice, liberatory theory was generated in the Third World by Mao, Ho Chi-Minh, Che Guevara, Franz Fanon, Amílcar Cabral, and others.

However, national liberation would prove easier to obtain than ending imperialist exploitation. The anti-colonial movements were well aware that the struggle to develop the forces of production was a continuation of national liberation. Following the Algerian revolution's military victory, the key question became the production front. In a speech on December 23, 1964, in Algeria, Che Guevara said:

> This is a time for construction, something much more difficult, and seemingly less heroic, but demanding all the nation's forces...It is necessary to work, because at times like these that is the best way of struggling...Fatherland or death.[13]

To echo Che in 2006, the Vice-President of Bolivia, Garcia Linera, launched the slogan "industrialization or death."[14] While the Cuban "Fatherland or death" expresses the identity, in specific circumstances, of the class and national struggle, "industrialization or death" expresses the idea that political independence proves illusory if not sustained by economic independence sustained by the development of the productive forces.[15]

In Algeria, Frantz Fanon posed the problem of a national liberation movement's transition from the politico-military to the politico-economic. The worker replaced the guerrilla as the revolutionary subject.

> Today, national independence and nation building in the underdeveloped regions take on an entirely new aspect...every country suffers from the same lack of infrastructure...But also, a world without doctors, without engineers, without administrators...When a colonialist country, embarrassed by a colony's demand for independence, proclaims with the nationalist leaders in

---

13 Guevara, Che. In Losurdo. *Class Struggle*. p. 188.
14 Stefanoni, Pablo. "Bolivia a due Dimensioni." 2006. https://www.peacelink.it/latina/a/17714.html
15 Losurdo. *Class Struggle*. p. 319–20.

mind: "If you want independence, take it and return to the Dark Ages," the newly independent people nod their approval and take up the challenge. And what we actually see is the colonizer withdrawing his capital and technicians and encircling the young nation with an apparatus of economic pressure. The apotheosis of independence becomes the curse of independence. The sweeping powers of coercion of the colonial authorities condemn the young nation to regression…The nationalist leaders then are left with no other choice but to turn to their people and ask them to make a gigantic effort. An autarkic regime is established and each state, with the pitiful resources at its disposal, endeavors to address the mounting national hunger and the growing national poverty. We are witness to the mobilization of people who now have to work themselves to exhaustion while a contemptuous and bloated Europe looks on. Other Third World countries refuse to accept such an ordeal and agree to give in to the terms of the former colonial power. Taking advantage of their strategic position in the cold war struggle, these countries sign agreements and commit themselves. The formerly colonized territory is now turned into an economically dependent country.[16]

After the end of the Second World War and the subsequent tide of decolonization, over a hundred new nations were born. But these countries weren't big like the Soviet Union and China, where more diverse economic land reforms, a planned economy, and "delinking" from the world market had created viable national economies. Most of the newly independent countries in the Third World remained dependent on exporting to the global market to survive. They were not able to develop their productive forces in a capitalist world market, trapped by dependency and exploited via unequal exchange caused by their low wages. To acquire foreign exchange for technology imports, they had to export their raw materials and agricultural products at world market prices.

Political independence led, in most cases, to capitalist applications of "development economics." Unlike their western colonial predecessors, they could not transfer the costs of industrialization and welfare to other nations, and therefore most were caught in the "development trap," leading to huge debt and sliding back to an exploited position in global capitalism.

The Soviet Union, China, and Cuba had to transfer the social costs of industrialization internally—meaning to the rural communities—or mitigate the problem of capital scarcity by mobilizing a large amount of labor at a low cost in the construction of state projects. It contributed to

---

16 Fanon, Frantz. *The Wretched of the Earth*. Grove Press, 2004. p. 53–55.

China's successful industrialization that the Communist Party, through voluntarism, was able to substitute capital with labor. In decades after the revolution, millions of people were willing to sacrifice themselves for the socialist primitive accumulation. This created the foundation for China to escape the polarizing tendency within global capitalism, between a rich core and a poor periphery.

CHAPTER 15

The Cultural Revolution

The Cultural Revolution was not a sudden or isolated phenomenon. The launch of the Cultural Revolution must be viewed in the context of a dialectical relation between evolving global and internal Chinese contradictions. On the global level, we saw the intensified contradiction between U.S. imperialism and the national liberation struggles, as well the growing hostility between the Soviet Union and China. The latter disagreed on how to develop socialism on the national level as well as the stance to take on imperialism—and how to continue a world revolutionary process. China resented that its economy had become dependent on the Soviet mode of production. After delinking from the Soviet Union, China used labor as a substitute for the lack of capital. But the adopted Soviet system of planning and management, without corresponding financial and technological support, became alienated from the economic base. The Cultural Revolution has to be contextualized in this contradiction.

On the national level, the Cultural Revolution was a continuation of the political struggles in the 1950s, centered on how to move towards socialism. To simplify: how might China use voluntarist means to mobilize the masses to construct infrastructure, develop industry, and increase agricultural production in service to the common good? Or how might it use economic incentives and the market mechanism to develop the economy? At the same time, this dispute was a critique of the Soviet superstructure, which according to Mao, had led to a degeneration of the Party, the development of a ruling bureaucracy, and accommodation to imperialism. Mao argued that the road toward socialism was going through a chain of revolutions in the superstructure. The way the economic system was managed in the 1950s was incompatible with the new "self-reliance" line, and therefore a radical transformation of the superstructure became imperative—a cultural revolution.

Mao had been critical of the Soviet strategy for revolution and the development of society since "The Long March," and he responded by developing his "sinification" of Marxism. Coming to power in 1949, Mao insisted on a Chinese version of socialism, in which the modernization of industry and the collectivization of agriculture would go hand in hand. However, despite a different "economic base," China had followed the pattern of the Soviet Union's "superstructure" in management, its educational system, and cultural life. It was not until 1956, under Khrushchev, that Mao realized that it was this pattern that should be broken if China was to avoid following the Soviet Union's path away from the political preconditions of socialism.

Mao's main critique of the Soviet Union was that it denied class struggle would continue under socialism. The Soviet leadership claimed that class society had ended and that the state belonged to the people. In Mao's view, a new bourgeoisie had risen to power in the Soviet Union. He saw the same development in China under the leadership of Liu Shaoqi, who had gained a major influence in the Party, during the crises of the Great Leap Forward. Mao's response was to launch "The Great Proletarian Cultural Revolution."

The enactment of the revolutionary spirit at the beginning of the Cultural Revolution, with students taking to the streets, and Party leaders being overthrown and subjected to mass criticism for being capitalist roaders, proved to the world that China took the idea of continuous revolution seriously. It wanted to prevent the emergence of a bureaucratic class that acted in its own interest, as had happened in the Soviet Union.

Up until the beginning of the 1960s, China's planned economy developed according to the Soviet model. Thirty-eight thousand Chinese engineers were trained in the Soviet Union, and 11,000 Soviet experts helped build infrastructure and the industrial sector. China received blueprints and know-how to construct everything from trucks to nuclear power stations.[1] This certainly helped with the development of

---

1   Rosen, Steven and Kurth, James. *Testing Theories of Economic Imperialism.*

China, but it also fostered a technocratic elite with special privileges, similar to what had occurred in the Soviet Union. Significant factions in the Communist Party of China, however, were eager to counteract the bureaucratization of the revolution and the emergence of a new ruling class. The first attempt was a radical experiment in direct democracy. In 1957, Mao famously stated, "Let a hundred flowers bloom and a hundred schools of thought contend," encouraging the people to criticize the practices of the Communist Party and its leaders. In 1962, a large-scale "Socialist Education Campaign" was developed in the rural areas of China as a forerunner of the Cultural Revolution, to experiment and seek out the correct method. Thousands of unemployed urban youth, workers, and intellectuals were sent to the rural communities as a "soft landing" site for the economic crises in the wake of the Great Leap Forward, absorbing redundant labor power from the city to assist agricultural production, and at the same time, strengthen a socialist consciousness. Mao understood how tightly capitalism and imperialism were connected. He knew that China might easily be absorbed by the capitalist world system and feared that this would turn China itself into a capitalist and imperialist power. He hoped that a Cultural Revolution would help prevent this. In 1964, he wrote:

> Class struggle, the struggle for production, and scientific experiment are the three great revolutionary movements for building a mighty socialist country...If, in the absence of these movements, the landlords, rich peasants, counter-revolutionaries, bad elements and monsters of all kinds were allowed to crawl out, while our cadres were to shut their eyes to all this and in many cases fail even to differentiate between the enemy and ourselves, but were to collaborate with the enemy and were corrupted, divided and demoralized by him, then it would not take long, perhaps only several years or a decade, or several decades at most, before a counter-revolutionary restoration on a national scale inevitably occurred, the Marxist-Leninist party would undoubtedly become a revisionist party or fascist party, and the whole of China would change its color.[2]

Mao denounced the cadres who wanted to use capitalist methods to restore China's national power, calling them "capitalist roaders." Yet his strategy did not at first succeed within the Party; while the Party leader-

Lexington Books, 1974. pp. 261–81.

2   Zedong, Mao. "We Must Prevent China From Changing Colour, July 14, 1964." https://www.marxists.org/reference/archive/mao/selected-works/volume-9/mswv9_24.htm.

ship applied Mao's class struggle rhetoric against traditional class enemies such as landowners, capitalists, and foreign imperialists, it refused to apply it to the party leadership itself. The new political elite felt they were entitled to certain privileges and were unwilling to let them go. Mao's status within the party had been weakened by the economic problems generated by the Great Leap Forward. At the Lushan party conference in 1959, defense minister Peng Dehuai attacked Mao's failed economic policy, which turned the peasants against the party. Peng's open attack cost him his position, but Mao was under pressure. To regain strength, Mao chose to address the masses of workers, peasants, and students directly, in a Cultural Revolution initiative launched under the slogan "it is right to rebel," which encouraged the people to "Bombard the Headquarters!" It turned out to be an effective strategy. However, Mao would hardly have thrown himself into a struggle of such great magnitude if he had not secured the support of the new defense minister Lin Biao and the army.

Mao's formulation of the Cultural Revolution was summarized in a document known as the "Sixteen Points."[3] It defined three stages: to engage in a struggle against the authorities, to criticize capitalist ideas, and to carry out reform. The people of China were urged to rise against established ideas and habits, especially those espoused by old and new elites. All state institutions needed to be reformed. Criticism and self-criticism were declared the basis of progress. Mao was not alone in this project. During the Cultural Revolution, a faction of the Communist Party of China headed by Zhang Chunqiao promoted a socialist political economy, which would move China toward egalitarianism and eliminate capitalist values.

In May 1966, Mao sent a letter to Lin Biao, head of the People's Liberation Army.[4] Mao demanded that regular soldiers, as well as officers, should engage not only in military training, but also in cultural studies

---

3   Peking Review. "Decision of the Central Committee of the Chinese Communist Party Concerning the Great Proletarian Cultural Revolution (Adopted on August 8, 1966)." https://www.marxists.org/subject/china/peking-review/1966/PR1966-33g.htm.

4   Zedong, Mao. "Notes on the Report of Further Improving the Army's Agricultural Work by the Rear Service Department of the Military Commission." *Long Live Mao Tse-tung Thought*. 1966. https://china.usc.edu/mao-zedong-"notes-report-further-improving-army"-agricultural-work-rear-service-department-military.

and agricultural production. It was a challenge to the mentality of capitalist wage labor: work was not merely completed to earn money, but was pursued to become a revolutionary agent. Mao knew that the division of labor could not be entirely abolished. Yet, any worker could do some agricultural work, and any peasant could do some industrial work. Soldiers, students, and Party officials were expected to line up alongside the workers and peasants in their efforts—not only to assist them, but to develop their own consciousness and respect for the hardships of the proletariat.[5]

The Cultural Revolution became exceptionally visible during the summer of 1966, when the "Red Guards" stepped forward. The first to respond to the call to "rebel" was a Red Guard group, formed at Tsinghua University's attached Middle School. These young people played a huge role in the first chaotic phases of the Cultural Revolution. They shook things up; they attacked all obsolete feudal and bourgeois phenomena in society. One example was "careerism" in the educational system. This instilled in the students a feeling of being "better" than the common working population. The graduates from higher education could look forward to living in prosperity, miles ahead of the average industrial worker. Higher education concentrated upon creating "experts"—not upon educating politically conscious people wishing to serve the people. This was not just rhetoric. During the Cultural Revolution, within the "Young Intellectuals Going to Countryside" movement, 20 million urban youth were sent to production teams in people's communes.[6] The young people went to the countryside and gave up the advantages of urban life to integrate intellectual and manual workers, to have them become one and the same person.

It was not until 1966 that the Cultural Revolution spread from Beijing to other Chinese cities where factional battles between students would be supplemented by more widespread mobilization of the working classes. To break down the expert mentality and its manifestations in the planning of production, a change in mentality was required from both technicians and ordinary workers. Here the Red Guards also played their part in moving the process forward by placing *dazibao* [big-character posters] at workplaces. This would then be followed by a discussion between the

---

5   Gao. "Why Is the Battle for China's Past Relevant to Us Today?" pp. 4–16.
6   Tiejun. *Ten Crises.* p. 158.

workers, the technicians, and the administration personnel to create a new attitude toward work. Administrators were required to participate in manual labor, while workers began making administrative decisions—an integration of all efforts.

Prior to this, the "self"—that is, individual material advantages—had been prioritized, following the Soviet example. The management used differences in wages, "material incentives," money rewards, and bonus arrangements to encourage workers to engage in cost-reducing work. During the Cultural Revolution, emphasis was placed upon politics, ideology, and the individual's conscious attitude toward the collective and the whole of society. The workers', the technicians', and the bureaucracy's political understanding of the importance of "serving the people" became the ideal.[7]

In November 1966, the "Rebel Headquarters of Red Workers" was formed in Shanghai. Unlike the student groups, it was not a small group organized around a few institutions, but a huge network with over 400,000 members. This trend was not limited to Shanghai. In the same month, similar organizations spread like a prairie fire all over the country, forming the "All-China Red Laborer Rebels' Headquarters," a reference to the state-controlled "All-China Federation of Trade Unions" (ACFTU). The Red Laborer Rebels organized sit-ins at ACFTU and Ministry of Labor headquarters.[8] The peak of this mobilization, called the "January Storm," came in Shanghai in the winter of 1967, leading to the formation of the "Shanghai Commune" in early February 1967.

As these tumults spread, a window opened in which workers were able to take direct, often chaotic, control over production and day-to-day life. One of the most important accomplishments of the Cultural

---

7   Che Guevara was sympathetic to Mao's positions. He cheered the idea of developing a "socialist man" (sic) to serve the people. The aversion of the Cubans to manual labor had to be eradicated. One would work for all and all for one. The collective interest would supersede the individual one. Che Guevara emphasized the superiority of moral over material incentives; he lashed out at "economism" described as "the tendency to consider that men produced more and better as they received more and better." See Guevara, Che. "Socialism and Man in Cuba." *The Che Reader*. Ocean Press, 2005. https://www.marxists.org/archive/guevara/1965/03/man-socialism.htm.

8   Wu, Yiching. *The Cultural Revolution at the Margins*. Harvard University Press, 2014. p.108.

Revolution was the empowerment of ordinary people and the democratization of Chinese society, in terms of everyday life at the factory, farm, army, and school. This established a strong sense of egalitarianism. People's mindsets and outlooks were fundamentally changed—indeed, it was a *cultural* revolution. With the re-evaluation of norms, this political movement hardly left a single Chinese person untouched. It caused debates and discussions, accusations and counter-accusations, and even violent clashes between different groups.

When Mao initiated the Cultural Revolution, he did not have a master plan. Much was left to improvisation and spontaneity, which led to unexpected developments and turns of events.[9] Fred Engst, an American who grew up in China after his parents moved there in the 1950s to be part of the revolution, cites the "immaturity of the working class" as the main reason for the Cultural Revolution's shortcomings:

> They could not overcome contradictions between themselves. They could not avert factional fights. At the beginning of the Cultural Revolution, the problem was how to make the masses rise up. After the masses rose up, overcoming factionalism became the key issue. The immaturity of the working class was demonstrated most vividly by the conservatives who did not hesitate to use arms to suppress the rebels who criticized the leader. When you use arms to suppress others who criticize the leader, you give up your own right to criticize. That is why I talk about the "immaturity of the working class." The working class was divided. The capitalist roaders were united. The number of cards that revolutionary leaders could play were getting fewer and fewer. So, they got backed into a corner.[10]

To restore order when local authorities had collapsed, the army was called in "to take control of communication and transportation facilities, supervise political stabilization and economic production, and conduct ideological education."[11] The organization of the Shanghai Commune was seen as too excessive, hampering the efficiency of production, and Mao recommended it be replaced by "three-in-one revolutionary committees," run by military officers, party cadres, and representatives from

---

9 Gao. "Why Is the Battle for China's Past Relevant to Us Today?" pp. 4–16.

10 Ülker, Onurcan. "The Struggle for Actually Building Socialist Society: An Interview with Fred Engst." *Research Unit for Political Economy*. https://rupeindia.wordpress.com/2018/01/19/the-struggle-of-actually-building-socialism-an-interview-with-fred-engst/.

11 Wu. *The Cultural Revolution at the Margins*. p.125.

the rebel organizations. These committees became the new organs of power and rebuilt the political order to solidify the Cultural Revolution.

The Cultural Revolution was meant to ensure that the struggle against capitalist influence in Chinese society and the Communist Party would not falter. It was seen as mandatory for building socialism. Predictably, the Cultural Revolution deepened the divide between Mao's more voluntarist line with emphasis on continued class struggle and reoccurring revolutions and those who wished to emphasize the need to develop economic incentives, represented by Liu Shaoqi and Deng Xiaoping. All three wanted to restore China as a world power but differed strongly in their thoughts on how to develop the productive forces and the road toward socialism. However, it is important to mention that the conflict within the Communist Party of China did not take the extreme form as the conflict within the Soviet Communist Party in the 1930s. It was no dinner party, but it did not have mass incarceration and liquidation. During the Cultural Revolution, Liu Shaoqi and Deng Xiaoping were ridiculed, but remained in the party and would be able to make a comeback.

In the process of the Cultural Revolution, two main groups became crystallized. One group was headed by Liu Shaoqi, who remained an advocate of the Soviet model. This group was opposed by Mao's cultural revolutionary group. The conflict hardened and simplified into the existence of two lines: the revolutionary and the revisionist, the socialist and the capitalist. This division was correct—as far as Liu Shaoqi and his faction had been following the Soviet line—but it is an oversimplification, because Mao had also followed the same line for China's reconstruction after 1949. This simplification turned Mao's writing into a universal dogma.

"Mao Zedong Thought"

In the turbulent situation of a Cultural Revolution in a post-revolutionary society, the concept of "Mao Zedong Thought" was established as the yardstick with which one could and must measure everything. Mao Zedong Thought was concentrated in *The Little Red Book: Quotations from Chairman Mao Zedong*, published in 1964, first to be used in the army, but it quickly spread to the entire society. It gained an enormous influence. In 1966, it was translated and sold in more than a hundred countries. Over one billion official volumes were sold between 1966 and 1969 alone, as well as untold numbers of unofficial local reprints and unofficial translations.[12] In Denmark, the organization to which I belonged published it in Danish in 1967, and in just two years we sold 25,000 copies in a country with five million citizens.

It was Lin Biao who coined the term "Mao Zedong Thought" as a tendency of Marxism, in the same way Stalin coined "Leninism." In the preface, Lin wrote:

> Comrade Mao Zedong is the greatest Marxist-Leninist of our era. He has inherited, defended and developed Marxism-Leninism with genius, creatively and comprehensively and has brought it to a higher and completely new stage.[13]

In a speech to the Politburo on May 18, 1966, Lin called Mao a "genius" and Mao Zedong Thought "universal truth and our guide for action."[14] In an editorial of *Jiefangjun Bao* (*Liberation Army Daily*) on June 7, 1966, Lin writes:

> The attitude towards Mao Zedong's thought, whether to accept it or resist it, to support it or oppose it, to love it warmly or be hostile to it, this is the touchstone to test and the watershed between true revolution and sham revolution, between revolution and counter-revolution, between Marxism-Leninism and revisionism. He who wants to make revolution must accept Mao Zedong's thought and act in accordance with it.[15]

The idea of Chairman Mao as a "genius" and his words as "universal truth" is a side of the idealistic current that came to dominate part of the Cultural Revolution. However, this is not the philosophy of Mao. When Lin became Mao's "close comrade in arms," it is because their interests

---

12 Cook, Alexander. *Mao's Little Red Book: A Global History*. Cambridge University Press, 2014. p. xiii.

13 Biao, Lin. *Foreword to the Second Edition of Quotations of Chairman Mao*. 1966. https://www.marxists.org/reference/archive/lin-biao/1966/12/16.htm.

14 Biao, Lin. "Address at the Enlarged Meeting of the CPC Central Politburo, 18 May 1966." *Chinese Law & Government*. Vol. 2, no. 4, 1969, pp. 42–62.

15 Biao, Lin. "Mao Zedong's Thought is the Telescope and Microscope of Our Revolutionary Cause." *Liberation Army Daily*. June 7, 1966. https://www.bannedthought.net/China/MaoEra/GPCR/GreatSocialistCulturalRevolutionInChina-03-1966.pdf   .

coincided. They both regarded the right wing of the party as an acute danger threatening a military coup, and Mao needed more than a student revolt to carry out the Cultural Revolution. Mao and Lin had common opponents, but their philosophy was different.

Lin Biao's Mao Zedong Thought changed in 1967 from being advice for action to moral teaching, a wisdom to bow down to, exemplified in ritual public readings from *The Little Red Book*. In his struggle against the right wing of the Party, Mao teamed up with a man whose philosophical position seemed unsustainable. In a private letter to Jiang Qing (his wife) Mao reveals his thoughts on Lin Biao:

> Some of his methods always leave me unsettled. I have never believed that those booklets of mine have that sort of magical power. Now if he praises to the sky, the whole party and country do so too...I expressed my difference with that sort of pronouncement [of Lin Biao's].[16] But what was the use? When he went to Beijing, at the May conference [of 1966], he still spoke that way, and the press even more fiercely so, simply exaggerating to the point of fantasy...This matter cannot be made public at present. The entire left and the broad masses all are speaking in this way.[17] Making it public would pour cold water on them and help the right. And the present task is for the entire party and country to achieve a general defeat (it cannot be a complete one) of the right, and then in seven or eight years to have another movement for sweeping away the monsters and demons...
>
> If the Rightists stage an anti-Communist coup d'etat in China, I am sure they will know no peace either and their rule will most probably be short-lived because it will not be tolerated by the revolutionaries, who represent the interests of the people making up more than 90% of the population. ...Wherever the rightists are arrogant, they are defeated and then their downfall is even more miserable, and the left then gains in strength. This is a nationwide maneuver in which the left, right and wavering unstable middle factions, all will acquire their own respective lessons. The conclusion is still the two familiar comments: The future is bright; the road is tortuous.[18]

---

16   This refers to Lin Biao, promotion of the Quotations of Chairman Mao and Lin's "Genius Theory" in which he referred to Mao as "a genius that only comes around every few thousand years."

17   Reference to the promotion of the use of the Quotations from Chairman Mao Zedong.

18   Zedong, Mao. "Letter to Jiang Qing July 8, 1966." https://www.bannedthought.net/China/Individuals/MaoZedong/Letters/Mao'sLetterToJiangQing-660708-Alt3.pdf. For examples of Mao's many repudiations of this practice, see Zedong, Mao. "A Few Opinions of Mine." 1970. https://bannedthought.net/USA/

By the end of the Cultural Revolution, Mao and Lin Biao began to disagree over the issue of China's relationship with the United States and the Soviet Union. Lin believed that both superpowers were equally threatening to China. Zhou Enlai and Mao believed that China should become closer to the United States to mitigate the threat posed by the Soviet Union.[19] Mao approved Zhou's efforts to rehabilitate officials who had been purged during the first years of the Cultural Revolution and supported Zhou's efforts to improve China's relationship with the United States.[20] In July 1971, Mao decided to remove Lin from power. Zhou attempted to moderate Mao's resolution to act against Lin but failed. Lin may have tried to stage a military coup to counter Mao. Lin died when his aircraft crashed in Mongolia on September 13, 1971; the circumstances of the crash are still debated. After his death, Lin was labeled as a traitor by the Party, and a purge of his followers was conducted.[21]

Lin's transformation of Mao's writings on specific matters into universal truth also had an international dimension. To stress Mao Zedong Thought as a development of Marxism is correct if what is meant is that Mao's application of the Marxist method demonstrates how reality can be studied and acted upon. The Vietnamese applied the Maoist guerrilla strategy and people's protracted war with great success. However, the use of Mao Zedong Thought becomes wrong if it is thereby meant that Mao's specific judgments on concrete international and Chinese situations and phenomena, at certain moments, can be applied as if they were of univer-

---

MCU/RedPages/issue_two/a-few-opinions-of-mine/. Regarding Mao's criticism of Chen Boda and Lin Biao's "genius theory," see Zedong, Mao. "Recommendation of Chairman Mao to Regulate the Wasteful and Superficial Dissemination of Figures and Sayings of Chairman Mao as well as Statue Construction and Associated Central Committee Document Series 67, Number 219: July 5, 1967." https://www.bannedthought.net/China/MaoEra/GPCR/Chinese/RecommendationOnDisseminationOfMaoFiguresAndSayings-CCP-CC-1967-Chinese.pdf.

19   Ross, Robert. "From Lin Biao to Deng Xiaoping: Elite Instability and China's U.S. Policy." *The China Quarterly*. No. 118, June 1989, p. 268.

20   *Ibid.* pp. 265–99.

21   In recent years there have been more balanced evaluations of Lin Biao. Lin's name and picture have re-appeared in Chinese history textbooks, recognizing him as one of the Red Army's best military strategists. In 2007, a portrait of Lin was included in a display of the "Ten Marshals," a group considered to be the founders of China's armed forces and displayed at the Military Museum in Beijing.

sal validity. This was the approach being taken in China, to some extent, and among many Maoists around the world in the 1970s.

These Maoist organizations took Mao's specific analysis as universal law and used them in a reality that did not necessarily conform to the situation in which they were made. One of the weaknesses of Indian Maoism, for example, has been the poor theorization of Indian state power. Capitalism was much more developed in India in the 1960s than in China in the 1930s and the Indian state was much more robust than the Chinese—which more or less collapsed during the Japanese invasion.

The copy-pasting of Maoism became grotesque when it was transferred to the imperialist heartland. In late 1966, the Chinese press, which hitherto had been almost silent about the working class of the imperialist countries, suddenly started writing about the poor and exploited Western workers who were awakening to the revolutionary struggle against their oppressors. Mass rallies were held in support of white American workers' purely economic strike actions, and the British dock workers were hailed for their heroic struggle against ruthless exploitation.[22] Even more peculiarly, the Maoist groups in North America and Europe talked about the peasants, fishermen, and workers in the same terms as Mao did about these classes in China in the 1930s. The use of Mao's concrete statements as if they were universal truths distorted the Maoists' views of the world around them. I still encounter Maoists (of the old cultural revolutionary school), who, with reverence for Mao Zedong Thought, put the working class in the global North and South on the same footing.

There are similarities between the Chinese attitude in the late-1960s and the former Soviet attitude under Stalin. China, on its own, and some others' opinion, had taken over the position occupied by the Soviet Union in the world, as the "native country of socialism." When Lenin, in the last years of his life, assessed perspectives on the future of socialism in the Soviet Union, he stressed that the decisive problem was whether Soviet power could hold out until the proletariat in the more advanced countries had accomplished their revolution. From this perspective, he concluded that the Bolsheviks had to do everything within their power to maintain workers' power until the European working class had completed their revolution. The COMNINTERN's interpretation of this in

---

22 Lauesen. *The Principal Contradiction*. p. 175.

the 1930s was that the most important task for all communists was to preserve the power of Soviet workers. The "touchstone" for a Marxist was one's attitude toward the Soviet Union.

The Chinese overtook this position: the "touchstone" for a Marxist became their attitude toward China, specifically toward the Cultural Revolution, and Mao Zedong Thought, while China was awaiting the proletariat in the Third World to follow their path to socialism. Nevertheless, the thesis was just as wrong when applied to China as it was to the Soviet Union. The "touchstone" for Marxists is the ability to develop a revolutionary theory for their own country based on the specifics of that country and how it is situated in the capitalist world system. This was what Lenin did. This was what qualified Mao in the period when the COMINTERN and Stalin had quite different theories for the Chinese Revolution. Mao stressed that to be a Marxist in China meant to know, understand, and correctly influence Chinese reality.

The use of the term "Mao Zedong Thought" during the Cultural Revolution corresponds closely to the Soviet use of the term "Leninism" under Stalin. Mao Zedong had to directly oppose this "Leninism" to secure the Chinese revolution's victory. We must use Marxism, including the Chinese experience, and Mao's works, as Lenin stated:

> ...[to] seek, find and correctly determine the specific way or the exact turn of events, which will lead the masses on to the real, decisive and final revolutionary fight in our own country.[23]

"Leninism" and "Mao Zedong Thought" correspond to two different stages in the worldwide development of socialism. The experience of the Cultural Revolution, positive and negative, has brought China a step further in the direction of socialism. It was a lesson in how to carry on the class struggle after the Communist Party had taken state power. The Cultural Revolution gave China new possibilities, which the Soviet Union never witnessed. However, China in the 1970s, just like the Soviet Union at the beginning of the 1920s, was facing the problem of whether it could "hold out" until the tide of revolutionary movements might materialize into socialist countries around the world. Just as Lenin's hopes were in vain, so too were the hopes of the Chinese.

---

23 Lenin, Vladimir Ilyich. "Left-wing Communism, an Infantile Disorder." *Collected Works*. Vol. 31. Progress Publishers, 1975. p. 17.

The national liberation struggles in the Third World during "the long sixties" did not proceed into a socialist world revolution. Global capitalism had not yet exhausted its development opportunities. Just like the Soviet Union, China took the "wrong" track of Dengism. "Wrong" is in quotation marks because it is meaningless to refer to unavoidable historical processes as "right" or "wrong." The reason why the Cultural Revolution did not materialize into a socialist economic development has both an internal Chinese explanation and a global explanation. China had to change its course.

The Cultural Revolution and the End of the Long 1960s

Let us now zoom out and take a look at the Cultural Revolution from a more global perspective. How did it interact with the principal contradictions during the Long 1960s?

China's decision to try to be the leader and inspiration for revolutionaries worldwide relied on both the example set at home and on the stance of China upon the global stage. Domestically, the Cultural Revolution promoted egalitarian social reforms that corresponded with communist values. In its foreign relations, China's willingness to support liberation movements abroad, and its efforts to promote its interpretation of Marxism internationally, likewise played an important role in its ability to serve as a radical example. At the time, China had nothing to lose concerning its relations with the West, which had isolated it since 1949.

As the Russian Revolution waited in vain for revolutions in the advanced capitalist countries, the Chinese Cultural Revolution waited for supplemental revolutions in the Global South to develop their own socialism and continue the world revolution. Lin Biao laid out this strategy in 1965 in "Long Live the Victory of People's War!" He expounded upon the experience of the Chinese Revolution, in which peasants had encircled and taken over urban areas, to the entire globe:

> ... comrade Mao Zedong's theory of the establishment of rural revolutionary base areas and the encirclement of the cities from the countryside is of outstanding and universal practical importance for the present revolutionary struggles of all the oppressed nations and peoples, and particularly for the revolutionary struggles of the oppressed nations and peoples in Asia, Africa and Latin America against imperialism and its lackeys...Taking the entire

globe, if North America and Western Europe can be called "the cities of the world," then Asia, Africa and Latin America constitute "the rural areas of the world." Since World War II, the proletarian revolutionary movement has for various reasons been temporarily held back in the North American and West European capitalist countries, while the people's revolutionary movement in Asia, Africa and Latin America has been growing vigorously. In a sense, the contemporary world revolution also presents a picture of the encirclement of cities by the rural areas. In the final analysis, the whole cause of world revolution hinges on the revolutionary struggles of the Asian, African and Latin American peoples who make up the overwhelming majority of the world's population.[24]

When Mao, with Lin's support, launched the Cultural Revolution, it was in a global context where the revolutionary forces were on the offensive all over the world. By the end of the 1960s, it was not unthinkable that there would be a series of revolutionary breakthroughs, which would support China's new course and vice versa. The Cultural Revolution was in line with revolutionary global developments. Cultural Revolution-era China hoped that the wave of revolutionary activities would result in a world order under which the Chinese way of developing socialism could become an example for others to follow. Revolutions erupted in Cuba, Algeria, Vietnam, Angola, Mozambique, Guinea-Bissau, Namibia, Zimbabwe, Nicaragua, and so on, but despite their socialist aspirations, they hardly left the ground concerning the construction of socialism. Therefore, it was not only the Cultural Revolution that lost its steam through the 1970s, it was revolutionary movements all over the world. This indicates that there was a deeper transformation occurring in world capitalism, which was reflected in global class struggles. Undoubtedly there were specific, localized reasons for the downturn of socialism within each country; here, however, we will examine the changes occurring in the global structures.

National self-determination and the ambition to create socialism were not enough to bring about socialism in reality. The conditions were even more difficult for the smaller Third-World countries than it had been for huge countries like Russia and China—particularly in terms of economic diversity and mounting a defense against hostile imperialist

---

24 Biao, Lin. "Long Live the Victory of People's War! In Commemoration of the 20th Anniversary of Victory in the Chinese People's War of Resistance Against Japan." *Peking Review*. No. 36, September 1965.

encirclement.

Most important, however, was the polarizing dynamic, caused by the "Unequal Exchange" in global capitalism.[25] Raw material and agricultural products produced by low-wage labor in the Third World were exchanged by industrial products produced by relatively high-wage labor in the imperialist center. The newborn revolutionary states did not have the power to change these dynamics. They could not simply increase wages and prices for the raw materials and agricultural products they supplied to the world market. They stood in competition with one another and were forced into a race to the bottom. Without the necessary development and diversity of the productive forces, delinking themselves from the world market and trying to produce solely for the domestic market in the interest of the workers and peasants risked throwing their economies into ruin. They had inherited the economic structures established by their former colonial oppressors—these were not designed to serve their interests. They were stuck with monocultures and industries limited to processing a few raw materials. No matter their aspirations, the economies of the newly independent countries were determined by the dominant capitalist realities.

Today, it is easy to say that this was inevitable and that the anticolonial movements should have known better. However, they had little choice. Seizing state power was necessary to at least change the balance of international relations. The various attempts to strengthen the political position of the former colonies and newly independent nations show that, at the time, it seemed possible to collectively make a difference. Up until the mid-1970s, global capitalism was actually under pressure, culminating in the so-called oil crises. However, as mentioned by Marx:

> No social order is ever destroyed before all the productive forces for which it is sufficient have been developed, and new superior relations of production never replace older ones before the material conditions for their existence have matured within the framework of the old society.[26]

As it turned out, capitalism had the potential for yet another round in the ring. It fought its way out of the economic and political crises through neoliberal reforms and the globalization of the production pro-

---

25 Arghiri. *Unequal Exchange.*
26 Marx. *A Contribution to the Critique of Political Economy.*

cess itself by basing it on low-paid labor in the South. It triggered the rapid development of the productive forces, both qualitatively (computers, communications, new transnational management regimes and container transports) and quantitatively, by industrializing the Third World, integrating hundreds of millions of new proletarians into the world economy.

What terminated this revolutionary period in China and on the global level, and ushered the counter-offensive of capital in the form of neoliberalism? The answer is the same as what generated the revolutionary 1960s—changes in the global principal contradiction's interaction with local contradictions.

Let me be more specific. The struggle against colonialism and imperialism grew stronger as U.S. neocolonialism penetrated the Third Word, replacing the old colonial powers, in the first two decades after the Second World War. This contradiction of imperialism versus anti-imperialism interacted with the confrontation between the U.S. and the "actually existing socialism" of the Soviet Union. Although the split between China and the Soviet Union weakened the socialist bloc and socialist movements overall, the two positions, in some peculiar ways, supplemented each other on the ground during the 1960s. While China's Cultural Revolution and Vietnam's armed struggle provided a new revolutionary spirit, the Soviet Union was the necessary nuclear military power which could counterbalance U.S. imperialism on a global scale, so that the revolutionary spirit could receive the necessary space to flourish without being crushed. The Soviet Union's ability to reciprocate a nuclear attack prevented the outbreak of a devastating global nuclear war and deterred the U.S. from using nuclear weapons in its imperialist wars.

Vietnam took advantage of "the best of both worlds." The Soviet Union provided them with anti-aircraft missiles and heavy artillery alongside existential guarantees to counterbalance the U.S. and avoid a nuclear attack on Hanoi. At the same time, Vietnam waged a "protracted people's war" on the ground without compromise, until its final victory, in tune with Maoist principles.

A supplemental force constituting "the long sixties" was the student and youth rebellion in the Global North, culminating in 1968. It was a series of protests against authoritarian regimes in the workplace, schools, families, and society in general. The 1968 uprisings in the West broadened the spectrum of liberation from the proletariat to race, gender, sexual minorities, and the indigenous peoples' struggle. It also offered a critique of "actually existing socialism" from a left perspective, creating not only Maoist-inspired groups, but a host of new left-wing organizations. I was a member of such a Maoist group in Copenhagen, Denmark. It was our hope that the liberation movements, like those taking place in Vietnam, would prevail, cutting the pipes of imperialism and creating a revolutionary situation in the imperial core. These forces would interact or merge with the rebellions in Europe and the U.S. and create a new global movement for socialism. I think Mao shared this hope in the 1960s, wishing that China would lead this new world revolutionary process. As it happened, the new global wave which came into being was not a world socialist revolution, but neoliberalism. Capitalism still had options for expansion—a new spatial fix. The forces of the Third World were too fragmented. The socialist camp was split and the '68 Rebellion in the West was, in the end, more rhetoric than deeds.

Explanations for the end of the revolutionary wave in the Sixties are typically given on a country-by-country basis as an example of domestic state repression: co-option of rebellious elements by reformists, CIA-financed reactionary forces, and exhaustion of rebellious energies. These factors contributed to extinguishing the revolutionary transformation.[27] However, the most important overarching factor was the inability of "actually existing socialism," both the Soviet and Chinese versions, and "the newly liberated states" in the Third World to develop their productive forces to a sufficient degree so as to break the power of the global capitalist market, which blocked the road to the development of socialism. Because of this, the neoliberal counter-offensive was able to do what the U.S. army could not in Vietnam: put the Third World on its knees.

Just as the revolutionary energy of China played a role in the emergence of the global uprisings in the 1960s, the decline of the Cultural Revolution played a role in the ending of the wave.

I do not think the Communist Party of China's change of strategy in the mid-1970s was a result of treason, or that Mao lost the internal power struggle in the Party. I think "the great helmsman" himself was part of this new strategy, shifting the course from port to starboard to

---

27   Rothwell. "The Road Is Tortuous." p. 2490.

avoid sailing too close to the wind of the looming storm of global capitalism. Instead, he chose a course which would give a steady tailwind in developing the productive forces of China. It was Mao, in person, who ended the Cultural Revolution by receiving columns of Red Guards on parade at Tiananmen. It was Mao himself who initiated a new policy by receiving Nixon in Beijing in 1972 and thus began the opening of transnational capital.

Chinese domestic and foreign policies were confronted with a similar dilemma as Lenin's Russia had been in the 1920s. On one hand, trying to develop socialism implies a need to defend China from foreign aggression and to generate resources to develop the economy. On the other hand, China needed to promote the spread of communist and national liberation struggles globally, which in the end is a precondition of building "genuine socialism." The dilemma is whether to defend socialism in one country, with the risk of the erosion of socialist values, or promote the world revolution, which could provoke imperialist aggression but safeguard China's own revolution in the long run. As the revolutionary 1960s faded into the neoliberal counteroffensive of the early 1970s, China chose the first option, as Stalin had before them in the 1930s, in order to face the threat from the West.

The specific circumstances, which would cause China's turn away from supporting a world revolutionary process and opening towards Western capitalism, were already present in 1968–69. The escalation of the Vietnam War made it seem likely that China could be drawn into direct conflict with the United States as it had been in Korea. On the eastern front, tensions continued to simmer on the Indian border, where a war had been fought in 1962. On the northern frontier with the Soviet Union, a troop build-up on both sides resulted in two direct military clashes between Soviet and Chinese forces.

In this critical situation, it was as if the Communist Party, with Mao as its "helmsman," lost its sense of direction. The harsh critique of the Soviet Union went from a debate on how to continue the construction of socialism in a post-revolutionary society to a theory of the principal contradiction in the world, the so-called "Three World Theory." In 1974, Mao defined the three worlds as follows:

> I hold that the U.S. and the Soviet Union belong to the First World. The

middle elements, such as Japan, Europe, Australia and Canada, belong to the Second World. We are the Third World...The U.S. and the Soviet Union have a lot of atomic bombs, and they are richer. Europe, Japan, Australia and Canada, of the Second World, do not possess so many atomic bombs and are not so rich as the First World, but richer than the Third World...All Asian countries, except Japan, belong to the Third World. All of Africa and also Latin America belong to the Third World.[28]

According to Mao's theory, there are two superpowers, the United States and the Soviet Union, which constitute "The First World," fighting each other to obtain world domination. In this makeup, China regarded the Soviet Union as the aggressive party. The Soviet Union was no longer just a revisionist bureaucratic state. The Soviet Union had not only restored capitalism, but it had also become "the most dangerous and aggressive social-imperialist power in the world;" so dangerous that the "Third World" had to ally with the "Second World"—Western Europe, Japan, and even the United States—to neutralize "Soviet imperialism" and avoid a nuclear war.

Based on the reasoning that "my enemy's enemy is my friend," China supported anti-Soviet forces worldwide, often in cooperation with the U.S. and reactionary forces. China was one of the first to recognize the government of Chilean dictator Augusto Pinochet following the coup against the Socialist Allende government. China, together with the CIA, supported Mobutu in Zaire, and Jonas Savimbi's National Union for the Total Independence of Angola in the civil war against the People's Movement for the Liberation of Angola, which was backed by Cuba.

However, there was no evidence that the Soviet Union was the most aggressive power in the confrontation with the U.S. in the mid-1970s. Already at this point, the Soviet Union was under economic, political, and military pressure from the United States, trying to keep up in the arms race. China made its national conflict with the Soviet Union into *the* global principal contradiction. Claiming that the Soviet Union was richer than the countries in the "second world" was incorrect—the Soviet Union belonged to the semi-periphery of the world-system. Neither was the Soviet Union an imperialist power in its relationship with Eastern

---

28 Zedong, Mao. "On the Question of the Differentiation of the Three Worlds, Conversation with Kenneth Kaunda (February 22, 1974)." *Mao Zedong on Diplomacy.* Foreign Languages Press, 1998.

Europe and the Third World, at least not in any economic significance. The Soviet Union was already in a defensive mode in the mid-1970s, culminating in its collapse 15 years later.

This anti-Soviet policy was combined with the Sino-American rapprochement, which Mao initiated in the late 1960s, and continued up until his death in 1976. The pragmatic faction of the Communist Party, led by Zhou Enlai and Deng Xiaoping, which had managed to hold its positions of power during the Cultural Revolution despite criticism, now gained a base of support within the party that wanted social stability. When Mao died in 1976, it was only a matter of weeks before the "Gang of Four" was arrested, and a purge was carried out against what was labeled the far left-wing faction of the party.

The changes created confusion in Maoist circles outside China. Albania had been China's ideological ally during the Mao years, but in 1978 Albania published Hoxha's *Imperialism and the Revolution*, which polemicized against Mao's theoretical work and accused China's post-Mao leadership of aspiring to turn China into a new imperialist power.

Given the decline of the Cultural Revolution and the confusion over the direction that the new Chinese leadership was heading, some former Latin American Maoists, such as the Communist Party of Peru–Red Flag *(Partido Comunista del Perú–Bandera Roja)* and Colombia's third largest guerrilla group, the People's Liberation Army *(Ejército Popular de Liberación)*—led by the Communist Party of Colombia (Marxism-Leninism) [*Partido Comunista de Colombia (Marxista-Leninista)*]— reoriented in the direction of Hoxhaism. Taking things one step further, the Communist Party of the Philippines and its New People's Army, which had been waging guerrilla warfare since 1969, sought a new relationship with the Soviet bloc itself.[29]

The opening towards global capitalism in China, combined with Hoxhaist factional activity within the Maoist ranks, greatly diminished the Maoist forces globally. By the end of the 1970s, it was hard to imagine

---

29 Sison, José María and Rosca, Ninotchka. *Jose Maria Sison: At Home in the World. Portrait of a Revolutionary*. Open Hand Publishing, 2004. pp. 152–53. After the collapse of the Soviet Bloc in 1990, the Communist Party of the Philippines (CCP) rediscovered its Maoist roots and conducted a rectification campaign, turning back to its old Maoist position. The CPP regards China as a capitalist and imperialist state.

the force that Maoist ideology had exercised on the global communist movement just a decade earlier.[30]

The End of the Cultural Revolution

While Mao still seemed to be in political control of the country in 1968, Liu Shaoqi and Deng Xiaoping's influence within the Communist Party increased. Many party members were concerned with the chaos that the Cultural Revolution had created in workplaces and institutions as well as by the sharp division it had created within the Communist Party. At the 1969 Party Congress, Mao felt power slipping away from him. He was well aware of the fact that socialism's final victory still lay several generations ahead, and he emphasized that not one, but several revolutions must take place in the superstructure to spur on socialist development.

On the global level, the revolutionary movements in the Third World had lost their momentum; capitalism had initiated its neoliberal offensive. Because China had failed to achieve a position as the leader of the new world socialist movement, Deng began to draw China out of its isolation and develop its productive forces with the assistance of transnational capital. Mao's more voluntarist line was abandoned. As far as socialism was concerned, Deng had a very pragmatic approach. Back in 1962, he stated: "It doesn't matter whether a cat is white or black, as long as it catches mice."[31]

The politics of the Cultural Revolution were dismantled after a political struggle in China, where the global contradiction became decisive. The principal contradiction shifted from U.S. imperialism versus Third World liberation movements to neoliberalism versus the power of the nation-state.

Neoliberalism was the political expression of a new international division of labor. As a response to the growing cost of labor in the center, labor-intensive industries were transferred to low-wage countries. At the same time, the financial structure of capitalism changed. The U.S. had financed the Vietnam War by printing dollars it could no longer prom-

---

30 Rothwell. "The Road Is Tortuous." pp. 2494–95.

31 Xiaoping, Deng. "Speech at the Communist Youth League Conference on July 7, 1962." *China Daily*. August 20, 2014.

ise to exchange for gold, which led to the disintegration of the Bretton Woods system. The astronomical expansion of the U.S. money supply catalyzed a financialization of capitalism, in which unfettered speculation and exchange of money became as important as investment in production for profit.

After the Cultural Revolution, China stood alone with its improved political preconditions for the development of socialism. However, the national liberation struggles in the Third World did not transform into a viable counterweight to global capitalism. In a capitalist-dominated world, without a sufficiently developed economic base, China had to become part of the world economy. It had to build up its productive forces under conditions which would almost certainly be a threat to the hard-won political preconditions, since capitalist norms and values would penetrate society.

While under pressure from neoliberal globalization, China had to build its peculiar form of state capitalism and market economy in order to maintain its national project. It could not continue the development of its productive forces without investments and trading with capitalist countries. It needed to begin the transfer of technology from the imperial countries.

The transfer of technology can take two forms: a direct form, in which the developing country buys turnkey advanced factories, together with knowledge to run them. The second form is indirect. This implies that the developing country opens up to transnational companies to invest and by so doing obtains a transfer of their technology. It is a mistake to think that the quest for advanced technology is a post-Maoist feature. After the break with the Soviet Union, China imported machines and turnkey factories from the West. Deng just opened up a second form of technology transfer—investments from transnational capital. Mao was not at all against foreign technology:

> The fact that we are developing small and medium-size industries on a large scale, although accepting that the large undertakings constitute the guiding force, and that we are using traditional technologies everywhere, although accepting that foreign technologies constitute the guiding power, is essentially due to our desire to achieve rapid industrialization.[32]

---

32   Hu, Chi-his. *Mao-Zedong et la Construction du Socialisme*. Le Seuil, 1975. p. 85.

ne can regret the new course, since it led away from socialism. But it was a necessary detour. The question is whether maintaining the cultural-revolutionary line was possible and could lead to success, particularly at a time when global capitalism went from crisis to new dynamics. If China had isolated itself to save its political system, it would not have developed its productive forces at the necessary speed, and thereby it would have run the risk of being overrun—either collapsing like the Soviet Union or becoming isolated like North Korea.

Only by contextualizing the actors can we understand the choices made at a particular historical moment, rather than putting ideological labels on them as either true revolutionaries or renegades.

Let me conclude this chapter by summarizing the results of Mao's leadership of China, which are indeed remarkable. Starting from one of the poorest countries in the world in 1949, China emerged at the end of the Mao period as one of the six largest industrial producers in the world. The higher yields obtained on family farms during later years would not have been possible without the vast irrigation and flood-control projects. China's GDP grew between 1952 and 1978 at an average annual rate of 6.2 percent. By the end of this period, it had tripled; industrial production contributed more to GDP than agriculture, despite the problems created by the Sino-Soviet split.[33] China's economic growth rate was 6.8% between 1970 and 1979, more than double that of the United States during the same period (3.2%).[34] China's GDP growth rate started to exceed 10% in the 1980s, before the decision to open it to the world system.[35]

On a per capita basis, the index of national income (at constant prices) increased from 100 in 1949 to 440 in 1978.

Over the last two decades of the Maoist era, from 1957 to 1975, even taking into account the economic disasters of the Great Leap, China's national income increased by 63 percent per capita, more than doubling

---

33 Maddison. *Chinese Economic Performance in the Long Run.*
34 Long, Zhiming, and Herrera, Rémy. "The Enigma of China's Growth." *Monthly Review.* Vol. 70, no.7, December 2018. https://monthlyreview.org/2018/12/01/the-enigma-of-chinas-growth/
35 *Ibid.*

overall.[36] This economic development is exceptional compared with the colonial-supported industrialization of Western Europe and North America. Even a World Bank report from 1983 acknowledged this:

...China's most remarkable achievement during the past three decades has been to make low-income groups far better off in terms of basic needs than their counterparts in most other poor countries. They all have work; their food supply is guaranteed through a mixture of state rationing and collective self-insurance; most of their children are not only at school but being comparatively well taught; and the great majority have access to basic health care and family planning services. Life expectancy is...outstandingly high for a country at China's per capita income level.[37]

By 1976, China was unique among developing countries in being unburdened by either foreign debt or internal inflation. The Communist Party had reunited the largest population on earth, modernized it, and ended the reoccurring years of famine that had haunted China for centuries, increasing grain production by three hundred percent. In 1949, life expectancy in China was 38 years. In 1970, it was 68.[38] This accomplishment is undeniable.

Before I continue with the changes in China, I will return to the development of the Soviet Union.

---

36 Meisner, Maurice. *Mao Zedong: A Political and Intellectual Portrait*. Polity Press, 2006. p. 153.

37 The World Bank. *China: Socialist Economic Development*. Vol. 1, 1983. https://documents1.worldbank.org/curated/en/192611468769173749/pdf/multi-page.pdf. p. 11.

38 Chen, Meixia. "The Great Reversal: Transformation of Health Care in the People's Republic of China." Cockerham, William. *Blackwell Companion to Medical Sociology: Second Edition*. Blackwell, 2004.

CHAPTER 16

USSR 1956–90: THE END OF "ACTUALLY EXISTING SOCIALISM"

Up to the late 1950s and early 1960s, the five-year plans brought the Soviet Union closer to catching up with the West. This model, however, fell into crisis in the 1970s. Not only did production stagnate, but the superstructure continued to erode.

As a response to this conflict between the base and superstructure, Khrushchev led the Soviet Union further along the path of competition with the West using capitalist standards, rather than acknowledging that class struggle continues in a post-revolutionary society and carrying out his own form of cultural revolution to change the superstructure and reconnect with the masses to reestablish trust in the Communist Party.

In the 1950s, the Soviet economy was growing rapidly using crude figures. However, it was an unbalanced and uncoordinated growth that complicated the possibility of further expansion; centralized planning was unable to control the system because there was a lack of reliable information being relayed from the factories on what they were actually capable of producing. Waste and scarcity increased, and quality declined. The growth rate plummeted during the mid-1960s; between 1978-1980 it was zero, and then went below zero.

The way Stalin handled conflict between different political lines turned the Party into a hierarchical power structure—a nomenklatura, a list of names of those to be appointed to key positions throughout the governmental system. This system was unable to rectify error and develop the economy. Coextensive with the nomenklatura was the growth of patron-client relationships. An official in the bureaucracy could not advance without the assistance of a patron. In return, the client carried out the policies of the patron. Khrushchev was a protégé of Lazar Kaganovich, who had been close to Stalin. Leonid Brezhnev was a client of Khrushchev, his predecessor. This creates inertia and conservatism.

It was during the Brezhnev regime that things really went wrong. Anatoly S. Chernyaev, who was Deputy Director of the International Department of the Central Committee, kept an extensive diary from 1971-1991. In his 1982 volume, he describes the decaying system. Diary entries are devoted to the absence of food and basic consumer goods in the stores. He chronicles the pervasive corruption in the upper echelons of power and in Brezhnev's family.[1] When Brezhnev finally died in November 1982, and Yury Andropov was selected as the new General Secretary, there was hope that he would pull the country out of its stupor. Andropov began to fight violations of the Party, state, and labor discipline. He initiated an anti-corruption campaign against Brezhnev's cronies, and criminal cases against high-level Party and state officials were initiated. However, Andropov's term in office became too short to make a difference. He suffered kidney problems and died after only 15 months as General Secretary. Andropov was succeeded by Chernenko, yet another man with severe health problems who served even less time in office, only 13 months.

The brutality of the regime through the Stalin years also seriously harmed the relationship between the Party and the population. There was no longer any application of the principle that, according to Marx, drove development towards socialism: remuneration according to the quantity and quality of work delivered.[2] The enthusiasm and commitment to production and work weakened. In the last years of its existence, the Soviet Union was characterized by massive absenteeism and disengagement in the workplace. The saying was: "We pretend to work, and they pretend to pay." The tight control exercised by the political powers over civil society coincided with a substantial amount of anarchy in

---

[1] Melyakova, Anna and Savranskaya, Svetlana. "The Chernyaev Diary, 1982: The Run Up to Perestroika." *The National Security Archive*. 2022. https://nsarchive.gwu.edu/briefing-book/russia-programs/2022-05-25/chernyaev-diary-1982-run-perestroika

[2] Marx. *Critique of the Gotha Programme*. pp. 13–30.

workplaces. All these factors produced a weak order unable to resist the pressure from the West.

Chernenko was followed by Gorbachev in 1985. In his first year, 14 of the 23 heads of department in the secretariat were replaced. By doing so, Gorbachev secured dominance in the Politburo within a year, faster than either Stalin, Khrushchev, or Brezhnev.[3] Gorbachev used the term *perestroika* for a series of reforms to restructure society and the economy. In a speech in September 1986, he embraced the idea of reintroducing market economics.[4] In the second year of his leadership, Gorbachev began speaking of *glasnost* (openness) in media and culture.[5] Some in the Party thought Gorbachev was not going far enough in his reforms; a prominent liberal critic was Boris Yeltsin.

The economic problems remained. By the late 1980s, there were still widespread shortages of basic goods, rising inflation, and declining living standards. To reduce the heavy drinking that led to absenteeism from work and poor health, Gorbachev initiated restrictions on alcohol. This—and the general tightening up of work discipline—led, in the first couple of years of his government, to some improvement in economic growth. It had, however, side effects. Since sales of vodka could no longer take place in government shops, a black market of illegally distilled vodka sprang up, controlled by the criminal underworld, like in the U.S. during Prohibition. The criminal class turned out to be a very dangerous enemy.[6] In February 1990, both the liberal faction headed by Yeltsin, and the "old school" hardliners, intensified their attacks on Gorbachev.

Throughout 1991, with the Soviet budget deficit climbing, Gorbachev tried to obtain loans from the West in return for his political concessions. He managed to get an invitation to the G7 meeting in July 1991, where he continued to call for financial assistance. Most G7 members were reluctant, instead proposing the Soviets receive "special associate" status—rather than full membership—to the World Bank and Interna-

---

3 McCauley, Martin. *Gorbachev: Profiles in Power*. Longman, 1998. pp. 50–52.
4 Doder, Dusko and Branson, Louise. *Gorbachev: Heretic in the Kremlin*. Futura, 1990. p. 166.
5 *Ibid.*, p. 75.
6 Cockshott, Paul. "Crisis of Socialism and Effects of Capitalist Restoration." *Monthly Review*. Vol. 71, no. 11, April 2022. p. 25.

tional Monetary Fund. Instead of helping Gorbachev, they would rather await total collapse and then take over. Gorbachev seemingly harbored the hope that peaceful coexistence between the Soviet Union and the capitalist West could be established, in which both parties could harvest a huge peace dividend. The world could then enter a peaceful and prosperous era. For a General Secretary of the Communist Party, such ideas about the nature of capitalism seemed optimistic.

Yet, Gorbachev delivered his part of the deal. The Berlin Wall fell, and he accepted the reunification of Germany. Gorbachev hoped this would lead to economic cooperation with Europe. The Warsaw Pact was dissolved and NATO prevailed. The U.S. and Western Europe quickly converted Eastern Europe into a semi-periphery for investments and cheap labor, and prepared to consolidate its position by enlarging NATO eastwards.

At home, Gorbachev became more and more isolated. Yeltsin rallied against him from a neoliberal position. Hardliners within the army and security forces were urging Gorbachev to arrest vocal liberals in the media. By mid-November 1990, much of the press was calling for Gorbachev to resign and was even predicting the outbreak of civil war.[7] Fearing civil disturbances, Gorbachev banned demonstrations and ordered troops to patrol Soviet cities alongside the police. This further alienated the liberals, but was not enough to win over hardliners.

On August 20, 1991, a group of senior Communists Party members launched a coup to seize control of the Soviet Union. Gorbachev was kept under house arrest. The coup plotters announced that he was ill, and therefore Vice President Yanayev would take charge of the country.[8] Yeltsin, now President of the Russian Soviet Federative Socialist Republic, took refuge inside the Moscow White House. Tens of thousands of protesters amassed outside it to prevent the coup troops from storming the building to arrest him.[9] At that moment, the coup's leaders realized that they lacked support and ended their efforts. On the evening of August 21, Gorbachev returned to Moscow, where he thanked Yeltsin and

---

7 Taubman, William. *Gorbachev: His Life and Times*. Simon and Schuster, 2017. p. 532.
8 McCauley. *Gorbachev*. p. 237.
9 *Ibid*. p. 238.

the protesters for helping to undermine the coup. Two days later, he resigned as General Secretary and called on the Central Committee of the Communist Party to dissolve.[10] On August 29, 1991, the Supreme Soviet indefinitely suspended all Communist Party activity, effectively ending Communist rule in the Soviet Union.

Following that suspension, the Soviet Union collapsed with dramatic speed. By the end of September, Gorbachev had lost the ability to influence events outside of Moscow. By the end of 1991, Yeltsin began to take over the remnants of the Soviet government, including the Kremlin itself. Without Gorbachev's knowledge, Yeltsin met with the Ukrainian and Belarusian Presidents on December 8, 1991 and signed a declaration proclaiming the Soviet Union ceased to exist and announced the formation of the Commonwealth of Independent States (CIS) as its successor. On December 20th, the leaders of 11 of the 12 remaining republics, all except Georgia, signed a declaration agreeing to dismantle the Soviet Union, and to formally establish the CIS.

Accepting the *fait accompli* of the Soviet Union's dissolution, Gorbachev formally announced his resignation as Soviet President on December 25th. The Soviet Union officially ceased to exist at midnight on December 31, 1991 after 74 years. The red flag was lowered at the Kremlin and the Russian white, blue, and red tricolor was hoisted to mark the restoration of full-blown capitalism.

When Boris Yeltsin agreed to the neoliberal "shock therapy" order by the West, neither the remaining elite of the Party nor the working class wanted to defend "actually existing socialism," which had abolished poverty, developed an advanced health and educational system, yet lost its competition to the West in delivering consumer goods. Soviet citizens took the social advantages for granted and dreamt of tropical fruit, electronic devices, private cars, and travel to foreign countries, without realizing that these goods are largely available and affordable due to the imperialism of the West, and Russia would not enter the capitalist system in the center, but as a semi-periphery—a site to deliver raw materials and cheap energy.

The Soviet version of Marxism-Leninism in the late 1980s had already begun their transformation into a version of "modernization the-

---

10   Taubman. *Gorbachev.* pp. 614–15.

ory," according to which the Soviet Union should return to the "main path of capitalist development" by cooperating with the West. The disintegration of the Soviet Union and the Communist Party from 1989-91 was mainly a top-down process governed by the ruling elite and not a bottom-up political process dictated by the people of the Soviet Union. It was the nomenklatura wanting the same lifestyle as the upper echelons in the West that was to seal the fate of the Soviet system.

Gorbachev's main instrument, the Communist Party, proved to be useless for transmitting his reform projects to the people. Most people believed that the regime was falling apart, and that "socialism" could not be saved by *perestroika* and *glasnost*. Few were prepared to defend the old apparatus. Yeltsin and part of the Soviet working class harbored the naive dream that the Soviet Union would develop into a capitalist welfare state, but the reality was quite different.

From 1989 onwards, the old Party elite and the newly established oligarchs robbed the state. Individuals with a nomenklatura background continue to dominate Russia. According to one 2022 estimate, 60% of the elites in Putin's regime have nomenklatura backgrounds.[11] Instead of the promises of U.S. consumption patterns and a capitalist welfare state, the Russian population got the worst effects possible from neoliberal shock therapy. Following IMF privatizations, real income was reduced to half by 1995.[12] The birth rate fell by 36% between 1989 and 1993, and life expectancy in 1993 was 57.3 years, compared to 65.5 in 1990.[13] The world's second superpower had a bankrupt economy with decimated industrial production, contributing to increased poverty, hunger, homelessness, and alcoholism.

The Communist Party of China closely followed the decay of the Soviet Union, and the emerging neoliberalism in the late 1970s, and they began to set another course to combat the offensive of globalized capitalism.

---

11 Snegovaya, Maria and Petrov, Kirill. "Long Soviet Shadows: The Nomenklatura Ties of Putin's Elites." *Post-Soviet Affairs*. Vol. 38, no. 4, 2022.

12 Hedlund, Stefan. *Russia's "Market" Economy: A Bad Case of Predatory Capitalism*. UCL Press, 1999. pp. 345–72.

13 *Ibid.* pp. 345–348, 356.

Between Mao and Deng

After the Cultural Revolution the Communist Party had to find a new way forward. This difficult task is reflected in the frequent changes of leadership in the party, with Zhou Enlai as the usual mediator between different political lines.

In 1971, China began rapprochement with the U.S. to exit isolation. Henry Kissinger made a secret visit to China and met Zhou Enlai. The U.S. lifted its blockade in October 1971, and China was reinstalled in the United Nations. After Mao's meeting with Nixon in Beijing in 1972, Zhou launched the economic strategy of "four modernizations" (economy, agriculture, scientific and technological development, and national defense). In 1973, China acquired industrial facilities from western countries for $4.3 billion. With this, China took the first steps to upgrade its level of technology and implement a more balanced industrial sector between heavy industry and a diversified production of consumer goods.[14]

However, the cost of introducing expensive Western technologies was high. It was not like the assistance from the Soviets, which had saved China technological costs. China now had to pay expensive service fees, on top of the price of hardware, to the West. Additionally, all payments had to be made in foreign currency. The result was a huge fiscal deficit in 1974, leading to an economic crisis and the closing of many factories. To solve the problem, the state once again mobilized urban surplus labor in a "Up to the Mountains and Down to the Countryside" movement. Between 1974–1976, millions of laborers who had not been absorbed by the urban economy were sent to rural collectives. But since the Cultural Revolution had ended, their enthusiasm was lacking, and urban youth were reluctant to leave cities. As a result, the campaign did not run as smoothly as on previous occasions. Social discontent was mounting.[15]

Mao had believed in the strategy of relying on China's own force, based on the premise that accelerated economic growth could be achieved with the same methods used in revolution: mass mobilization and the will to self-sacrifice. Yet the Great Leap Forward and the Cultural Revolution showed that appeals to the heroism of the masses couldn't be

---

14   Tiejun. *Ten Crises.* p. 194.
15   *Ibid.* p. 195.

made constantly and eternally.[16]

In 1976, Zhou Enlai, Zhu De, and Mao Zedong passed away one after the other, opening up a new analysis of the world, and a new strategy for China's development. The appointed new leadership, headed by Hua Guofeng, continued to buy Western industrial equipment. In 1978 alone, China signed contracts for 22 projects with the West, costing $7.8 billion.[17]

Isabella M. Weber, in the book *How China Escaped Shock Therapy*, described the debate that took place within the Communist Party involving young Chinese economists and Western neoliberal economists. The latter pushed for neoliberal "shock therapy"; however, they did not prevail, and what emerged was an experimental economic reform that drew from the experience of Chinese economic statecraft. The leadership in China were still first-generation revolutionaries and approached the economic change differently than Gorbachev or Yeltsin.[18]

---

16   Losurdo. *Class Struggle*. pp. 193–194.
17   Tiejun. *Ten Crises*. p. 195.
18   Weber, Isabella. "Interview: How China Escaped Shock Therapy in the 1980s." *LeftEast*. July 29, 2022. https://lefteast.org/how-china-escaped-shock-therapy/

CHAPTER 17

THE CHINESE ENCOUNTER WITH NEOLIBERAL GLOBALIZATION

Deng Xiaoping took over in 1978. His approach was not about just buying turnkey industries from the West; it was centered on a liberalization of China's internal economy, opening up for direct investments by foreign transnational capital and Chinese participation in the capitalist world market.

This does not mean that Deng wanted to turn China into a capitalist state, nor was he personally a capitalist opportunist. Deng studied and worked in France in the 1920s. Here he became a Marxist and joined the Communist Party of China in 1924. In 1926, Deng was sent to Moscow to study communism and became a political commissar in the Red Army upon his return. In 1929, Deng led the Red Army uprisings in Guangxi. In 1931, he was demoted within the Party due to his support of Mao and his conflict with the COMINTERN commissars in the Party. However, he was promoted again once Mao's line prevailed. Deng played an important role in the Long March and the following liberation war. He was second-in-command after Mao in the 1950s. Deng presided over the economic reconstruction following the Great Leap Forward. His economic policy during this period caused him to fall out with Mao, and he was purged during the Cultural Revolution. However, following Mao's death in September 1976, Deng quickly returned to the inner circles of the Party. Deng had been working with ailing Premier Zhou Enlai to bring order to the economy after nearly a decade of turmoil. Deng finally became de facto leader of China in December 1978.

In a conversation on October 10, 1978, Deng argued that the technological gap with advanced countries was growing.[1] Deng criticized the model of using political calls for mass mobilization because the recent practice had shown that it was incapable of developing the productive forces, and therefore could not genuinely satisfy the economic needs of China:

> Our experience in the 20 years from 1958 to 1978 teaches us that poverty is not socialism, that socialism means eliminating poverty. Unless you are developing the productive forces and raising people's living standards, you cannot say that you are building socialism.[2]

Deng had a pragmatic approach to the development of socialism. He wanted to use elements of capitalism to create a strong and prosperous nation under the leadership of the Communist Party. Deng believed that initiative couldn't be aroused without economic means. A small number of politically advanced people might respond to the moral appeal, but such an approach can only work for a short time. Further, China had to learn from the advanced countries in the fields of technology and science.

Deng Xiaoping drew on ideas from the New Economic Policy (NEP) in his reforms. During his stay in the Soviet Union in 1926, Deng became acquainted with the NEP (1923-28), an experience that he tried to apply between the years of 1949 and 1952, when he was in charge of the Regional Committee of the Party in Southeastern China. In the aftermath of The Great Leap Forward, he recommended it again. In 1978, now in control of the Party, he finally got the chance to implement his policy across the country. In a speech from 1978, Deng explained the background for his ideas:

> Only if we make our country a modern, powerful socialist state can we more effectively consolidate the socialist system and cope with foreign aggression and subversion; only then can we be reasonably certain of gradually creating the material conditions for the advance to our great goal of communism. The first point is the necessity of understanding that science and technology are part of the productive forces. More than a century ago, Marx said that expansion of the use of machinery in production requires the conscious application of natural science. Science too, he said, is among the productive forces.

---

1 Xiaoping, Deng. "Carry Out the Policy of Opening to the Outside World and Learn Advanced Science and Technology from Other Countries." *Selected Works: Vol. 2.* p. 143.

2 Xiaoping, Deng. "We Shall Expand Political Democracy and Carry Out Economic Reform." *Selected Works: Vol. 3.* p. 122.

The development of modern science and technology has bound science and production ever more tightly together. Modern science and technology are now undergoing a great revolution...Profound changes have taken place and new leaps have been made in almost all areas. A whole range of new sciences and technologies is continuously emerging. A series of new industries, including high-polymer synthesis, atomic energy, electronic computers, semiconductors, astronautics and lasers, have been founded on the basis of newly emerging sciences. Modern science opens the way for the improvement of production techniques and determines the direction of their development. In particular, the development of cybernetics is rapidly raising the degree of automation in production. With the same manpower and the same number of man-hours, people can turn out scores or hundreds of times more products than before...Our science and technology have made enormous progress since the founding of New China and have played a vital role in economic construction and in building up our national defence...But we must be clear-sighted and recognize that there is still an enormous gap between the level of our science and technology and that of the most advanced countries... One must learn from those who are more advanced before he can catch up with and surpass them... Independence does not mean shutting the door on the world, nor does self-reliance mean blind opposition to everything foreign. Science and technology are part of the wealth created in common by all mankind.[3]

According to Deng, only by opening up and realizing Zhou Enlai's "Four Modernizations" would it be possible to abolish poverty and create common prosperity. He insisted on the political continuity between Mao's era and the era of reform which united the leadership of the Communist Party. In a 1980 interview with the Italian journalist Oriana Fallaci, Deng says "Let's start with pointing out that, in the final analysis, the principle of our national construction is the same which was formulated by Chairman Mao. While taking international assistance, we'll mainly rely on our own efforts...Then of course, there will be some decadent influence of capitalism brought into China. We are aware of this, but I think that it is not so terrible, and we are not afraid of it." Deng insists that Mao's "contributions are primary and his mistakes secondary... We will not do to Chairman Mao what Khrushchev did to Stalin."[4]

---

3   Xiaoping, Deng. "Speech at the Opening Ceremony of the National Conference on Science March 18, 1978." https://dengxiaopingworks.wordpress.com/selected-works-vol-2-1975-1982/

4   Xiaoping, Deng. In "Deng: A Third World War is Inevitable: Interview by Oriana Fallaci." *The Washington Post*, September 1, 1980. https://www.washingtonpost.com/archive/politics/1980/09/01/deng-a-third-world-war-is-inevitable/a7222afa-

Deng's reform strategy does not stem from a neoliberal perspective. Deng advocated for the acceleration of foreign investment capital in a planned way, believing that planning and markets could be used to serve the development of a socialist system. Neither did Deng introduce economic shock therapy, the way Yeltsin did in Russia. Rather, elements of capitalism were introduced gradually. "Crossing the River by Feeling for the Stones," became a popular slogan.[5]

The most important question in the early years of the economic reform was how to develop the countryside. Success in agricultural reform was the key to other reforms. The reform plans were made by young economists who, during the Cultural Revolution, had been sent to the countryside, where they lived for years and acquired a knowledge of the rural economy. They formed an alliance with the first generation of China's communist leaders who had a deep connection to the countryside. These two generations had a common experience, and they shared the view that the countryside was critical for successful reforms.[6]

These reforms gradually dismantled the people's communes—the political and economic backbone of the former economy. Instead, family households were formed, which worked together in cooperatives. The households had to deliver their share of the planned quota for agrarian goods, which were distributed at subsidized prices. If they were able to produce more, they could produce it for the market at market price. This formed a dual-track price system. On the one hand was planned fulfillment, which gave secure and cheap prices of food for the cities, and on the other hand were market prices for other products to expand production. This meant that the peasants earned more cash and were able to purchase consumer goods from urban industrial areas—goods like bicycles, motorcycles, or sewing machines. This dual-track price system gave the rural economy a dynamic expansion while keeping secure and cheap food for the working class in the cities.

When the urban industrial economy later became the focus, the dual track plan and price system that had emerged in the countryside was

---

5   Brandt, Lauren and Rawski, Thomas. *China's Great Economic Transformation*. Cambridge University Press, 2008. p. 98.

6   Weber. "Interview: How China Escaped Shock Therapy in the 1980s."

transposed to the industrial economy. Each company would have to fulfill its plan, but could produce beyond the plan for sale in the market. In addition, the industry was divided into an essential primary sector and a secondary industrial production. The steel, cement, energy industry, and transport were considered crucial, whereas the production of some consumer products was considered secondary. The logic was to keep the essential parts of the industry under the strict control of the plan to ensure the strength of the economy, while part of the secondary sector, producing consumer goods, could grow into the market. Finance and banking remained public under the planned economy. The logic was to unleash new dynamic forces through market experimentation and then to channel it into the planned economy. Rather than destroying the plan to make way for the market, the liberalization of some sectors added something to the economy.

In the industrial sector, there was a shift in strategy from heavy industries to light industry and export-led growth. Light industrial output was vital for China, which came from a low capital base. Foreign-exchange export earnings generated by light manufacturing were reinvested in technologically more advanced production and further capital expenditures.

These reforms were a reversal of the Maoist policy of economic self-reliance. However, by attaining foreign funds, and thereby advanced technologies and management, economic development began accelerating. In the 1980s, Deng's reform policy attracted foreign companies to Special Economic Zones in South China, where foreign investment and market liberalization were encouraged.[7] In 1988, the ban on internal labor migration was lifted, prompting the migration of millions of low-wage laborers from rural areas to the industrial zones in the country's south.[8] This led to China becoming the world's leading industrial producer.

In 1986, Deng explained that some people and regions could first

---

7   Stoltenberg, Clyde. "China's Special Economic Zones: Their Development and Prospects." *Asian Survey*. Vol. 24, no.6, June 1984, pp. 637–54.

8   Lin, Yi-min. "Postrevolution Transformations and the Reemergence of Capitalism in China." Chu, Yin-wah. *Chinese Capitalisms: Historical Emergence and Political Implications*. Macmillan, 2012. p. 88.

become prosperous in order to bring about common prosperity, popularized by the slogan: "Let some people get rich first." With a reference to the NEP in the Soviet Union, Deng said that "Socialism does not mean shared poverty." In a CBS interview from 1986, he explained his approach:

> During the "cultural revolution" there was a view that poor communism was preferable to rich capitalism...According to Marxism, communist society is based on material abundance. Only when there is material abundance can the principle of a communist society—that is, "from each according to his ability, to each according to his needs"—be applied...There can be no communism with pauperism, or socialism with pauperism. So to get rich is no sin. However, what we mean by getting rich is different from what you mean. Wealth in a socialist society belongs to the people. To get rich in a socialist society means prosperity for the entire people. The principles of socialism are: first, development of production, and second, common prosperity. We permit some people and some regions to become prosperous first, for the purpose of achieving common prosperity faster. That is why our policy will not lead to polarization, to a situation where the rich get richer while the poor get poorer. To be frank, we shall not permit the emergence of a new bourgeoisie.[9]

Deng's promise did not quite keep. The rich got richer, and a new bourgeoisie emerged. In the second half of the 1980s, the defenders of the dual-track approach came under pressure from the more neoliberal-minded faction of the Communist Party, headed by Zhao Ziyang, and vanished from the scene of policymaking as liberalization and privatization intensified. Weber writes:

> Throughout the 1990s, the economics profession in China was remodeled to align with the international neoclassical mainstream. Neoliberal reformers made deep inroads in the arenas of ownership, the labor market, and the healthcare system, among others. But the core of the Chinese economic system was never destroyed in one big bang. Instead, it was fundamentally transformed by means of a dynamic of growth and globalization under the activist guidance of the state.[10]

In that period, most of the country's small and medium-sized companies were privatized and sold for prices below their actual value. The

---

9 Xiaoping, Deng. "Interview with Mike Wallace of CBS 60 Minutes. CBS, September 2, 1986." https://china.usc.edu/deng-xiaoping-interview-mike-wallace-60-minutes-sept-2-1986

10 Weber, Isabella. *How China Escaped Shock Therapy: The Market Reform Debate*. Routledge, 2021. p. 397.

buyers were political officials, former managers of state-owned companies, and private capitalists with good connections to the regime.[11]

The pressure to introduce capitalism in China also came from the process of external neoliberal globalization. Many large transnational companies—located in North America, Western Europe, and Japan—became capable of controlling production activities on a global level through new communication and transport technology. This reduced the entities involved to subcontractors, consequently siphoning these subcontractors' profit toward themselves. Transnational capitalism required low-wage labor power to continue its expansion, and China possessed a huge proletariat and developed infrastructure, all ready to be connected to global capitalism. However, transnational capital could not just demand "structural adjustment" to get free access to China, as in the rest of the Third World. China's encounter with neoliberalism was different from the rest of the world. Weber writes:

> What was at stake in China's market reform debate is illustrated by the contrast between China's rise and Russia's economic collapse...Russia and China's positions in the world economy have been reversed since they implemented different modes of marketization. Russia's share of world GDP almost halved, from 3.7 percent in 1990 to about 2 percent in 2017, while China's share increased close to sixfold, from a mere 2.2 percent to about one-eighth of global output. Russia underwent dramatic deindustrialization, while China became the proverbial workshop of world capitalism. The average real income of 99 percent of people in Russia was lower in 2015 than it had been in 1991, whereas in China, despite rapidly rising inequality, the figure more than quadrupled in the same period, surpassing Russia's in 2013. As a result of shock therapy, Russia experienced a rise in mortality beyond that of any previous peacetime experiences of an industrialized country.[12]

---

11 Møller, A. M.. *Hegemonic project, interventions on the politics of communist elite legitimation in China, 2008–2015*, Ph.D. thesis. Department of Political Science, University of Copenhagen, 2016. pp. 108–9.

12 *Ibid.* p. 21.

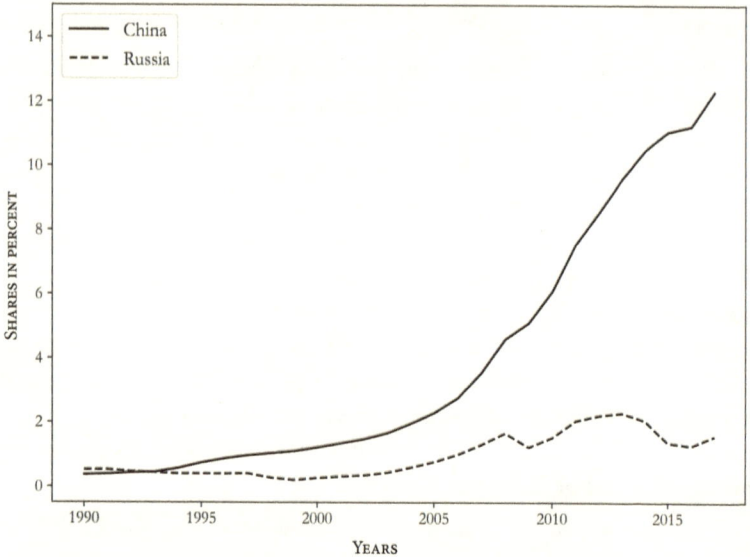

FIGURE 1. *China and Russia's Shares (in percent) in World GDP, 1990–2017. Source: World Bank, 2019.*

China was keen on avoiding unconditional integration into global capitalism. The government defended its sovereign economic planning by forcing any global capital that wished to enter the country to conform to their policies, not vice versa.

It was important for the Chinese government to control private capital within the framework of a planned economy. The aim was to develop a diverse industrial sector based on joint ventures with transnational corporations, and according to a strategic plan. The planned economy also controlled infrastructure projects: housing for millions of new urban proletarians, as well as the construction of new roads, ports, dams, and power lines required for industrialization. Strategic industrial sectors, such as energy, transport, and defense industries, remained state-owned.

A strong planning instrument is the state ownership of land. It is used to plan the location of industry and is essential for the agricultural sector. The Chinese state still guarantees access to land for the peasantry. Agricultural production changed from collective farms to family plots during "Dengism," but the agricultural sector as a whole remained under the control of the state, as land cannot be privately owned, and the family plot was still organized in cooperatives. The persistence of public ownership of land distinguishes the agrarian situation in China from other countries such as India, Brazil, and South Africa, where the agrarian question still causes huge difficulties for the development of the productive forces.

Another tool that enhances the Chinese government's autonomy is that of fiscal policy; the financial system and its foreign exchange management are still under state control. China has strong national banks and a national currency with increasing international importance. Finally, China is not engaged in an arms race to the detriment of the national economy, as had happened with the Soviet Union. Its per capita military expenditure is much lower than the NATO countries. Former U.S. president Jimmy Carter, in a conversation with former President Donald Trump in April 2019 about China, made the following remarks to Trump, who was concerned that China was getting ahead of the U.S.:

> China's peace dividend has allowed and enhanced its economic growth... How many miles of high-speed railroad do we have in this country? China has around 18,000 miles (29,000 km) of high-speed rail lines while the U.S. has wasted, I think, $3 trillion on military spending. According to a study by Brown University's Watson Institute of International and Public Affairs, the U.S. has spent $5.9 trillion waging war in Iraq, Syria, Afghanistan, Pakistan, and other nations since 2001. It's more than you can imagine...China has not wasted a single penny on war, and that's why they're ahead of us in almost every way.[13]

THE TIANANMEN UPRISING

Deng's project was not without danger. Not only did neoliberalism have enormous economic power; it was also an ideological challenge. Nineteen eighty-nine was the zenith of neoliberalism. It saw the fall of the Berlin Wall and the dissolution of the Soviet Union. In the summer of 1989, it seemed that this destructive process would continue in China.

---

13   Carter, Jimmy. In Wilkins, Brett. "Jimmy Carter Lectures Trump: US 'Most Warlike Nation in History of the World.'" *Telesur*. April 18, 2019. https://www.telesurenglish.net/opinion/Jimmy-Carter-Lectures-Trump-US-Is-Most-Warlike-Nation-in-History-of-the-World-20190418-0020.html

Export-led growth was not yet on track. To accelerate economic growth, China still needed to increase the imports of foreign capital goods and technologies. The Party and state bureaucrats, the emerging capitalist class, and the growing urban middle class also desired to have imported consumer goods. Chinese imports grew rapidly in the 1980s, but exports failed to catch up, resulting in trade deficits by the second half of the 1980s. To finance the trade deficits, China borrowed money, and foreign debt surged from 16 billion dollars in 1985 to 53 billion dollars in 1990.

Similar to the effects of Soviet assistance, this new influx of Western technology and management changed the superstructure. In the 1950s, it was the formation of a Soviet superstructure, which took a Cultural Revolution to try and correct. Likewise, the new flow of investments since the late 1970s required universities to run courses in neoliberal economics to educate the new managers.

In 1988, Milton Friedman, one of the world's leading neoliberal economists, visited China and met with Zhao Ziyang, who was then the General Secretary of the Communist Party of China and was in charge of implementing Deng's reform program in 1986. Zhao was very impressed by Friedman.[14] After the meeting, Zhao decided to liberalize all prices of consumer goods within a short period. The consumer price inflation rate surged to 21 percent in 1988. In addition to the surging inflation, growing corruption led to the escalation of social discontent.

The protests in Tiananmen Square began on April 15, 1989, precipitated by the death of pro-reform General Secretary Hu Yaobang. While the protests lacked a unified cause or leadership, participants raised the issue of corruption within the government. Some voiced calls for more economic liberalization and liberal democratic reforms. A replica of the Statue of Liberty was raised. Many of the protesters came from universities in Beijing. Minqi Li, author of *The Rise of China and the Demise of the Capitalist World Economy*, recalls his participation in the events.

> I was a student at the Economic Management Department of Beijing University during the period 1987–90…western classical liberalism and neoliberal economics, as represented by Friedrich Hayek and Milton Friedman, had become the new, fashionable ideology…and in early 1989, restiveness grew on

---

14   Li, Minqi. *China and the 21st Century Crisis*. Pluto Press, 2016. p. 20.

university campuses...As the student demonstrations grew, workers in Beijing began to pour onto the streets in support of the students, who were, of course, delighted...I could not help experiencing a deep sense of irony. On the one hand, these workers were the people that we considered to be passive, obedient, ignorant, lazy, and stupid. Yet now they were coming out to support us. On the other hand, just weeks before, we were enthusiastically advocating "reform" programs that would shut down all state factories and leave the workers unemployed. I asked myself: do these workers really know who they are supporting? Unfortunately, the workers did not really know. In the 1980s, in terms of material living standards, the Chinese working class remained relatively well-off. There were nevertheless growing resentments on the part of the workers as the program of economic reform took a capitalist turn. Managers were given increasing power to impose capitalist-style labor disciplines (such as Taylorist "scientific management") on the workers. The reintroduction of "material incentives" had paved the way for growing income inequality and managerial corruption...Given the collaboration of official media and the liberal intellectuals (and certainly aided by mainstream western academia and media), it should not be too surprising that many among the Chinese workers would accept the mainstream perception of capitalism naively and uncritically. The dominant image of capitalism had turned from one of sweatshop super-exploitation into one synonymous with democracy, high wages and welfare benefits, as well as the union protection of workers' rights. It was not until the 1990s that the Chinese working class would again learn from their own experience what capitalism means in real life.

While many Chinese workers might be ready to accept capitalism in the abstract from its depiction on television, in reality they certainly understood where their material interests lay. They cherished their "iron rice bowls" (that is, lifetime job security and a full set of welfare programs) and their initial support of the student demonstrations was partly based on the belief that the students were protesting against corruption and economic inequality. However, once politically and ideologically disarmed, the Chinese working class was not able to act as an independent political force fighting for its own class interest. Instead, they became either politically irrelevant or coerced into participating in a political movement the ultimate objective of which was diametrically opposed to their own interests...By mid-May 1989, the student movement became rapidly radicalized...showdown between the government and the student movement was all but inevitable.[15]

As the protests developed, the authorities responded with both conciliatory and hardline tactics, exposing divisions within the Communist Party. During the demonstrations, General Secretary Zhao supported

---

15   Li, Minqi. *The Rise of China and the Demise of the Capitalist World Economy.* Pluto Press, 2008. pp. x–xv.

the demonstrators and distanced himself from the rest of the Politburo. On May 19, Zhao appeared in Tiananmen Square and wandered among the crowd of protesters, delivering a speech to the students in which he referenced the leadership of the Party, saying: "We are already old, and do not matter."[16]

This was the last public appearance of Zhao Ziyang. The day after Zhao's May 19th visit to Tiananmen Square, Premier Li Peng declared martial law and Tiananmen Square was cleared on the 4th of June. There was no "massacre on Tiananmen Square" as the story goes but the clearing of the square led to the deaths of hundreds of protesters and soldiers in street fighting in western Beijing. Only a few days later, on the 9th of June, Deng responded to the uprising in a speech broadcast by national television:

> This storm was bound to come sooner or later. This is determined by the major international climate and China's own minor climate...It was just a matter of time and scale...It was also inevitable that the situation would further develop into a counterrevolutionary rebellion...They have two main slogans: One is to topple the Communist Party, and the other is to overthrow the socialist system. Their goal is to establish a totally Western-dependent bourgeois republic. The people want to combat corruption. This, of course, we accept. We should also take the anti-corruption slogans raised by people with ulterior motives as good advice and accept them accordingly...Is our basic concept of reform and openness wrong? No. Without reform and openness, how could we have what we have today?...The positive results of ten years of reforms and opening to the outside world must be properly assessed, even though such issues as inflation emerged. Naturally, in carrying out our reform and opening our country to the outside world, bad influences from the West are bound to enter our country, but we have never underestimated such influences...
>
> Furthermore, we must persist in integrating a planned economy with a market economy. In practical work we can place more emphasis on planning in the adjustment period. At other times, there can be a little more market regulation, so as to allow more flexibility. The future policy should still be an integration of a planned economy and a market economy.[17]

---

16 Ziyang, Zhao. "Chinese Communist Party General Secretary Zhao Ziyang Visiting and Talking to Protesting Students Gathered on Tiananmen Square before the June 4th Incident, (May 19, 1989)." https://web.archive.org/web/20110716222958/http://www.theasiamag.com/cheat-sheet/zhao-ziyangs-tiananmen-square-speech

17 Xiaoping, Deng. "Speech to Martial Law Units." 1989. Online. http://www.tsquare.tv/chronology/Deng.html

Two weeks later, from June 19-21, an enlarged meeting of the Politburo was held in response to the June 4th uprising. Zhao was dismissed from all his positions and placed under house arrest. Deng declared that:

> The entire imperialist Western world plans to make all socialist countries discard the socialist road and then bring them under the monopoly of international capital and onto the capitalist road.[18]

If victorious, the uprising in Tiananmen Square in 1989 would have meant the rise to power of a Chinese Yeltsin like Zhao Ziyang, and a similar development as in the Soviet Union. It was not a left-wing democratic and egalitarian movement—it was pro-neoliberal. The events in Tiananmen took place at the very moment when neoliberalism was triumphing in Eastern Europe. To promote and support the Tiananmen Square protesters as progressive is abandoning analysis of class—domestic and international—and replaces it with mythological credence in the redemptive value of any "popular rising" despite its content. As Losurdo points out:

> In absolutizing the contradiction between masses and power, and condemning power as such, populism proves incapable of drawing a line of demarcation between revolution and counter-revolution. Perhaps it would be better to learn the lesson of old Hegel, who, with the Sanfedista and anti-Semitic agitation of his time in mind, observed that sometimes "courage consists not in attacking rulers, but in defending them." The populist rebel who would be bound to consider Hegel insufficiently revolutionary could always heed Gramsci's warning against the phraseology of "primitive, elementary 'rebellionism,' 'subversionism' and 'anti-statism,' which are ultimately an expression of de facto 'a-politicism.'"[19]

In contrast to the revisions introduced by Khrushchev, which in the end led to the dissolution of the Communist Party of USSR, China's communists managed to stay in power. There were inter-party divisions, but nothing resembling the Twentieth Congress of the Soviet Party in 1956. Whatever compromise China made to the markets, and whenever it backfired, the Communist Party managed to readjust its policy.

Deng's Comeback

The uprising in June 1989 created a crisis in Deng's leadership. The bal-

---

18 Fewsmith, Joseph. In MacFarquhar, Roderick. *The Politics of China: Sixty Years of The People's Republic of China*. Harvard University Press, 2011. p. 481.

19 Domenico. *Class Struggle*. p. 337.

ance of power shifted within the Communist Party. Chen Yun, who was in favor of a state-led economic model with limited roles for the private sector, reversed some of the reforms. Then Deng, who formally retired and kept a low profile after Tiananmen, bypassed Beijing to make his "Southern Tour" in January and February 1992. According to Deng's plan, Shanghai would be the leading city in a new round of market-oriented economic reforms. Jiang Zemin, who became the General Secretary of the Communist Party after the 1989 events, swiftly shifted his political allegiance and became a follower of Deng Xiaoping. In October 1992, at the Fourteenth Congress, the Communist Party promoted Deng Xiaoping's "Theory on Socialism with Chinese Characteristics" as the guiding principle of the Communist Party of China and decided that the goal of reform was to build a "socialist market economy."

This decision revived the marketization agenda. The first step was the far-reaching price liberalization of 1992–1993, targeting commodities such as grain, steel, coal, and oil. By the end of the 1990s, many state-owned enterprises were privatized. State sector employment peaked in 1995 at 113 million. It fell to 81 million by 2000 and 64 million by 2007. After the dismantling of the People's Communes, tens of millions of people from the countryside began to seek new employment opportunities in industry and services in the cities. By 2000 the number of migrant rural workers surged to 106 million.[20] As a massive surplus labor force, the migrant workers were forced into low wages and harsh working conditions. Sweatshop exploitation became the standard practice in China's export-oriented manufacturing industries in Southern China. The intense exploitation of a large cheap labor force allowed transnational capital and Chinese capitalists to have high profit-rates and capture a growing share of the world market. China's merchandise exports surged from 62 billion dollars in 1990 to 249 billion dollars in 2000.

After Deng died in 1997, Jiang Zemin continued in his footsteps. In December 2001, China joined the World Trade Organization (WTO). Its admission was viewed in the West as a confirmation of Margaret Thatcher's claim that "There Is No Alternative" to the new neoliberal order under U.S. hegemony. China's inclusion in the WTO further accelerated investment in the export industry. China's share of the world's total

---

20   Li. *China and the 21st Century Crisis*. p. 21.

merchandise exports was 1.8 percent in 1990. By 2012, it had surged to 11.1 percent, equivalent to 2.05 trillion dollars. Since 2010, China has been the world's largest exporter of goods.[21]

CLASS STRUGGLE IN CHINA DURING DENG

Class struggle in China, which Mao pointed out incessantly, is far from over. The Communist Party might not deny this, but they certainly downplay it, stressing the importance of a "harmonious society." When private businesses were reintroduced in China, there was a shift toward the right. It was not only business people who were making fortunes, but also corrupt Party officials cooperating with capital.

Attempts by Chinese state-owned enterprises to introduce capitalist-style management to increase labor intensity and reduce workers' control were met with strong resistance by the workers.[22] However, the privatization wave in the 1990s changed the balance of power in favor of capital. On the global level, China's reintegration into the capitalist economy provided the system with a fresh supply of cheap labor. This helped to turn the balance of power in favor of the capitalist classes at a global scale in the late twentieth century.

This did not stop labor unrest in China. Since Deng's policy created inequality, deterioration of working conditions, and degradation of the environment, class struggle in China put pressure on the Communist Party to change course. According to the data from the Chinese Ministry of Public Security, "social order violations" increased from 3.2 million in 1995 to 13.9 million in 2012.[23] In some large-scale "mass incidents," a term used by the Chinese government to describe social protests—including strikes, sit-ins, marches, and riots—tens of thousands of people occupied local governments for days.[24]

---

21   *Ibid*. pp. 20–21.

22   *Ibid*.

23   Tanner, Murray Scot. "China's Social Unrest Problem: Testimony before the U.S.-China Economic and Security Review Commission, May 15, 2014." http://www.uscc.gov/sites/default/files/Tanner_Written%20Testimony.pdf

24   Tong, Yanqi and Lei, Shaohua. "Large-Scale Mass Incidents and Government Responses in China." *International Journal of China Studies*. Vol. 1, no. 2, October 2010, pp. 487–508.

The ongoing conflict between factions of the Communist Party has always been reflected in the shifting political lines of the state apparatus. From 2000–2010, there were improvements in pensions, health insurance, social welfare programs, and labor market regulations as a direct response to workplace uprisings.

A sizable Chinese middle class emerged because of industrialization and market reforms. Parts of the Chinese middle-class are convinced that prosperity will come from copying the economic and political systems of the Global North.[25] However, not everyone in the middle class shares this view. Many young unemployed, marginalized intellectuals criticize China's collaboration with capital. Some of them end up becoming political radicals.[26]

Likewise, China's peasants do not support neoliberalism. The Chinese revolution was a peasant revolution. Unlike in Russia, peasants were never a reactionary force. While collectivization has been abolished, land is still public. The peasants are direct producers whose subjective identification and objective positioning could lead socialist renewal.[27]

The New Rural Reconstruction Movement, which advocates communal life, is critical of the capitalist growth imperative. Its ecological outlook also appeals to urban laborers, who suffer as much from environmental degradation as farmers do.[28] They consider it unjust that those "who got rich first" will escape the brunt of the climate crisis by importing food, installing expensive air conditioners, or moving to less polluted areas.

Evaluation of the Deng Era

From a purely economic perspective, Deng's policy was a success. New

---

25   Møller, A.M. *Hegemonic Project: Interventions on the Politics of Communist Elite Legitimation in China, 2008–2015.* [Ph.D. thesis]. University of Copenhagen, 2016. p. 522.

26   Hambides, Zac. "China's Growing Army of Unemployed Graduates." *World Socialist Website.* 2010. https://www.wsws.org/en/articles/2010/10/chin-o04.html

27   Chun, Lin. *China and Global Capitalism: Reflections on Marxism, History, and Contemporary Politics.* Palgrave, 2013.

28   Møller. *Hegemonic Project.* p. 359.

industrial jobs have been created for 400 million people (roughly, the population of Europe). China's economy has become diverse and highly developed. It produces consumer electronics, cars, high-speed trains, robots, and airplanes. China went from being a relatively poor, primarily agricultural country to being the world's most important producer of industrial goods.

From a purely socialist perspective, Deng policy has a more dubious record. The new capitalist class was legitimized by the Communist Party of China in 1992 when it decided that its members would be allowed to become managers of private companies.[29] At its Sixteenth Congress in 2002, it was made clear that the Party represented not only the interests of the "masses of the people," but also those of the "most advanced productive forces"—a euphemism for the new capitalists.

With regards to the economy, during the epoch of Deng, China changed from being one of the world's most equal countries to one of the world's most unequal countries. In 2006, according to the World Wealth Report, 0.4% of the richest families in China controlled 70% of the national wealth. In 2006, 3,200 people had personal capital of over 100 million yuan (roughly US$15 million). Two-thousand nine hundred (90%) of these people were the children of leading government and Party officials.[30] The prosperity of the new capitalist class is based on the wealth accumulated by state-owned companies and collectives during the Mao era. Former Prime Minister, Wen Jiabao, became one the richest people in China, while his son owns one of China's largest private companies, and his wife Zhang Beili is known as the "diamond queen."[31] These Party officials have come a long way since the time of Mao, who had no personal possessions and left nothing when he died.[32]

If we take the global perspective on Deng's strategy towards neoliberalism, it was a rational choice—bend to the pressure from the capitalist offensive without breaking the power of the Party, as had happened in

---

29   *Ibid.* pp. 108–9.

30   Li, Minqi. "The Rise of the Working Class and the Future of the Chinese Revolution." *Monthly Review.* Vol. 63, no. 2, June 2011, p. 38.

31   *Ibid.* p. 39.

32   Han. "The Socialist Legacy Underlies the Rise of Today's China in the World."

the Soviet Union, and use the dynamic power of neoliberalism against itself, by first allowing it to develop China's productive forces, and then turn away from neoliberalism, using the advance in technology to develop the prerequisites for socialism in China. But to prevent capitalism from achieving a totality, it was necessary to manage this process carefully. Deng was aware of this balance.

The prerequisite for the success of this controlled opening towards neoliberalism was the development of the economic base during the Mao era. An agricultural sector able to feed the population, well-developed infrastructure, a heavy industrial sector, public banking, and a high level of education and public health, were all central pillars that have decisively contributed to the dynamism of the economy.

After completing this basis created solely by the Chinese people and delinked from global capitalism, China made an effort to partake in globalization, with an extraordinary effect. China once mainly exported textiles, shoes, and fireworks; not anymore. After acquiring technological and scientific knowledge, China is a leading exporter of high-end products such as industrial robots, consumer electronics, solar panels, electric cars, and high-speed trains. Chinese engineers are today constructing infrastructure projects in the Global South, changing the colonial North-South trading routes to South-South trade, and thereby diminishing the unequal exchange between Global North and South.

However, China's opening was costly. Deng often compares his reform with the NEP, however, there is a difference between the NEP in the Soviet Union and Deng's reforms. The NEP lasted from 1921 to 1928. It was firmly subjected to the needs of the planned economy and was under the complete control of the Communist Party. The Chinese reforms were much more comprehensive and lasted for 40 years, creating a significant capitalist class and capitalist mentality within China.[33] Globally, the opening gave capitalism a new golden era for three decades leading up to the financial crisis in 2008. No matter the ideological dressing, China's integration into global capitalism was a "re-linking" which entailed a transfer of surplus labor to the imperialist center. Low-cost Chinese labor created huge profits for capital, and cheap goods for con-

---

33   Park, Henry. "Postrevolutionary China and the Soviet NEP." *Research in Political Economy*. No. 9, 1986, pp. 219–233.

sumers, in the North.

China's industrialization was complementary to the U.S.'s deindustrialization and financialization, linked by the "dollar circuit." Dollars paid for Chinese goods exported to the U.S. are recycled back to the U.S. through China's purchasing of treasury bonds. This reifies the "dollar hegemony," whereby the U.S. obtains what it desires from other countries with an infinite credit.

The change in the agricultural sector, along with the industrial export strategy, forced millions of migrant workers to new urban capitalist enterprises. It was these millions of new workers who paid the price for the rapid development of China's productive forces, development that also had environmental consequences. It wasn't just industrial production, which was outsourced from North to South; it was also the pollution that comes with it. China's industrial cities were plagued by air pollution, and water shortages were a growing problem.

Thirty years of neoliberalism also had an impact on values and norms in society. Individualism, competitive mentalities, and corruption were spreading. The new middle class was copying consumer patterns from the West, adopting "the imperial mode of living," with its growth of meat consumption, cars, and air transport. Neoliberalism is not only an economic force, but also a mentality that permeates our thinking.

In the 1990s, many in the West, both neoliberals and leftists, were certain that China would disintegrate like the Soviet Union. But they were wrong. The Chinese system did not collapse as a result of the global neoliberal offensive. The Communist Party remained at the helm, even though its course changed, exercising what Ali Kadri calls "the discreet rule of the proletariat."[34]

The status of the Communist Party in China is very different from the late years of the Soviet Union. It is much more embedded in the population. With 98 million members, it is organized in 5.1 million urban street committees and rural village councils, and the Party has the respect of the population. About 89 percent of the Chinese respondents trusted the government in 2022, listed in first place among 28 surveyed countries in 2022. On average, about 51 percent of respondents showed trust in

---

34   Ali. *China's Path to Development*. p. 1.

their government globally.³⁵

After its encounter with neoliberalism, China emerged as a major economic power. This is an epochal change in the world-system. China was able, for the first time in two hundred years, to break the polarizing dynamic of capitalism between the West and the rest of the world.

This polarizing dynamic led the "dependency" theorists of the 1970s to conclude that the industrialization of the Third World was impossible within the imperialist system. They assumed that a substantial domestic market for consumer products had to be developed before industrialization could occur. They underestimated the development of the productive forces that made the globalization of production and consumption possible. The multinational companies (MNC) industrialized in the Global South with the primary aim of exporting to the affluent markets in the Global North. In 1976, Emmanuel anticipated the future role of MNC in China:

> Since the main problem of capitalism is not to produce but to sell, less traditional capital was attracted by the low wage rates of certain countries than was discouraged by the narrowness of the local market associated with such wages. This lack of capital in turn prevented growth and hence wage increases. The result was a deadlock. In theory the solution was production for exports alone. But except for standardized primary products, such an operation appeared to transcend the fief of the traditional capitalist. In any case, it has never occurred. The MNC, with its own sales network abroad and, even more, its own consumption in the case of a conglomerate, would not be put off by the lack of "pre-existing" local outlets. It would take advantage of both the low wages of the periphery and the high wages of the centre. I have no idea of the relative importance of the phenomenon. Here, as elsewhere, statistical information is lacking... All I can say is that, if this is so, this gives us, for the first time, the possibility of breaking the most pernicious vicious circle which was holding up the development of the Third World. It is rather a matter for rejoicing.³⁶

---

35 Statista Research Department. "Level of Trust in Government in China from 2016 to 2023." 2024. https://www.statista.com/statistics/1116013/china-trust-in-government-2020/

36 Emmanuel, Arghiri. "The Multinational Corporations and Inequality of Development." *International Social Science Journal*. Vol. 28, no. 4, 1976, p. 766.

THE DECLINE OF NEOLIBERALISM

Looking back at the zenith of globalization in the mid-1990s, when Russia and Eastern Europe were incorporated into the world market, capitalism had a foothold in China, and socialism, globally, was in crisis, it is no wonder that capitalism seemed victorious. Transnational capital dreamt of a globe managed by transnational institutions. In that sense, Negri and Hardt's thesis of the establishment of a single global *Empire* was the left-wing version of Fukuyama's thesis that capitalism was "the end of history." However, both versions missed the dialectical nature of the development of neoliberalism.

The rise of neoliberalism took place within the world system of states, as an effort of transnational capital to avoid state interference and control the movements of capital. The effort to erode the borders of the nation-state is one aspect of the contradiction of neoliberalism. The other aspect is that nation-states persist in managing society within borders. Capital is not a system in balance, it needs the state to regulate and keep security, not to end in chaos. From the mid-1970s until the turn of the millennium, transnational capital was the offensive aspect of the contradiction. At first, it weakened the state "at home" through the deregulation of transnational movements of capital and trade, privatization, and cuts in welfare. Then transnational capital outsourced jobs to low-wage countries for higher profits. However, the social consequences of these acts began to change the balance between aspects. The outsourcing of jobs, erosion of the welfare state, and migration problems generated nationalism in the North, demanding a stronger national state as a bulwark against the negative impact of global market forces. The "structural adjustments" of neoliberalism in the Global South had the same effect. By the turn of the millennium, the negative social consequences of neoliberalism began to weaken the political dominance of its institutions. The financial crisis of 2007-2008 further strengthened the demand for state control of capital. The balance tipped towards nationalism and the nation-state.

The shift of contradictory balance in neoliberalism became a problem for the capitalist mode of production, which for decades ran smoothly using the global production-chain, providing high profits for capital and cheap goods for consumers. The rejection of neoliberal policies and the shrinking size of the world market as a consequence of trade war, embargos, and sanctions due to national conflicts in the world system, hampered the continuity of capital accumulation. The heyday of neoliberal capitalism and U.S. hegemony was over. This meant an increasing discordance between global capitalism and China's national project of development. In terms of foreign policy, this was expressed by China's attempt to reshape international politics away from U.S. hegemony and towards a multi-polar world-system.

China avoided severe consequences from the financial crises primarily because its banking system was state-owned, and not an integrated part of the global financial house of cards that collapsed. Secondly, China quickly expanded investments in the state-owned sector to replace a flailing private capitalist sector. However, China's growth strategy was still based on exports to the U.S. and European markets, which had declined. More than 20 million workers lost their jobs. However, most of these migrant workers could return to their rural homes, where they had the right to housing and basic social services.

The financial crisis was a wake-up call to the Chinese leadership. They realized that neoliberalism was no longer a dynamic force to develop the productive forces, but increasingly a problem in the form of economic stagnation, social inequality, and environmental problems. These conditions led to a reemerging Marxist critique in China, challenging the influence of neoliberal thought.

Left or Right?

The state sector workers' anti-privatization struggles, and strikes in the export-oriented manufacturing sectors, suggested that working-class militancy was growing, and the regime of cheap labor exploitation was not sustainable. There was also growing concern about China's various ecological problems. This led to strategic debates within the Communist Party. One faction, led by Bo Xilai, advocated more state control of the economy and redistribution of wealth from the capitalist class to the working class under the slogan of "common prosperity." In 2007, Bo was appointed as the Party Secretary of the Municipality of Chongqing and a member of the Politburo of the

Communist Party of China. He initiated a massive anti-corruption campaign and confronted the mafia-connected local capitalist class. Bo emerged as the leader of the anti-neoliberal faction. Under his leadership, Chongqing achieved one of the highest economic growth rates among all provinces, and income inequality declined. Bo's experiment was met with opposition from the supporters of continued neoliberal policies in the Communist Party. The "liberal" media within China portrayed what was going on in Chongqing as an attempt to revive the Cultural Revolution.

In the heat of this struggle, something strange happened. On February 6, 2012, Chongqing's police chief suddenly went into the U.S. consulate and demanded political asylum. In April, Bo was stripped of his membership in the Politburo of the Communist Party. His wife was accused of murdering Neil Heywood, a British spy. What actually happened remains unclear. But the neoliberal faction of Communist Party leadership had conspired for months to get rid of Bo Xilai, and the incidents certainly served their political purpose.[37]

---

37   Li. *China and the 21st Century Crisis*. pp. 36–38.

CHAPTER 18

XI JINPING

Instead of Bo Xilai, whom many had seen as the next General Secretary of the Communist Party, the 18th Central Committee elected Xi Jinping in November 2012. However, it turned out not to be the hoped-for victory for the pro-neoliberal faction of the Party.

Born in 1953, Xi's father held a series of high posts in the Communist Party. During the Cultural Revolution, his father was purged from the Party. Xi's experience during the Cultural Revolution had a great influence on his view of politics. In an interview in 2000, he said:

> People who have little contact with power, who are far from it, always see these things as mysterious and novel. But what I see is not just the superficial things: the power, the flowers, the glory, the applause. I see the bullpens [Red Guards' detention houses during the Cultural Revolution] and how people can blow hot and cold. I understand politics on a deeper level.[1]

In 1968, Mao ordered millions of young people, including Xi, into the countryside to be "educated." For several years, Xi was in the countryside, building wells, digging fields, and herding sheep. Looking back, the time in the village was transformative for Xi. He ended up as the local Party chief in the village. He developed an affinity to China's rural poor, as well as a pragmatism in politics, in his dealings with village life.[2]

The Xi family was reunited in 1972, under orders from Zhou Enlai. His father was rehabilitated in 1978 and resumed his work establishing

---

1 Page, Jeremy. "How the U.S. Misread China's Xi: Hoping for a Globalist, It Got an Autocrat". *The Wall Street Journal.* December 23, 2020. https://www.wsj.com/articles/xi-jinping-globalist-autocrat-misread-11608735769

2 *Ibid.*

China's first Special Economic Zone to attract foreign investment. Xi himself became a member of the Communist Party in 1974. Xi's personal experience during the Cultural Revolution did not generate an aversion toward Mao. Since becoming General Secretary, he has sought to resurrect Mao's image.

After a degree in engineering in 1979, Xi served in several posts in the provinces. In 1990, he became the leader of the Party School in Fuzhou. From 1998 to 2002, Xi studied Marxist theory and ideological education at Tsinghua University. In 2002, he was elected a member of the Central Committee.

Already by 2009, secret U.S. cables sent by Center for New American Security (CNAS) to Washington, revealed by Wikileaks, stated that Xi knew very well that corruption, commercialization, and loss of value had emerged. It was suggested that when Xi would take the helm of the Party, he might aggressively attempt to address those evils, perhaps at the expense of the new moneyed class.[3] The West's dream for the rise of a "Chinese Gorbachev" was eviscerated on November 15, 2012 when Xi was elected to the post of General Secretary of the Communist Party.

Xi had the task to rectify the many problems inherited from "opening up."

He started with an anti-corruption campaign, fighting the cronyism that market development had introduced. Inspection teams initiated investigations of high-ranking officials. Over 100 provincial-ministerial level officials were implicated. These included leading figures of state-owned enterprises and highly ranked generals, who were subsequently dismissed. In addition to this, over 200,000 low-ranking officials received warnings, fines, and demotions within the first two years of the campaign, and a hard line on corruption has continued since.[4]

The Xi period is sometimes referred to as China's Third Revolution. The first being Mao's and the second Deng's. The periods are linked together through the creation of "Socialism with Chinese Characteristics,"

---

3   Hunt, Luke. "The World's Gaze Turns to the South Pacific." *The Diplomat.* September 4, 2012. https://thediplomat.com/2012/09/the-worlds-gaze-turns-to-the-south-pacific/

4   Heilmann, Sebastian. *China's Political System*. Rowman & Littlefield, 2017. pp. 62–75.

as explained by Xi in 2013:

> For our Party…there are two historical periods: before "reform and opening up" and after "reform and opening up." These are two interrelated periods that also have major differences, but the essence of both periods is that our Party was leading the people in the exploration and practice of building socialism. "Socialism with Chinese characteristics" was created in the new historical period of "reform and opening up," but it was created on the basis of New China having already established the basic socialist system and carried out more than twenty years of work…If our Party had not taken the decision in 1978 to carry out "reform and opening up"…socialist China would not be in the good situation it is today—it is even possible it could have faced a serious crisis like the Soviet Union and Eastern Europe…Although the ideological direction, policies and practice of building socialism in these two historical periods were very different, these two periods are not separate from each other, and are not at all fundamentally opposed…The practice and exploration of socialism before "reform and opening up" built up the conditions for the practice and exploration of socialism after "reform and opening up"; the practice and exploration of socialism after "reform and opening up" is to maintain, reform and develop the previous period.[5]

During Deng's Era, the national principal contradiction was defined as "the ever-growing material and cultural needs of the people versus backward social production." However, despite the development of the productive forces under Deng, it produces, according to Xi, an unbalanced development, characteristic of the capitalist growth model, marred by deepening class inequality, rural/urban divisions, promotion of economic development at the expense of cultural development, and an unsustainable relation to the environment.[6] In 2017, Xi declared at the 19th National Congress of the Communist Party:

> What we now face is the contradiction between unbalanced and inadequate development and the people's ever-growing needs for a better life…The evolution of the principal contradiction represents a historic shift that affects the whole landscape and that creates many new demands for the work of the Party and the country…(developing people's) access to childcare, education, employment, medical services, elderly care, housing, and social assistance, as well as social fairness and justice. While China's overall productive forces

---

5 Jinping, Xi. In Batson, Andrew. "What Xi Jinping Really Said About Deng Xiaoping and Mao Zedong." May 31, 2016. https://andrewbatson.com/2016/05/31/what-xi-jinping-really-said-about-deng-xiaoping-and-mao-zedong/

6 Jinping, Xi. In Foster, John Bellamy. "The New Cold War on China." *Monthly Review*. Vol. 73, no.3, July–August 2021. p. 1.

have significantly improved and in many areas our production capacity leads the world, our problem is that our development is unbalanced and inadequate. Despite the evolution of the principal contradiction, China is still and will long remain in the primary stage of socialism.[7]

Four decades of "opening up" towards neoliberalism has left its mark, not only in terms of increased inequality, but also in terms of worse working conditions, especially for the workers in the export zones. The values and norms of neoliberalism have also left their mark. Individualism, a competition mentality, along with greed, have made their inroads at the expense of solidarity and community. It requires a long, tough pull to change mentality. It is not done by words alone, but foremost by changing the way of living—in production, in the education system, and everyday life—to make the socialist values and norms rational.

Thus, a shift toward equality, self-sufficiency, ecological balance, rural revitalization, and the forging of a "dual circulation" with more emphasis on the domestic market—designed to reduce China's dependence on foreign markets—are all seen as crucial to China's emergence as a "great modern socialist society."[8]

Sliding to the Left

The crisis of neoliberalism became a turning point in Chinese politics. Instead of economic growth based on exports to America, Europe, and Japan, China began expanding the Chinese domestic market. The growing domestic market was based on rising wages in industry, putting more emphasis on the public welfare system and an effort to eliminate poverty in the countryside, which had been neglected since the end of the Cultural Revolution. Chinese workers' wages more than tripled over the last 12 years, from around an average of 32,000 to 107,000 Yuan between 2009 and 2021.[9] The growing domestic market meant that workers who lost their jobs during the 2007-8 crisis could find new employment, and

---

7   Jinping, Xi. "Principal Contradiction Facing Chinese Society Has Evolved in New Era. Statement at the 19th National Congress of the Communist Party." http://english.www.gov.cn/news/top_news/2017/10/18/content_2 81475912458156.htm

8   Jinping. In Foster. "The New Cold War on China." p. 14.

9   "China Average Yearly Wages." Trading Economics. https://tradingeconomics.com/china/wages. https://tradingeconomics.com/china/wages

that China's growth could continue despite the economic recession in the rest of the capitalist world.

Growing hostility from the U.S., seen in its trade war and technology blockade, have alerted China to its dependency on the U.S. and moved it in the direction of a soft delinking process. The Fourteenth Five Year Plan (2021-25) set forward the principle of independent scientific research capacity and technological self-sufficiency as the foundation of the nation. The aim is to build a digital China with its independent IC chip, 5G, new energy technologies, and new material science.[10]

According to the Communist Party of China, the current form of market socialism has three goals: to establish a highly developed and diversified industrial sector; to establish balance with the agricultural sector; and to make a planned national economy an important factor in the world capitalist system.[11]

Besides the technological development and expansion of the industrial sector, the agricultural production and rural areas have been reconstructed. In the decade from 2003 to 2013, China increased its grain output by about 50 percent. From 2013 to 2019, the number of towns with supply-marketing cooperatives in rural China increased from 50 percent to 95 percent, as part of the revitalization of the countryside, contributing to the elimination of extreme poverty.[12] It is essential to maintain collective ownership of land, and a solid cooperative economy for rural social stability, which in turn is vital for the stability of Chinese society as a whole.[13] Rural community cooperatives are also an important agent of environmental protection. Whereas the urban economy is more driven by a market economic rationality (which often leads to irrational behavior), the rural community is maintained by cooperative rationality. For decades Chinese rural society has served as the buffer for crises generated in the cities.

Signifying that the government has turned its attention to the ru-

---

10   Tiejun. *Ten Crises.* p. 419.

11   Amin, Samir. "China 2013." *Monthly Review.* Vol. 64, no. 10, March 2013. p. 4.

12   Scholten, Joe. In Foster, John Bellamy and Clark, Brett. "Socialism and Ecological Survival: An Introduction." *Monthly Review.* Vol. 74, no. 3, p. 27.

13   Tiejun. *Ten Crises.* p. 437.

ral sector, the government proposed a rural rebuilding strategy in 2017, consisting of:

1. A diversion from the policy of accelerating urbanization and instead giving priority to agriculture.

2. An assertion that rural revitalization is the most creative aspect of China's development in the twenty-first century.

3. An abandonment of the path of dependence on quantitative growth and a turn towards eco-friendly (quality) growth and development.[14]

In 2021, Xi called on China to promote "common prosperity." This term is not new. The phrase first appeared in 1953, when "common prosperity" was stated as a goal of China's socialist construction.[15] In 1979, the People's Daily carried an article entitled: "A Few Getting Rich First and Common Prosperity," echoing Deng's policy.[16] The dethroned Bo Xilai also used the term frequently. However, it is now back in force. In January 2021 Xi Jinping said:

> Realizing common prosperity is more than an economic goal. It is a major political issue that bears on our Party's governance foundation. We cannot allow the gap between the rich and the poor to continue growing...We must be proactive about narrowing the gaps between regions, between urban and rural areas, and between rich and poor people. We should promote all-around social progress and well-rounded personal development, and advocate social fairness and justice, so that our people enjoy the fruits of development in a fairer way.[17]

To move in the direction of common prosperity, China is increasing wages, especially for low-income groups, and addressing excessively high incomes through a new income distribution and tax system. The government has also pursued the common prosperity agenda with a series of related reforms. China's Ministry of Human Resources and Social

---

14   Ibid. p. 444.

15   Bandurski, David. "A History of Common Prosperity." *China Newspeak*. August 27, 2021. https://chinamediaproject.org/2021/08/27/a-history-of-common-prosperity/

16   Xiaoping, Deng. "Unity Depends on Ideals and Discipline, 7th March 1985." *Selected Works: Vol. 3 (1982–1992)*. People's Publishing House, 2014.

17   Dunford, Michael. "On Common Prosperity." 2021. https://socialistchina.org/2021/10/17/on-common-prosperity/

Security and the Supreme People's Court jointly declared it illegal for companies to make employees work extended hours and then terminate their contracts if they had excruciating work schedules, commonly known as "996"—9 a.m. to 9 p.m., six days a week.[18] Furthermore, there has been a crackdown on tech firms and other monopolies, such as online food delivery, car-hailing, recruitment, and speculation in real estate. As a result of the liberalization of the past, the costs of housing, education, and health have grown. Speculative capital was allowed to penetrate the housing sector, causing real estate prices in major cities to become unaffordable for most people.

In 2017, Xi announced that "houses are for living in and not for speculation." In subsequent years the government sought to control housing prices and subsidize rental housing. The government has also mandated local authorities scrutinize all the activities of developers from the arrangement of finance to the transfer of ownership titles.[19]

There are other echoes of Bo Xilai's Municipality of Chongqing. In June 2021, the State Council drafted a plan for the construction of a "common prosperity zone" in Zhejiang. The plan sets guiding principles for the zone: urban and rural income should increase and narrow the income gap, it should provide strategic support to the state-owned economy and prevent the disorderly expansion of capital. The new zone should make sure that houses are for living and not for speculation, and develop a rural revitalization with an ecological, collectively owned, and cooperative rural economy.[20]

Finally, in 2013, Xi launched the "Belt and Road Initiative," the resurrection of the ancient Silk Road trade route, building train lines, roads, and airports to connect South and Central Asia to the Middle East and Europe. This is coupled with a Maritime Silk Road that would connect China to Southeast Asia, the Middle East, Africa, and Europe via various sea lanes. In 2017, China further extended its Maritime Silk Road to Lat-

---

18 Yiying, Fan. "China's Top Court Says Grueling '996' Work Schedule Illegal." *Sixth Tone*. August 27, 2021. https://www.sixthtone.com/news/1008375/chinas-top-court-says-grueling-996-work-schedule-illegal

19 Dunford. "On Common Prosperity."

20 The State Council Information Office of the People's Republic of China. In Dunford, "On Common Prosperity."

in America. Thirty-nine countries in sub-Saharan Africa, thirty-four in Europe and Central Asia, twenty-five in East Asia and the Pacific, eighteen in Latin America and the Caribbean, seventeen in the Middle East and North Africa, and six in South Asia are now affiliated with One Belt, One Road.

This project, in combination with the intergovernmental organization BRICS, ultimately involves shifting power away from the U.S./EU/Japan dominated North-South hierarchy, towards a South-South economic cooperation and a multipolar political world system.

THE GOVERNANCE OF CHINA

The Communist Party of China is described in Western media as a centralized authoritarian regime, seeing liberal parliamentarianism as the only way to practice democracy—a discursive label shared, to some extent, by the mainstream left wing. It ignores the rule of capital over politics in the West itself, as well on global affairs. The Communist Party is on its side, trying to develop a democratic form of governance suitable for "socialism with Chinese characteristics" and to become more pervasive than capitalist liberalism. This has been a long process going back to the revolution and the development of the "mass line," and still has high priority, as reflected in the title of a four-volume collection of speeches and articles by Xi Jinping, *The Governance of China*.[21]

In Western discourse, it is claimed that democracy and liberal market capitalism are linked together as conjoined twins. However, liberal capitalism thrives when linked with fascism, as we have seen in Nazi Germany, Franco's Spain, and Pinochet's Chile.

If the development of liberal democracy is linked to something, then it is linked to colonialism. The super-profits from colonialism helped make possible the molding of "the dangerous classes" into loyal citizens of the state, who were then allowed to vote for parliament, as they no longer posed a danger for the rule of capital.

European democracy became a resource-allocation mechanism,

---

21   See Jinping, Xi. *The Governance of China: Vol. I–IV*. Foreign Languages Press, 2014–2022.

creating welfare for sections of the Northern working class to cement capital's rule and expand empire. Within the framework of a multiparty, representative parliamentary democracy, the population of Europe has voted for colonialism and imperialism up through the 20th century. A vote for the Euro-American wars of encroachment is not a vote for democracy; it is a vote for a share of imperialist rents.

The Eurocentric universalization of multiparty liberal parliamentarism as the essence of democracy not only overlooks its historical roots and how it is exercised on the global level, but it also fails to question the rule of capital in liberal democracy. It presents democracy as a purely procedural phenomenon and masks the underlying political and economic content—the exploitation needed for capitalist production and environmental destruction. However, you cannot isolate the political form of management from the laws of the economic sphere.[22]

China has no use for capitalist liberal democracy. Since China is developing the economic preconditions for "Socialism with Chinese Characteristics," it is also in the process of developing its own form of democracy, more pervasive than the Western model. Socialist democracy is linked to popular collective ownership of the means of production. Democracy means to decide how to produce, what to produce, and how the social product shall be divided. The essence is not to cast a vote once every fourth year in parliamentary elections after watching discussions in a closed circuit between politicians and media.

Democracy is defined by the extent to which people can control and shape their lives daily, to steer resources toward the betterment of living conditions on national and global levels. Once latched to the institution of the state, the organs of labor oversee each step in the social production and redistribution process.[23] China does not claim that it has reached that stage. However, they are trying. The current Chinese form of governance is popular democracy, as Samir Amin stressed, which imparts autonomy.[24] Control of value-flows and autonomous industrialization are the principal features of the Chinese development experience.

---

22   Kadri. *China's Path to Development*. p. 147.

23   *Ibid*. p. 157.

24   Amin, Samir. In Kadri, Ali. *Development Challenges and Solutions After the Arab Spring*. Palgrave, 2016.

The Communist Party is not a monolith. It has always consisted of several factions with different political lines, changing the policies and being able to correct mistakes. This political system has been superior to the West when it comes to generating development plans with a long-term vision, medium-term goals, and short-term policies. Most importantly, it also has the ability to execute those plans.[25]

The policy of the Communist Party must be seen as reflective of the interaction between the global principal contradiction and the contradictions inside China, rather than power struggles between different individuals.

The changing principal contradiction has been the main reason for the shifting course of the CPC against the headwind of the capitalist world system. If capitalism is controlled, it can contribute to the development of the productive forces and better conditions for building a socialist society. But for this to happen, it is of vital importance that the working class and the peasantry retain state power. The "opening up" of China created capitalist billionaires, but as a class, they do not rule the country.

The Return of Marxism

In the past decade, the Communist Party has emphasized Marxist and dialectical conceptions. Marxism is part of Chinese education from primary school to universities. Discussions in Chinese academia on Marxism are diverse, as reflected in articles in many journals both in Chinese and English. In 2018, on the occasion of Marx's 200th birthday, Xi Jinping held a lecture that engaged with the works of Marx and Engels and applied them to China. Xi ended the lecture by declaring that Marx is the thinker of modern times and China is dedicated to realizing his vision of communism.[26] At the one-hundredth anniversary of the Communist Party of China in 2021, Xi, dressed in Mao-style clothing, emphasized that the CPC is a Marxist party.[27] This is not just empty rhetoric, such an

---

25 Hernández, Carlos Miguel. "On the Sinicization of Marxism." 2022. https://socialistchina.org/2022/05/25/on-the-sinicization-of-marxism/

26 Jinping, Xi. "Speech at the Conference Celebrating the 200th Anniversary of Marx's Birth, Beijing, 4 May 2018." *Qiushi*. Vol. 10, no. 3, July–September 2018.

27 Jinping, Xi. "Speech at a Ceremony Marking the Centenary of the CCP." 2021. http://www.xinhuanet.com/english/special/2021-07/01/c_1310038244.htm

embracing of Marxism from the bottom to the top of society makes an impact. It empowers people to analyze society and develop strategies to strengthen the power of the proletariat.

The path forward will not be easy. The development of the productive forces during the Deng era promoted the possibility of socialism, but it also generated a capitalist class that is committed to the preservation and defense of capitalism. This heralds inevitable contradictions within Chinese society. These are to be found in the inequality created by the "opening up" policy, which still exists, and in the exploitation of labor employed by companies such as Foxconn.[28]

What Xi has referred to as the "principal contradiction"—the unequal distribution of wealth and the uneven development between rural and urban communities—is evident in class struggles taking place at all levels of society.

The Communist Party tries to build bridges and avoid major divisions between the different currents of society through a process of reforms to redistribute wealth, the reduction of the gaps between incomes and regional development, fighting poverty, and promoting "common prosperity."

On the 16th of October 2022, Xi delivered a report to the 20th National Congress and was reelected for another four-year term. The report confirms the course of Xi's policy in the past decade: the pursuit of economic growth, but also the pursuit of quality growth that reduces inequality, tackles corruption, increases collective prosperity, and restores ecological integrity.[29]

CHINA 1949–2023

China has been an advanced civilization for millenia, both in technology and governance. Imperialism created a break in this continuity between 1840 and 1949. Neither the traditional ruling class nor the indigenous

---

28 Enfu, Cheng. *China's Economic Dialectic: The Original Aspiration of Reform*. International Publishers, 2023. pp. 287–93.

29 Jinping, Xi. "Report to the 20th National Congress of the Communist Party of China, 16 October 2022." *Qiushi*. October 26, 2022. Accessible online at: http://en.qstheory.cn/2022-10/26/c_824626.htm

capitalist class was able to reverse China's national decline. Only the Communist Party was able to mobilize the peasants and the urban workers to create the conditions required to develop the productive forces and raise China within the capitalist world system.

By defeating imperialism—including the rural landlord class and the nationalist capitalist class—it became possible to rebuild the economy to the benefit of the Chinese people. In the past 70 years, China has developed from one of the poorest countries to one of the leading powers in the world. This process has been realized without the exploitation of other nations. This result has been obtained solely by the effort of the Chinese people.

To move from a defensive to offensive position within the world system, the socialist-oriented countries have to develop their productive forces to an advanced level so they can break the power of the capitalist world market to develop socialism—and defend themselves in the process—in a hostile capitalist world system. The era of Mao (1949-76) both developed the productive forces and mobilized socialist values. To carry on the transition from capitalism to socialism, it was necessary to abstain from the utopianism and idealism that has been a characteristic of many socialists, which then became disappointed by the subsequent development in China.

The thesis of the restoration of capitalism in China after Mao is too simple. The policy of the Communist Party after Mao reflects the changes in the principal contradiction in the world system and the development of internal contradictions in China's economy. In the first part of the Deng era, from 1976 to the early 1990s, after the tumult of the Cultural Revolution, Chinese leaders were preoccupied with getting the economy running again and upgrading the level of technology. At the same time, capitalism launched neoliberal globalization, with the demand for capitalist investment connected with the outsourcing of industrial production from the global North to the South. But China did not accept the demand for "structural adjustments." The Communist Party had its own strategy to maintain the Chinese national project. If the transnational companies wanted access to the Chinese labor force and infrastructure, then China demanded access to the technology and science behind production. With this, China would be able to develop the next generation of technology by itself. The transnational companies were so eager to take advantage of low-wage labor that they accepted Chinese partners in the companies. The result is that China today produces the most advanced solar power systems, 5G networks, smartphones, artificial intelligence, industrial robots, high-speed trains and electric cars.

This was made through the exploitation of the working class and peasants. This tradeoff, between the extreme exploitation of the Chinese working class on one side, and the development of the forces of production on the other side, was done consciously by Deng. The Chinese working class had to endure the hardships of capitalist exploitation for a generation in order to continue the transfer toward socialism.

This may seem to be a cynical position. But was there an alternative at the time? The anti-imperialist wave of the 1960s was running out of steam; the world revolution was a distant goal. The left wing was in crisis globally. The Soviet Union had entered its death-spiral and the global neoliberal offensive seemed unstoppable.

China needed to develop its productive forces. Not only to eradicate poverty in China itself, but also because it is necessary to possess the most developed technology to break the dominance of capitalism, and thus promote a global transformation towards socialism.

Yet by neoliberalism's crisis in 2007-8, China was capable of producing not only simple industrial products but also advanced electronics. More importantly, Chinese leadership was aware that internal contradictions started to erode the power of neoliberalism. The world market could no longer be the driver of Chinese economic development. China has to change its economic strategy both on the national and global levels. On the global level, it had to reduce its dependency on exports to the U.S. to avoid being dragged down by crises in the capitalist world economy. On the national level, it had to roll back neoliberal policies and repair the damage done to Chinese society—a kind of "soft delinking," following Samir Amin's advice for engaging with the capitalist world system on the way towards socialism:

> ...the organization of a system of criteria for the rationality of economic choices based on a law of value, which has a national foundation and a popular content, independent of the criteria of economic rationality that emerges from the domination of the law of capitalist value that operates on a world

scale.³⁰

The Communist Party charted a zig-zag course in terms of delinking and relinking strategies according to the economic and political developments in the world system. From 1949 until 1971, delinking was presented as a policy of self-reliance, but it was more the result of necessity than of choice.

The relinking from 1978 was a reaction to the challenge of neoliberal globalization, to modernize China, and to counter imperialist domination in the longer run. It was for sure a deviation from the strict socialist course. It made China the "factory of the world," but with the consequences of environmental degradation, rural-urban inequalities, and an enlarging gap between the rich and the poor. The course had to be adjusted by adopting policies of "rural reconstruction," "dual circulation," "elimination of extreme poverty," and "common prosperity." All policies which are "putting people's needs first." In this sense, the state is rejecting the capitalist law of value.

I have presented the Chinese revolution and its effort to build socialism as a long process influenced by the interaction of the principal contradictions in the world system with local contradictions. It has created breaks, but there is also a continuity, as Ali Kadri states:

> The past is alive in the present. It is neither the person of Mao nor Deng who endures, but the revolutionary ideology that charted the recent course of history. Whether Deng's cat was catching mice or whether China was feeling the stones as it crossed the river, it did so under the ironclad fist of the Communist Party. To falsify the structural continuity in modern Chinese history is an ideological position that aligns with imperialism.³¹

No other country has managed to develop its productive forces both in qualitative and quantitative terms faster than China. Most importantly, China has broken the polarizing dynamic in the capitalist world system, which for centuries, on one hand, has relegated the Third World to poverty, and on the other hand, concentrated wealth and power in the

---

30   Amin, Samir. "A Note on the Concept of Delinking." *Review*. Vol. 10, no. 3, 1987. pp. 435–44.

31   Kadri. *China's Path to Development*. p. 18.

imperialist center. This gives new prospects for the development of socialism and heralds the end of capitalism. No small achievement for a political party. There is a saying that "in China, they sew with long thread." In a speech on January 5, 2018, at a seminar for new Central Committee members and other leading cadres, Xi Jinping summarized the quest for socialism very well:

> Both history and reality tell us that a social revolution often requires a long historical process to achieve ultimate victory. Only by looking back at the road taken, comparing the road of others, looking far ahead of the road, to figure out where we came from, [can we see] where to go...The main problem here is that building socialism in a semi-colonial and semi-feudal society like ours is an unprecedented undertaking, and there is no ready-made model to follow. Engels pointed out that the so-called "socialist society" is not something that is set in stone, but should be seen, like any other social system, as a society that changes and reforms frequently.
>
> Socialism with Chinese characteristics was founded in the new period of reform and opening up, but to understand its formation and development, its historical inevitability and scientific truth, we should stretch the time scale and grasp it in the course of the evolution of socialism in the world. One-hundred and seventy years ago, Marx and Engels, on the basis of in-depth investigation and study of the basic contradictions of capitalist society, inherited and abandoned the (utopic) ideas of Saint-Simon, Fourier and Owen. They put forward the materialistic view of history and the doctrine of surplus value, laid a scientific theoretical foundation for socialism, which led socialism from an ideal to a science...
>
> After the end of the Second World War, a number of socialist countries were born...which led scientific socialism from practice in one country to development in many countries. At that time, the socialist camp was flourishing, and together with the anti-imperialist and anti-colonialist struggles of Asian, African and Latin American countries, it formed a basically evenly matched pattern with the capitalist world, which is why Comrade Mao Zedong said that "the east wind overwhelmed the west wind." However, historical development is never straight, but full of twists and turns. In the late 1980s and early 1990s, the collapse of the Soviet Union, the fall of the Communist Party of the Soviet Union...brought a serious impact on the vast number of developing countries that aspired to socialism, and many of them were forced to take the path of copying the Western system...As Lenin profoundly pointed out in commemorating the fourth anniversary of the October Revolution: "This first victory is not yet final, but we have already begun this enterprise. It does not matter when and for what period the proletarians of which country will carry this cause to its conclusion. What is important is that the ice has been broken, the voyage has been opened, the way has been shown."

History always evolves according to its own logic. The great success of socialism with Chinese characteristics in China shows that socialism has not perished, nor will it perish, and that it is flourishing with vitality and vigor. The success of scientific socialism in China is of great significance to Marxism and scientific socialism, and to socialism in the world. It is conceivable that if socialism had not achieved the success in China today, if the leadership of the Communist Party of China and our socialist system had also collapsed in the domino change of the collapse of the Soviet Union, or had failed for other reasons, then the practice of socialism might again have to wander in the darkness for a long time, and again as a ghost, as Marx said, wandering in the world...

This means that it will take a long historical period for us to build socialism with Chinese characteristics. In this long historical process, it is a challenge to ensure that the Communist Party of China does not collapse, and the Chinese socialist system does not fall. Once upon a time, the Soviet Communist Party was so strong, the Soviet Union was so powerful, but now it has long been "the old country cannot look back at the bright moon." A generation does the work of a generation, but without historical perspective, without a long-term vision, also cannot do the things of the moment.[32]

In differentiating between a capitalist or socialist course, the crucial questions are: Is the plan or the market the dominant factor in the economy? Are human needs or profit prioritized? Which of these determines the location of the factors of production and the rules of distribution for products? Who oversees the commanding heights of the economy: the dictatorship of the proletariat or the capitalist class? Samir Amin considers that the period of transition towards socialism should support collective ownership of the land; the construction of a modern industrial system; the maintenance of state ownership over key sectors of the economy, and above all, over the financial-credit sector; the preservation of planning criteria together with the use of commercial relations; and an integration into the world market, in which economic sovereignty is preserved, technology transfer is taken advantage of, and surplus is retained.[33]

These points reflect China's policies very well. The future will be decided by the class struggle in China. A continued movement toward

---

32 Jinping, Xi. "Consistently Develop and Uphold Socialism with Chinese Characteristics, 5 January 2018." https://socialistchina.org/2022/09/26/xi-jinping-consistently-develop-and-uphold-socialism-with-chinese-characteristics/

33 Amin. "China 2013." pp. 14–33

socialism will require the mobilization of peasants and workers by social movements or factions inside the Communist Party. For Mao, the class struggle in China was not over with the proclamation of the People's Republic. The question of continued class struggle was central to the Sino-Soviet dispute in the 1960s. In the Soviet Union, class struggle was considered over, while the Chinese saw "Soviet revisionism" as proof that it wasn't, and that a new class had seized power. For Mao, the revolution was a process characterized by waves; setbacks on the long road to socialism were followed by progress.

With the history of the Chinese working class, I believe there is potential for socialist development in China. The economic development successes achieved in recent years—the struggle against the pandemic and overcoming poverty—show the organizational skills and mobilizing capacity of the CCP. It must deepen this capacity and get involved in the struggles on the ground level—it must "go to the masses" and formulate new politics to advance towards socialism.

A socialist-orientated China will be of great importance for a transition towards global socialism. Compared to the former Soviet Union, the economy of China is more developed. This gives China the strength to balance the surrounding capitalist world headed by the U.S. The global military capability of the U.S. is superior, but China has sufficient strength to counter direct U.S. aggression. Like the Soviet Union, a strong socialist China will create possibilities for anti-capitalist struggles within the remaining capitalist world system.

Just as the Soviet Union played a role as a strategic ally for national liberation struggles throughout the twentieth century, China must play a role in the South's struggle against global neoliberalism in the twenty-first century. This can only happen if China resists national chauvinism. With China's new central position in the world system, the importance of socialist-oriented development in China can hardly be overestimated. It can tip the global balance of power decisively in favor of a socialist world order.

PART III
THE TRANSITION TO SOCIALISM

CHAPTER 19

Additional Historical Lessons

The past two hundred years of attempts to build socialism is not just history. It reaches into the future. The process is ongoing. Our reading of the Paris Commune, the Russian, and Chinese revolutions has an impact on our strategies, and thus on our future actions. The past, the present, and the future are not just a chronological set of events. They are dialectically connected and interdependent. The transformation toward socialism is a process stretching backward and forward. The struggle is not just about the future, it is about the realization of the historical ideas of socialism. From the ideas of Marx and Engels to the struggle of the Third World revolutionary movements still have a hopeful impact, which drives us to act and realize those hopes in the future. Our struggle should not be led by utopian goals, but by strategies built upon historical materialism. The recurrent debates about whether the Soviet Union, China, Cuba, or any state in the process of developing socialism is/was a worker's state or just an elite-ruled authoritarian state represent a mode of thinking that tries to fit the real world into a preconceived ideal. One imagines a socialist society and contrasts the problematic reality of building socialism with utopia. No matter how impressive progress is, it will always remain below expectations.[1]

Anti-imperialist strategy must contain an actually existing counter-hegemonic force capable of challenging the dominant power structure. Western Marxists are often trapped in a utopian world where the idea of socialism is superior to the transitional regimes and modes of production—many of which have emerged in the past hundred years, strug-

---

1   Amin. "China 2013." p. 69.

gling against a dominant capitalist world system. The Brazilian communist Jones Manoel writes:

> Nothing is socialist transition, and everything is state capitalism...The contradictions, the problems, the failures, the mistakes, sometimes even the crimes, mainly happen during this moment of building the new order. So, when the time comes to evaluate the building of a new social order—which is where, apparently, the practice always appears to stray from the purity of theory—the specific appears corrupted in the face of the universal.[2]

The transition from capitalism to socialism will be a long process. The transition to capitalism was a process that took centuries, from the Italian city-states, to the Dutch Empire, to the breakthrough of industrial capitalism in England at the beginning of the nineteenth century. Since capitalism developed globally, the transition towards socialism is also global. But not a simultaneous transformation; the transition contains many revolutions. The balance between capitalism and socialism has tilted back and forth since the mid-nineteenth century. The dialectical relationship between economic laws and class struggle creates tendencies and counter-tendencies, which interact with one another.

This transformational process has also contained socialist movements and states. Movements are a first step towards state power, but they are also a transformative power in themselves, changing our norms and values, as seen in the 1968 rebellion.

This process of transformation takes place within the framework of the world system of states. Although the economy of capitalism is transnational, its political system is divided into nation-states. The nation-state is thus an inevitable factor in the transformation from capitalism to socialism. We need the power of the state to defend the socialist project in a hostile world system.

Throughout the 20th century, there were several attempts to develop socialism within the framework of the nation-state, which inevitably clashed with the surrounding capitalist world. To defend their project, these states have been caught in the dilemma between supporting the world revolution, which in the long run is necessary for the success of building socialism, and the need to survive in the shorter

---

2   Manoel, Jones. "Western Marxism Loves Purity and Martyrdom, But Not Real Revolution." *Black Agenda Report*. June 10, 2020. https://www.blackagendareport.com/western-marxism-loves-purity-and-martyrdom-not-real-revolution

run—exemplified by the Soviet strategy of "socialism in one country." Historical periods do not follow one another in a clear-cut manner; they interpenetrate and combine over a long period. In the long transition from capitalism, different forms of "socialism under construction" have and will appear according to the different histories, cultures, and positions of each country in the world-system. As Engels put it in 1890:

> So-called "socialist society" is not, in my view, to be regarded as something that remains crystallized for all time, but rather in the process of constant change and transformation like all other social conditions.[3]

Instead of seeing each attempt to build socialism in the past two hundred years as mistakes, I see them as steps in a long transitional process. These steps have contributed to the transition by changing capitalism, and have acted as learning-processes for the forces of socialism. As we see advances and retreats, we must evaluate them in the context of the different stages of capitalist development.

The crises in capitalism occur when the development of the productive forces is blocked by the mode of production. The driver of the transition process is the class struggle, initiated by exploitation, which is necessary for the continued accumulation of capital. However, until now, capitalism has been able to solve the contradiction within the system. It has adapted—and rolled back attempts—to the construction of socialism. Thus, transition is a process of trial and error, and of trying again. Communism is a practical struggle with a bevy of trials containing the praxis of past revolutions from which we can learn. In the following, I summarize the main lessons from the preceding historical chapters.

THE REVOLUTIONS OF 1848

In 1848, the main problem for the socialist movement was how to organize the proletariat. The construction of a future socialist society was only addressed in abstract terms. The focus was on *taking* state power, not on how to use it.

The participants in the 1848 upheaval were the proletariat in the major cities of Europe, led by liberal capitalists and middle-class intellectuals

---

3   Engels. "Letter to Otto von Boenigk, 21 August 1890." Marx and Engels. *Collected Works: Vol. 49.* p. 18.

whose goals were to eliminate remaining feudal structures and establish republican nation states. They had little concern for socialism.

The lesson from the 1848 revolutions were that liberals and the middle classes could not be trusted. The proletariat had to organize themselves and not rely on parliamentarians to implement their demands. Future revolutions would not be peaceful. In 1850, Marx wrote:

> You will have to go through 15, 20, 50 years of civil wars and national struggles not only to bring about a change in society but also to change yourselves and prepare yourselves for the exercise of political power.[4]

The 1848 revolutions were social and national uprisings, which led to the formation of bourgeois nation-states in Europe—a necessary criterion for the development of capitalism. On one side, capitalists hate the state as it interferes with the economic dispositions of capital; however, on the other side, capital needs the state to mitigate its contradictions and to administer its expansion. Capitalism builds its superstructure as a world-system of national states. The imperialist dimension of capitalism divided this world system into a center of capitalist nation-states and a periphery of colonies.

The struggle for the establishment of nation-states and socialism has often been interwoven because the nation-state is the modern economic and political unit. Thus, the transition towards socialism has to go through the nation-state.

Nationalism can be progressive or reactionary, depending on the classes involved and the position of the nation in question within the global order. There is a difference between nationalism espoused by an imperialist nation and the national struggle of an oppressed one.

The internationalism promoted in 1848 by Marx and Engels in *The Communist Manifesto*, is the conviction that the class position is more important than the national identity in the consciousness of the proletariat. Unfortunately, this has not always been the case. Imperialism weakened class identity and strengthened nationalism. The current wave of nationalism in Europe and North America is reactionary, and utilized to defend privileges. But this does not make the struggle for national independence reactionary per se. The national liberation struggles fought

---

4   Marx. "Revelations Concerning the Communist Trial in Cologne." Marx and Engels. *Collected Works: Vol. 11.* p. 403.

against imperialism are still progressive—see, for example, the Palestinian liberation struggle.

The struggle for national sovereignty will continue to factor into the struggle for socialism. Capitalism will not end simultaneously in all corners of the world and make way for socialism. It will come one after the other in a world-wide struggle. Additionally, socialism will not be the same in all countries. There will be internal conflicts—as well as conflicts between countries. The revolutions of 1848 revealed that the globalization of socialism requires national liberation to undermine the global capitalist system.[5]

The Paris Commune

The Commune was the first explicit socialist uprising. The Communards proved that a conflict between capitalist nation-states could be used to bring a national class struggle to a head. Social tensions grew due to the hunger, unemployment, and overall misery caused by the Franco-German War. A revolutionary situation emerged, and the Communards seized the opportunity.

It was a self-organized initiative from below and a pluralist movement, in which a range of supporters participated: from Proudhon to Marx and the First International to libertarians and Jacobins to Blanquists and "social republicans." The representatives of the Commune were democratically elected in their neighborhoods and subjected to the permanent control of their popular base. However, the leadership turned out not to be effective. There was no coordinated strategy on how to mobilize the rest of France or how to defend and develop the revolution. They also lacked an ability to manage production in Paris. Factories were handed over to the workers without a common plan on how to carry out the production and distribution of goods.

The Commune is the first case in which the proletariat assumed the task of transforming society. Based on the experience of the Commune, Marx concluded that the bourgeois state must not

---

5   For a discussion on the role of the nation state in the imperialist system, see, Kuhn, Gabriel. "Oppressor and Oppressed Nations: Sketching a Taxonomy of Imperialism." 2017. https://kersplebedeb.com/posts/oppressor-and-oppressed-nations/

only be "conquered," but broken, and a new kind of state constructed. The Communards managed to take power in Paris, but not France. The uprising was put to an end when the Germans retreated and French troops could turn their attention to the communist rebels. Why did the Germans ease their military pressure on France at that moment? The answer is simple: they did not want Paris to set a revolutionary example that could spread to Germany. The Paris Commune revealed the need to defend socialist revolutions in a sea of capitalist states.

The Split of the Second International

The growing split in the Second International represented the rise of reformism within the socialist movement in Europe in the form of Social Democratic parties. A dynamic and growing national capitalism means a bigger "cake" to share, hence the Social Democrats' support of colonialism. The value transfer from the colonies solved the contradiction between expanded production and consumption in the center, as it provided the basis for a rising wage level. Through accommodating reformism, capitalism strengthened itself, like a virus adapting to weak medicine. European reformism divided the global proletariat, but it also had severe consequences for the center. Social Democrats' support for colonialism meant support for inter-imperialist rivalry. The Social Democrats supported the build up of their national state's military, leading up to the First World War. Social Democrats also led the repression of the Spartacist uprising in Germany after the war. Instead of trying to transform capitalism, social democratic reformist economic policy pulled capitalism out of crises in the late-1920s and early-1930s. The Social Democrats declined an alliance with communists against fascism in the 1930s, facilitating the rise of Nazi-Germany. Social Democrats were prominent anti-communists during the "Cold War," and continue to be supporters of NATO and U.S. attempts to uphold global hegemony. The Social Democrats represent Western working-class commitment to imperialist wars in order to protect these privileges. As Ali Kadri observes.

> The Western liberal omitted that the finance for reform must originate in equalizing global production conditions rather than a cut from imperialist profits—a share from the sphere of circulation. Reform is the payoff for "well

to do" labour to bomb "less well to do" labour.[6]

Learning the lessons of collaboration with Social Democrats is still relevant. In spite of the historical lessons, many on the mainstream left still believe that Social Democrats are an ally in the struggle for socialism and that social democratic capitalist welfare states are a step towards socialism, as the U.S. senator Bernie Sanders proclaims.

German Revolution

The German revolution was a spontaneous, messy affair, lacking unity in action. If you do not know where you are heading, there is no road forward. The indecisiveness of the revolutionaries gave the reactionary forces time to gather strength and crush the revolution. The result might have been different if the revolutionaries had had solid strategy and coordinated leadership.

The defeat of the German revolution was a turning point in the struggle between capitalism and socialism on the global level. Had it succeeded, other European countries might have followed the revolutionary track, placing the Soviet Union and world revolution in a more favorable position. Instead, the development of fascism, followed by liberal capitalist welfare states in Western Europe, created a secure center for capitalism and prolonged its life span. The German uprising was the last revolutionary attempt in the center and the struggle for socialism then moved to the periphery.

Russian Revolution

Lenin's answer to the question "How to escape defeat?" was years of preparation. Sixteen years before the revolution, Lenin wrote *What is to Be Done?* insisting that a vanguard party of dedicated revolutionaries spread Marxist ideas among the workers.[7] The October Revolution was well planned, led by central command, and executed like a military operation more than a spontaneous mass uprising.

The Bolshevik vanguard party was an effective instrument in carry-

---

6   Kadri. *China's Path to Development.* p. 32.
7   Lenin. "What is to Be Done?"

ing out the revolution and waging a civil war but was less successful in handling political differences within the Party while constructing a state to build socialism. When the revolution failed to occur in the advanced Western European countries, the Soviet Union stood alone in its own form of state capitalism in an attempt to create economic preconditions for socialism in a hostile world.

Socialism from Utopia to Reality

As attempts to build socialism developed throughout the 20th century, there emerged a gap between the ideals of socialism and the reality of actually existing socialism. The nation, the state, the market, inequity, and religion did not wither away. The idealist socialist idea of the withering away of the state was contradicted by the practice of socialist revolutions building strong states—called "statism" by its critics. State building was a defense mechanism against the surrounding capitalist world system, but it also created tension between the other socialist states scattered in the world-system, rather than creating a community free of tensions.

Nationalism played a decisive role in the dissolution of the "socialist camp." In 1948, there was a split between the Soviet Union and Yugoslavia. In interviews given shortly before his death in 1980, Tito acknowledged that what provoked the split with Stalin's Soviet Union in 1948 was the national question. The opposition of Yugoslav socialist self-management to Soviet state planning had merely served to justify Belgrade's defiant stance.[8]

In the 1960s, a split between the Soviet Union and China culminated in a bloody incident on the Sino-Soviet border in 1969. In the beginning of the 1970s, Mao designated the Soviet Union as "the most dangerous imperialist power" in the world-system.

In 1989, when Deng met Gorbachev in Beijing, he explained that the reason for the split was the attitude adopted by the Soviet Union:

> When victory in the Second World War was in sight, the United States, Britain, and the Soviet Union signed in Yalta a secret agreement dividing up spheres of influence among them, greatly to the detriment of China's interests...As soon as the [People's Republic of China] was founded...the threat

---

8   Losurdo. *Class Struggle*. p. 242.

came from the United States. Glaring examples were the Korean War and then the Vietnam War...The Soviet Union supplied us with arms but asked us to pay for them, albeit at half price. In the following years Sino-Soviet relations deteriorated, and China was beset with economic difficulties...In the 1960s the Soviet Union strengthened its military presence all along the borders between China and the Soviet Union and Mongolia...In 1963 I led a delegation to Moscow. The negotiations broke down...I don't mean it was because of the ideological disputes; we no longer think that everything we said at that time was right. The basic problem was that the Chinese were not treated as equals and felt humiliated.[9]

In 1989, it was too late to turn the page for the Soviet Union.[10] Three years later, Fidel Castro, a firm supporter of internationalism all his life, concluded that: "We, socialists, made a mistake in underestimating the strength of nationalism."[11]

In *The State and Revolution,* written a few months before the October Revolution, Lenin still believed that the withering away of the state was possible. However, in "Better Fewer, but Better," written in 1923, he moved away from the language of withering and instead "insisted" on the need to "improve our state apparatus...create a republic that is really worthy of the name of Soviet and socialist...[a task requiring] many, many years."[12]

This practice was in contradiction with the ideals of socialism, but accorded with realistic needs. The first theoretical rethinking of the passage from capitalism to socialism emerged here, the need for a transitory mode of production governed by a transitory state, a process that would go on for many years.[13]

Internationalism and Nationalism

The October Revolution was assumed by the Bolsheviks to be the first step of the world revolution to follow. In concluding the First Congress

---

9   Xiaoping, Deng. "Let Us Put the Past Behind Us and Open Up a New Era, 1989." *Selected Works: Vol. 3.* Foreign Languages Press, 1992. pp. 286–87.

10   Losurdo. *Class Struggle.* p. 242.

11   Schlesinger, Arthur Jr. "Four Days with Fidel: A Havana Diary." *New York Review of Books.* March 26, 1992. p. 25.

12   Lenin. "Better Fewer, But Better." pp. 487–502.

13   Losurdo. *Class Struggle.*

of the Communist International, Lenin optimistically declared: "the victory of the proletarian revolution on a world scale is assured. The founding of an international Soviet republic is on the way."[14]

However, his prediction did not materialize; the relationship between nationalism and internationalism is complicated. In 1848, Marx and Engels asserted in the Communist Manifesto that, "The working men have no country." Yet, at the same time, Marx, Engels, and the International Working Men's Association supported national struggles of oppressed peoples as part of the struggle for socialism. Marx emphasized that it was possible, as in the case of Ireland, for the "social question" to take the form of the "national question." The struggle against national oppression can be a form of class struggle. On the relationship between national and international struggle, Engels remarked in 1882:

> Generally speaking, an international movement of the proletariat is possible only as between independent nations...The International...had first to learn from events, and must still do so daily, that international co-operation is possible only among equals.[15]

Engels repeated this position in 1893:

> Without restoring autonomy and unity to each nation, it will be impossible to achieve either the international union of the proletariat, or the peaceful and intelligent cooperation of these nations toward common aims.[16]

In December 1919, Lenin stressed in an open letter to the workers and peasants of Ukraine that:

> Capital is an international force. To vanquish it, an international workers' alliance is needed. We are opposed to national enmity and discord, to national exclusiveness. We are internationalists. We stand for the close union and the complete amalgamation of the workers and peasants of all nations in a single world Soviet republic...the working people must not forget that capitalism has divided nations into a small number of oppressors, Great-Power (imperialist), sovereign and privileged nations and an overwhelming majority of oppressed, dependent and semi-dependent, non-sovereign nations. The war of 1914-18 still further accentuated this division and as a result aggravated

---

14   Lenin. "First Congress of the Communist International." *Collected Works: Vol. 28.* pp. 476–77.

15   Engels. "Letter to Kautsky, 7 February 1882." Marx and Engels. *Collected Works: Vol. 46.* pp. 191–92.

16   Engels. "Preface to the Italian Edition (1893) of the Manifesto of the Communist Party." Marx and Engels. *Collected Works: Vol. 27.* p. 366.

> rancor and hatred...We want a voluntary union of nations—a union which precludes any coercion of one nation by another—a union founded on complete confidence, on a clear recognition of brotherly unity, on absolutely voluntary consent...
>
> We must, therefore, strive persistently for the unity of nations and ruthlessly suppress everything that tends to divide them, and in doing so we must be very cautious and patient, and make concessions to the survivors of national distrust...And what the bourgeoisie of all countries...try most of all to accomplish is to disunite the workers of different nationalities, to evoke distrust, and to disrupt a close international alliance of the workers. Whenever the bourgeoisie succeeds in this the cause of the workers is lost.[17]

The specific reason for the letter was a conflict between the communist parties of Russia and Ukraine on whether Ukraine should be an independent state, or it should pursue an amalgamation of Ukraine with Russia. Lenin continued his letter to the Ukrainian Communist Party with the words:

> The Communists of Russia and the Ukraine must therefore by patient, persistent, stubborn and concerted effort foil the nationalist machinations of the bourgeoisie and vanquish nationalist prejudices of every kind and set the working people of the world an example of a really solid alliance of the workers and peasants of different nations in the fight for Soviet power, for the overthrow of the yoke of the landowners and capitalists, and for a world federal Soviet republic.[18]

The change from headquarters of world revolution to socialism in one country a few years later signaled the passage from internationalism to nationalism in Soviet policy. When Nazi-Germany invaded the Soviet Union in 1941, Ukrainian nationalists took the opportunity to form a Ukrainian state, which, as stated in the text "Act of Proclamation of Ukrainian Statehood":

> ...will work closely with the National-Socialist Greater Germany, under the leadership of its leader Adolf Hitler, which is forming a new order in Europe and the world.[19]

However Russian patriotism defeated Hitler's plan to colonize and

---

17   Lenin. "Letter to the Workers and Peasants of the Ukraine: Apropos of the Victories over Denikin, 28 December 1919." *Collected Works: Vol. 30*. pp. 293–97.

18   *Ibid*. p. 297.

19   Hunczak, Taras. In Torke, Hans-Joachim and Himka, John-Paul. *German-Ukrainian Relations in Historical Perspective*. University of Alberta, 1994. p. 178.

enslave the peoples of Eastern Europe and the Soviet Union. Losurdo concludes:

> To summarize, the revolutionary class struggle which...should have inaugurated the withering away of state and nation, actually witnessed the emergence of an "aristocracy of statesmen" and a patriotism that saved state and nation from a horrific catastrophe.[20]

It seems that a future socialist world will consist of an assembly of nations developing socialism with different national characteristics, and moving from this stage towards "a single world Soviet republic" envisioned by Lenin. It has become a condition of an advanced socialism, in a world system with so many states in possession of an arsenal of nuclear weapons which can destroy the world, and inequality, ecological and climate problems that need a global solution.

Capitalist Methods in Socialist Development

Another violation of socialist ideals by "actually existing socialism" is the use of capitalist methods in the development of the productive forces, from the NEP to Dengism. The revolutionary movements often entrusted their economic development to proletarian sacrifice and heroic "Stakhanovism" as a driver for economic development, but this was transient. Bertolt Brecht said, in his play *Galileo*: "Blessed are the people that need no heroes."[21] Heroics are required for the transition from a state of emergency to some kind of normality, and thus should only be used to the extent that they render themselves superfluous.

A market economy has, to a certain extent, existed in all attempts to build socialism. Again, if one cringes at this statement, it illustrates a discrepancy between ideals and reality. According to the theory of socialism, market forces belong to capitalism, and planning belongs to socialism. But in reality, as socialism arose in the semi-feudal peripheries with less developed capitalism, in order to revive the productive apparatus of such a country, the market had to be expanded. Market forces can be used as a dynamic factor in certain sectors, such as food production and consumer products, but must be ensconced within a planned economy,

---

20   Losurdo. *Class Struggle*. p. 234.
21   Brecht, Bertolt. "The Life of Galileo." *Collected Plays: 5*. Trans. Willett, John. Methuen, 1980. Scene 12.

where the strategic basic industry is governed by and for workers.

The communist movement did not manage to develop an understanding which might bridge the ideals of socialism of the early nineteenth century with the practical attempts to construct socialism in the twentieth century. The disappointments of the result of "actually existing socialism," and the inability to remold and even erase the state, nation, religion, market, inequality, and so forth, made a decisive contribution to the general crises of socialism in the past decades. In the intensive and dramatic struggle for socialism in the twentieth century, the ideals of socialism, according to Losurdo:

> ...acts like a kind of drug, burdening the struggle for social change with excessive expectations. Intoxication gave way to exhaustion. And on the eve of its collapse, the condition of real socialism in Eastern Europe was one of exhaustion.[22]

One of the tasks today is to draw conclusions from the experience of socialist construction in the past and develop it into a theory and strategy for the transition to socialism in this century. It is not a revival or rejection of the old socialist ideals, but an attempt to turn them into practice. This requires specifying that the socialist mode of production is not an ideal utopia—it is a realistic solution to the problems of capitalism. The task is to develop a praxis of societal management. How do we produce, divide, and consume the social product to solve global inequality and ecological problems?

National and International Inequality in Building Socialism

When the hopes of an anti-capitalist revolution in Europe vanished, the Bolsheviks realized that the inequality of nations was a problem as profound as the inequality of classes. In building socialism, they had to deal with both problems. As a nation on the periphery, the Soviet Union was far behind the more advanced countries. Lenin emphasized:

> You must remember that our Soviet land is impoverished after many years of trial and suffering and has no socialist France or socialist England as neighbors which could help us with their highly developed technology and their highly developed industry. Bear that in mind! We must remember that at present all their highly developed technology and their highly developed in-

---

22 Losurdo. *Class Struggle*. pp. 242–43.

dustry belong to the capitalists, who are fighting us. We must remember that we must either strain every nerve in everyday effort, or we shall inevitably go under. Owing to the present circumstances the whole world is developing faster than we are. While developing, the capitalist world is directing all its forces against us. That is how the matter stands!...We must see to it that everyone who works devotes himself to strengthening the workers' and peasants' state. Only then shall we be able to create large-scale industry.[23]

Lenin encapsulated the aims of the October Revolution as "Electrification [Plus the] Soviets."[24] The first task was to develop the productive forces and end national inequality and the second task was the ability to defend the revolution against attacks from the West. The latter protects the revolution from sliding back into capitalism.

The problem of overlapping national and international inequality arose regularly in the periphery. In the 1960s, Che Guevara observed:

> Ever since monopoly capital took over the world, it has kept the greater part of humanity in poverty, dividing all the profits among the most powerful countries. The standard of living in those countries is based on the extreme poverty of our countries...In the economic field we must conquer the road to development with the most advanced technology possible...We have to make the great technological leap forward that will reduce the current gap between the more developed countries and ourselves. Technology must be applied to the large factories and also to a properly developed agriculture...
>
> Above all, its foundation must be technological and ideological education, with a sufficient mass base and strength to sustain the research institutes and organizations that have to be created in each country, as well as the men and women who will use the existing technology and be capable of adapting themselves to the newly mastered technology...
>
> A great technological leap is required to reduce the difference that exists today between our countries and the more developed ones...We must create a genuine international division of labour, based not on the history of what has been done so far, but on the future history of what should be done.[25]

The struggles against national and international inequality are in-

---

23   Lenin. "The New Economic Policy and the Task of the Political Education Departments Report to the Second All-Russia Congress of Political Educations Departments, 17 October 1922." *Collected Works: Vol. 33*. p. 72.

24   Lenin. "The Task of the Youth Leagues." *Collected Works: Vol. 31*. p. 289.

25   Guevara, Che. "At the Afro–Asian Conference in Algeria, 24 February 1965." *The Che Reader*. Ocean Press, 2005. https://www.marxists.org/archive/guevara/1965/02/24.htm

terlinked; in the case of the Soviet Union 1920, "electrification" would jolt the countryside out of isolation from the cities. Technological and scientific development would reduce the disparity in both the economic and military balance of power. To acquire tech, it was necessary to attract foreign capital. Albeit unavoidable, the acquisition of the most advanced technology involved significant costs. The dilemma was the same in China fifty years later.

A Revolution of the West or the East?

The notion that the October Revolution was premature due to a lack of capitalist and working class development is a purely Eurocentric stance, hence why revolutionaries in the periphery had a different perspective than Western European socialists. Revolutionaries on the periphery analyzed the October Revolution through the lens of nationality and self-determination, factors that were linked with the progression of the "awakening of Asia" and the anticolonial struggle.

Lenin's understanding of revolution included the struggle between capital and the proletariat as well as the perspective of national inequality created by imperialism. The revolution in Russia occurred because it was the weakest link in an imperialist chain, fractured by internecine struggle during the First World War. Russian revolutionaries invoked the "Eastern Question," a question centered on the struggle of oppressed peoples against imperialism. The lineage of Asian revolutions is almost invisible in Western left discourse. The Russian Revolution is seen as derivative of the European revolutionary tradition. As far as the subjective forces, this is correct; Lenin and the leading Bolsheviks were linked to the European Marxist tradition. Yet, if we look at the objective conditions, the October Revolution could be placed within the ranks of an "awakening Asia." Could we not trace some trajectories from the 1907 Iranian Revolution, the 1909 Turkish Revolution, and, above all, the 1911 Chinese Revolution?[26]

The Bolsheviks themselves sought to use their Revolution as an example in the East. On January 25, 1918, the Third All-Russia Congress of Soviets announced the "Declaration of Rights of the Working and Ex-

---

26 Hui. "The Prophecy and Crisis of October." pp. 669–706.

ploited People," drafted by Lenin, Stalin, and Bukharin, in which they proclaimed the right to self-determination for the oppressed people in the colonies and semi-colonies and announced a "complete break with the barbarous policy of bourgeois civilization."[27] In this way, the Bolsheviks had placed oppressed peoples in the subjectivity of "revolutionary classes." The revolutions of the twentieth century were thus not only revolutions of the idealized (Eurocentric) industrialized working classes, but also included oppressed peoples as revolutionary subjects, much to the chagrin of the Western Left. The reconfiguring of revolutionary classes matched the concrete conditions of the imperialist epoch and had great importance for the development of communism in China and in the Third World in general.[28]

COMINTERN

The possibility of a successful transition towards socialism will be limited if it only takes place in one country. There has never been one socialist country at any point in history. Not in the Soviet Union nor China or elsewhere. A transfer from capitalism to socialism has to involve the majority of states in the world system, hence the need for internationalism in the socialist movement. Despite the call "Proletarians of all countries, unite!" in *The Communist Manifesto*, nationalism has had a strong grip on the socialist movement. The Second International was split between the social democratic emphasis on citizenship and the nation-state as the framework for developing socialism, while the communist faction insisted on class struggle and the world revolution as a condition for the development of socialism.

Following the foundation of the COMINTERN in 1919, class struggle was framed as a binary between a unified global proletariat and capital. The statutes approved by the Second Congress of the COMINTERN on August 4, 1920 state that:

> The emancipation of the workers is not a local, nor a national, but an international problem...the Communist International must, in fact and in deed, be a single communist party of the entire world. The parties working in the

---

27   Lenin. "Declaration of Rights of the Toiling and Exploited People." *Collected Works: Vol. 26*. p. 424.
28   Hui. "The Prophecy and Crisis of October." pp. 669–706.

various countries are but its separate sections.[29]

The Fifth Congress in 1924, now led by Stalin, called for the creation of a homogenous Bolshevik world party:

> The world party of Leninism must be strongly fused, not by mechanical discipline, but by unity of will and action...Every party must give its best forces to the international leadership. It must be brought home to the broadest masses that in the present epoch serious economic and political battles of the working class can be won only if they are led from one centre and on an international scale.[30]

But the civil war in China in the 1930s, and fascism in Europe, revealed that conflicts could assume the most diverse configurations with multiple contradictions involving different class alliances and national struggles. The "pure" proletariat-capitalist class struggle rarely existed.[31] Later, in the 1930s, the Soviet Union itself changed its emphasis on the world revolution to the nationalist "socialism in one country."

The organizational model of the COMINTERN proved inadequate to accommodate this complexity of struggles and was finally dissolved by Stalin in 1943 to avoid antagonizing his capitalist allies during World War II.

Since then, we have lacked effective international coordination of the struggle for socialism; not necessarily the world communist party envisioned in 1919, but even coordination of struggle on the national level in a global perspective. The consequence of the lack of an International has been significant. The cooperation between the different national liberation movements and the newly independent states could have been more effective. On top of this, the split between the Soviet Union and China made it much easier for the U.S. to terminate the revolutionary wave during "the long sixties."

A more recent attempt to develop transnational cooperation between socialist movements has been the World Social Forum. The enthusiasm was great during the first meeting in 2001; however, the "open space" method in meetings, and its horizontal structure, made it impos-

---

29   Degras, Jane. *The Communist International, 1919–1943: Documents. Volume 1: 1919–1922.* Oxford University Press, 1955. pp. 163–64.

30   *Ibid.* pp. 154, 199.

31   Losurdo. *Class Struggle.* p. 170.

sible to move from talking to action. "A little less conversation, a little more action, please."[32]

The experience of former Internationals is that nationalism has been a "Trojan horse" that has divided the global proletariat. To avoid this, it is important to emphasize that movements on the national level must take a global perspective on their struggles. Production is organized in globally integrated chains. Commodities are traded on a highly integrated world market. The global contradictions influence the outcome of national struggles. Our struggles must contribute to pushing the principal contradiction in a direction that favors the transformation towards socialism.

But how should such an international struggle be coordinated today? The COMINTERN was established by rather uniform communist parties, with the backing of the first socialist state, and with the esteem of Lenin. The situation today is quite different. The socialist and communist movements are fragmented and divided into a multitude of political lines and issues. A new International cannot be constructed as a master plan from above as in 1919. It must be built from below. It requires that each organization and movement have the global perspective prioritized in their strategy, developing transnational networks of action. In that way, it is possible to establish transnational organizations of workers in global production chains, peasant movements, indigenous/oppressed people, anti-imperialists, climate movements, and so on. These sub-internationals could then be coordinated into more holistic Internationals, again focusing on unified action. With this common global perspective in mind, this process can be initiated here and now—by any organization, from different locations and issues—merging into more formalized forms of coordination and institutions.

THE NATIONAL LIBERATION STRUGGLE DURING THE LONG 1960S

From around 1965 to 1975, the contradiction between U.S. imperialism and the anti-imperialist movements—from Vietnam to Nicaragua—was the principal contradiction in the world. Some of the movements were victorious, establishing pro-socialist states. However, the newly indepen-

---

32 This is a reference to lyrics in an Elvis Presley song released in 1968.

dent Third World had economies that had been adapted to imperialist needs during colonization. Economic liberation proved much more difficult than attaining political independence.

The national liberation struggles were not able to unite in practical, coordinated internationalism. A common front against the imperialist system, which would have been necessary to topple it, was never established.

By the mid-1970s, despite the victories in Vietnam and the Portuguese African colonies, anti-imperialism began to wane, and neoliberal globalization was on its way. An example of this shift is the change in policy of the African National Congress (ANC) in South Africa. From the 1960s to the late 1980s, the ANC was committed to socialism. It had close connections to the South African Communist Party and the Soviet Union. Accordingly, the ANC was labeled as a communist terror organization by the West. However, when Nelson Mandela was elected president in 1994 and the ANC became the ruling party in South Africa, socialism was gone. The ANC did not change the class character of the state; they were subsumed by neoliberalism. However, this was contrary to the Chinese strategy of using neoliberalism for their own purpose to the benefit of the proletariat. Mandela changed from prisoner to president, and the policy of the ANC changed from socialist to neoliberal capitalism. No wonder Bill Clinton and other Western leaders celebrated the inauguration of Mandela. This is not a "know it all" critique; it is simply an assessment of how strong neoliberal globalization and U.S. hegemony were at the time. Even South Africa, with developed productive forces and rich natural resources, would have struggled to pursue socialist transformation in the 1990s; Mozambique, Angola, Guinea-Bissau, and Zimbabwe have also not had much success.

However, it was not that the ANC, FRELIMO, MPLA, PAIGC, and ZANU made poor choices which prevented them from building socialism. Rather, it was the world-system that limited their choices on the path toward independence at the time.

CHINA—HOW TO BUILD SOCIALISM?

A lesson from the Chinese experience is that you cannot copy revolutions from one context to another. On the advice from the COMINTERN, the Chinese communists prioritized mobilizing the urban proletariat and allied with the bourgeois nationalist Kuomintang. This strategy ended in disaster in Shanghai in 1927. Instead, following Lenin's demand for "a concrete analysis of a concrete situation," the Communist Party relied on the peasants and lumpenproletariat to lead the revolution. Based on their praxis and specific analysis, the Communist Party developed its military strategy "the people's protracted war" and guerilla tactics. Marxism, as the praxis of change, is not encapsulated in its application in Russia, China, or any other country, movement, or individual. The praxis of Marxism is conditioned and limited by the circumstances in which it works. Marxism embodies all the analysis, praxis, and lessons learned in the course of its development. Marxism is a living and constantly developing synthesis of theory and praxis.

The Chinese communists had a different perception of the post-revolutionary period than the Soviets. They have not at any point, as Stalin did in 1936, declared that socialist construction has been completed. In the perception of the Communist Party of China, the transformation to socialism is a much longer process in which the class struggle continues. It requires several transformations of the superstructure. The Chinese communists have mapped their own winding road towards "socialism with Chinese characteristics."

In the same way, as a precondition for success, other attempts to build socialism have to analyze the specific national conditions during the transition process; for example, in Latin America, the development of socialism has Cuban, Venezuelan, or Chiapan characteristics. Similarly, we might see the development of socialism with special Palestinian or South African characteristics, and so on.

Another lesson from the Chinese experience is the handling of the contradiction between the development of the productive forces and the development of a socialist mode of production. To move ahead, there is a need to develop the productive forces beyond the need to defeat poverty. At the same time, there is also the need to change the values and norms of the past into socialist values of community and solidarity, both on the individual level and in institutions of government.

Humans produce and consume differently under particular social relations, which necessarily affects their consciousness. Under capitalist relations of production, workers are fragmented, degraded, and alienated. The capitalist market creates a selfish and competitive mentality. In the socialist mode of production, it is different. Marx writes in *Capital*:

> When numerous workers work together side by side in accordance with a plan, whether in the same process, or in different but connected processes, this form of labour is called co-operation...Not only do we have here an increase in the productive power of the individual, by means of co-operation, but the creation of a new productive power, which is intrinsically a collective one...when the worker co-operates in a planned way with others, he strips off the fetters of his individuality, and develops the capabilities of his species.[33]

There is an interregnum between capitalism and socialism, in which elements of the old interact, and collide, with the new. As Marx describes:

> ...a communist society, not as it has developed on its own foundations, but, on the contrary, just as it emerges from capitalist society; which is thus in every respect, economically, morally, and intellectually, still stamped with the birthmarks of the old society from whose womb it emerges.[34]

Neither communist nor capitalist elements exist in pure form. Cuba has, much like China, been caught between capitalism and socialism, in what Castro has called "the struggle to the death between the Future and the Past."[35] The future must subordinate the elements inherited from the past, but the new system is inevitably defective as it emerges from capitalism. It is no mystery why "actually existing socialism" has difficulties in the development required to move to socialism for real.[36] For Che Guevara, the central need was to build the "future":

> We understand that the capitalist old categories are retained for a time and that the length of this period cannot be predetermined, but the characteristics of the period of transition are those of a society that is throwing off its

---

33   Marx, Karl. *Capital: Volume I.* https://www.marxists.org/archive/marx/works/1867-c1/ch13.htm

34   Marx. "Critique of the Gotha Programme." Marx and Engels. *Selected Works: Vol. 3.* pp. 13–30.

35   Castro, Fidel. "Speech at the Second Anniversary of the Cuban Revolution." 1961. http://lanic.utexas.edu/project/castro/db/1961/19610105.html

36   Lebowitz, Michael. "The Struggle between the Future and the Past: Where is Cuba Going?" *Monthly Review Online.* July 3, 2022. https://mronline.org/2022/07/03/the-struggle-between-the-future-and-the-past-where-is-cuba-going/

bonds in order to move quickly into the new stage.[37]

To do this, Che warned against relying solely on material incentives:

> ...the temptation is very great to follow the beaten track of material interest as the lever with which to accelerate development...We do not deny the objective need for material incentives, although we are reluctant to use them as the main lever...the tendency should be, in our opinion, to eliminate as fast as possible the old categories...or, better, to eliminate the conditions for their existence...The pipe dream that socialism can be achieved with the help of the dull instruments left to us by capitalism (the commodity as the economic cell, profitability, individual material interest as a lever, etc.) can lead into a blind alley. And you wind up there after having traveled a long distance with many crossroads, and it is hard to figure out just where you took the wrong turn.[38]

That is why Che stressed that:

> To construct communism the new man has to be created as well as the material base. At times of extreme danger, it is easy to promote moral incentives; to maintain their force, it is necessary to develop a consciousness whereby new values are acquired and society as a whole is transformed into one enormous school.[39]

Che, like Mao, believed that voluntary labor for the common good was part of this process, to create community, aversion to inequity, and international solidarity.

THE NEED TO WALK ON TWO LEGS

According to Che, socialist consciousness is built through practice, by creating space for collective work and the spread of the commons in society. When relying solely upon material incentives, the "past" capitalist values tend to crowd out the "future." The material interest as an economic lever is "the Trojan horse of socialism,"[40] reinforcing the alienation and self-orientation inherited from capitalism. Che stressed that the individual learns to transform work from a disagreeable human necessity into a moral necessity for the common good. Michael Lebowitz com-

---

37   Yaffe, Helen. In Lebowitz. "The Struggle between the Future and the Past."
38   Tablada, Carlos. In Lebowitz. "The Struggle between the Future and the Past."
39   Guevara, Che. In Barrio, Hilda and Jenkins, Gareth. *The Che Handbook*. MQ Publications, 2003. p. 221.
40   Lebowitz. "The Struggle between the Future and the Past."

mented on Che's position:

> But the important thing was balance—the necessity to walk on two legs. Changing consciousness, he insisted, was essential as part of the dual aspect of the construction of socialism. Building socialism is neither a matter of work alone nor of consciousness alone. It combines work and consciousness—expanding the production of material goods through work and developing consciousness.[41]

In developing socialism, you should not rely exclusively upon material incentives, but stress the idea of socialism in workplaces, communities, and society as a whole to emphasize a balance between the simultaneous developments of productive forces and the creation of socialist human beings. Che's legacy is the recognition that if the "future" is to prevail, it is essential to build it now by creating socialist consciousness.

In the struggle between the "future" and the "past" lie two methods of developing socialism. The first is the updating of the economic model, sometimes by using capitalist instruments to create the necessary productive forces to sustain a socialist society. The other is to use moral incentives and to develop a mode of production which enhances the development of socialist attitudes.

Cuba has tried to uphold a balance between the two methods. Being a small country in a hostile world, they have achieved remarkable results because they have created a socialist morale. Cuba has survived attacks and blockades from the U.S. and the collapse of the Soviet Union. Not only that, but Cuba has been the prime example of internationalism since 1959.

In China, we have seen a zig-zag course between the two methods, navigating in a sea of changing contradictions. In the era of Mao, the economy was developed using moral incentives, in the form of voluntary work and political campaigns. In the Great Leap Forward and the Cultural Revolution, Mao appealed to the masses to develop socialism through radical practices. However, as Che foresaw, no one can call upon the masses to sacrifice themselves all the time. This method must remain the exception and never become the rule. Mao's radical mobilization and campaigns were unsustainable in the long term.

During Deng's "opening up," "market-socialism" was introduced,

---

41 *Ibid.*

leading to the rapid development of the productive forces using elements from capitalism and the encouragement of individual material incentives. However, Dengism also lost sight of socialist values and created inequality, corruption, individualism, and degradation of solidarity.

In the history of the Communist Party of China, there has been struggle and unity between the two different approaches to the development of socialism. Depending on the Chinese and global contradictions at hand, Mao himself changed between the two methods. After nearly 40 years of Dengism, the Communist Party under Xi has to rectify the side effects of "opening up" to the world market. China is once again sliding to the left, trying to balance the need to develop the productive forces with the development of socialist values in society.

Even though Mao underlined that socialism's final victory still lies several generations ahead, and that several revolutions must take place in the superstructure, the fact is that China must remain a part of the world economy, which is still dominated by capitalism. China had to go through its own form of state capitalism to create its large-scale, high-tech industry. A socialist mode of production cannot use outdated, underdeveloped technology, but must use the most advanced technology, because it can produce more goods of sustainable, higher quality, with less labor power.[42] Robot industries are better than assembly line factories. Windmills and solar energy are better than fossil energy-fueled power plants.

If China had isolated itself to save Mao's state socialist system, it could not have developed the productive forces at the necessary speed, and it would have run the risk of being overrun, both economically and politically. In order to stay in power, the Communist Party chose to arrange production along a more capitalist pattern. Gradually, capitalist values infected the Chinese population and the Communist Party itself.

Are the Chinese leaders to be blamed for this? No, it is not their fault that the proletarian revolution has not yet taken place in the advanced countries. But one can, and one ought to, blame the Communist Party for not describing the situation with the same ruthless honesty as Lenin did about the NEP in his day. The truth is that the encounter with neoliberalism has strengthened capitalist values and norms, and a mobiliza-

---

42   Emmanuel. *Appropriate or Underdeveloped Technology?*

tion of the workers and peasants is needed to change direction. But the truth is that China, through a revolution, fundamentally altered life for one of the most poverty-stricken peoples in this world, and in so doing has enriched our knowledge about developing socialism. The Chinese and Russian Revolutions are steps in the development toward world socialism. In the words of Lenin:

> ...that only by a series of attempts—each of which, taken by itself, will be one-sided and will suffer from certain inconsistencies—will complete socialism be created by the revolutionary co-operation of the proletarians of all countries.[43]

The Soviet Union and China are both attempts of this kind, made possible by history's devious road of development in this century. Without the Soviet Union, there may not have been a revolution in China. Without learning from the negative experiences in the Soviet Union, there would be no Cultural Revolution. And without learning the positive and negative lessons from Deng, there can be no future revolution. The different revolutions changed the nature of the entire world system. Capitalism today is a product of these changes; like in a game of chess, it has reacted strategically to the moves of its opponent.

CLASS STRUGGLE IN THE TRANSITIONAL STATE

A central thesis in the Chinese perception of the development of socialism is that class struggle continues in the post-revolutionary society. It is a long process that might continue for several revolutions. This was also in contrast to the perception in the Soviet Union, which announced that class struggle was over, and that socialism was implemented in 1936.

However, if China is heading towards socialism, why is the Communist Party not at the forefront of the class struggle, on the side of the workers against national and transnational capital? Why does the Communist Party allow companies like Foxconn to exploit Chinese workers in the most ruthless way? Why does the Party allow real estate speculation on such a large scale to make housing expensive for people, and so on? To explore such questions, we must look at the functioning of the *transitional state*.

---

43   Lenin. "The Tax in Kind."

What is the Transitional State?

The capitalist mode of production accumulates on a global scale. However, its political governance is made through the system of competing nation-states in the world system. As long as the capitalist mode of production is vital, and developing the productive forces, the capitalist states will dominate the world system. As Marx said:

> No social order is ever destroyed before all the productive forces for which it is sufficient have been developed, and new superior relations of production never replace older ones before the material conditions for their existence have matured within the framework of the old society.[44]

Hence states, seeking to develop socialism within this capitalist dominated world-system, can only establish a transitional mode of production, to develop the preconditions to move towards socialism. To facilitate this, and to survive as a state in the world system, they had to establish a corresponding transitional state, in which the power of state rests in the hands of the proletariat.

A ruling class–whether it is the capitalists or the proletariat–needs state power to uphold its mode of production and ease class conflict, so that society does not disintegrate into conflicting chaos. The state is the product and manifestation of class contradictions.

In the struggle for state power, the communist party represents the interests of the proletariat. However, if this includes a struggle against imperialism, communists can enter alliances with political forces representing other classes, such as the petit bourgeoisie and the national bourgeoisie, as we have seen in the Chinese revolution.

When achieving state power, Communist Parties have usually formed so called "party-states," meaning that the respective Communist Party forms governments and rules state institutions. In the current case of the People's Republic of China (PRC), Xi Jinping is General Secretary of the Communist Party and also president of the PRC. The difference is not pro forma but rather reveals two different organizations in terms of who they represent, their working-methods, goals, and discourse. The Communist Party represents the proletariat, and its goal is socialism on the national and world level. The party-state and its government repre-

---

44   Marx, Karl. *A Contribution to the Critique of Political Economy.*

sent the people—all classes, including the national capitalists and the interests of resident transnational capital. The tasks of the state institutions are national development, stability, and harmony. The state also takes care of foreign economic and political relations. The task is again to enhance national development and the security of the transitional state in the world system. The discourse is not class struggle and world revolution, but mutual benefit and respect.

On the one hand, the party-state has the political, economic and institutional instruments to ensure that the contradictions between the proletariat and the bourgeoisie do not spin out of control, risking state power and the development of the productive forces. On the other hand, the Communist Party must lead the proletarian class struggle, in order to ensure that development advances in the direction of socialism. To a certain extent, these tasks are reflected in the two organizational layers. Sometimes the distance between the layers is greater and sometimes they move towards each other—sometimes even blending together, depending on the national and global contradictions.

The History of Governance in China

For the transitional states, the survival within a capitalist dominated world-system has historically been a priority. Their strategy has changed between confrontation to more or less peaceful coexistence and adaptation to capitalism.

The strategy, practice, and discourse of the two layers—party and state institutions—have been shaped by the interaction between the changing principal contradiction in the world-system and the internal national contradiction. Hence, the transitional states have taken different forms in their interaction with capitalism in the history of the world-system. The Soviet Union fluctuated between confrontation, alliance, attempted peaceful coexistence, and cooperation, leading to dissolution. The Democratic People's Republic of Korea developed a form of defensive isolation after the Korean War. The Cuban state has also been pressed into a defensive, isolated national position, but at the same time chose an offensive anti-imperialist foreign policy. Many post-revolutionary party-states have given in to the economic, political and military pressure from the surrounding capitalist world-system, sliding back into a capitalist mode of production and a bourgeois state.

Here, let us focus on how national and international class struggle has been handled by the Chinese transitional state. In the long revolutionary process from 1921 to 1949, class analysis and class struggle against feudalism, the national bourgeoisie represented by the Kuomintang, and international capitalism, in the form of Western and Japanese imperialism, was the central theory and praxis of the Communist Party.

However, when the Communist Party declared the People's Republic of China in 1949 and established the party-state, Mao did not only speak as the chairman of a revolutionary party, but also as the leader of a very poor country, torn apart by decades of war, in a world-system dominated by capitalism with the US as the new hegemonic power. The Communist Party had to make the difficult transition from "breaking" to "making."

Going from revolutionary struggle to building socialism, class contradiction had to be handled differently. China needed stability, unity, and economic development to improve the condition for the masses. Hence the policy of "New Democracy" built on four social classes, namely the peasantry, proletariat, petit bourgeoisie and national bourgeoisie. In foreign policy, China kept a revolutionary profile, more or less forced by the imperialist isolation of the country, for example in the military confrontation with the US in the Korean War.

As the Soviet-Chinese "Treaty of Friendship" signed in 1950 began to work, the Chinese government became less dependent on the national capitalists, leading Mao to launch political campaigns, including the "anti-Rightist Campaign" (1957–1959), under the headline of "the continuing class struggle under socialism." As the split between the Soviet Union and China evolved up through the sixties, Mao mobilized the grassroots to struggle against "capitalist roaders" within the Communist Party, which led to the Cultural Revolution.

With slogans like *"It's Right to Rebel! Making Revolution is No Crime! Bombard the Headquarters!"* Mao, in the name of class struggle, mobilized against any authority within the party or state institutions, who was deemed to be taking "the capitalist road." For Mao the Cultural Revolution was a struggle to maintain the proletariat at the helm of state power, against a sneaking capitalist counterrevolution.

It was a much-needed showdown with bureaucracy, expert mentality, and hierarchy generated by the years of Soviet influence, but it did also generate a severe split in the Communist Party, the breakdown of state institutions, dysfunctional economic development, and increased tensions with the surrounding capitalist system. However, was it a class struggle between capital and the proletariat?

The capitalists in China in the late sixties were a small minority, and not organized as a class in the party or in state institutions. What was labeled "capitalist roaders" were a faction in the Communist Party, which wanted to use market forces and other capitalist enticements to "open up" China towards the world market in order to speed up development of the productive forces.

During the Cultural Revolution, contradictions that existed within the people and within the Communist Party were handled as if they were antagonistic class contradictions, between proletariat and capital. However, in reality there were two different strategies within the Communist Party on how to handle the contradiction between dominating global capitalism and a transitional state, such as China.

This is not to say that that the difference between the strategies were not that important, but the shift from Mao's mobilization of the people by reference to the socialist moral, to the use of material enticements and "opening up," also reflect the change in the surrounding world-system, from the revolutionary spirit of the "long sixties" to capital's counter-offensive in the form of neoliberal globalization. An indication of the non-antagonistic character between the two lines within the Communist Party is that it was Mao himself who ended the Cultural Revolution and initiated contact with the U.S. in 1971.

After Mao's death in September 1976, Deng Xiaoping replaced Mao's class struggle theory with an economic-oriented pragmatism. The opening towards transnational capital's globalization, initiated in 1978, made transformations in the structure of property relations. Domestic and foreign private owned relations of production expanded. As existence determines consciousness, it had consequences in terms of the values and norms in Chinese society. It was no longer "serve the people"; self-interest and a competition mentality increased, as well as the pursuit of material interests. The new bourgeois and petty-bourgeois classes—the ones who "got rich first"—together with the ideological and cultural apparatus of the intrusion of transnational capital, generated an ideological trend which was called "bourgeois liberalization." The Chinese economist and former member of the Central Committee (1982-1992) Liu Guoguang–looking back–stated in 2017:

> Bourgeois liberalization occurs not only in the political field, but also in the economic field. Privatization, liberalization, and marketization; opposition to public ownership, government intervention, and opposition to socialism, these are all things that are all related to the economic field. It is not enough to oppose bourgeois liberalization, politically. To prevent bourgeois liberalization in the economic field is to prevent the economic field from deteriorating. If the economic field deteriorates (is privatized, turned into capitalism), the political field will also deteriorate. This is a basic common principle of Marxism.[45]

As capitalist relations of production increased, "bourgeois liberalization" gained force. The conception of class struggle that was in force during the period of the Cultural Revolution was criticized. In 1978, the Communist Party broke with the previous position that class struggle during the development of socialism is the main contradiction and promoted "socialist modernization" as the new line. The official Party line maintained that class struggle still continues to exist, but within certain limits. However, a faction of the Communist Party led by General Secretary Zhao Ziyang, who was in charge of implementing Deng's reform program from 1986, was heavily influenced by neoliberal ideas, claiming that the Marxist concept of class struggle is outdated. Accompanying reforms in the economic sphere, reforms in the political sphere calling for liberal democracy emerged in society and inside the Communist Party, in line with what happened in the Soviet Union during the time of Gorbachev. This trend led to the Tiananmen Square uprising of 1989. After that, Deng Xiaoping realized the danger of the "bourgeois liberalization" stating that:

> It seems that one Cold War has come to an end, but that two others have already begun: one is being waged against all the countries of the South and

---

45 Guoguang, Liu. In Martinez, Gabriel. "Ideological Work in the New Era of Socialism in China." *The International*. https://internationalmagz.com/articles/ideological-work-in-new-era-of-socialism-in-china-part-1

the Third World, and the other against socialism. The Western countries are staging a third world war without firearms. By this I mean that they want to promote the peaceful evolution of socialist countries to capitalism.[46]

It became clear that the Party had to focus more on the ideological front, pointing out that class struggle still exists in China. Jiang Zemin, the new General Secretary (1989-2002), in his speech commemorating the 78th anniversary of the Party's founding in 1991, stated:#Class struggle is no longer the main contradiction in our country, but for a certain period it will continue to exist within a certain limit; moreover, under certain conditions, it may intensify.[47]

It did so in the new factories run by transnational capital in Southern China, in the struggle over privatization of state companies, and because of the introduction of market forces and declining social welfare and security.

Hu Jintao, General Secretary (2002-2012) tried to calm things down by upholding the principle of a "harmonious society" for the development of a socialist China. The central point in this social contract between classes was that the contradiction between the socialist principle of political rule over economy versus the power of the market economy had to be solved in such a way that the dynamics of the market may serve socialism. On one hand, private property of productive forces had to be recognised and protected; on the other hand, the dark sides of capitalism, the damage to the society caused by the "disorderly expansion of capital" had to be tamed, and this was difficult.

China's "opening up" for transnational capital, the outsourcing of industrial production and the accompanying transfer of technology had a positive effect on the development of the productive forces, but as private property increased it had negative effects on social life. The condition of labor in the national and transnational capitalist companies, inequality, the worsening of ecological problems, internal labor migration, the housing problems in the major cities, the general level of stress, and the

---

46   Xiaoping, Deng. "We Must Adhere to Socialism and Prevent Peaceful Evolution Towards Capitalism, 23 November 1989." *Selected Works: Vol. 3.* https://dengxiaopingworks.wordpress.com/2013/03/18/we-must-adhere-to-socialism-and-prevent-peaceful-evolution-towards-capitalism/

47   Zemin, Jiang. In Martinez. "Ideological Work in the New Era of Socialism in China."

competition mentality all worsened.

After the crises of neoliberalism in 2006-7, it became clear that the negative effect of neoliberalism had outweighed the positive effects. The Communist Party began to change course, tackling the negative effects of the intrusion of capitalism. As a result of the new posture, several changes occurred: a shift from an export oriented economy to emphasizing the domestic market, erasing poverty in rural areas, and an insistence that class struggle is still an issue. Xi Jinping's coming to power in 2012 repeated Jiang Zemin's position. In 2014 Xi explains:

> The political position of Marxism is primarily a class position, which implements class analysis. Some people say that this idea no longer corresponds to the present era, which is a mistaken point of view. When we say that the class struggle in our country is not the main contradiction, we are not saying that in our country the class struggle within certain limits no longer exists, or that in the international sphere it doesn't exist either.[48]

The capitalist class is not a politically well-organized force which can challenge the state power of the proletariat, but the expansion of private property and the accompanying mentality, in the form of norms and values in society—the "bourgeois liberalization"—remains a challenge. When Xi talks about ideological "struggles," it is not "class struggle" in the traditional sense. Xi warns against "money worship, hedonism, ultra individualism, and historical nihilism." He states that: "the formation of firm ideals and beliefs is neither achieved overnight nor once and for all but must be constantly tempered and tested in concrete struggle."[49] He says that:

> It will be no easy task like a walk in the park; it will not happen overnight, or through sheer fanfare. We must always keep a long-term perspective, remain mindful of potential risks, maintain strategic focus and determination, and 'attain to the broad and great while addressing the delicate and minute.'[50]

After forty years of "opening up" towards neoliberal globalization it

---

48   Jinping, Xi. In Martinez. "Ideological Work in the New Era of Socialism in China."

49   Jinping, Xi. Resolution of the CPC Central Committee on the Major Achievements and Historical Experience of the Party over the Past Century. *Xinhua*, November 16, 2021. Beijing 2021.

50   Jinping, Xi. New Year Address. December 31, 2021, https://www.fmprc.gov.cn/mfa_eng/zxxx_662805/202112/t20211231_10478096.html

would be a mistake to diminish the role of class struggle in China. Given the expansion of capitalist relations of production in the past decades, it is obvious that class contradictions would intensify.

The problems facing China today are different from the 1970s, when the main contradiction was between the low level of development of the productive forces, and the growing demands of the masses. However, according to Xi, this development was characterized by an unbalanced capitalist growth deepening inequality, rural/urban divisions and creating an unsustainable relationship to the environment. The values and norms of neoliberalism have also left their mark. Individualism, a competition mentality, and greed have made their inroads at the expense of solidarity and community. Xi now redefined the main contradiction as the unbalanced and inadequate development and the growing needs of the people for a better life.

To ease contradictions, Xi emphasizes the policy of "Common Prosperity" instead of Deng's "some get rich first." New tax laws to redistribute wealth, a huge campaign to eliminate rural poverty, new laws to regulate the working condition, and rules to reduce speculation in the real estate sector were all introduced. However, at the same time, Xi Jinping stressed the need to promote the unity and struggle of the Chinese people and to promote harmonious class relations.[51] *The Governance of China* is also the title of the four-volume collection of Xi Jinping speeches and writings.[52]

Xi, as a member of the communist party since his youth, is a schooled Marxist, and knows all about class struggle as the driver for change. He often affirms the party's adherence to Marxism, but seldom discusses the specific class struggle in China and the future of the national capitalist sector, national and transnational. Xi is also president of the People's Republic of China, which needs class harmony to continue the economic development to fulfill the needs of the people.

---

51 At the Central United Front Work Conference, Xi Jinping emphasized that we should promote the unity and struggle of the Chinese people at home and abroad and gather great strength for the great rejuvenation of the Chinese nation 习近平在中央统战工作会议上强调 促进海内外中华儿女团结奋斗 为中华民族伟大复兴汇聚伟力—时政—人民网 (people.com.cn).

52 The concept "governance" became popular in political science in the 1980s, meaning the act or process of overseeing the direction of a country.

This blend of understanding the transformative role of class struggle, and promoting class harmony, is not schizophrenic or revisionist. It reflects the real dilemma—or balancing exercise—between the need for the development of the productive forces in a transitionary state within a world still dominated by the capitalist mode of production on the one side and on the other side, the need of proletarian class struggle to maintain state power and push towards a socialist mode of production. This takes into account the concrete reality that class struggle in China between labor and capital, and the ideological struggle between bourgeois ideas, norms and values and socialist values is a long-lasting struggle, which will go on as long as capitalist relations of production plays a major role in China.

It is important to understand and differentiate between the phases in the transformation process. We have to distinguish between when we are talking about the development of the productive forces–in a transitionary state–in a world system still dominated by the capitalist mode of production, or when we are talking about the final transformation of the mode of production, from capitalist to socialist.

In the first case we can use capitalist management and the market to move towards socialism. In the second case we have to eliminate residual elements of the capitalist mode of production as they no longer play a progressive role in the development of the productive forces, but are blocking and even destroying human development.

This is the tipping point, when it is time to move from taking advantage of the capitalist mode of production to eliminating it, and to release the socialist mode of production from the constricting residual bind of capitalism. We are approaching the point where the need for another mode of production becomes more and more pressing as the destruction of global ecology and climate accelerates under capitalism.

The Transformation Towards Socialism at the National and Global Level

The dialectic of the transitional state is represented by, respectively, the nationalist development perspective and the universal socialist perspective. An advanced socialist mode of production must be global, as the capitalist mode of production is globalized both in terms of geography and in function. But the global transformation has to go through the national state, as the world-system is politically organized in national states. The national framework constitutes a historical constraint that must be taken into account as a necessity, not something we should make into a virtue.

Hence, China, or any other transitionary state should not attempt to avoid contact with globalized capitalism, as they cannot carry on the transformation process towards socialism in isolation from a capitalist mode of production which is still developing the productive forces and hence a source of useful advanced technology. In addition, the transitional state's interaction with global capitalism is part of the transition process, as it modifies capitalism and presents itself as an alternative to capitalism.

So China can, and has to, continue part of the way to socialism on the national road, as "Socialism with Chinese Characteristics," but also must keep in mind that a developed socialist mode of production has to be realized on the global level, as it has to solve the historically inherited problem of inequality between center and periphery in the world system, as well as the global ecological and climate problems.

As we step towards that advanced stage in socialism, we will see the development of different socialisms with national characteristics, based on different histories and cultures. However, it is essential to move on from the nationalist version towards global socialism, as the national component contains material for future national disputes. For the transitional state it is important to keep the right balance between the national interest and socialist transformation in relation to the surrounding world system. The nationalist aspect should not dominate the socialist perspective, as I think happened when China launched "The Three World Theory" around 1974. The confrontation with the Soviet Union, and the opening towards the U.S. in 1971, led China to pursue a nationalist foreign policy.

Nationalist disputes between transitional states will not only benefit capitalism, but will also increase the risk of nuclear warfare and slow down solutions to the urgent environmental and climate problems. It will block the transition towards advanced global socialism.

The fact that humanity has transitioned from scattered local places, then from states and empires, towards a more and more globalized world-system, equipped with advanced productive forces, means that we have developed a way of living that has damaged the planet, and acquired weapons with the ability to destroy human life. But it has also contributed the knowledge and ability to organize and manage the world system as a whole, needed for an advanced social mode of production.[53] The transformation of the relations of production towards socialism does not mean going back to productive forces organized within a national framework. World unification has ceased to be an option. It has become a condition of its existence.

For us, remaining in capitalist states in the world-system, an understanding of the dialectic of the transitional state is important. The understanding of the dilemmas and the balance between the need for national development versus advancing socialism nationally and globally (in class terms, the contradiction between national class unity versus the class struggle nationally and globally) is important and a guide for us, in the Global North, on how to relate to the transitional states, in order to defend them against imperialism, but also advance the transition to socialism. We must support the transitional states' respective nationalist aspects, against the hostile capitalist states. Not only to defend their attempt to develop socialism, but also because they are an essential anti-imperialist component, balancing imperialism, providing breathing space for socialist movements in the remaining capitalist world system. However, we must also push for a socialist transformation by class struggle, wherever we can, to ensure that the socialist aspect dominates the national aspect in the contradictions of the transitional state.

As we approach this revolutionary "end game" the class struggle between proletariat and bourgeoisie at a national and global level will be accentuated. It will be a dangerous game. Mao called imperialism a "paper tiger":

> Imperialism and all reactionaries, looked at in essence, from a long-term point of view, from a strategic point of view, must be seen for what they are—paper tigers. On this, we should build our strategic thinking. On the other

---

53 Shigong, Jiang. *A History of Empire Without Empire*. Preface to the Chinese edition of Darwin, John. *After Tamerlane: The Global History of Empire Since 1405.* 2008.

hand, they are also living tigers, iron tigers, real tigers that can devour people. On this, we should build our tactical thinking.[54]

Capitalism can be ended, but in the struggle we must be careful, and should not be adventurous in our actions, as global nuclear war will be catastrophic. But neither can we allow ourselves to give in to imperialism's threats.

---

54 Zedong, Mao *Speech at the Wuchang Meeting of the Political Bureau of the Central Committee of the Communist Party of China'*, in *Selected Works of Mao Zedong, Vol. IV*. Foreign Languages Press, Beijing, 1958. pp. 98–99.

CHAPTER 20

THE END GAME

After this comprehensive overview through the history of the struggle between capitalism and socialism, I begin this chapter by summarizing the history of the capitalist mode of production through the lens of the fundamental contradiction in historical materialism. This serves the purpose of explaining why I think capitalism has entered the end phase.

THE HISTORY OF THE CAPITALIST MODE OF PRODUCTION

The mode of production to satisfy our material needs—to sustain human life—is the fundamental condition of all history.[1] Marx identified two interdependent structures, which describe how humans interact with nature in the process of producing their subsistence: the forces of production and the relations of production. The forces of production are everything that humans use to produce the things that society needs. In order to carry out production and exchange, humans enter into relations of production determined by the development of the existing forces of production, present at any given time in history.

The fundamental contradiction in history is between the development of the productive forces and the relations of production. At a certain stage of their development, the forces of production come into conflict with the existing relations of production—the property relations within which they had been at work before. From the forms of the forces of production, these relations turn into their fetters. Then comes a period

---

1 Marx, Karl. "The German Ideology." In *Marx-Engels Collected Works, Volume 5*. Progress Publishers, Moscow 1976. p. 49.

of social revolution. However, no social order can disappear before the totality of its productive forces have been developed; additionally, new relations of production never appear before the material conditions of their existence have matured in the womb of the old society.[2] Keeping this in mind, we can formulate the short "historical materialist" story of capitalism. (See *Figure 2* [X].)

In the first part of the 19th-century, the capitalist mode of production had its breakthrough in Western Europe after centuries of European colonialism, which provided the primitive accumulation of capital.

In a dialectical way, Marx, on one hand, affirmed the positive, progressive features of capitalism, new technology, and development of science, industrialization, urbanization, mass literacy, and so on; on the other hand, he denounces the exploitation, the human alienation, the commodification of the social relations, the false ideology, the imperialism and its connected mass extermination—all inherent in the modernization process.

These two perspectives on capitalism represent the difference between analyzing the development of productive forces from within the framework of capitalist relations to the need for their "appropriation by the people"—the establishment of a new mode of production. This dialectical perspective on historical development permeated Marx's and Engels' writings. In *The Communist Manifesto,* they describe the rise of capitalism as a progressive stage of historical development. In the first pages they describe "modern industry," "modern bourgeois society," "modern workers," "modern state power," "modern productive forces," and "modern relations of production."[3] In the preface to *Capital,* Marx writes that the "purpose" of the book is to "disclose the economic law of motion of modern society."[4] Marx defended modernity because it prepared the way to a more fully developed modernity—socialism.[5]

---

2   Marx, Karl "Contribution to the Critique of Political Economy," In *Collected Works. Vol. 29*, Progress Publishers, Moscow, 1977. p. 263.

3   Marx, Karl, and Engels, Frederick. "The Communist Manifesto," In *Marx/Engels Selected Works, Volume 1*. Progress Publishers, Moscow, 1969. pp. 12–13.

4   Marx, Karl. *Capital, Volume I.* Progress Publishers, Moscow. 1962.

5   Therborn, Göran. "Dialectics of Modernity: On Critical Theory and the Legacy of Twentieth Century Marxism." *New Left Review*, 215. Jan/Feb 1996.

The imperialist aspect of capitalism united and polarized the world-system into a center-periphery structure, characterized by the super-exploitation of the labor force in the periphery, and a rising wage, hence its expanded consumption power in the center. This value-transfer entailed a dynamic development of the productive forces in the center, and at the same time, blocked development in the periphery. Consequently, there was no "need"—and no successful—revolutions in the center; capitalism had "not played out its role." In the periphery, on the other hand, capitalism eroded feudal and other pre-capitalist modes of production, but the development of the productive forces was blocked by super-exploitation and the flow of value towards the center. Only a revolutionary process could get the wheels of the economy running again, by initiating the development of a "transitionary mode of production" on the road towards socialism. It had to be "transitionary mode" because the world-system was still dominated by capitalism—economic, political, and military. The lack of development of productive forces in the periphery, and the hostile world-system, hindered an immediate transition to a socialist modernity. This is the history of the Soviet and Chinese revolutions, and their effort to develop socialism in the 20th century.

Lenin and Mao had the same dialectical approach to the development of the productive forces as Marx had. From an historical materialist point of view, the answer to this development is not an attempt to roll back the productive development of the productive forces. As Lenin approvingly quotes Hilferding: "The reply of the proletariat to the economic policy of finance capital and to imperialism cannot be free trade, but socialism."[6] The answer to this new phase of imperialism cannot be a struggle for maintaining the old forms of more national based capitalist economics, but the struggle for a more social treatment of the productive forces, a more social version of internationalization. As Lenin said:

> The questions as to whether it is possible to reform the basis of imperialism, whether to go forward to the further intensification and deepening of the antagonisms which it engenders, or backward, towards allaying these antagonisms, are fundamental questions in the critique of imperialism.[7]

Wanting to fight against the internationalization of production,

---

6   Lenin, V.I (1916) "Imperialism, the Highest Stage of Capitalism." In *Lenin Collected Works Vol. 22*. Progress Publishers, Moscow, 1965. p. 289.
7   *Ibid.* p. 287.

trade, and finance means demanding a return to a situation out of which the present one has grown. In other words, it is reactionary. According to Lenin, Kautsky's critique of monopoly capitalism was the result of a "petty bourgeoisie opposition to imperialism, caused by the general reactionary tendency in society."[8] At the present time, we are experiencing the same opposition and general reaction to transnational globalization in society. Both are forms of right-wing national conservatism and left wing populism longing for the "Paradise Lost" of small-scale national capitalism. Lenin called the newly emerged trusts of his time "progressive phenomena," in spite of the suffering they caused. He knew that one does not struggle for socialism by striving to stop economic development. This will only lead to the intensification of the contradictions of imperialism which will make the transformation towards socialism inconvertible.

The transnational companies, and the globalization of production they stand for, are in that sense progressive. They want the creation of new social productive forces. This is not to say that technical progress is independent, or that they take priority over the organization of social relations. Not at all. What we are discussing is the development of productive forces *within the capitalist mode of production,* and if the current transitional mode of production in what we call "socialist" countries are some form of state capitalism with markets relations, then it must also apply to them. Emmanuel says that we should not:

> ...slide from the criticism of capitalism in general to the denial of development within capitalism. In other words, this trend forgets that if capitalism is hell there exists a still more frightful hell: that is, less developed capitalism. This is because, if capitalism has not got a historical mission, it nonetheless has a place in human history; it is not a bad dream. By its very nature, it develops the productive forces, and if this development does not ipso facto lead to the satisfactions of social needs, it nonetheless constitutes...a much more favourable framework for a certain satisfaction of these needs than those of the past class regimes.[9]

As stated by Marx, no social system is destroyed until all the possibilities for the development of the productive forces which it contains have been exhausted. Neoliberal globalization was such a possibility par excellence. It created the framework for yet another gigantic development of

---

8   *Ibid.*

9   Emmanuel, Arghiri. *Appropriate or Underdeveloped Technology?* John Wiley & Sons, New York, 1982. p. 105.

the social productive forces. In a historical materialist perspective, this means that the neoliberal globalization has brought the day closer when capitalism will have exhausted all its possibilities and will suffer a profound crisis—this time not only national, but global. As this crisis will affect most countries simultaneously, this will make it easier for the working class to carry through and maintain the revolution.

Neoliberal globalization, from the end of the 1970s onwards, was the counter offensive from capital against the challenges of different kinds of "transitional modes of productions" in the Socialist Bloc, nationalists in the Third World, and in the form of Social Democratic welfare states in the center. Neoliberalism globalized the production process itself. It relocated hundreds of millions of industrial jobs from the Global North to the low-wage countries of the South in search of higher profits. Neoliberal globalization gave capitalism forty golden years of high profit and cheap goods for consumers in the Global North. It dissolved the so-called "actually existing socialism" in Soviet and East Europe and penetrated deep into the Chinese economy.

However, in our examination and evaluation of neoliberal globalization, transnational companies and transnational production chains, we must adopt a dialectical approach towards the development of the capitalist mode of production, between the progressive role it has and the agony it produces. We must also distinguish between when we are analyzing the development of productive forces *within* the global capitalist system and when we are discussing the contradictions leading to the transformation of the relations of production.

Capitalism is characterized by an enormous development of the productive forces, with an extensive division of labor, accompanied by an increasing concentration of capital in still larger transnational companies. The neoliberal globalization marks a further step along this road. The new technological revolutions in computers and communications, new management systems, the new large scale transnational operations in production, and all that this involves, could not be sufficiently developed under the old conditions. It was the development of the productive forces themselves, which acted independent of the will of the individual capitalist, and demanded to be treated increasingly transnational—to be globalized.

On one hand, the result of neoliberal globalization was an increased transfer of value to the North. On the other hand, the immense development of the productive forces in the Global South began to turn the table. China became the crank in the global system of production as an unintended side effect of the capitalist desire to exploit the Chinese proletariat. In its encounter with neoliberalism, China kept the command of its economy and its national project. China managed to break two centuries of polarized development in the world system of global capitalism and develop its productive forces to an advanced level. The transformation of the relations of production towards socialism does not mean going back to productive forces organized within a national framework. On the contrary, socialism implies equalization of international inequalities and global solutions to ecological and climate issues—a globalization of another kind.

The development of the productive forces in the second half of the 20th century has globalized production and trade to a new level, but it has also globalized nuclear warfare and environmental destruction to a new level. This has an impact on our consciousness. We are now able to grasp the world as a whole and relate to our planet earth in a new way. The image of our green and blue planet in the dark universe, as seen from a spaceship, contributed to this. But it is also the knowledge of how our mode of production has damaged the planet, and that our weapons have the ability to destroy human life. This has also contributed to the formation of this consciousness.

The fact that humanity has transitioned from small communities to states, then empires, towards a more and more globalized world-system, equipped with advanced productive forces, means that we have the knowledge and ability to organize and manage the world system as a whole. The transformation of the relations of production towards socialism does not mean going back to productive forces organized within a national framework. World unification has ceased to be an option. Rather, it has become a condition of its existence.

With the crises of global neoliberalism, the decline of U.S. hegemony, the rise of China, and the development of a multipolar world system, it seems that capitalism is reaching the limits of its ability to exploit humans and nature. There is no longer a "territorial fix" to the problem. The capitalist mode of production is not only blocking, but destroying, the development of human life on planet earth.

What does this change imply? That "the end game" is on, and it is possible and necessary to move from "the transitionary" relation of production to a socialist relation. It is getting rid of exploitative capitalist relations of production and patterns of consumption, which conflict with the global ecosystem. It is the development of investment and trade to promote global equality. It is the development of common prosperity, instead of privatization and extreme individualism. It is solidarity instead of competition. This mode of production requires that the majority in the world-system join the effort.

So, how does this general and rather abstract contradiction—the development of productive forces against the mode of production—unfold as specific economic and political contradictions on the global and local level?

The Contradiction of the End Game

The Soviet proletariat seized power during World War I before the preconditions for socialism were present. The Chinese proletariat achieved the same. Cuba, Vietnam, and other decolonized countries in the Third World have crafted their own histories outside the narrow Eurocentrism of the Western Left.

Since the decline of the Long 1960s, and throughout the half-century of neoliberalism, revolutionary socialist movements have been unable to forge new political organizations of significant strength. But this is not the end of socialism. Forty-six years separated the Paris Commune from the October Revolution, with another 32 years between it and the Chinese Revolution.

Marx underestimated the longevity of capitalism, as did Lenin and Mao. Many of us in the "1968 generation" have predicted the end of capitalism several times, and our hopes for world revolution were frustrated. This has led to the mistaken belief that capitalism can assimilate all critiques and innovate out of all problems.

Universalization of the present denies the historical specificity and transitory character of capitalist social relations.[10] History has shown that all modes of production have a beginning and an end. Capitalism is no different, and we might be at the turning point.

It is easier to evaluate the past than predict the future of capitalism, but both are necessary to formulate strategies for change. Historical materialism teaches us that capitalism has a lifespan. It has successfully reproduced its existence for 200 years, but there are limits to this reproduction. It is not a system in balance. Its historical impurities have enabled it to reproduce itself. Trade union struggle gave the European working-class higher consumption power; the growth of mass consumption in the center without a drop in the profit rate was financed by exploitation of the periphery. However, this dynamic has been challenged by the rise of China.

Like the late Immanuel Wallerstein, I believe that the decline of U.S. hegemony forebodes the end of capitalism.[11] This will not take place within a decade, but it seems clear that the twenty-first century is the autumn of the capitalist system. The industrialization of the Global South in recent decades signals a significant change in the dynamics of global capitalism itself. The system is losing the balancing force of the center-periphery dichotomy.

Certainly, an industrialized Global South is not to be as prosperous as capitalism in Northwestern Europe and North America. Neither China, India, Indonesia, nor Brazil has a periphery to exploit that is substantial enough to feed the development of welfare capitalism, and ecologically, the world cannot sustain such a capitalist world-system. However, the development of the productive forces in the Global South will threaten the privileged positions of the United States and the European Union and accelerate the crises of global capitalism.

In "the end game," global capitalism will be haunted by crises generated by the old contradiction between the need to expand production and the inability to consume the produced goods. The "unequal exchange"

---

10   Foster, John Bellamy. "Ecology and the Future of History." *Monthly Review*. Vol 74. No. 3, 2022. p. 122.

11   Wallerstein, Immanuel. "Structural Crisis, or why capitalists may no longer find capitalism rewarding." In *Does Capitalism have a Future?* Oxford University Press, Oxford, 2013. pp. 23–24

of trade, which has transferred value from South to North, reached its zenith in 2011 and is now declining, as wages are rising in China and global trade patterns are changing. The creation of consumption-power by debt—pushing the problem into the future—is also reaching its limit. Profits will decline and accumulation will come to a halt. As Marx predicted:

> ...[crises will] become more frequent and more violent, if only because, as the mass of production, and consequently the need for extended markets, grows, the world market becomes more and more contracted, fewer and fewer [new] markets remain available for exploitation, since every preceding crisis has subjected to world trade a market hitherto unconquered or only superficially exploited.[12]

The development of the productive forces of China and other countries in the Global South signals not only a shift in dynamics within capitalism, but also enhances the material conditions for the development of socialism. On devious roads for more than a hundred years, capitalism is finally approaching a dead end. We may now see the realization of Engels' prophecies in a letter to Kautsky in 1894:

> It is again the wonderful irony of history: China alone is still to be conquered for capitalist production, and in so doing at long last the latter makes its own existence at home impossible.[13]

China's revolution fundamentally contributed to the global transition from capitalism to socialism.

The Principal Contradiction

What is the driving force in this transition? Who are the subjective forces in the process? What will trigger the revolutionary situation? The first step in answering such questions is to identify the principal contradiction. We have to be specific in our analysis, to develop a strategy, which can be used for intervention. We must investigate both aspects, and struggle between them to decide which way the contradiction will move. The principal contraction is not fixed; it changes as the balance of its

---

12   Marx, Karl. "Wage labour and capital." *Marx/Engels Collected Works Vol. 9*, Lawrence Wishart, London, 1982. p. 197.

13   Engels, Frederick. "Letter to Karl Kautsky 1894." In *On Colonialism*, Foreign Languages Publishing House, Moscow, 1963. p. 346.

aspects changes, and interacts with other contradictions.

Since the 1970s, the principal contradiction has been between transnational capital's neoliberal globalization project and the nation-state's attempt to domesticate capitalism and try to dampen the negative effects of outsourcing and privatization—to regulate capitalism. Until the turn of the millennium, transnational capital was the dominant aspect of this contradiction. However, the economic consequences of neoliberalism, in both the Global North and South, generated nationalist demands for a stronger state, as bulwarks against globalization. In the past decades, globalized capitalism and its institutions came under increasing pressure from both right and left-wing nationalist political forces.

The new international division of labor, created by neoliberal outsourcing, changed the power structure in the world system. Northern transnational capital turned China into "the factory of the world," but it did not turn China into a permanent periphery of the center. China broke the historical polarizing tendency in the capitalist mode of production. China used the neoliberal intrusion to develop its national project—"socialism with Chinese characteristics." In May 2020, Newsweek Magazine published an article with the telling headline: "America Is in a New Cold War and This Time the Communists Might Win," which lines up with the situation:

> China is economically powerful, and deeply integrated with both the developed and developing worlds. That was never the case with the former Soviet Union, which was largely isolated economically, trading only with its east bloc neighbors...[China] is sophisticated across a wide range of critical technologies, including telecommunications and artificial intelligence. It has set as a national goal—in its so-called Made in China 2025 plan—preeminence not just in quantum computing and AI, but in biotech, advanced telecommunications, green energy and a host of others.[14]

During the height of neoliberalism, U.S. hegemony was based on economic and technological superiority. This advantage is now challenged by China. William Barr, U.S. Attorney General, expressed this concern:

> 5G technology lies at the center of the technological and industrial world

---

14 Powell, Bill. "America Is in a New Cold War and This Time the Communists Might Win." *News Week Magazine* 2020. https://www.newsweek.com/2020/06/05/america-new-cold-war-this-time-communists-might-win-1504447.html

that is taking shape. In essence, communications networks are not just for communications anymore. They are evolving into the central nervous system of the next generation of the internet, called the "Industrial Internet," and the next generation of industrial systems that will depend on that infrastructure. China has built up a lead in 5G, capturing 40 percent of the global 5G infrastructure market. For the first time in history, the United States is not leading the next technology era.[15]

We see the U.S. increasingly utilizing trade blockades, sanctions, and military pressure to uphold its dominant position. The economic competition, which characterized the neoliberal era, has been replaced by territorial disputes. With the coming to power of Trump in 2017, the world entered another phase of mercantilism: a sharp increase in trade/sanctions wars and a new arms race.

The U.S./NATO proxy war in Ukraine against Russia is also an attempt to destabilize and encircle China and apply pressure to any state that challenges U.S. hegemony. Get a regime-change in Russia and then in China. However, this is tearing apart the neoliberal world market, which is necessary for the continued accumulation of transnational capital.

The transition from neoliberal economic-driven imperialism towards old-fashioned territorial imperialism is not in the interest of transnational capital, which is dependent on global production chains to generate surplus value, and access to the entire world market to realize the profit. If the 2007–8 crisis was the crisis of financial neoliberalism, then the current crisis is the crisis of globalized production. The interests of U.S. transnational capitalism and the state are increasingly at odds. However, transnational capital cannot distance itself from its political leadership, which provides security for its operation. There is no way out of the dilemma for transnational capital, as it is the crises of neoliberalism itself which has created this situation. The immediate need of political imperialism overrides the interests of transnational capital. U.S. policy is becoming self-destructive; it shatters the world market, upon which America has built its power since the end of the Second World War.

The disintegration of globalization is a reconfiguration of the power structure in the world system. In retrospect, China was admitted into the

---

15   Tiejun, Wen. *Ten Crises. The Political Economy of China's Development (1949–2020)*. Palgrave Macmillan, Singapore, 2021. p. 416.

global trade regime in 1972 because of the U.S. rivalry with its chief opponent, the Soviet Union. Beating the Soviets first, then China, was the plan. U.S. superiority in technology and finance, at the time, gave it the confidence to open its global trade regime to any country willing to play the game, regardless of ideology. At this phase, the globalization regime was a gigantic profit machine based on global production chains and the extraction of cheap production factors from the global South. Today, as the U.S. is no longer economically competitive, instead it uses its military power and an ideological alliance with Europe and Japan for geopolitical struggle to rule the world system.

The former principal contradiction between transnational globalization and nationalist states is being replaced by a new emerging principal contradiction between the forces which want to uphold U.S. hegemony and the forces which seek a multipolar world order, headed by China. Transnational capital in the Global North is forced by the changing winds in the world-system to join with nationalist and conservative political forces in the North.

The U.S., the EU, Japan, New Zealand, and Australia, have united to uphold U.S. hegemony. They constitute one aspect of the principal contradiction. The other aspect is headed by China, the upcoming economic and political world power, and its ambition to build "socialism with Chinese characteristics." China is allied with a conglomerate of states which, for various reasons, are opposed to the continuation of U.S. hegemony and want a multipolar world system. They are united in the ambition to change the North-South structure, which has dominated the world-system for the last two centuries and expand South-South and East-West relations.

It seems that the only way to uphold U.S. hegemony and solve the crises of neoliberalism is to "reconquer" China for a third time, which means subjecting China to the interest of Western transnational capital. The first time was the Opium Wars in the mid-nineteenth century; the second time was the opening of China in the 1990s. Hence, the U.S. political elites have identified China as the main rival in the future.

As China turned from a pool of low-wage workers to a competitor on the world market, the Obama administration began its policy of "Asia-Pacific Rebalance", also known as the "Pivot to Asia." The Trump

Administration launched a trade war, technology sanctions, and a series of military maneuvers. Joe Biden has followed that track.

The U.S. strategic competition with China is full scale: technology, trade, currency, geopolitics, and ideology. The U.S. is increasingly adopting Cold War rhetoric, describing its engagement with China as a rivalry between two opposite ideologies, and even civilizations. At the same time, the U.S. pressures other actors to take its side against China.

As a response, China is establishing an alternative trade and finance system: The Belt and Road Initiative" and BRICS. If China can delink softly from its dependence on U.S. and EU markets, we will see the emergence of two economic cores, with separate financial and monetary institutions, but to some extent, overlapping supply chains and markets. If the contradiction escalates and takes on an antagonistic character, we could see a hard delinking, raising the probability of military confrontation.

For the time being, the U.S. is well aware that direct military intervention in China is not an option. Instead, the U.S. is trying to create a crisis to overthrow the Communist Party of China and install a pro-Western regime to subject China to Western capital interests, keeping it in a permanent subaltern status. The U.S. has tried to create tensions around Taiwan, Tibet, Hong Kong, and the Xinjiang Uyghur Autonomous region. It has also covertly supported Uyghur separatists in Turkey and Syria to draw China into conflicts with Islamist groups.[16]

For the U.S. to confront China is very different from the confrontation with the Soviet Union in decline. China is not a falling star. In fact, China is too important for the world economy to collapse. The United States and China are economically interdependent, with trade between the two nations reaching half a trillion dollars in 2020; and China holds hundreds of billions of dollars of U.S. bonds. Thus, the U.S. seeks to change China's political system while keeping the economy running.

This is a dangerous game. It is a conflict on how to organize the world system and the future. It can generate wars and will hamper efforts to solve ecological and economic problems as international cooperation and diplomacy become stalled by cold and hot wars.

---

16 Lin May, Christina. *Chinese General: Anti-Chinese Uyghurs are in Syria's Anti-Assad Force.* ISPSW Strategy Series: Focus on Defense and International Security, no. 353, May 2015. Berlin.

In the Long 1960s, we hoped that the Third World liberation movements would build socialist states to cut off the pipelines of value transfer to the center. We were too optimistic. Neoliberal globalization still offered an escape route. It seems today that from the North, the U.S., in its desperate struggle to uphold hegemony, is disrupting the imperialist pipeline system. From the South, China has succeeded in diminishing the imperial rent of unequal exchange, while simultaneously breaking the technological monopoly of Western capital. Chinese economists have calculated that:

> Between 1978 and 2018, on average, one hour of work in the United States was exchanged for almost forty hours of Chinese work. However, from the middle of the 1990s...we observed a very marked decrease in unequal exchange, without it completely disappearing. In 2018, 6.4 hours of Chinese labor were still exchanged for 1 hour of U.S. labor.[17]

Since 2011, the global value transfer of unequal exchange from South to North has begun to decline, partly due to rising wages in China, partly due to declining North-South trade as the neoliberal world market erodes.[18]

The U.S. is still the dominant aspect. However, the erosion of the neoliberal world market, and alternative political and financial institutions without the dollar as the world trade currency, may shift the balance of the contradiction. As time passes the U.S. will become poorer, and the economic crises in the remaining neoliberal sector will generate disagreements between the U.S. and its allies.

Whether U.S. hegemony is in terminal decline, or its military offensive will allow it to preserve its hegemony for the next several decades, the contradiction between U.S. and China will affect all other contradictions. No aspect of the global economy, political movement, or state will be untouched by this contradiction.

The U.S. confrontation with China will be different from the Cold War with the Soviet Union in the 1950s. China's economy is resilient

---

17   Long, Zhiming, Feng, Zhixuan, li, Bangxi, and Herrera, Rémy. "U.S.-China Trade War. Has the Real 'Thief' Finally Been Unmasked?" *Monthly Review*, Vol. 72, No. 5, October 2010. pp. 8–9.

18   Hickel, Jason, Sullivan, Dylan & Zoomkawala, Huzaifa. "Plunder in the Post-Colonial Era: Quantifying Drain from the Global South through Unequal Exchange, 1960–2018." *New Political Economy*, Vol. 26, No. 6, 2021. pp. 1030–47.

and more self-sufficient. It can replace exports by expanding its internal market using planning techniques. China's GDP will be overtaking that of the U.S. in the next decade. China is investing heavily in domestic infrastructure and the development of new technology. It has the Belt and Road Initiatives. It is China which has plans and visions for the future, while the U.S. is a destabilizing factor, creating chaos in the world system.

Let us look at the main actors in the new "regionalization," and how their internal contradiction interacts with the principal contradiction.

The U.S.

The U.S. envisages a permanent unipolar world, governed by its huge military force. Since 1945, the United States has engaged in 211 interventions in 67 countries. It currently maintains 250,000 soldiers stationed in 700 bases distributed throughout 150 nations—an unprecedented imperium. Direct invasions have been replaced by proxy wars, economic sieges, and destabilization of targeted countries. These hybrid wars also include more pervasive media campaigns than the old anti-communist propaganda. The U.S. uses a network of foundations and NGOs on social media. The official U.S. "defense" budget in 2022 was $765.8 billion, four times that of China, twelve times that of Russia, and thirty times that of Iran.[19] NATO expanded and rearmed its forces in Europe in their confrontation with Russia. However, NATO has also expanded its area of operations globally, mobilizing its allies to form an anti-China geopolitical alliance. The 2022 Strategic Concept of NATO stated:

> The People's Republic of China's (PRC) ambitions challenge our interests, security and values…The PRC seeks to control key technological and industrial sectors, critical infrastructure, and strategic materials and supply chains…We will work together responsibly, as Allies, to address the systemic challenges posed by the PRC to Euro-Atlantic security and ensure NATO's enduring ability to guarantee the defense and security of Allies. We will boost our shared awareness, enhance our resilience and preparedness, and protect against the PRC's coercive tactics and efforts to divide the Alliance.[20]

---

19   Chipman, John and Hackett, James. *The Military Balance 2022*, Internationalal Institute for Strategic Studies, London. 2022.

20   NATO. *The 2022 Strategic Concept*, adopted at the Madrid Summit. 29–30 June 2022. https://www.nato.int/strategic-concept/

The UK, the U.S., and Australia formed the AUKUS pact in 2021 to encircle China. From Australia through the Pacific, to South-East Asia, Japan, Korea, and across Eurasia, to Afghanistan and India, the U.S. bases form the perfect noose.[21] This military superiority is not without cost. America's military spending and wars have left its treasury indebted to foreign governments and their central banks.

It is not only in its confrontation with China that U.S. dominance is challenged, but also eroded from the inside by the split in the political elite, which cuts through society. It is not just an ordinary political dispute between the Democratic and Republican parties. The Democrats are trying to get the former President Trump imprisoned—changed with treason and staging a coup. The 2024 presidential election may develop into a major crisis, whether a Democrat or Republican wins, if the electorate refuses to acknowledge the result as legitimate.

Europe

The European Union, after the shocks of Brexit and the growth of populist nationalism in almost all member states, is struggling to regain its footing. Lacking a strong united administration, and without its own armed force, the EU cannot deal with the overspill of conflicts in proximal regions, not to speak of the global level. The EU is left on the frontline of America's confrontations.

In the past fifteen years, European countries have integrated with the Russian energy market and expanded their trade with China. The piped natural gas through Nord Stream 2 was cheaper and less dangerous than liquefied natural gas from the Persian Gulf and the Gulf of Mexico. Several European countries also joined the Chinese Belt and Road Initiative.

All this is to the frustration of the U.S., which has tried to prevent or delay that process. The financial crisis of 2007–08 was a sign to the rest of the world that the U.S. economy was untrustworthy. The Trump presidency did not help American credibility in European eyes. In 2018, Trump criticized NATO's general secretary, the Norwegian Jens Stoltenberg:

---

21 Pilger, John. "Another Hiroshima is coming – unless we stop it now." 2020. https://www.rt.com/op-ed/497096-john-pilger-hiroshima-china-us/

...we're protecting Germany. We're protecting France. We're protecting all of these countries. And then numerous of these countries go out and make a pipeline deal with Russia, where they're paying billions of dollars into the coffers of Russia...Germany is a captive of Russia...I think it's very inappropriate.[22]

The war in Ukraine and the EU's boycott of Russian gas and oil have created inflation and made EU products less competitive in global markets. The EU's foreign-policy chief Josep Borrell acknowledged this in October 2022:

> Our prosperity has been based on cheap energy coming from Russia...cheap and supposedly affordable, secure, and stable. It has been proved not [to be] the case. And the access to the China market, for exports and imports, for technological transfers, for investments, for having cheap goods. I think that the Chinese workers with their low salaries have done much better and much more to contain inflation than all the Central Banks together...You—the United States—take care of our security. You—China and Russia—provided the basis of our prosperity. This is a world that is no longer there... [There is] messy multipolarity. There is the US-China competition. This is the most important "structuring force"...The second characteristic is a competitive world where everything is being weaponized.[23]

The proxy war against Russia on Ukraine's soil was an opportunity for the U.S. to discipline Europe and strengthen the NATO alliance under its command—an alliance that now also includes Finland and Sweden. In another case of "the second time as farce," we are seeing a re-enactment of the summer of 1914, when the European labor movements nearly all rallied to their national warmongers. However, it is not just about Ukraine and Russia, but about preventing the EU's integration with China. This development has been costly for the EU. Not only are they forced to increase their military budgets by hundreds of billions, but their economy is also hurt. The U.S. policy is dragging Europe down—a price Europeans seem to be willing to pay to protect their "imperial mode of living" for the time being. However, NATO membership is not a la carte, Europe must swallow the U.S. global menu, including its Middle East and China policy, and what if military expenditures occur at the

---

22 Trump, 2018. https://www.atlanticcouncil.org/blogs/natosource/trump-believes-us-paying-a-lot-of-money-to-protect-nato-allies/

23 Borrell, Josep. "Speech at EU Ambassadors Annual Conference 2022." https://www.eeas.europa.eu/eeas/eu-ambassadors-annual-conference-2022-opening-speech-high-representative-josep-borrell_en

expense of healthcare and social services? What if the U.S. political system becomes unstable? What if the U.S. threatens to drag Europe into a direct war with Russia or China? Will the NATO alliance continue to be stable?

Asia and Oceania

A similar dilemma is unfolding in Asia. The cooperation between China, Japan, Korea, and Association of Southeast Asian Nations (ASEAN) countries appears to be beneficial for all countries in the region. However, Japan and South Korea, firmly under U.S. dominance, have to struggle with the dilemma of whether to befriend China, with which they have close economic ties, or yield to U.S. pressure and downsize relations. The ASEAN countries, likewise, have a close economic connection with China. However, they have been drawn into conflict by disputes in the South China Sea. Australia, Japan, New Zealand, and South Korea attended the NATO summit in 2022 for the first time. Australia and Japan, along with India and the U.S., are part of the Quadrilateral Security Dialogue (Quad), called the Asian NATO. Quad, the AUKUS pact between the UK, U.S., and Australia, along with 400 American military bases with missiles, bombers, warships, and nuclear weapons have created a complete encirclement of China.

Africa

Western imperialism is under duress in Africa today. Colonial exploitation and oppression are not forgotten. There is a revival of Pan-Africanism across the continent. Particularly important is the resistance to "Françafrique" and the U.S. military and economic presence across the continent. In West Africa, military governments in Mali, Burkina Faso, and Niger have seized power, riding waves of anti-imperialist sentiment, fueled by resentment at the IMF-sponsored structural adjustment programs of the 1990s neoliberalization, as well as continued French control of the currency through the CFA Franc. The rhetoric of figures like Burkina's Ibrahim Traoré seems to harken back to older anti-imperialists like Thomas Sankara. Russia is increasingly involved militarily, creating a possible conflict with the U.S. Ethiopia joined BRICS in August 2023.

The entire continent and its largest countries, such as the Congo, South Africa, and Nigeria are faced with Western alignment or growing engagement with China. This principal contradiction will interact with movements that challenge the remaining legacy of colonialism, apartheid, and extraction of raw materials.

The Middle East

U.S. influence in the region remains high after the invasions of Iraq and meddling in the civil war in Syria. The Israeli settler-state is "the battleship on ground" to protect U.S. interests. Iran is the U.S.'s main enemy in the region; however, the U.S. sanctions on Iran are crippling. The conflict between Iran and Saudi Arabia, and their proxy war in Yemen, has ended due to Chinese diplomacy. The Saudi discussion of possibly selling oil in Yuan rather than dollars will weaken the latter's position as world currency. Saudi Arabia, Iran, Egypt and the United Arab Emirates membership in BRICS will contribute to the establishment of a multipolar world.

The Palestinian struggle remains on the ground. The Hamas attack of October 7, 2023 is an example of how unstable the world system is. A relatively small military operation, consisting of around 1,500 persons equipped only with small arms, occupied a few villages for two days and set off an avalanche of events—not only the war in Gaza, but also in pushing the contradictions in the region and on a global scale. The former contradiction between Sunni and Shia muslims have been toned down—Iran and Saudi Arabia are united in support for the Palestinian struggle. The rapprochement between the Gulf states and Israel has come to a sudden stop.

Because of the support of NATO countries to the Israeli war in Gaza, the West is losing credibility everywhere. As a senior diplomat says:

> We have definitely lost the battle in the Global South. All the work we have done with the Global South [over Ukraine] has been lost…Forget about rules, forget about world order, they won't ever listen to us again.[24]

---

24 Foy, Henry. "Rush by west to back Israel erodes developing countries' support for Ukraine." 2023. https://www.ft.com/content/e0b43918-7eaf-4a11-baaf-d6d7fb61a8a5

Latin America

Latin America is no longer just the "backyard" of the U.S., ruled by the "Monroe Doctrine." Lula's return as president in Brazil has revitalized its membership in BRICS and relations to China, which is Brazil's main trading partner. In general, China is developing economic and political relations with countries in Central and South America. Columbia and Mexico have elected left-wing presidents. The U.S. did not manage to overthrow President Maduro in Venezuela. In Bolivia and Ecuador, Indigenous struggle for land and sovereignty has become increasingly important—as further exemplified by the Zapatistas in Chiapas. Cuba remains a bastion of socialist development. Cuba's relationship with China can ease the problems of the U.S. blockade, as China can provide high tech industrial products.

Russia

Russian capitalism has some specific properties acquired during the process of the dissolution of Soviet socialism. The inauguration of Boris Yeltsin as president was a decisive moment in the development of Russian capitalism. Yeltsin pushed through a Russian constitution in 1993, which gave more power to the president. The highly centralized political system became the basis of the Russian corporate oligarchy.

The new oligarchs—who were often involved in the criminal black economy (about 15 percent of Soviet gross domestic product in the 1980s)—mixed with former high-ranking members of the Communist Party. During the Yeltsin regime, these two groups seized the former Soviet industries, operating as a comprador bourgeoisie of the West. The neoliberal "shock therapy" caused the Russian economy to decline by 50 percent between 1990-2000. Russian capital has expanded in the post-Soviet epoch in countries like Kazakhstan and Belarus, conflicting with Western capital pursuing the same goal. However, on the main, the Russian economy continued to contribute to the development of the capitalist core countries—with exports of cheap gas and oil to Europe, and by the large-scale participation of foreign capital in all sectors of the Russian economy, and by allowing the huge outflow of capital to the West. From the end of the 1990s, the economy in Russia lost $10–20 billion annually in capital flight. In 2014, the net capital outflow exceeded $150 billion, which was equal to 7.5% of the Russian GDP. Thus, according to the Central Bank of the Russian Federation in 2014, Russia allocated over $82 billion to the economy of the British Virgin Islands, 77 times more than the annual GDP of the islands. Hardly a productive investment. Cyprus, Liechtenstein, and Luxembourg also acted as "transshipment points" for Russian capital.[25]

In that sense, Russia was a semi-peripheral nation in the world system in the first decade of the 21st century. However, the decline of economic growth in the past decades indicates that Russia might even drift towards a peripheral position. The degradation of the Russian economic system is accompanied by attacks on labor rights, privatization of education and health care, raising of the retirement age, and the constant reduction of social benefits.

This trend has generated a conservative nationalist response in Russia, both in the working class and in part of the oligarchy. Russian capitalists wanted to be more than just a comprador bourgeoisie of the Western transnational capital; they wanted to transform the former Soviet Union into their own sphere of influence within global capitalism. This soon created a renewed rivalry between the U.S. and Russia.

In December 1999, Vladimir Putin, a former KGB officer, succeeded Yeltsin. In his first years in office, Putin hoped for a relaxed relationship with NATO. In 1994, Russia joined the "Partnership for Peace" program with NATO, and through the early part of the 2000s, NATO and Russia signed several additional agreements of cooperation. However, successively frustrated by the expansion of NATO towards the east and the NATO bombing of Belgrade, Putin became eager to push back the influence of the U.S. military in the region. Russian support of Bashar al-Assad in Syria was the first sign of this policy. Given the pressure from NATO, Russia drew a geopolitical "red line" against Ukraine's desired affiliation with NATO. Because of the war in Ukraine, and a total break of economic relations with the West, Russia is trying to build a Eurasian alternative in the east, bringing it closer to China.

However, even if Russia aims to establish a national economy inde-

---

25 Komolov, Oleg. "Capital outflow and the place of Russia in Core-periphery relationships." *World Review of Political Economy* Vol. 10, No. 3. Fall 2019. pp. 328–29.

pendent of the U.S. and the EU, the oligarchs have no interest in restoring socialism. According to Samir Amin, there is no immediate possibility of Russia moving from an oligarchic structure to some kind of socialist-directed economy. Amin argues that, in the conflict between Russia and the West, elements of the Russian elite might gravitate toward state capitalism with a social dimension—if only for survival—severing the power structure of the oligarchy currently ruling the country.[26] The conflict between Russia and the U.S./EU alliance is a classic conflict between capitalist powers over territory, market, and resources. Russian capitalists are trying to defend their shrinking Empire. In that sense, they are at odds with the U.S. Due to the Soviet Union's long confrontations with the West, Russia possesses nuclear weapons to match the U.S., which China does not have. The West's isolation of Russia has turned it towards China. The combined military capacity of Russia, and the economic rise of China, has changed the global power structure, which, since the Second World War, has been characterized by U.S. hegemony. When Xi Jinping visited Moscow in March 2023 he stated: "Right now there are changes—the likes of which we haven't seen for 100 years—and we are driving these changes."[27]

In Chinese foreign policy, national sovereignty is a priority, and as such, they are against the Russian invasion in Ukraine, and seek a peace settlement the sooner the better. However, as the war on Ukrainian soil increasingly becomes a confrontation between Russian and NATO, led by the U.S., China will support the Russian side. Russia is the only country equal to the U.S. in terms of nuclear weapons, and China's relationship with Russia prevents the U.S. from a direct military attack on China.

The aim of the U.S. in Ukraine is to bring about a regime change in Russia, which would suit its geo-political confrontation with China. Sergei Glazyev, the Russian commissioner of the Eurasian Economic Union explains the U.S. strategy:

---

26   Amin, Samir. "Russia and the Ukraine crisis: The Eurasian Project in conflict with the triad imperialist policies." *Monthly Review Online*. 2022. https://mronline.org/2022/05/07/russia-and-the-ukraine-crisis-the-eurasian-project-in-conflict-with-the-triad-imperialist-policies/

27   Al Jazeera. "China's Xi tells Putin of 'changes not seen for 100 years.'" 2023. https://www.aljazeera.com/news/2023/3/22/xi-tells-putin-of-changes-not-seen-for-100

After failing to weaken China head-on through a trade war, the Americans shifted the main blow to Russia, which they see as a weak link in the global geopolitics and economy. The Anglo-Saxons are trying to implement their eternal Russo-phobic ideas to destroy our country, and at the same time to weaken China, because the strategic alliance of the Russian Federation and the PRC is too tough for the United States.[28]

Catastrophe as a Possible Principal Contradiction

For the time being, the principal contradiction between U.S. hegemony and a multipolar world order headed by China seems to shape the world system.

However, the endgame of capitalism takes place within a framework of its structural crisis—economically, politically, and ecologically. The structural crisis entails that the system is out of balance and that conjunctions do not come in regular waves, but by sudden uncontrollable swings. Three unpredictable possibilities in the transitional process could complicate the struggle in the coming years: climate change, pandemics, and nuclear warfare. It is not so much the effects of these that are unpredictable; it is the timing of these dangers that is unknown.

We have reached the stage in the history of planet earth where capitalism is the main driver of systemic changes, disrupting ecological balances and expediting gradual changes that before would take over millennia and now occur in decades. The devastating flood, drought, storms resulting from climate change will worsen, and "green capitalism" is the emperor without clothes.

A revolutionary break with capitalism is not just a question of removing capitalism's fetters on human development; it is necessary to stop the destruction of the earth. Already we understand Engels' warning in *Dialectics of Nature*:

> Thus at every step we are reminded that we by no means rule over nature like a conqueror over a foreign people, like someone standing outside nature—but that we, with flesh, blood and brain, belong to nature, and exist in its midst, and that all our mastery of it consists in the fact that we have the ad-

---

28   Glazyev Sergey. "'Events like This Happen Once a Century': Sergey Glazyev on the breakdown of epochs and changing ways of life" *The Saker*. 2022. https://thesaker.is/events-like-this-happen-once-a-century-sergey-glazyev-on-the-breakdown-of-epochs-and-changing-ways-of-life/.

vantage over all other creatures of being able to learn its laws and apply them correctly.[29]

Climate change is a reality; it is the rate of destruction that is unclear. Where will the next disaster strike, and how big will it be? The growing ecological and climatic problems, as well as the scramble for the Earth's natural resources, can trigger revolutionary situations, as it changes living conditions, causing natural disasters and refugee migrations. We are running out of time. Some kind of "lifeboat socialism" may be the only system with the ability to solve climate change.

Another effect of the contradiction between nature and capitalism are the recent pandemics. Global medical knowledge has advanced to bring many diseases under control, but the way we produce food has given germs new ways to resist our medicines. The list is long: AIDS, MERS, SARS, Ebola, and recently COVID-19. As long as medical production is for profit, the distribution of medicines will be unequal. The same goes for health systems, which have been increasingly privatized during the past 40 years of neoliberalism. All this makes it difficult to combat pandemics. COVID-19 has ceased to be a major problem but what about the next pandemic? It will surely come if we continue with our current farming methods.

The planetary character of ecology and the climate question also makes it dependent upon geopolitical developments. There is the danger of nuclear war in a world system with territorial rivalry. Many states have, and more states are acquiring, nuclear weapons, along with the means to launch them. This mathematically increases the risks of mass destruction. Wars between the world's leading powers could very well become the world's principal contradiction if they escalate into the use of nuclear weapons. While nuclear weapons are essentially defensive weapons, the decision to use nuclear weapons is in the hands of individual, sometimes irrational, human beings. The struggle for peace, when the ruling class calls for war, is of critical importance, and offers a revolutionary perspective as the survival of humanity takes precedence over the system.

Things may develop faster than we expect. Global capitalism can either collapse in brutal chaos, or we can manage to achieve an orderly transformation towards a fairer and more sustainable mode of produc-

---

29   Engels, *Dialectics of Nature*. p. 461.

tion. That depends entirely on us. The next decades will be dramatic and dangerous—a revolution is not a tea party. We will see sudden changes in political alliances, and in this scenario, we need to stay the course and stick to a clear socialist perspective. At the same time, we are running out of time due to climate change. The majority of the world's population will have to change their production and consumption habits by 2050. Once this date has passed, the only option will be a transition to a kind of "lifeboat socialism," where we must struggle to get through one natural disaster after the other instead of developing a world more prosperous for all.

CONCLUSION

Towards a Strategy for the Transition to Socialism

I am not a utopian socialist. I cherish the socialist ideals, but I do not insist on immediate perfection. Nevertheless, we must progress towards realizing them. As I began working practically with Third World liberation movements in the 1960s, I experienced the difference between ideals and the pragmatic compromises necessary for the everyday struggle. Practice leads to knowledge. Take, for instance, the Popular Front for the Liberation of Palestine (PFLP), which we supported in the 1970s and 1980s. During this period, they gradually moved from a small radical movement with a high revolutionary spirit, to a more mature organization with greater responsibility for the protection of Palestinian refugee camps in Lebanon and Syria. This forced them to compromise with non-socialist regimes like Lebanon and Syria. During the late-1970s onwards, the PFLP developed close relations with the Soviet Union, which we considered a dubious ally. However, the Soviet Union was the only power which counterbalanced the U.S., the main ally of the Zionist occupation. Furthermore, the Soviet Union educated many PFLP members and offered practical, material support. As we learned more about the dilemmas in the daily work of a revolutionary organization, we became less rigid in our evaluation of this cooperation. You may get dirty hands when you get work done.

The utopian socialists in the beginning of the 19th century used all their energy to paint an image of ideal socialisms, while the path towards realizing it remained hidden. Marx instead studied the real existing forces of capitalism to discover a path forward, to unite the wishes for a better world with a knowledge-based realistic strategy based on existing conditions and social movements—a concrete dream.

The strategies of transformation have to be realistic, but cannot be confused with reformism. They have to be based on the existing conditions. We must think of the struggle for socialism as practical politics in specific historical contexts; political movements, institutions, and forms of praxis will reflect their unique conditions in the capitalist world system.

The strategies and organizations used in the past two centuries are not necessarily effective today and in the future struggles. We must learn from history that there are no universal forms of struggle or organizational representations of socialist principles. The Paris Commune, the worker's councils in the German revolution, the Soviet model of "actually existing socialism," and the Cultural Revolution in China were all historically-conditioned attempts at socialism. To attribute these historically specific forms of praxis to some kind of universality, to gain support for immediate strategies, is dangerous. The rejection of bureaucracy does not mean that planning is no longer part of socialism. On the contrary, planning economic decision-making—politics dominating economics—is essential for any form of socialism. We need a democratically constituted planned economy which can reconcile human needs with the reproduction of nature.

In the global transformational process from capitalism to socialism, such a model has to take place within a state structure. Ideas of direct democracy, taken from anarchism and workers' councils, should be used *within* this state structure, as these ideas have failed to develop structures that have the necessary transformative power within world state systems.

A rigid, idealist, and utopian perception of national and international struggles obscures the complexity and changeability of current class behaviors and interests. An anti-imperialist strategy must contain *real existing* counter-hegemonic forces capable of challenging the dominant power structure. It is not enough to wish for some socialist workers movement to take state power from below if you cannot point to its real existence. Western Marxists have for long been trapped in a perception of the world where the idea of socialism is superior to the transitional regimes and modes of production, which have emerged in the past hundred years. In this way Western Marxists have no real path towards socialism, only criticisms of the movements and states struggling to build socialism, and in that way they are siding with capitalism.[1]

On the "left" there exists an idealist perception that "working and oppressed classes" in "pure emancipatory struggles," must be the ones that accomplish the transition to socialism. The perception of the masses flushing out the old regimes by pouring into the streets in mass protests organized from below, and general strikes are perceived as the only real revolution. As soon as they get more organized, assume state power, and exercise that power (or relate to state powers) they somehow become sullied. In this perception, revolutions turn into just one more oppressive regime, as in the case of the Soviet Union, China, Cuba, or Venezuela.

However, in the transition process from capitalism to socialism, there is a close relation between the movements of the "working and oppressed classes" and the power of states in the world system. Take again the example of The Popular Front for the Liberation of Palestine. In its struggle, it had to take into account its relation to the Syrian and Lebanese states, which hosted them, as well as the geopolitical struggle between the U.S., Soviet Union, Iran, Saudi Arabia, and China. If you insist on purity and ideals in relation to the state powers involved, you will not get far. A "pure" movement of "workers and oppressed people" does not exist as a transformative power. It appears in the complex interplay between economic and political contradictions in the world system.

Why is China So Important?

Why do I put so much trust in China's role in the transformation from capitalism to socialism? For one, political power is concentrated in the Communist Party. The Communist Party of China is one of the largest "political management machines" in human history, with more than 96.7 million members. Its organizational structure reaches every corner of the world's most populous country of more than 1.4 billion people. The survival and achievements of the Party throughout one hundred years indicates that it is in touch with the popular base.

---

1 Ness, Immanuel. "Western Marxism, Anti-Communism and Imperialism." Forthcoming.

When defining the character of China, it is also important to keep in mind that despite the influx of capitalism under Dengism, over 70% of workers are still self-employed (peasants) or employed in non-capitalist enterprises and non-market-oriented public organizations.[2] Public ownership and control of finance, along with a hands-on approach to market regulations, ultimately left the economy in the hands of the state.[3]

The Communist Party has over seven decades of demonstrable evidence that it can take and enact decisions on how to develop the world's largest nation. Its actions are not dependent on the will of millions of independent capitalists, whose actions are guided by profit motives. China can carry out political decisions, in accordance with plans and a vision, which can change the world. This is why China is important.

The national state is the political and economic framework of the world system. This has been the model for the past several centuries and will persist in the endgame. Thus, the transition towards socialism will partly be determined by the struggle between nation-states. The nation-state remains necessary, as it provides essential security from the surrounding hostile world. During the transitional process, the socialist states will be on the defensive as long as capitalism dominates the world market and the politics of the world system.

But the nature of the nation-state and its ability to engage in the transition toward socialism will be determined by the class struggle. The strength of the state is dependent on a pro-people policy to secure the backing of the people. In addition to this, it is of vital importance that the socialist-orientated states cooperate to achieve a critical mass of economic and political power to defy capitalism on the global level.

I am aware of the criticism of both the former Soviet Union and China for "state-ism." The development of an authoritarian state limits the freedom of any form of opposition. The state machinery has certainly not been "withering away" in states which have attempted to build socialism during the past hundred years. On the contrary, they have built "strong states." Remember the difference between Lenin's writings on the nature

---

2 Gabriele, A. *Enterprises, industry and innovation in the People's Republic of China–questioning socialism from Deng to the trade and tech war*. 2020. Springer Press.

3 Kadri, Ali. *China's Path to Development: Against Neoliberalism*. 2021. Springer Press. p. 9.

of the socialist state in *State and Revolution* in August 1917, and the realities that led the Bolsheviks to build a "strong state" just a few months later. The discrepancy is not due to treason against the ideals of socialism. But the Lenin of August 1917 seemed to forget that the mission of the dictatorship of the proletariat is not limited to upholding internal national security. There is also the question of the capitalist world system, which became evident with the intervention of the allied imperialist forces during the civil war in January 1918. Only strong states can offer the necessary protection against the hostile capitalist world while moving toward socialism. Only when the global transition from capitalism to socialism has reached the turning point, in which the socialist states are in the dominant position, can the process of the withering away of the state take place.

The attempt to build socialism inside capitalist societies on the micro-level, without state building, has a long history, first associated with the traditions of cooperatives and anarchism; and later with the New Left collectives in the 1960s, autonomous movements and squatters collectives in the 1980s, and today with ecological attempts to build sustainable collectives. Marx recognized cooperatives as a vital part of the labor movement, empowering the workers as part of the wider struggle against capital. There is an unceasing dialectic between the tasks of transforming oneself, one's immediate surroundings, and restructuring the larger society. This question is also related to the relationship between creating a socialist human being and transforming society, discussed above. We are at once individual separate human beings and units of a collectivity on different levels. These levels are linked together in the individual, national, regional, and global levels.

How do I relate to nature and other people—from my neighbor to the ones who produce my coffee and smartphone? What do I eat? How do I transport myself? All these considerations have a global impact. These observations draw us back to a familiar argument: How can I change the world if I cannot change my own way of living? Let us start with ourselves! It also expresses a certain impatience with the abstract socialist agenda in general, and suggests that we focus on transforming our immediate surroundings here and now rather than aiming at state power and global transformation. However, I do not see a social praxis inside capitalist society—or any other "non-state" movement—with the sufficient power to break the capitalist system without aiming at state power.

This is why China is important. Due to the level of its productive forces, China has the potential to be a game changer, which can tip the balance of the world system in favor of socialism.

A multi-polar world-system, representing 90% of humanity, offers a better chance for global equality and a way out of the climate crisis, than the most privileged 10%—North America and Western Europe. A multipolar world might also be a world with the best chanced for social transformation

China has become the principal force in the effort to establish a multipolar world system and a new international economic order not dominated by the Bretton Woods financial institution and the dollar as the world currency. This is the reason why the development of "socialism with Chinese characteristics" becomes crucial, not only for China but also for other nations breaking with capitalism.

This is what Samir Amin calls the strategy of "Disconnection in a Polycentric World System."[4] Countries in the global South that want to delink from global capitalism and develop socialism, or are under sanctions from the U.S., stand in a better position today than during the Cold War. In the '70s, the Third World demanded a "New World Order," which came to nothing. Today the Global South is creating a new world order. Instead of centuries of exploitative North-South relations, we see the emergence of mutually beneficial South-South investment, trade, and political relations. Today it is within the capacity of the Global South to delink and cut the pipelines of imperialism if they have the commitment.

China can push for a multipolar world order from a position of strength. It can give material and diplomatic support to countries in the Global South that are facing the U.S., much like the Soviet Union once did, but with even greater resources at its disposal. The monopoly of global financial institutions, technology, and science held by the West is broken.

---

4   Amin, Samir. *Delinking: Towards a Polycentric World*. Zed Books. 1990. London.

Anti-Imperialism—Past and Present

Anti-imperialism today is not, and cannot, be the same, as in the Long 1960s. History does not repeat itself, it moves ahead. The high revolutionary spirit, and the success of the anti-colonial struggle from the late-1940s until mid-1970s, were due to a combination of contradictions in the world-system at the time. This contradiction was between the Socialist Bloc and the U.S., as well as the contradiction between the emergence of the Third World on one side, and the U.S. trying to implement neocolonialism on the other. There was an intense wish in the Third world to get out of the grip of the West, reflected in the Bandung Conference in 1955 and the formation of the Non-Alignment Movement. This set of interlinked global contradictions opened up the wave of anti-imperialist liberation struggles with a socialist perspective across Asia, Africa, and Latin America.

All this changed with the counter offensive of imperialism, beginning in the mid-1970s, which revitalized capitalism for decades. However, neoliberal globalization was not the end of history. The changes in the international division of labor produced the decline of U.S. hegemony and the rise of China, together with the other BRICS members in the world economy, and promoted a multipolar world system.

The BRICS cooperation between Brazil, India, Russia, and South Africa was founded in 2009, as a result of the financial crises in 2006-7, which revealed the weakness of Western financial institutions. In September 2023, it was enlarged to include Argentina, Egypt, Ethiopia, Iran, Saudi Arabia, and the United Arab Emirates. BRICS now comprises 46% of the world's population and 32% of the world economy. Its future prospects of growth outweigh those of the G7.[5]

The BRICS countries pursue individual strategies to enhance their economic and political regional and world position as U.S. hegemony declines. In that effort, they are at odds with the current rules of the global economy, established to ensure the flow of value to the centers of imperialism. At the same time, they are in need of capital to develop their productive forces. However, to get access to financial resources, they find that the IMF and World Bank require that they open their economies to

---

5   Statista. "BRICS and G7 countries' share of world GDP in PPP." 2023. https://www.statista.com/statistics/1412425/gdp-ppp-share-world-gdp-g7-brics/.

the interests of the West. The trade of the Global South is carried out in dollars: investments are in dollars, reserves are held in dollars, their debt is to be in dollars; the BRICS are subject to dollar hegemony. Instead of this they want to work together and take advantage of complementarities in each other's production and markets, to trade and invest amongst themselves for mutual benefit, in order break the unequal North-South structure of finance and trade. They cannot pursue that strategy on their own, but acting together, they can begin to challenge the "rules-based international order" of the imperialist system. BRICS is not an anti-capitalist or socialist organization; it is an organization trying to create an alternative and fairer system of finance and trade. Following the BRICS+ summit in September 2023, 30 heads of state and representatives from the G77+China group met in Cuba and stressed the urgent need for a comprehensive reform of the international financial architecture.[6]

Once again, this does not mean that BRICS is anti-capitalist, and members like Russia are for sure repressive regimes. India is participating in the military alliance Quad, together with U.S., Japan, India and Australia directed against China. Iran kills communists and are brutally suppressing women. Saudi Arabia and the United Arab Emirates are exploiting Southern migration labor in the most extreme way. How can this project be progressive?

The emerging multipolar world system consists of a complex of contradictory currents—between hegemonic and counter-hegemonic, capitalist and socialist forces. The challenge is to navigate these interconnected struggles in the world system. This is what China tries to do, encouraging anti-hegemonic movements among states of the Global South, with the BRICS as a significant support. The lesson from the Chinese revolutionary process was that a rigid view of class relations can obscure the complexity and changeability of class behaviors and interests, and that the conditions for revolution need to be understood in assessing the overall situation and identifying the principal contradiction.[7] In the

---

6 Havana G77. "Declaration on current development challenges: The role of science, technology, and innovation." 2023. https://www.diplomacy.edu/resource/g77-havana-declaration-on-current-development-challenges-the-role-of-science-technology-and-innovation/.

7 Clegg, Jenny. 2023. "The BRICS and China: towards an International New Democracy." Paper presented to a conference hosted by the Shanghai University of

anti-imperialist struggle against Japan, the communists were allied with the national bourgeois Kuomintang. The newborn People's Republic in 1949 adopted the "New Democracy" concept, which also included the national bourgeoisie. According to Mao, the revolutionary advance went through stages, moving first against the international bourgeoisie to clear the path for national development, with the help of capital, and through this "dealing unrelenting blows to imperialism," it served to "clear a path even wider for socialism."[8] One can see China's current international strategy as "New Democracy," played out on the global level. Like the national bourgeoisie in China, Modi in India or the Saudi King Salman may be unreliable, and fall under the influence of U.S., but they should be seen as possible allies with China helping to weaken the U.S. hegemonic grip, and develop the productive forces in the Global South, to prepare the ground for future socialist advances.[9] A decline in U.S. hegemony will furthermore provide more space for "working and oppressed classes" to move ahead in their struggles towards socialism. We should support the struggles against oppression and exploitation in any BRICS country, whether the current rulers like it or not, as it will strengthen the socialist trend in the Global South.

The current phase in the world system is undermining the United State's hegemonic grip and thereby providing the ground for a socialist transition within this century. The failure to grasp this is to misread the potential of the situation, with momentum gathering in the Global South and pressure mounting for more international cooperation. States outside the imperialist triad of the United States/Canada, Europe, and Japan, comprising more than 80% of the global population, have refused to join the West's sanctions against Russia. Similarly, most countries in the Global South are opposed the U.S.'s aggressive policy towards China. The war in Gaza and the U.S. drive to maintain control over the Middle East through the settler-colonial state of Israel, has further undermined the credibility of the West, increasing discourse on democracy, human rights, and a rule-based world system.

Finance and Economics in September 2023. https://socialistchina.org/2023/12/06/the-brics-and-china-towards-an-international-new-democracy/.

    8   Zedong, Mao. "On New Democracy." 1940. https://www.marxists.org/reference/archive/mao/selected-works/volume-2/mswv2_26.htm.

    9   Clegg, Jenny. "The BRICS and China."

Like in the 1960s, this contradiction between the "West" trying to uphold its hegemony and the "Rest" resisting it can create space for movements struggling for socialism, and open opportunities for nations wishing to develop socialism. The development of the productive forces in the Global South in the past several decades has placed them in a much better position to move towards socialism than during the 1960s. The "West" does not have a monopoly on high-tech development any longer and they do not dominate global trade because the "Rest" has been expanding South-South development and trade.

On the surface, the ideological struggle between China and the U.S. is different from the 1960s. The U.S. is not talking about the struggle against communism, but "liberal democracy versus authoritarianism," and China is not talking about the socialist world revolution, but the establishment of a multipolar world system.

In the 1960s, China had an explicitly communist anti-imperialist policy, supporting revolutionary movements around the world. Currently, Chinese foreign policy is pragmatic with an emphasis of "non-interference" in other states. China has its reason for this pragmatism. It wants to build "Socialism with Chinese characteristics" in a calm international atmosphere. It no longer believes it would be effective to "stamp" its version of socialism on other movements and countries; instead China encourages them to develop socialism in accordance with their own national characteristics. However, this policy is still a threat to the accumulation of global capital, and as such, is still a class based anti-imperialist struggle, even though the ideological tone is turned down.

During the 1960s, it was the European colonial powers and the U.S. versus the Third World. Today, it is the same imperialist powers versus the Global South. The North is still the dominant aspect, but the South is again on the offensive. While the transformative power of the Third World, in the sixties, was based on the "revolutionary spirit"—the attempted ideological dominance over economic development, the current transformative power of the Global South, in particular China, is based on its economic strength. As the totality of the relations of production, this is a much better position for the future struggle.[10]

---

10 Kadri, Jude. "Comparing the Two 'Cold Wars' Through Gramsci, Althusser and Mao." *Journal of Labor and Society*. Vol. 26, Iss. 2. 2022. pp. 185–222.

How should we—as anti-imperialists in the capitalist center—deal with the contradiction between declining U.S. hegemony and a multipolar world system? We need a balanced approach. We must support the Chinese peasants and workers in their class struggle to move society towards socialism. I believe this struggle is possible within the current political framework, as the Communist Party has been moving steadily to the left in the past decade. If one chooses to support a struggle for socialism against the Communist Party, one must be very sure that the critique is from the left, and not a liberal democratic pro-capitalist movement, which will serve the interests of upholding U.S. hegemony.

On the other hand, anti-imperialists must defend China against U.S.-led imperialism. Just as the Soviet Union balanced imperialism, which made decolonization possible, China is today the only power that can balance the U.S., which is a prerequisite for strengthening the anti-imperialist struggle globally. A strong and socialist China can be of decisive importance for a global transformation from capitalism to socialism, and will be necessary to avoid the collapse of the system into a chaotic abyss.

Nationalism and Internationalism

Internationalism is of strategic interest because the realization of socialism has to involve the majority of the world system. We need to unite internationally to make multi-polarity possible and provide this new world-order with a socialist content.

However, it is difficult to foster internationalist solidarity within a world-system in which the working class live under very different circumstances, and are struggling not only against national capitalism but also against the exploitation of one nation by another.

Anti-imperialism must be an integrated part of the national struggle, not only in words, but also in deeds. One may rightly focus and engage in community-level struggles, but without prioritizing anti-imperialism and taking the global perspective, the struggle fragments and the achievements in one part may undermine the advance of the whole.

The primary revolutionary actor of the coming decades will be the proletariat of the Global South. Given the globalization of production, it has the potential to develop a global perspective. Its struggle cannot succeed if it remains confined to nation-state boundaries. This would only create a race to the bottom between the national working classes. There is a place for national tactics and strategies, but they must be embedded in international organizing. If industrial workers organize along the transnational production chains, they can achieve more strength than only organizing along national lines. The logistics of globalized capitalism depend upon the workers in container transport, harbors, and airports; they could block the system if they chose.

In the Global South, the peasants are still the largest class, comprising around 60% of the population. The growing importance of eco-socialist struggle is foreshadowed by peasant movements, including the Landless Workers' Movement (MST) in Brazil; the international peasant's alliance "La Via Campesina"; the Farmers' Revolt in India; and China's rural reconstruction movement. The ecological aspect is also the focus of indigenous peoples' struggles throughout the Americas. These movements are finding ways to unite with workers' struggles and call for a New International of workers and people.[11] Indigenous resistance is an important inspiration in the environmental-proletarian revolt, as they take a global perspective. As Nick Estes writes:

> There is a capaciousness to Indigenous kinship that goes beyond the human... Whereas past revolutionary struggles have strived for the emancipation of labor from capital, we are challenged not just to imagine, but to demand the emancipation of the earth from capital. For the earth to live, capitalism must die.[12]

In the absence of a Communist International, we need at least a transnational anti-systemic movement.[13] How do we organize such a movement? It can be done here and now, starting with creating a network through which participants could share resources, experiences, and information; coordinate protests, strikes, and actions; mobilize solidarity

    11   Amin, Samir and Manji, Firoze. "Toward the Formation of a Transnational Alliance of Working Oppressed Peoples." *Monthly Review*. Vol. 71, No. 3, July–August 2019. p. 120–26.

    12   Estes, Nick (2019) *Our History Is the Future: Standing Rock versus the Dakota Access Pipeline, and the Long Tradition of Indigenous Resistance*. 2019. Verso. p. 256–57.

    13   Amin, Samir. "It is Imperative to Reconstruct the International of Workers and Peoples." 2018. http://www.networkideas.org/featured-articles/2018/07/it-is-imperative-to-reconstruct-the-internationale-of-workers-and-peoples/

and support; in short, organizationally erase the boundaries between isolated struggles and connect them into one common struggle.

The specific areas of the transnational struggle can be multiple: the transnational trade union struggle (across global commodity chains); transnational climate and ecological struggles; movements against imperialist wars; anti-racist, anti-fascist, and anti-colonial struggles; the global movement for basic living conditions, etc.

From the times of the *Communist Manifesto* onward, it was understood that the only way to implement socialism was a world revolution. Lenin believed that the Russian Revolution could only survive if revolutions in the most advanced capitalist countries would follow. Likewise, China hoped that the revolutionary spirit in the Long 1960s would draw the Chinese socialist project out of its isolation.

However, nationalism had a stronger appeal in Europe, where social democratic parties identified the interests of the working class with the interests of the nation. Eventually, nationalist sentiments grew strong in the Soviet Union as well. Nationalism was also a key factor in Third World liberation struggles: in fighting for their political independence, oppressed nations pitted a progressive nationalism against the reactionary nationalism of the imperialist nations.

The failed attempt to develop the national liberation struggle into an economic liberation from imperialism by establishing socialist states in the Third World during the Long 1960s, together with the dissolution of the Soviet Union and the Chinese opening to neoliberalism, proved Marx and Engels statement in the *Manifesto* right. Even if some kind of "socialist transition" would occur in one country within a dominating capitalist world system, it would still be part of the global division of labor, transnational production chains, and it would have to compete in the global market. This can only lead to the implementation of exploitative practices that benefit the capitalist world economy, as we have seen in China.

This requires us to return to socialism's global ambition—the only realistic one. The principal contradiction in the world system determines to a large extent the outcome of national and local struggles. While we cannot ignore the political reality of nation-states, our strategy must be a global one. The national struggle should contribute to moving the principal contradiction of the world systems in the right direction. Socialism can only flourish when it becomes the dominant mode of production globally. To achieve this situation, the struggle for socialism has to develop from movements, parties, and other kinds of organizations to govern states. The socialist state can begin to develop a mode of production on the national level, but just as importantly, they can support the struggle for socialism within the entire world-system.

The existence of "actually existing socialism," with all its flaws, secured a balance of power with U.S. imperialism, which made other struggles for socialism possible. The existence of the Soviet Union contributed to the victory of China, Vietnam, and the survival of the Cuban Revolution (which itself was important for struggles in Angola, Bolivia, the Congo, and more).

Today, a socialist-orientated China can be of great importance for a possible transition towards global socialism. China should not be isolated and forced to retreat into nationalism, but take part in the international struggle for the global transition to socialism.

Besides internationalism, the struggle has to have a radical, anti-capitalist perspective. There is no social democratic road to socialism. Social democracy is a mutation of socialism generated by imperialism and can only prosper in the Global North as a capitalist welfare state. If reforms in the Global North are not accompanied by the deconstruction of imperialism, then they are not a step forward—they are parasitic. Time is running out for reforms. The capitalist mode of production threatens the balance of the global ecosystem. We do not have all the time in the world.

Climate Change and the Transition Towards Socialism

Capitalism, especially the past fifty-years of neoliberal globalization, has created serious environmental problems. This has already affected the living conditions of millions of people in the Global South and led to the formation of movements for a radical change. The Global North is trying to reduce global warming without significantly changing the lifestyle that is causing global warming. As usual, capitalism assimilates critique and is now developing "green capitalism," which innovates new products and grows in parallel with continuing fossil capitalism. "Green capitalism" is a contradiction in terms. The competition between capital and states within the world system forces each capitalist and state to expand capital accumulation. The current conflict level in the world system reinforced this competition, and the prospect of reaching international agreements which could diminish global warming seem to have vanished.

Alternatively, there should be an economic system based on the social ownership of the means of production, which makes political decisions that control how and what to produce. Instead of using surplus products for extended capital accumulation, they can be used for decarbonization, environmental cleaning, or projects to reduce inequality.

The climate movement sometimes tends to view the environment and climate as issues separate from class relations, yet climate change is connected to capitalism and imperialism, and therefore is class related. Citizens in the Global North are able to mindlessly consume the globe's resources and throw out the trash only because the rest of the world cannot.[14] The climate struggle must be linked to the development of an equal world. It is not possible to raise the living standards of billions of poor people in the Global South to the level of the U.S. or Germany within the capitalist mode of production, due to the simple lack of natural resources. To accommodate their needs, it is not only a change in the relations of production and patterns of consumption which is needed to develop socialism on a global scale—it is also a continued development of the productive forces. On this Emmanuel writes:

> Steel, aluminum and copper of which the masses of the center consume today in such extravagant quantities, do not serve only to produce automobiles and gadgets. They produce doctors or books as well (it takes a tremendous amount of steel, cement, and energy to produce a doctor or school or village).[15]

A global and sustainable socialism cannot be developed by under developing technology. It needs the most advanced forms of technology.

---

14 Emmanuel, Arghiri. "Unequal Exchange Revisited." IDS Discussion Paper, no. 77. 1975. University of Sussex. p. 66–67.

15 Emmanuel Arghiri. "Europe-Asia Colloquium. For the use by the Commission on International Relations. Some guidelines for the 'problematiqe' of world Economy." IEDES. 1976. Manuscript found in Emmanuel's archive. Green portfolio marked "Imperialism." p. 3–4.

The ruling class cannot and will not save the environment. Instead of pleading with rulers, we need to anchor our understanding of the climate crisis in class analysis. Without the mobilization of the proletariat and peasants, there is no abolition of capitalism, and thus no social-ecological transformation of society.

The global scale of the climate crisis must be countered by centralized and global planning, which presupposes a global transformation towards socialism. The global movement for socialism must include environmental struggles, while environmental movements must equally take on a class and global perspective. John Bellamy Foster writes:

> Hundreds of millions of people have now entered actively into the struggle for a world of substantive equality and ecological sustainability, constituting the fundamental meaning of socialism and the future of history in our time. Yet, the planetary revolt of humanity in the twenty-first century will prove "irresistible and irreversible," and thus succeed against all odds, only if it takes the form of a more unified, revolutionary human subject, emanating from "the wretched of the earth," an environmental proletariat. It is time to exit the burning house.[16]

I may only add the need to construct a new house. Instead of appeals to the capitalist state to act sensible in terms of climate change, the struggle has to go through the establishment of pro-socialist states. And in terms of transition, we are running out of time due to our climate problems.

THE END GAME

The end game will be characterized by intense and sometimes chaotic fluctuations. Today, capitalism *is* in crisis: an economic crisis aggravated by the erosion and split up of the world market and wars. The crisis is ecological. Scientific studies tell us that we are heading toward catastrophe in the form of natural disasters, storms, floods, droughts, and shrinking harvests. A development that is increasing migration and exacerbating the economic crisis. There is political crisis because the bourgeoisie is divided between those who wish to resume neoliberal globalization—change everything to keep everything the same—and paleo-conservative factions

---

16 Foster, John Bellamy. "Ecology and the Future of History." *Monthly Review*, Vol 74, No. 3. 2022. p. 132.

who want to return to a nation-based accumulation of capital, authoritarian rule, and warfare to secure the lion's share of the global spoils.

The split in the bourgeoisie continues down through the middle class and the working class in the Global North, between groups linked to transnational capital and groups linked to national sectors. New national-conservative alliances arise. The Trump-dominated Republican Party in the United States, together with right populism throughout Europe, are all signs of this split and the confusion it causes. The old politicians in the Global North are desperately seeking to overcome the gap between the need for transnational capital for continued neoliberal globalization and a growing desire of the electorate to return to the capitalist nation-based welfare state. It is a difficult task. Production and consumption have become globalized. You cannot just dismantle the transnational production chain without a serious loss of profit for capital.

Based on the evaluation of the past and present, the following is a possible scenario in the following decades: U.S. hegemony is in decline. The U.S. has lost its economic superiority, its political elite is divided and there is no revival of the "American century." China is on the rise. It will continue its development of "socialism with Chinese characteristics." Externally, it will pursue the establishment of a multipolar world-system. Professor Cheng Yawen from the School of International Relations and Public Affairs in Shanghai has reintroduced the strategy of the encirclement of the cities from the countryside as part of China's foreign policy:

> One hundred years ago, the leaders of the Communist Party of China proposed the revolutionary path of "encircling the city in the countryside." At this time of "unprecedented changes," China and the developing countries need to break the center-periphery order of the contemporary world and the Western countries' prevention and suppression of non-Western countries, as well as to improve solidarity and cooperation in the global "rural" areas.[17]

The Belt and Road Initiative was launched in 2013. By February 2022, 146 countries have signed up to join the initiative. In combination with BRICS, China will create South-South and East-West relations to change the old North-South structure of the world-system.

There is a wish in many countries in the Global South to change the

---

17   Yawen, Cheng. "The peace dividend is over, and China has to prepare for a full decoupling" 2022. *Monthly Review Online*. https://mronline.org/2022/06/14/building-the-new-three-rings/

U.S. dollar-centered international financial system for several reasons. Due to its hegemonic position, the U.S. had the exorbitant privilege of printing dollars to be used as world money for exchange—dollars which never return to the U.S. for claiming goods. The U.S. also uses the status of the dollar as world money and international financial architecture to sanction countries, as trading denominated in dollars has to transit through a U.S. bank and the SWIFT system. A change to this will further weaken U.S. hegemony, which depends on these structures.

A multipolar world system, alternative economic institutions, and the existence of a major technologically developed state—China—will provide space for social movements and states in the Global South to move in the direction of socialism. We may see the development of a different kind of socialism, incorporating the historical and cultural background of each nation. These movements and states will intensify their corporation, tipping the balance in the world-system from capitalism towards the direction of socialism.

Socialist advances will originate in the Global South, where the popular forces understand that it is not possible to turn the development of the productive forces into a system that benefits the people without a transformation from capitalist to socialist relations of production. These struggles are necessarily arising in specific contexts, embodying environmental, as well as economic and cultural realities. They will develop not just Socialism with Chinese characteristics, but Socialism with South African characteristics, Brazilian characteristics, and Palestinian characteristics. This is not just a tribute to diversity; diversity is necessary for success in developing socialism in different contexts.

As global capitalism begins to collapse, the immediate concern for future socialist governments in the Global South will be how to organize the economy to meet people's basic needs without worsening the ecological crisis. In this transitional period, future socialist-orientated governments may again take up the strategy of "delinking" from the remains of the capitalist world market and its law of value. The strategy of "delinking" would help socialist governments to establish a state monopoly over domestic markets and reduce the pressure from the capitalist world market. The establishment of an international alternative to the capitalist financial system and its dollar tyranny will also improve the maneuvering space for socialist governments to socialize the economy and implement socially and environmentally progressive policies. They will face the task of cleaning up the global environment and developing new ways to produce and consume which will lead to long-term sustainability.[18]

We are at the threshold of decisive struggles. The transition from capitalism to another mode of production can take two qualitatively different forms. The first is an uncontrolled implosion of capitalism into ecological and political chaos.[19] The second is a transition in which the strategy of the struggling classes captures the reality of the situation and solves the contradiction to unblock development of the productive forces. In this case, we have a transition with a clear vision. However, socialism is not predetermined to follow after capitalism, as the more mechanical rendition of dialectical materialism suggests. It is not a given fact that there is a happy ending.

The crisis of capitalism makes objective conditions for change excellent. In a structural crisis, where the system is unstable, the "agent" plays a decisive role. The problem is the development of the subjective forces for change. We were too optimistic in the 1970s. However, I believe that we are too defensive and pessimistic today. In the introduction, I pointed out that without anger and a burning desire to change the world, it is not possible to mobilize the forces that will create radical change. This anger exists, as spontaneous uprisings across the globe signify. The problem is the strategy that can turn these feelings from the streets into socialist transformation. The pessimism in the mainstream left is understandable given previous failures. But pessimism gets in the way of revolutionary hope: "Capitalism survives every crisis," "All attempts to establish socialism have ended in disaster," and so forth. The result is a cynical, toothless critique of capitalism without a perspective of radical change. Therefore, I choose to be an optimist. This choice is part of the ideological struggle both within the left and against the capitalist system. When I say optimism, I do not mean naivety. It is not simply a matter of time until "the masses get it right." What I mean is *realistic optimism*, taking into account the structural crises and instability of global capitalism, as well

---

18   Li, Minqi. *China and the Twenty-First Century Crisis.* 2016. Pluto Press. p. 191–192.

19   Amin, S. "The Communist Manifesto, 170 Years Later." Page 1–14. *Monthly Review,* Vol. 70, No. 5. October 2018. p. 1–14.

as the hundreds of millions of new proletarians in the Global South who have "nothing to lose but their chains," and are becoming ever more conscious of their power. The development of the productive forces in the Global South places the working class in a central position and creates a much stronger foundation for the development of a socialist society than was the case in the decolonization era.

Even if the "brand" of socialism is damaged by the many failed attempts and the mixed experiences of "actually existing socialism," I think socialism has a chance to replace capitalism, simply because it has a core of rationality which is needed to solve the problems confronting humanity.

What is to be Done?

Support a multipolar world system against U.S. hegemony to promote a more peaceful and democratic world, with an empowered and reformed United Nations.

Support the Global South's struggle for a more equal world against the West, which have ruled the world through colonialism and imperialism for the last five hundred years.

Support the countries and movements developing socialism, to end the exploitation of humans and the destruction of planet earth.

What specifically can the left in the Global North do? After all, we will not be the driving force in the transition toward global socialism. However, it is not enough to wait for the proletariat of the Global South to create a revolutionary situation in our part of the world. We must be more than passive bystanders. We must make sure that the North is no safe "hinterland" for imperialism, which means struggle against right-wing national chauvinism, racism, and imperialist political and military intervention. Anti-war campaigns will be an essential part of anti-imperialism in the coming years. We will be considered national traitors—but that is better than being class traitors.

We must support socialist movements and states, not only in words, but in deeds and material means. To the extent possible, we should promote workers' struggles along the global production chains. We must build an international climate and solidarity organization. The specific ways, and which means to use in the struggle, depend on the type of organization, and the specific political situation and place. It will range from mass movement to direct-action groups, from parliamentary work and civilian disobedience to armed struggle.

We will be a minority, but an important minority. In our political work, we often feel what we are doing is too little—unimportant in terms of changing the world. However, there are no "small" struggles, no "small" resistances. There are separate sets of actions and interventions that sometimes converge to force "big" changes. The capitalist system is out of balance. Small actions can produce an avalanche of events.

We should keep in mind that revolution is not a "tea-party." Capitalism will not just lay down. If our struggle is more than words, it will have consequences. We should plan and be prepared for this, on the personal and the organizational level.

On a personal level, it is not easy to be at odds—not only with the state but also mainstream society. There are strong forces, which aim to integrate us into the system—our imperial way of living. Our participation in the real estate market and our pension funds link us to the well being of capitalism. The massive news media and cultural influence inject the norms and values of liberal capitalism into our body and soul. It can be difficult to maintain a clear-cut opposition to the system and accept that deep economic and political crises are part of the endgame of capitalism, and we should welcome it. The end game is not a walk in the park.

On an organizational level, we will have to prepare for how the global struggle will develop in the next 2 to 5 years. What should our strategy be? How can I, and my organization, fit into the analysis of the objective and subjective forces of transition? What kind of support can we deliver? How can we best be a cogwheel in the big machine of transformation from world capitalism towards socialism?

There Will Come a Day

Let me end this long book as I began—on a personal note. I wish to paraphrase the handbill "There will come a day," handed out in May 1968 at

Burmeister & Wains Shipyard in Copenhagen,[20] a text that in many ways set the course for my political trajectory.

The handbill states that the mobilization and transformation of the working class in the capitalist metropolis into a revolutionary force requires a crisis, and the working class needs to realize that radical change is necessary. Only then can we undertake struggles for emancipation. Lenin said:

> Revolution is impossible without a nationwide crisis affecting both the exploited and the exploiters. It follows that, for a revolution to take place, it is essential, first, that a majority of the workers (or at least a majority of the class-conscious, thinking, and politically active workers) should fully realize that revolution is necessary, and that they should be prepared to die for it.[21]

Unless blindfolded by illusions or dogmatism, no one will maintain that the majority of the working class of the Global North is "prepared to die" for the socialist revolution. Rather, the majority are prepared, if not to die, then to struggle to defend their "imperial mode of living."

This has been the case since the end of the Second World War, and it will be like this for some time to come. How will the Global North working class react when—because of the struggle for the emancipation of the oppressed nations and people—"the imperial mode of living" is no longer possible?

We have seen racism and right-wing populism spreading in Europe and North America in the past decades. When the middle-class comes under pressure, it often moves to the right and Social Democrats have a historical record of allying with capital during crises. This might lead to military intervention against emerging socialism in the Global South, in an effort to reconstruct imperialist dominations. Seldom has someone hit the bull's eye better than Lenin when he wrote:

> ...there (in the West) the craft-union, narrow-minded, selfish, case-hardened, covetous and petty-bourgeois "labour aristocracy," imperialist-minded, and imperialist-corrupted, has developed.[22]

---

20   Appel, Gotfred. "There will come a day...Imperialism and the Working Class." 1971. Communist Working Circle. Copenhagen.

21   Lenin, V.I "Left-wing Communism: An Infantile Disorder." *Collected Works, Volume 31*. 1964. Progress Publishers. Moscow. pp. 17–118.

22   *Ibid.*

How has this come about? The answer is, as Engels wrote, that the Northern workers "have gladly taken their share of the booty" from the exploitation of colonized peoples. The British Prime Minister Disraeli, who was the champion of imperialism and defended the right of the "superior" races to subjugate "inferior" ones, extended suffrage to the popular classes in Britain in exchange for their support for colonial expansion. In this way, he defused the social question and class struggle in his own country:

> I say with confidence that the great body of the working-class of England... are English to the core. They are for maintaining the greatness of the Kingdom and the Empire, and they are proud of being subjects of our Sovereign and members of such an Empire.[23]

The popular masses respond to the dominant class's social reforms with patriotism and support for colonial expansionism. Losurdo writes:

> However progressive in itself, there is no class struggle that cannot be instrumentalized by the dominant power and integrated into a general project of a conservative or reactionary stamp. This is not a new phenomenon. But it has been accentuated and acquired a new qualitative potency in the wake of disenchantment at the results of twentieth-century revolutions and subsequent theoretical disorientation.[24]

Marx and Engels pointed to the connection between social reform and colonialism. Lenin extended the critique—but the social-democratic and communist parties of Western Europe kept silent about it. What have the Social Democrats done instead? They have been working for reforms, for shorter working hours, longer holidays, bigger unemployment subsidies, etc. What have the Communists been doing? They have raised demands for still higher wages, still longer holidays, still bigger unemployment subsidies, etc.

The Social Democrats have been boasting of the results achieved. The Communists have been saying that these results were too small. They are wrong. "Imperial socialism" will not lead to socialism. Lenin explained why:

> Only the proletarian class, which maintains the whole of society, can bring

---

23 Wilkinson, William John. *Tory Democracy*. 1980. Octagon Books. New York. p. 52.

24 Losurdo, Domenico. *Class Struggle. A Political and Philosophical History*. 2016. Palgrave Macmillan. New York. p. 280.

about the social revolution. However, as a result of the extensive colonial policy, the European proletarian partly finds himself in a position where it is not his labour, but the labour of the practically enslaved natives in the colonies, that maintains the whole of society...In certain countries this provides the material and economic basis for infecting the proletariat with colonial chauvinism.[25]

Social Democrats and Communists have been joining hands in making the workers believe that it is the working class itself, through class struggle, that has made the welfare state possible. It is, but it is also based on imperialism. Lenin called it a "parasite state."

However, it is important to remember that the "parasite state theory" is not *only a* state that the working class gains from imperialism.[26] The bourgeoisification was a historical phenomenon, created by specific historical, economic, and political development in capitalism, and since it is an historical phenomenon, it opens up the possibility of change in the position of the class.

The "parasite state theory" states that the working class in Western Europe and North America occupies a dual position. They are an object of exploitation, as they perform wage labor, which creates surplus value and thus profit for capital. However, by virtue of their relatively high wages, they are also able to acquire value through their consumption of goods, produced by low-wage labor in the Global South. Whether they are exploited or exploiter, in a global perspective, it is a matter of a balance between the acquisition of value—through consumption, exploitation, and their contribution of surplus value to capital.

Without this double perspective on the position of the working class, the "parasite state theory" becomes static and loses its revolutionary content. This theory can explain both the historical process of bourgeoisification and the working class's support for colonialism and imperialism through the 20th century. At the same time, it also maintains the future possibility of this class as the gravediggers of capitalism.

If one denies the significance and consequences of imperialism's transfusion of value to the working class in the Global North, one falls

---

25 Lenin, V.I. "The International Socialist Congress in Stuttgart." *Collected Works Vol. 13.* 1972. Progress Publishers. Moscow. p. 77.

26 Lauesen, Torkil. "The parasite state in theory and practice." *Labor and Society*, Vol. 21. 2018. pp. 285-300.

into the fog of seeing every economic struggle as a revolutionary struggle on the road to socialism. If one denies that the highly paid worker in the imperialist countries produces value, surplus value, and profit, then you reject the possibility that the working class in the imperialist center can ever play a role in the struggle against capitalism. Moreover, one loses sight of political activity in the Global North, and gives up the task set by Lenin:

> To be able to seek, find and correctly determine the specific path or the particular turn of events that will lead the masses to the real, decisive and final revolutionary struggle—such is the main objective of communism in Western Europe and in America today.[27]

The hallmark of a Marxist is to have an analysis, strategy, and praxis for the context in which one is situated. The communists in the Global North must include the anti-imperialist struggle, and thereby the struggle against their own states' imperialism, as a centerpiece in their strategy. The success of this task depends on their courage and their fighting spirit—on how deep into the quagmire of chauvinism and imperialism the working class can do battle.

When imperialism is defeated in the Global South, and the working class in the center once again faces only their own bourgeoisie, then they may overthrow the exploiters. Global socialism—the only possible socialism—needs intervention from both South and North. The new world order will emerge from fiery struggles. The stakes are high. Will the system self-destruct by catastrophe? Will we slide further into global apartheid under fascist rule? Or will strong anti-capitalist and anti-imperialist movements emerge?

---

27 Lenin, *"Left-Wing" Communism*, p. 112.

Appendix

Figure 2. *The History of the Development of Productive Forces in Capitalism.*

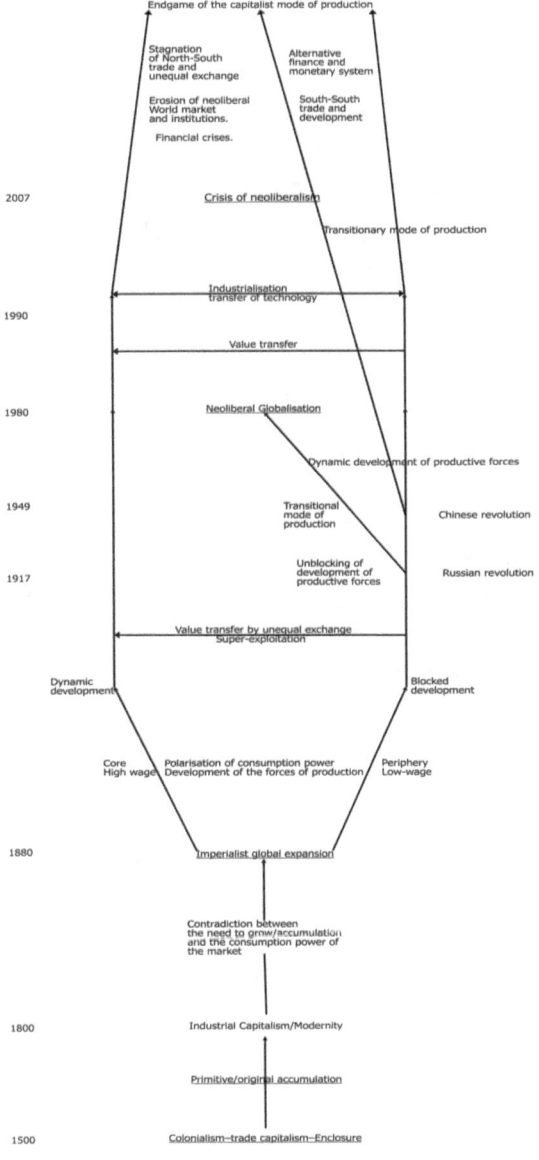

Bibliography

AL JAZEERA. "China's Xi Tells Putin of 'Changes Not Seen for 100 Years.'" *Al Jazeera*, March 22, 2023. https://www.aljazeera.com/news/2023/3/22/xi-tells-putin-of-changes-not-seen-for-100.

ALBRIGHT, Madeleine. Interview by Lesley Stahl. "60 Minutes." CBS, May 12, 1996. https://wellesleyunderground.com/post/55743079050/television-interview-60-minutes-may-12-1996.

AMIN, Samir, and Firoze Manji. "Toward the Formation of a Transnational Alliance of Working Oppressed Peoples." *Monthly Review* 71, no. 3 (July-August 2019).

——— "A Note on the Concept of Delinking." *Review* 10, no. 3 (1987): 435–44. Fernand Braudel Center.

——— "China 2013." *Monthly Review* 64, no. 10 (March 2013).

——— "Egypt: Failed Emergence, Conniving Capitalism, Fall of the Muslim Brothers—A Possible Popular Alternative." In *Development Challenges and Solutions after the Arab Spring*, edited by Ali Kadri. London: Palgrave, 2016.

——— "It is Imperative to Reconstruct the International of Workers and Peoples." *Ideas*, July 3, 2018. http://www.networkideas.org/featured-articles/2018/07/it-is-imperative-to-reconstruct-the-internationale-of-workers-and-peoples/.

——— "Russia and the Ukraine Crisis: The Eurasian Project in Conflict with the Triad Imperialist Policies." *Monthly Review Online*, May 7, 2022. https://mronline.org/2022/05/07/russia-and-the-ukraine-crisis-the-eurasian-project-in-conflict-with-the-triad-imperialist-policies/.

——— "The Communist Manifesto, 170 Years Later." *Monthly Review* 70, no. 5 (October 2018): 1–14.

——— *Delinking: Towards a Polycentric World*. London: Zed Books, 1990.

——— *The Law of Worldwide Value*. New York: Monthly Review Press, 2010.

——— *The Long Revolution of the Global South*. New York: Monthly Review Press, 2019.

APPEL, Gotfred. "There Will Come a Day." Handbill distributed for B&W, Shipyard, May 3, 1968. In *There Will Come a Day... Imperialism and the Working Class*, Communist Working Circle. Copenhagen: Futura, 1971.

ARENDT, Hannah. *The Origins of Totalitarianism*. New York: Meridian Books, 1958.

ARMSTRONG, Charles K. "The Destruction and Reconstruction of North Korea, 1950-1960." *Asia-Pacific Journal* 7, no. 0 (2009).

BADIOU, Alain. "The Paris Commune: Marx, Mao, Tomorrow." *Monthly Review* 73, no. 1 (May 2021).

BANAC, Ivo. *The Diary of Georgi Dimitrov, 1933–1949*. New Haven: Yale University Press, 2003.

BANDURSKI, David. "A History of Common Prosperity." China Newsspeak, August 27, 2021. https://chinamediaproject.org/2021/08/27/a-history-of-common-prosperity.

BANERJEE, Sumanta. *India's Simmering Revolution: The Naxalite Uprising*. London: Zed Press, 1984.

BARNOUIN, Barbara, and Yu Changgen. *Zhou Enlai: A Political Life*. Hong Kong: Chinese University of Hong Kong, 2006.

BARR, William P. "Keynote Address at the Department of Justice's China Initiative Conference, February 6, 2020." https://www.justice.gov/opa/speech/attorney-general-william-p-barr-delivers-keynote-address-department-justices-china.

BASHEAR, Suliman. *Communism in the Arab East, 1918–28*. London: Ithaca Press, 1980.

BAUER, Otto. *Zwischen zwei Weltkriegen? Die Krise der Weltwirtschaft, der Demokratie und des Sozialismus*. Bratislava: Eugen Prager, 1936. In *Western Marxism and the Soviet Union. A Survey of Critical Theories and Debates Since 1917*, edited by Marcel van der Linden. Historical Materialism Book Series, vol. 17. Leiden: Brill, 2007.

BERNSTEIN, Eduard. "Der Sozialismus und die Kolonialfrage." *Sozialistische Monatshefte*, 1900. https://www.marxists.org/deutsch/referenz/bernstein/1900.

——— *Die Voraussetzungen des Sozialismus und die Aufgaben der Sozialdemokratie*. Hamburg: Rowoht, 1969.

BIAO, Lin. "Address at the Enlarged Meeting of the CPC Central Politburo, May 18, 1966." Published in *Renmin Ribao*, June 1966. In *Chinese Law & Government* 2, no. 4 (1969): 42-62.

——— "Foreword to the Second Edition of Quotations of Chairman Mao Zedong." December 16, 1966. https://www.marxists.org/reference/archive/lin-biao/1966/12/16.htm.

——— "Long Live the Victory of People's War! In Commemoration of the 20th Anniversary of Victory in the Chinese People's War of Resistance Against Japan." *Peking Review* 36 (September 3, 1965). Peking: Foreign Languages Press, 1965.

——— "Mao Zedong's Thought is the Telescope and Microscope of Our Revolutionary Cause." Editorial of *Jiefangjun Bao* (Liberation Army Daily), June 7, 1966. https://bannedthought.net/China/MaoEra/GPCR/GreatSocialistCulturalRevolutionInChina-03-1966.pdf.

BLOCH, E. *Geist der Utopie*. Reprint, Frankfurt am Main: Suhrkamp, 1971.

BLOOM, Joshua, and Waldo E. Martin Jr. *Black Against Empire: The History and Politics of the Black Panther Party*. Berkeley: University of California Press, 2013.

BORRELL, Josep. "Speech at EU Ambassadors Annual Conference 2022, October 10, 2022, Brussels." https://www.eeas.europa.eu/eeas/eu-ambassadors-annual-conference-2022-opening-speech-high-representative-josep-borrell_en.

BRADLEY, James. *The China Mirage*. New York: Little Brown and Company, 2015.

BRADY, Anne-Marie. *Making the Foreign Serve China: Managing Foreigners in the People's Republic*. Lanham: Rowman & Littlefield, 2003.

BRECHT, Bertolt. *Life of Galileo*. Scene 12. https://quotepark.com/works/life-of-galileo-2377/.

BROWDER, Earl Russell. *The Meaning of Social-Fascism: Its Historical and Theoretical Background*. New York: Workers Library Publisher, 1933. https://stars.library.ucf.edu/cgi/viewcontent.cgi?article=1315&context=prism.

BROWN, Anthony Cave, and Charles B. Macdonald. *On a Field of Red: The Communist International and the Coming of World War II*. New York: G.P. Putnam's Sons, 1981.

CARTER, Jimmy. "On Trump's China Policy." *Telesur English*, April 18, 2019. https://www.telesurenglish.net/opinion/Jimmy-Carter-Lectures-Trump-US-Is-Most-Warlike-Nation-in-History-of-the-World-20190418-0020.html.

CASTRO, Fidel. "Speech at the Second Anniversary of the Cuban Revolution." January 5, 1961. http://lanic.utexas.edu/project/castro/db/1961/19610105.html.

CHEN, Meixia. "The Great Reversal: Transformation of Health Care in the People's Republic of China." In *Blackwell Companion to Medical Sociology*, edited by William C. Cockerham. 2nd ed. Oxford: Blackwell, 2004. https://s3.us-west-1.wasabisys.com/p-library/books/018636e47d5361dd1dc0bbfc5ac6ba20.pdf.

CHENG, Chu-Yuan. *Communist China's Economy, 1949-1962: Structural Changes and Crisis*. Seton Hall University Press, 1963.

CHI-HSI, Hu. *Mao-Zedong und die Kommunistische Partei Chinas*. Hamburg: Institut für Asienkunde, 1968.

CLAUDIN, Fernando. *The Communist Movement from Comintern to Cominform*. New York: Monthly Review Press, 1975.

COHEN, G.A. *History, Labour, and Freedom: Themes from Marx*. Oxford: Clarendon Press, 1988.

Cohen, Stephen F. *Bukharin and the Bolshevik Revolution: A Political Biography 1888-1938.* New York: Alfred A. Knopf, 1973.

Curtis, Kim. "Between Promise and Practice: Life in a Russian Factory Town." In *Capitalism and Socialism in Cuba: A Study of Dependency, Development, and Underdevelopment*, edited by Jean-Paul Dumont. New York: Monthly Review Press, 1972.

Day, Richard B. *The 'Crisis' and the 'Crash': Soviet Studies of the West (1917-1939).* London: New Left Books, 1981.

Djilas, Milovan. *Conversations with Stalin.* London: Penguin, 1963.

——— *The New Class: An Analysis of the Communist System.* New York: Praeger, 1957.

Draper, Hal. *Karl Marx's Theory of Revolution.* Vol. 1, *State and Bureaucracy.* New York: Monthly Review Press, 1977.

Du Bois, W.E.B. *Black Reconstruction in America 1860-1880.* New York: Harcourt, Brace and Company, 1935.

Eastman, Max. *Since Lenin Died.* New York: Boni & Liveright, 1925.

Eckstein, Alexander. *China's Economic Development: The Interplay of Scarcity and Ideology.* Ann Arbor: University of Michigan Press, 1975.

Engels, F. "Letter to Karl Kautsky 1894." In Marx, K., and Engels, F., *On Colonialism.* Moscow: Foreign Languages Publishing House, 1963.

——— "Letter to Karl Kautsky 1894." In *On Colonialism*, by K. Marx and F. Engels. Moscow: Foreign Languages Publishing House, 1963.

——— "Letter to Paul Lafargue, 22 November 1894." In *Marx & Engels Collected Works*, vol. 50. Moscow: Progress Publishers, 1985.

Engst, F. "The Struggle for Actually Building Socialist Society: An Interview with Fred Engst Conducted by Onurcan Ülker on April 7, 2017, in Beijing." Originally published by Research Unit for Political Economy (RUPE) on January 19, 2018. Accessed July 6,

2024. mronline.org.

ESTES, Nick. *Our History Is the Future: Standing Rock versus the Dakota Access Pipeline, and the Long Tradition of Indigenous Resistance.* London: Verso, 2019. In Foster, John Bellamy. "Ecology and the Future of History." *Monthly Review* 74, no. 3 (July-August 2022).

FANON, Frantz. *The Wretched of the Earth.* New York: Grove Press, 2004.

FEWSMITH, Joseph. "Reaction, Resurgence, and Succession: Chinese Politics since Tiananmen." In *The Politics of China: Sixty Years of The People's Republic of China*, edited by Roderick MacFarquhar, 468-526. Massachusetts: Harvard University, 2011.

FIGES, Orlando. *A People's Tragedy: The Russian Revolution 1891–1924.* London: Pimlico Random House, 1996.

FILTZER, Donald. *Soviet Workers and De-Stalinization: The Consolidation of the Modern System of Soviet Production Relations 1953-1964.* Cambridge: Cambridge University Press, 1992.

FINANCIAL TIMES, "Rush by West to Back Israel Erodes Developing Countries' Support for Ukraine." October 18, 2023. ft.com.

FISCHER, Louis. *The Life of Lenin.* London: Weidenfeld and Nicolson, 1964.

FITZPATRICK, Sheila. *Education and Social Mobility in the Soviet Union 1921-1934.* Cambridge: Cambridge University Press, 1979.

FOOT, Rosemary. *The Practice of Power: U.S. Relations with China Since 1949.* Oxford: Clarendon Press, 1995.

FOSTER, John Bellamy. "Ecology and the Future of History." *Monthly Review* 74, no. 3 (July-August 2022).

——— "Lukács and the Tragedy of Revolution: Reflections on 'Tactics and Ethics.'" *Monthly Review* 73, no. 9 (February 2022).

——— "The Planetary Rift." Interview by Haris Golemis. *Monthly Review* 73, no. 6 (2021).

FREIRE, Paulo. *Pedagogy of the Oppressed.* Translated by Myra Bergman Ramos. New York: Herder and Herder, 1970.

FRIEDMAN, Milton. *Capitalism and Freedom*. Chicago: University of Chicago Press, 1962.

FROST, Daniel. "Long Marches, Long Revolutions." *Red Pepper*, April 22, 2022. Accessed July 6, 2024. https://www.redpepper.org.uk/long-marches-long-revolutions/.

FURET, François. *The Passing of an Illusion: The Idea of Communism in the Twentieth Century*. Chicago: University of Chicago Press, 1999.

GABRIELE, Alberto. *Enterprises, Industry and Innovation in the People's Republic of China: Questioning Socialism from Deng to the Trade and Tech War*. Singapore: Springer Press, 2020.

GADDIS, John Lewis. *We Now Know: Rethinking Cold War History*. Oxford: Clarendon Press, 1997.

GAO, Mobo C.F. "Why Is the Battle for China's Past Relevant to Us Today?" *Aspects of India's Economy: Remembering Socialist China, 1949–1976*, no. 59–60 (October 2014). Accessed July 6, 2024. rupe-india.org.

——— *Gao Village: A Portrait of Modern Life in Rural China*. Honolulu: University of Hawaii Press, 1999.

GHODSEE, Kristen. *Second World, Second Sex: Socialist Women's Activism and Global Solidarity during the Cold War*. Durham: Duke University Press, 2019.

GHOSH, Jayati. *Never Done and Poorly Paid: Women's Work in Globalising India*. New Delhi: Women Unlimited, 2009.

GILBERG, Trond. *Nationalism and Communism in Romania: The Rise and Fall of Ceausescu's Personal Dictatorship*. Boulder: Westview Press, 1990.

GLAZYEV, Sergey. "Events like This Happen Once a Century." *The Saker*, March 28, 2022. Accessed July 6, 2024. https://thesaker.is/events-like-this-happen-once-a-century-sergey-glazyev-on-the-breakdown-of-epochs-and-changing-ways-of-life/.

GLEIJESES, Piero. *Conflicting Missions: Havana, Washington, and Africa, 1959-1976*. Chapel Hill: University of North Carolina Press, 2002.

GOLDSTEIN, Andrea. *Multinational Companies from Emerging Economies: Composition, Conceptualization, and Direction in the Global Economy*. Basingstoke: Palgrave Macmillan, 2007.

GONCHAROV, Sergei N., John W. Lewis, and Litai Xue. *Uncertain Partners: Stalin, Mao, and the Korean War*. Stanford: Stanford University Press, 1993.

GONZALEZ, Juan. *Harvest of Empire: A History of Latinos in America*. New York: Viking, 2000.

GOULDEN, Joseph C. *Korea: The Untold Story of the War*. New York: McGraw-Hill, 1982.

GRAEBER, David. *Debt: The First 5000 Years*. Brooklyn: Melville House, 2011.

GRAHAM, Helen. *The Spanish Republic at War, 1936–1939*. Cambridge: Cambridge University Press, 2002.

GRAMSCI, Antonio. "Letter of the Politburo of the Italian Communist Party to the Central Committee of the Soviet Communist Party." In *Building the Communist Party*, edited by S. Caprioglio. Turin: Einaudi, 1971.

——— *La Città Futura 1917–1918* (The Future Society 1917–1918). Edited by S. Caprioglio. Turin: Einaudi, 1982.

GRANDIN, Greg. *Empire's Workshop: Latin America, the United States, and the Rise of the New Imperialism*. New York: Metropolitan Books, 2006.

GROW, R. F. "Soviet Economic Penetration of China, 1945–1960: 'Imperialism' as a Level of Analysis Problem." In *Testing Theories of Economic Imperialism*, edited by S. J. Rosen and J. R. Kurth, 261–281. Lexington, Mass.: Lexington Books, 1974.

GUEVARA, Che. "At the Afro-Asian Conference in Algeria, February 24, 1965." In *The Che Reader*. Australia: Ocean Press, 2005.

——— "Remarks in Algeria to Jeunesse, December 23, 1964." Published in "Revolución," December 26, 1964.

——— "Socialism and Man in Cuba." In *The Che Reader*. Australia: Ocean Press, 2005.

——— *El Socialismo y el Hombre en Cuba, Obras Escogidas 1957-1967*, Tomo II. Casa de las Americas, 1970. In *The Che Handbook*, edited by Hilda Barrio and Gareth Jenkins. London: MQ Publications, 2003.

Guoguang, Liu. *Some Problems of the Political Economy of Socialism with Chinese Characteristics*, Jinan chubanshe, 2017. In Gabriel Martinez, "Ideological Work in the New Era of Socialism in China." *The International*. Accessed July 6, 2024. https://international-magz.com/articles/.

Haffner, Sebastian. *Die Verratene Revolution—Deutschland 1918/19*. Hamburg: Stern Buch, 1969.

Haggard, Stephan, and Marcus Noland. *Famine in North Korea: Markets, Aid, and Reform*. New York: Columbia University Press, 2007.

Halperin, Sandra. *In the Mirror of the Third World: Capitalist Development in Modern Europe*. Ithaca: Cornell University Press, 1997.

Hämäläinen, Pekka. "Revolution, Civil War, and Ethnic Relations: The Case of Finland." *Journal of Baltic Studies* 5, no. 2 (1974): 117–125.

Hambides, Z. "China's Growing Army of Unemployed Graduates." *World Socialist Website*, October 4, 2010. Accessed July 6, 2024. https://www.wsws.org/en/articles/2010/10/chin-o04.html.

Hammond, Ken. "Beyond the Sprouts of Capitalism: Toward an Understanding of China's Historical Political Economy and Its Relationship to Contemporary China." *Monthly Review Essays*, March 3, 2021. Accessed July 6, 2024. https://mronline.org/2021/03/03/beyond-the-sprouts-of-capitalism.

Han, Dongping. "The Socialist Legacy Underlies the Rise of Today's China in the World." *Aspects of India's Economy*, no. 59–60 (October 2014): Remembering Socialist China, 1949–1976. Accessed July 6, 2024. rupe-india.org.

Hanover Historical Texts Project, ed. *The Gotha and Erfurt Programs*. 1875. Accessed July 6, 2024. https://history.hanover.edu/courses/excerpts/111gotha.html.

HARDEN, Blaine. "The U.S War Crime North Korea Won't Forget." *Washington Post*, March 24, 2015. In Tim Beal, "The Continuing Korean War in the Murderous History of Bombing." *Monthly Review* 72, no. 8 (January 2021).

HARRISON, Mark. *Accounting for War: Soviet Production, Employment, and the Defence-Burden, 1940–1945*. Cambridge: Cambridge University Press, 1996.

HARSCH, Donna. *German Social Democracy and the Rise of Nazism*. North Carolina: University of North Carolina Press, 1993.

HARVEY, David. *A Brief History of Neoliberalism*. Oxford: Oxford University Press, 2005.

HASLAM, Jonathan. *The Soviet Union and the Struggle for Collective Security in Europe, 1933–1939*. London: Macmillan Press, 1984.

HAVANA G77, "Declaration on Current Development Challenges: The Role of Science, Technology, and Innovation." September 15-16, 2023. Accessed July 6, 2024. https://www.diplomacy.edu/resource/g77-havana-declaration-on-current-development-challenges-the-role-of-science-technology-and-innovation/.

HEBBEL, Friedrich. *Judith: A Tragedy in Five Acts*. Translated by Carl Van Doren. Boston: R. G. Badger, 1914.

HEDLUND, Stefan. *Russia's 'Market' Economy: A Bad Case of Predatory Capitalism*. California: UCL Press, 1999.

HEGEL, G.W.F. *Berliner Schriften*. Edited by Johannes Hoffmeister. Hamburg: Meiner, 1956. In Domenico Losurdo, *Hegel e la Germania: Filosofi a e Questione Nazionale tra Rivoluzione e Reazione*. Milan: Guerini/ Istituto Italiano per gli Studi Filosofici, 1997.

HEILMANN, Sebastian. *China's Political System*. Maryland: Rowman and Littlefield, 2017.

HERNÁNDEZ, Carlos Miguel. "On the Sinicization of Marxism." English translation of *La Sinización del Marxismo, las Ciencias Sociales y la Cuestión del Modelo Propio*. Política Internacional, Havana, Cuba, 2022. Accessed July 6, 2024. https://socialistchina.org/2022/05/25/on-the-sinicization-of-marxism/.

HERZL, Theodor. "Zionistisches Tagebuch." In *Briefe und Tagebücher*, edited by A. Bein et al., vol. 2. Berlin, Frankfurt am Main, and Vienna: Propyläen, 1984-85.

HICKEL, Jason, and Dylan Sullivan. "Capitalism, Global Poverty, and the Case for Democratic Socialism." *Monthly Review* 75, no. 3 (July-August 2023).

HICKEL, Jason, Dylan Sullivan, and Huzaifa Zoomkawala. "Plunder in the Post-Colonial Era: Quantifying Drain from the Global South through Unequal Exchange, 1960–2018." *New Political Economy* 26, no. 6 (2021): 1030-1047.

HILL, Christopher. *Lenin and the Russian Revolution*. London: Hodder & Stoughton, 1947.

HINTON, William. "On the Role of Mao Zedong." *Monthly Review* 56, no. 4 (September 2004).

——— *Through a Glass Darkly: U.S. Views of the Chinese Revolution*. New York: Monthly Review Press, 2006.

HOBSBAWM, E.J. *How To Change the World: Reflections on Marx and Marxism*. New Haven: Yale U.P., 2011.

HOFFMAN, David. *The Dead Hand: The Untold Story of the Cold War Arms Race and Its Dangerous Legacy*. New York: Doubleday, 2009.

HORNE, Gerald. *The Apocalypse of Settler Colonialism: The Roots of Slavery, White Supremacy, and Capitalism in Seventeenth-Century North America and the Caribbean*. New York: Monthly Review Press, 2018.

HOCHSCHILD, Adam. *King Leopold's Ghost: A Story of Greed, Terror, and Heroism in Colonial Africa*. London: Mariner Books, 1999.

HOUGH, Jerry F. *Soviet Leadership in Transition*. Washington, D.C.: Brookings Institution, 1980.

HOXHA, Enver. *Reflections on China*. 2 vols. Tirana: 8 Nëntori Publishing House, 1979-1984.

HUI, Wang. "The Prophecy and Crisis of October: How to Think about Revolution after the Revolution." *The South Atlantic Quarterly* (October 2017): 669-706. Columbia University.

HUNCZAK, Taras. "OUN-German Relations 1941-1945." In *German-Ukrainian Relations in Historical Perspective*, edited by Hans-Joachim Torke and John-Paul Himka. Edmonton, Alberta: Canadian Institute of Ukrainian Studies Press, University of Alberta, 1994.

HUNT, Luke. "The World's Gaze Turns to the South Pacific." *The Diplomat*, September 4, 2012. Accessed July 6, 2024. https://thediplomat.com/2012/09/the-worlds-gaze-turns-to-the-south-pacific/.

IMLAY, Talbot. *The Practice of Socialist Internationalism: European Socialists and International Politics, 1914-1960*. Oxford: Oxford University Press, 2018.

INTERNATIONAL WORKING MEN'S ASSOCIATION. "The First Address On the Franco-Prussian War." July 23, 1870. Accessed July 6, 2024. marxists.org.

——— "Address of the General Council To All the Members of The Association in Europe and the United States." May 30, 1871. Accessed July 6, 2024. marxists.org.

JAFFE, Hosea. *Progress and Nationality*. Milan: Jaca Books, 1990.

JAMES, C.L.R. *The Black Jacobins: Toussaint L'Ouverture and the San Domingo Revolution*. 2nd ed. New York: Vintage Books, 1963.

JAMESON, Frederic. "Future City." *New Left Review*, no. 21 (May-June 2003).

JESSOP, Bob. *The Future of the Capitalist State*. Cambridge: Polity, 2002.

JINPING, Xi. "Consistently Develop and Uphold Socialism with Chinese Characteristics." Speech, January 5, 2018. Accessed July 6, 2024. Dongsheng newsgroup.

——— "New Year Address." December 31, 2021. Accessed July 6, 2024. https://www.fmprc.gov.cn/mfa_eng/zxxx_662805/202112/t20211231_10478096.html.

——— "Principal Contradiction Facing Chinese Society Has Evolved in New Era." Statement at the 19th National Congress of the Communist Party. Accessed July 6, 2024. http://english.www.gov.cn/news/top_news/2017/10/18/content_281475912458156.htm.

——— "Report to the 20th National Congress of the Communist Party of China," October 16, 2022. In *Qiushi*, CPC Central Committee Bimonthly Journal. Accessed July 6, 2024. http://en.qstheory.cn/2022-10/26/c_824626.htm.

——— "Resolution of the CPC Central Committee on the Major Achievements and Historical Experience of the Party over the Past Century." Xinhua, November 16, 2021. Beijing, 2021.

——— "Some Questions on Maintaining and Developing Socialism with Chinese Characteristics." Speech from January 5, 2013. In Andrew Batson's translation, "What Xi Jinping Really Said about Deng Xiaoping and Mao Zedong," May 31, 2016. andrewbatson.com.

——— "Speech at a Ceremony Marking the Centenary of the CCP." Accessed July 6, 2024. http://www.xinhuanet.com/english/special/2021-07/01/c_1310038244.htm.

——— "Speech at the Conference Celebrating the 200th Anniversary of Marx's Birth." Beijing, May 4, 2018. Published in the English Edition of *Qiushi Journal*, July-September 2018|Vol.10, No.3, Issue No.36. Accessed July 6, 2024. https://rolandtheodoreboer.files.wordpress.com/2021/11/xi-jinping-2018-marxs-200th-anniversary.pdf.

——— "Speech at the School of the Central Committee of the Communist Party of China." February 17, 2014. Quoted in Zhou Xincheng: "Adhere in Using the Principles of Marxism in Investigating Economic and Social Problems." *Jingji ribao chubanshe*, 2016, p. 228. In Gabriel Martinez, "Ideological Work in the New Era of Socialism in China." *The International*. Accessed July 6, 2024. https://internationalmagz.com/articles/.

——— *The Governance of China*, vol. 1. Beijing: Foreign Languages Press, 2018.

——— *The Governance of China*, vol. 3. Beijing: Foreign Languages Press, 2020.

JOHNSON, Chalmers. *Revolutionary Change*. 2nd ed. Stanford: Stanford University Press, 1982.

JOLL, James. *The Second International, 1889-1917*. New York: Praeger, 1966.

JONES, Charles E. *The Black Panther Party (Reconsidered)*. Baltimore: Black Classic Press, 1998.

JOWITT, Kenneth. *New World Disorder: The Leninist Extinction*. Berkeley: University of California Press, 1992.

KADRI, Ali. *China's Path to Development: Against Neoliberalism*. Singapore: Springer, 2021.

KALDER, Daniel. *The Infernal Library: On Dictators, the Books They Wrote, and Other Catastrophes of Literacy*. New York: Henry Holt and Company, 2018.

KARSH, Efraim. *Islamic Imperialism: A History*. New Haven: Yale University Press, 2006.

KENNEY, Padraic. *Rebuilding Poland: Workers and Communists, 1945-1950*. Ithaca: Cornell University Press, 1997.

KHALIDI, Rashid. *The Iron Cage: The Story of the Palestinian Struggle for Statehood*. Boston: Beacon Press, 2006.

KING, Michael. *Being Pakeha: An Encounter with New Zealand and the Maori Renaissance*. Auckland: Hodder and Stoughton, 1985.

KOLKO, Gabriel. *Century of War: Politics, Conflicts, and Society since 1914*. New York: New Press, 1994.

KOMOLOV, Oleg. "Capital Outflow and the Place of Russia in Core-Periphery Relationships." *World Review of Political Economy* 10, no. 3 (2019): 328-41.

KOREAN COMMITTEE FOR SOLIDARITY WITH THE WORLD PEOPLE SOCIETIES FOR FRIENDSHIP WITH THE ASIA-PACIFIC PEOPLE. "67th Anniversary of Outbreak of Korean War." Pyongyang, June 24, 2017. Accessed July 6, 2024. timbeal.net.nz.

KORNAI, János. *The Socialist System: The Political Economy of Communism*. Princeton: Princeton University Press, 1992.

KORNBLUH, Peter. *The Pinochet File: A Declassified Dossier on Atrocity and Accountability*. New York: New Press, 2004.

KOTKIN, Stephen. *Stalin: Paradoxes of Power, 1878–1928*. London: Allen Lane, 2014.

KRAUSZ, Tamás. "Lenin's Socialism – From the Perspective of the Future: Some Considerations." *LeftEast*, January 21, 2022. Accessed July 6, 2024. kersplebedeb.com.

——— *Reconstructing Lenin: An Intellectual Biography*. New York: Monthly Review Press, 2015.

KUHN, Gabriel, ed. *Turning Money into Revolution*. Montreal: Kersplebedeb/PM Press, 2014.

——— "Oppressor and Oppressed Nations: Sketching a Taxonomy of Imperialism." Accessed July 6, 2024. kersplebedeb.com.

KURAN, Timur. *Islam and Mammon: The Economic Predicaments of Islamism*. Princeton: Princeton University Press, 2004.

LACLAU, Ernesto, and Chantal Mouffe. *Hegemony and Socialist Strategy: Towards a Radical Democratic Politics*. London: Verso, 1985.

LACOUTURE, Jean. *Ho Chi Minh: A Political Biography*. New York: Vintage Books, 1968.

LAFEBER, Walter. *America, Russia, and the Cold War, 1945-2006*. 10th ed. New York: McGraw-Hill, 2008.

LANDY, Marcia. "Culture and Politics in the Work of Antonio Gramsci." In *Antonio Gramsci: Intellectuals, Culture, and the Party*, edited by James Martin. New York: Routledge, 2002.

LATHAM, Michael E. *Modernization as Ideology: American Social Science and "Nation Building" in the Kennedy Era*. Chapel Hill: University of North Carolina Press, 2000.

LAUESEN, Torkil. "The Parasite State in Theory and Practice." *Labor and Society* 21 (2018): 285-300.

——— *Riding the Wave: Sweden's Integration into the Imperialist World System*. Montreal: Kersplebedeb, 2021.

——— *The Global Perspective*. Montreal: Kersplebedeb, 2018.

——— *The Principal Contradiction*. Montreal: Kersplebedeb, 2020.

LEBOWITZ, Michael A. "The Struggle between the Future and the Past:

Where Is Cuba Going?" *Monthly Review Online*, July 3, 2022. Accessed July 6, 2024. https://mronline.org/2022/07/03/the-struggle-between-the-future-and-the-past-where-is-cuba-going/.

Leffler, Melvyn P. *A Preponderance of Power: National Security, the Truman Administration, and the Cold War.* Stanford: Stanford University Press, 1992.

LeMay, Curtis. *Mission with LeMay: My Story.* New York: Doubleday, 1965. In Tim Beal, "The Continuing Korean War in the Murderous History of Bombing." *Monthly Review* 72, no. 8 (January 2021).

Lenin, V.I. "Better Fewer, But Better." In *Lenin Collected Works*, vol. 33. Moscow: Progress Publishers, 1965.

——— "Declaration of Rights of the Toiling and Exploited People." In *Collected Works*, vol. 26. Moscow: Progress Publishers, 1974.

——— "Economics and Politics in the Era of the Dictatorship of the Proletariat." In *Lenin Collected Works*, vol. 30. Moscow: Progress Publishers, 1965.

——— "Eleventh Congress of the R.C.P.(B.), March 27-April 2, 1922." In *Lenin Collected Works*, vol. 33. Moscow: Progress Publishers, 1965.

——— "Extraordinary Seventh Congress of the R.C.P.(B.) March 6-8, 1918. Political Report of the Central Committee." Accessed July 6, 2024. marxists.org.

——— "First Congress of the Communist International." In *Lenin Collected Works*, vol. 28. Moscow: Progress Publishers, 1965.

——— "Fourth Congress of the Communist International, November 5, 1922." In *Lenin Collected Works*, vol. 33. Moscow: Progress Publishers, 1965.

——— "Imperialism and the Split in Socialism." In *On Imperialism and Opportunism*. Montreal: Kerrsplebedeb, 2019.

——— "Imperialism, the Highest Stage of Capitalism." In *Collected Works*, vol. 22. Moscow: Progress Publishers, 1972.

——— "Karl Marx: A Brief Biographical Sketch with an Exposition of Marxism." Article in the Russian encyclopedia "Granat." Accessed

July 6, 2024. marxists.org.

——— "Letter to the Workers and Peasants of the Ukraine Apropos of the Victories over Denikin." Dated December 28, 1919. In *Lenin Collected Works*, vol. 30. Moscow: Progress Publishers, 1965.

——— "Letters to the Congress. VII: The Question of Nationalities or 'Autonomisation,' December 1922 - January 1923." In *Lenin Collected Works*, vol. 36. Moscow: Progress Publishers, 1965.

——— "Notebooks on Imperialism." In *Collected Works*, vol. 39. Moscow: Progress Publishers, 1965.

——— "On Ascending a High Mountain." In *Lenin Collected Works*, vol. 33. Moscow: Progress Publishers, 1965.

——— "On Cooperation." In *Lenin Collected Works*, vol. 33. Moscow: Progress Publishers, 1965.

——— "Our Revolution." In *Lenin Collected Works*, vol. 33. Moscow: Progress Publishers, 1965.

——— "Report of the Commission on the National and Colonial Questions." In *Lenin Collected Works*, vol. 31. Moscow: Progress Publishers, 1965.

——— "Review of the Journal Kommunismus." In *Lenin Collected Works*, vol. 31. Moscow: Progress Publishers, 1965.

——— "Review: J.A Hobson: The Evolution of Modern Capitalism." In *Collected Works*, vol. 4. Moscow: Progress Publishers, 1960.

——— "Socialism and War." In *Collected Works*, vol. 41. Moscow: Progress Publishers, 1965.

——— "Terms of Admission into Communist International." In *Lenin Collected Works*, vol. 31. Moscow: Progress Publishers, 1965.

——— "The Collapse of the Second International." In *Collected Works*, vol. 21. Moscow: Progress Publishers, 1965.

——— "The Immediate Tasks of the Soviet Government." In *Collected Works*, vol. 27. Moscow: Progress Publishers, 1972.

——— "The International Socialist Congress in Stuttgart." In *Collected Works*, vol. 13. Moscow: Progress Publishers, 1972.

——— "The New Economic Policy and the Task of the Political Education Departments: Report to the Second All-Russia Congress of Political Education Departments, October 17, 1922." In *Lenin Collected Works*, vol. 33. Moscow: Progress Publishers, 1965.

——— "The New Economic Policy and the Tasks of the Political Education Departments: Report to the Second All-Russia Congress of Political Education Departments, October 17, 1921." In *Lenin Collected Works*, vol. 33. Moscow: Progress Publishers, 1965.

——— "The Proletarian Revolution and the Renegade Kautsky." In *Collected Works*, vol. 28. Moscow: Progress Publishers, 1974.

——— "The Role and Functions of the Trade Unions under the New Economic Policy." In *Lenin Collected Works*, vol. 33. Moscow: Progress Publishers, 1965.

——— "The State and the Revolution. Chapter V: The Economic Basis of the Withering Away of the State. Part 2. The Transition from Capitalism to Communism." In *Collected Works*, vol. 25, 381-492. Moscow: Progress Publishers, 1970.

——— "The Task of the Youth Leagues." In *Lenin Collected Works*, vol. 31. Moscow: Progress Publishers, 1974.

——— "The Tax in Kind." In *Lenin Collected Works*, vol. 32. Moscow: Progress Publishers, 1965.

——— "The Taylor System - Man's Enslavement by the Machine." In *Collected Works*, vol. 20. Moscow: Progress Publishers, 1967.

——— "What is to be Done?" In *Collected Works*, vol. 5, 347-530. Moscow: Progress Publishers, 1967.

——— "What the 'Friends of the People Are' and How They Fight the Social-Democrats." In *Collected Works*, vol. 1, 129-332. Moscow: Progress Publishers, 1967.

——— *Left-Wing Communism, an Infantile Disorder*. In *Lenin Collected Works*, vol. 31. Moscow: Progress Publishers, 1975.

——— *Imperialism: The Highest Stage of Capitalism*. New York: International Publishers, 1939.

Levy, Jonah D. *The State After Statism: New State Activities in the Age of Liberalization*. Cambridge: Harvard University Press, 2006.

Lewin, Moshe. *The Making of the Soviet System: Essays in the Social History of Interwar Russia*. New York: Pantheon Books, 1985.

Li, Minqi. "The Rise of the Working Class and the Future of the Chinese Revolution." *Monthly Review* 63, no. 2 (June 2011).

——— *China and the Twenty-First-Century Crisis*. London: Pluto Press, 2016.

——— *The Rise of China and the Demise of the Capitalist World Economy*. London: Pluto Press, 2008.

Li, Ziyang. "Milton Friedman's Three Visits to China." Accessed July 6, 2024. http://blog.sina.com.cn/s/blog_4b7f5ebb0100067b.html. In Li Minqi, *China and the Twenty-First-Century Crisis*, 20. London: Pluto Press, 2016.

Lih, Lars T. "Political Testament of Lenin and Bukharin and the Meaning of NEP." *Slavic Review* 50, no. 2 (Summer 1991): 234-263. Cambridge: Cambridge University Press, 1991.

——— *Lenin Rediscovered: What Is to Be Done? in Context*. Leiden: Brill, 2005.

Lin May, Christina. "Chinese General: Anti-Chinese Uyghurs are in Syria's Anti-Assad Force." *ISPSW Strategy Series: Focus on Defense and International Security*, no. 353 (May 2015). Berlin, 2015.

Lin, Y.M. "Postrevolution Transformations and the Reemergence of Capitalism in China." In *Chinese Capitalisms: Historical Emergence and Political Implications*, edited by I. Chu, 73–99. Houndmills: Macmillan Publishers, 2012.

Lindeng, W. "People's Net, December 10, 2013." In Dongping Han, "The Socialist Legacy Underlies the Rise of Today's China in the World." *Aspects of India's Economy* no. 59–60 (October 2014): Remembering Socialist China, 1949–1976. Accessed July 6, 2024. rupe-india.org.

Lindqvist, Sven. *Exterminate the Brutes*. Copenhagen: Gyldendal, 1992.

LINEBAUGH, Peter. "Afterword to Karl Marx, Critique of the Gotha Program." PM Press, New York, 2021.

LIU, William Guanglin. *The Chinese Market Economy, 1000–1500*. Albany: SUNY Press, 2015.

LIU, Xiaobo. *No Enemies, No Hatred: Selected Essays and Poems*. Edited by Perry Link, Tienchi Martin-Liao, and Liu Xia. Cambridge: Belknap Press, 2012.

LOCKWOOD, Lee. *Castro's Cuba, Cuba's Fidel*. New York: Macmillan, 1967.

LONG, Zhiming, Feng Zhixuan, Li Bangxi, and Rémy Herrera. "U.S.-China Trade War: Has the Real 'Thief' Finally Been Unmasked?" *Monthly Review* 72, no. 5 (October 2020): 6-14.

LÓPEZ, Daniel Andrés. *Lukács: Praxis and the Absolute*. Chicago: Haymarket, 2019.

LOSURDO, Domenico. "Has China Turned to Capitalism? Reflections on the Transition from Capitalism to Socialism." *International Critical Thought* 7, no. 1 (2017): 15-31.

——— *Class Struggle: A Political and Philosophical History*. New York: Palgrave Macmillan, 2016.

——— *Stalin: History and Critique of a Black Legend*, Washington: Iskra Books, 2023.

LUKÁCS, Georg. "Bolshevism as an Ethical Problem." In *The Lukács Reader*. London: Blackwell, 1995.

——— *Lenin: A Study on the Unity of His Thought*. London: Verso, 2009.

——— *History and Class Consciousness: Studies in Marxist Dialectics*. London: Merlin Press, 1971.

——— *Tactics and Ethics*. London: New Left Books, 1972.

LUXEMBURG, Rosa. "Article in Rote Fahne, January 7, 1919." In Chris Harman, *The Lost Revolution: Germany 1918 to 1923*. London: Aakar Books, 1982.

——— "Order Prevails in Berlin!" In *Gesammelte Werke*, vol. 4. Berlin:

Dietz Verlag, 1970-75.

———. "Our Program and the Political Situation." In *Selected Political Writings*, edited by Dick Howard. New York: Monthly Review Press, 1971.

———. *The Accumulation of Capital*. London: Routledge, 1951.

———. *The Accumulation of Capital*. New York: Monthly Review Press, 1972.

———. *The National Question: Selected Writings*. New York: Monthly Review Press, 1976.

———. *The Russian Revolution*. Chapter 8, "Democracy and Dictatorship." Written in 1918, first published in 1922. Accessed July 6, 2024. https://www.marxists.org/archive/luxemburg/1918/russian-revolution/index.htm.

MAC MANUS, Patrick. "Engle findes ikke mere – åbent brev til Enhedslisten." (Eagles do not exist – letter to Enhedslisten). *Kommunistisk Politik*, 2006 nr. 6. Copenhagen, 2006.

MACFARQUHAR, Roderick, Timothy Cheek, and Eugene Wu, eds. *The Secret Speeches of Chairman Mao: From the Hundred Flowers to the Great Leap Forward*. Harvard Contemporary China Series no. 6. Cambridge: Harvard University Press, 1989.

MACHIAVELLI, Niccolò. *The Prince*. London: Penguin, 1961.

MADDISON, Angus. *Chinese Economic Performance in the Long Run: 960–2030 AD*, 2nd ed. Paris: OECD, 2007. Accessed July 6, 2024. http://piketty.pse.ens.fr/files/Maddison07.pdf.

———. *Chinese Economic Performance in the Long Run*. Paris: OECD, 1998. Accessed July 6, 2024. https://www.oecd.org/china/chineseeconomicperformanceinthelongrun-secondedition.htm.

MAKARENKO, Anton Semenovich. *The Road to Life*. Honolulu: University Press of the Pacific, 2001.

MANN, Michael. *The Dark Side of Democracy*. Cambridge: Cambridge University Press, 2005.

MANN, Thomas, ed. Kurzke, Hermann. *Essays, Volume II 1914-1926*.

Frankfurt am Main: Fischer Verlag, 2002.

MARER, P., J. Arvay, J. O'Connor, M. Schrenk, and D. Swanson. *Historically Planned Economies: A Guide to the Data*. Washington, DC: World Bank, 1992. In Zhiming Long and Rémy Herrera, "The Enigma of China's Growth." *Monthly Review* 70, no. 7 (December 2018).

MARINI, Ruy Mauro. *Procesos y tendencias de la globalización capitalista*. Buenos Aires: Prometeo, 1996.

———. *The Dialectics of Dependency*. New York: Monthly Review Press, 2023.

MARX, Karl, and Friedrich Engels. "Address of the Central Committee to the Communist League." Accessed July 6, 2024. https://www.marxists.org/archive/marx/works/1847/communist-league/1850-ad1.htm.

———. "Circular Letter to August Bebel, Wilhelm Liebknecht, Wilhelm Bracke and Others, September 1879." In *Marx/Engels Collected Works*, vol. 24. Moscow: Progress Publishers, 1985.

———. "Preface to the 1872 Edition of the Communist Manifesto." Accessed July 6, 2024. https://www.marxists.org/archive/marx/works/1848/communist-manifesto/preface.htm.

———. *The Communist Manifesto*. In *Marx/Engels Collected Works*, vol. 6. Moscow: Progress Publishers, 1976.

MARX, Karl, and Jules Guesde. "The Programme of the Parti Ouvrier." Accessed July 6, 2024. https://www.marxists.org/archive/marx/works/1880/05/parti-ouvrier.htm.

MARX, Karl. "Letter from Marx to Meyer and Vogt, April 9, 1870." In *Marx/Engels Collected Works*, vol. 43. Moscow: Progress Publishers, 1982.

———. "Letter to Engels, October 8, 1858." In *Marx/Engels Collected Works*, vol. 40. Moscow: Progress Publishers, 1987.

———. "The Election Results in the Northern States." *Die Presse*, no. 321 (November 23, 1862). In *Marx/Engels Collected Works*, vol. 19. Moscow: Progress Publishers, 1984.

———. *A Contribution to the Critique of Political Economy*. In *Marx/Engels Collected Works*, vol. 29. Moscow: Progress Publishers, 1977.

———. *Capital*, vol. 1. Accessed July 6, 2024. https://www.marxists.org/archive/marx/works/1867-c1/ch13.htm.

———. *Capital*, vol. 3. London: Penguin, 1991.

———. *Critique of the Gotha Program*. In *Selected Works*, vol. 3, 13-30. Moscow: Progress Publishers, 1970.

———. *Revelations Concerning the Communist Trial in Cologne*. In *Marx/Engels Collected Works*, vol. 11. Moscow: Progress Publishers, 1984.

———. *The Civil War in the United States*. In *Marx/Engels Collected Works*, vol. 19. Moscow: Progress Publishers, 1984.

———. *The Class Struggles in France, 1848 to 1850*. In *Marx/Engels Selected Works*, vol. 1. Moscow: Progress Publishers, 1969.

———. *The Eighteenth Brumaire of Louis Bonaparte*. Chapter 1. In *Marx/Engels Collected Works*, vol. 11. London: Lawrence & Wishart, 2010.

———. *The German Ideology*. In *Marx/Engels Collected Works*, vol. 5. Moscow: Progress Publishers, 1976.

———. *The Poverty of Philosophy*. In *Marx/Engels Collected Works*, vol. 6. Moscow: Progress Publishers, 1976.

———. *Wage Labour and Capital*. In *Marx/Engels Collected Works*, vol. 9. Moscow: Progress Publishers, 1977.

Mazumdar, Charu. "China's Chairman is Our Chairman: China's Path is Our Path." *Liberation* 3, no. 1 (November 1969): CPI (M-L) India.

McCauley, Martin. *Gorbachev: Profiles in Power*. London and New York: Longman, 1998.

Meisner, Maurice. *Mao Zedong: A Political and Intellectual Portrait*. Cambridge: Polity Press, 2006.

———. *Mao's China and After: A History of the People's Republic*. New York: The Free Press, 1977.

MELYAKOVA, Anna, and Svetlana Savranskaya. "The Chernyaev Diary, 1982 — The Run Up to Perestroika." *The National Security Archive.* Accessed July 6, 2024. https://nsarchive.gwu.edu/briefing-book/russia-programs/2022-05-25/chernyaev-diary-1982-run-perestroika.

MÉSZÁROS, István. "The Historic Anachronism and Necessary Supersession of the State." In *Beyond Leviathan: Critique of the State.* Accessed July 6, 2024. https://mronline.org/2018/11/25/the-historic-anachronism-and-necessary-supersession-of-the-state/.

MINH, Ho Chi. "The Path Which Led Me to Leninism." In *Selected Works*, vol. 4. Hanoi: Foreign Languages Publishing House, 1962.

MØLLER, A. M. "Appendix A: China's Historical Experience and Current Crises of Democracy—An Interview with Wang Hui." In *Hegemonic Project, Interventions on the Politics of Communist Elite Legitimation in China, 2008–2015*, Ph.D. thesis, Department of Political Science, University of Copenhagen, 2016.

────── *Hegemonic Project, Interventions on the Politics of Communist Elite Legitimation in China, 2008–2015*. Ph.D. thesis, Department of Political Science, University of Copenhagen, 2016.

MOURET, Sébastien, and Kevin Wang. "The Manchurian Crisis and Chinese Civil War." *PIMUN*, 2018. Accessed July 6, 2024. http://pimun.fr/wp-content/uploads/2017/12/HISTORICAL-CRISIS-TOPIC-GUIDE.pdf.

NATIONAL SECURITY ARCHIVE. "Declassified U.S. Embassy Jakarta Files Detail Army Killings, U.S. Support for Quashing Leftist Labor Movement." Washington, D.C., October 17, 2017. Accessed July 6, 2024. https://nsarchive.gwu.edu/briefing-book/indonesia/2017-10-17/indonesia-mass-murder-1965-us-embassy-files.

NATO. "The 2022 Strategic Concept, Adopted at the Madrid Summit, 29-30 June 2022." Accessed July 6, 2024. https://www.nato.int/strategic-concept/.

NAUGHTON, Barry. "A Political Economy of China's Economic Transition." In *China's Great Economic Transformation*, edited by L. Brandt and T.G. Rawski. Cambridge: Cambridge University Press,

2008.

———. *The Chinese Economy: Transitions and Growth*. Cambridge: MIT Press, 2007.

NESS, Immanuel. "Western Marxism, Anti-Communism and Imperialism." Forthcoming article, 2024.

NOLAN, Peter. *The Political Economy of Collective Farms: An Analysis of China's Postmao Rural Reforms*. London: Routledge, 1988.

NOVE, Alec, ed. *The Stalin Phenomenon*. London: Weidenfeld & Nicolson, 1993.

———. *An Economic History of the U.S.S.R.* New York: Penguin, 1990.

OBERMEYER, Ziad, Christopher J.L. Murray, and Emmanuela Gakidou. "Fifty Years of Violent War Deaths from Vietnam to Bosnia: Analysis of Data from the World Health Survey Program." *BMJ*, 2008. Accessed July 6, 2024. https://www.bmj.com/content/336/7659/1482.

ORLÉANS, L. *Science and Techniques in the People's Republic of China*. Paris: OECD, 1977.

OVERY, Richard. *The Dictators: Hitler's Germany, Stalin's Russia*. London: Penguin, 2005.

PAGE, Jeremy. "How the U.S. Misread China's Xi: 'Hoping for a Globalist, It Got an Autocrat.'" *The Wall Street Journal*, December 23, 2020. Accessed July 6, 2024. https://www.wsj.com/articles/xi-jinping-globalist-autocrat-misread-11608735769.

PANNEKOEK, Anton. *Die Entwicklung der Weltrevolution und die Taktik des Communismus*. Vienna: Arbeiterbuchhandlung, 1920.

PANTSOV, A., and S. I. Levine. *Deng Xiaoping: A Revolutionary Life*. New York: Oxford University Press, 2015.

PARK, Henry. "Post-revolutionary China and the Soviet NEP." *Research in Political Economy* no. 9 (1986): 219–233. Accessed July 6, 2024. https://www.prisoncensorship.info/archive/books/soviet-NEPvChina-ParkH.pdf.

PASHUKANIS, Evgeny B. "The General Theory of Law and Marxism." In

Selected Writings on Marxism and Law, edited by P. Beirne and R. Sharlet, London & New York, 1980.

PATNAIK, Utsa, and Patnaik, Prabhat. *Capital and Imperialism, Theory, History and the Present.* New York: Monthly Review Press, 2021.

PATNAIK, Utsa. "Revisiting Alleged 30 Million Famine Deaths during China's Great Leap." *Monthly Review Online,* June 26, 2011. Accessed July 6, 2024. https://mronline.org/2011/06/26/revisiting-alleged-30-million-famine-deaths-during-chinas-great-leap/.

PETERSSON, Frederik. "Imperialism and the COMINTERN." *Journal of Labor and Society* 20, no. 1 (March 2017).

——— "We Are Neither Visionaries Nor Utopian Dreamers: Willi Münzenberg, the League against Imperialism, and the COMINTERN, 1925–1933." Ph.D. thesis, Abo Akademi University, 2013. Published as vol. I-II, Queenstown Press, Lewiston, 2013.

PILGER, John. "Another Hiroshima is Coming – Unless We Stop It Now." Accessed July 6, 2024. https://www.rt.com/op-ed/497096-john-pilger-hiroshima-china-us/.

PIPES, R., ed. *The Unknown Lenin: From the Secret Archives.* New Haven: Yale University Press, 1996.

PONTING, Clive. *World History: A New Perspective.* London: Pimlico, 2001.

POWELL, Bill. "America Is in a New Cold War and This Time the Communists Might Win." *News Week Magazine,* May 18, 2020. Accessed July 6, 2024. https://www.newsweek.com/2020/06/05/america-new-cold-war-this-time-communists-might-win-1504447.html.

PRC ECONOMIC ARCHIVES (1949–1952). *Selection from PRC Economic Archives 1949–1952: Commerce.* Beijing: China Supplies Press, 1995. Pages 338 and 365. Here from: Tiejun, Wen. *Ten Crises: The Political Economy of China's Development (1949–2020).* Singapore: Palgrave Macmillan, 2021.

QIAN LONG. "The Emperors Letter to King George III, 1793." Accessed July 6, 2024. http://academics.wellesley.edu/Polisci/wj/

China/208/READINGS/qianlong.html.

Qiu, Jin. *The Culture of Power: The Lin Biao Incident in the Cultural Revolution*. Stanford, CA: Stanford University Press, 1999.

Redfern, Niel. "The COMINTERN and Imperialism." *Journal of Labor and Society* 20, no. 1 (March 2017).

Renan, Ernest. *Oeuvres complètes*. Edited by Henriette Psichari. Vol. 1. Paris: Calmann-Lévy, 1947.

Riskin, Carl. *China's Political Economy: The Quest for Development Since 1949*. Oxford: Oxford University Press, 1987.

Ross, Robert S. "From Lin Biao to Deng Xiaoping: Elite Instability and China's U. S. Policy." *The China Quarterly* no. 118 (June 1989): 265–299.

Roth, Gary. *Marxism in a Lost Century: A Biography of Paul Mattick*. Leiden: Brill, 2015.

Rothwell, Matthew. "The Road Is Tortuous: The Chinese Revolution and the End of the Global Sixties." *Revista Izquierdas* no. 49 (April 2020). Accessed July 6, 2024. https://peopleshistoryofideas.com/the-road-is-tortuous-the-chinese-revolution-and-the-end-of-the-global-sixties/.

Sakai, J. *Settlers: The Mythology of the White Proletariat from Mayflower to Modern*. Montreal: PM/Kersblebedeb, 2014.

——— *The "Dangerous Class" and Revolutionary Theory: Thoughts on the Making of the Lumpen/Proletariat*. Montreal: Kersplebedeb, 2017.

Salisbury, Lord Robert Cecil. "Speech at Albert Hall," May 4, 1898. In Roberts, Andrew. "Salisbury, The Empire Builder Who Never Was." *History Today* 49, no. 10 (1999).

Salvadori, Massimo L. *Karl Kautsky and the Socialist Revolution, 1880–1938*. London: New Left Books, 1978.

Sartre, Jean-Paul. "Preface to Fanon, F: Wretched of the Earth." Accessed July 6, 2024. https://www.marxists.org/reference/archive/sartre/1961/preface.htm.

Schlesinger, Arthur Jr. "Four Days with Fidel: A Havana Diary." *New York Review of Books*, March 26, 1992.

Scholten, Joe. "How China Strengthened Food Security and Fought Poverty with State-Funded Cooperatives." *Multipolarista*, May 31, 2022. Here from: Bellamy, John Foster, and Brett Clark. "Socialism and Ecological Survival: An Introduction." *Monthly Review* 74, no. 3 (2022): 27.

Service, Robert. *Stalin: A Biography*. London: Macmillan, 2004.

Shigong, Jiang. "A History of Empire Without Empire." Preface to the Chinese edition of John Darwin's *After Tamerlane: The Global History of Empire Since 1405*. Accessed July 6, 2024. https://redsails.org/jiang-on-empire/.

Shirer, William L. *Rise and Fall of The Third Reich: A History of Nazi Germany*. New York: Simon Schuster, 1959.

Sison, José María, and Ninotchka Rosca. *Jose Maria Sison: At Home in the World. Portrait of a Revolutionary*. Greensboro, NC: Open Hand Publishing, 2004.

Snegovaya, Maria, and Kirill Petrov. "Long Soviet Shadows: The Nomenklatura Ties of Putin's Elites." *Post-Soviet Affairs* 38, no. 4 (2022): 329-348.

Snow, Edgar. *Red Star over China*. New York: Grove Press/Atlantic Monthly Press, 1994.

Sophocles. *The Three Theban Plays: Antigone, Oedipus the King, Oedipus at Colonus*. Translated by Robert Fagles. New York: Penguin, 1986.

Stalin, J.V. "On the Draft Constitution of the U.S.S.R.: Report Delivered at the Extraordinary Eighth Congress of Soviets of the U.S.S.R., November 25, 1936." In *Works*, Vol. 14. London: Red Star Press Ltd., 1978.

——— "Problems of Leninism." New York: International Publishers, 1934. Accessed July 6, 2024. http://www.marx2mao.com/Stalin/POLtc.html.

——— "Report on the Work of the Central Committee to the Eighteenth Congress of the C.P.S.U.(B.), March 10, 1939." In *Works*, Vol. 14. London: Red Star Press Ltd., 1978.

———. "Speech at the Red Army Parade on the Red Square, Moscow, November 7, 1941." Accessed July 6, 2024. https://www.marxists.org/reference/archive/stalin/works/1941/11/07.htm.

———. "Speech to Industrial Managers, February 1931." In *Problems of Leninism*, 454-458. Moscow: Foreign Languages Publishing House, 1953.

Statista. "China: Trust in Government 2022." Accessed July 6, 2024. https://www.statista.com/statistics/1116013/china-trust-in-government-2020/.

STAVRIANOS, Leften Stavros. *Global Rift: The Third World Come of Age*. New York: William Morrow & Co., 1981.

STEFANONI, Pablo. "'Bolivia a due dimensioni.'" *Il Manifesto*, July 22, 2006. Accessed July 6, 2024. https://www.peacelink.it/latina/a/17714.html.

STERN, Geoffrey, ed. *Communism*. London: Amazon Publishing Ltd., 1991.

STERNBERG, Fritz. *Der Faschismus an der Macht*. Amsterdam: Contact, 1935.

STOLTENBERG, Clyde D. "China's Special Economic Zones: Their Development and Prospects." *Asian Survey* 24, no. 6 (June 1984): 637–654.

SULLIVAN, Dylan, and Jason Hickel. "Capitalism and Extreme Poverty: A Global Analysis of Real Wages, Human Height, and Mortality since the Long 16th Century." *World Development* 161 (January 2023).

SURI, Jeremi. *Power and Protest: Global Revolution and the Rise of Détente*. Cambridge, MA: Harvard University Press, 2003.

TABLADA, Carlos. *Che Guevara: Economics and Politics in the Transition to Socialism*. New York: Pacific and Asia Pathfinder, 1989. Here from: Lebowitz, Michael A. "The Struggle between the Future and the Past: Where Is Cuba Going?" *Monthly Review Online*, July 3,

2022. Accessed July 6, 2024. https://mronline.org/2022/07/03/the-struggle-between-the-future-and-the-past-where-is-cuba-going/.

TANNER, Murray Scot. "China's Social Unrest Problem: Testimony before the U.S.-China Economic and Security Review Commission, May 15, 2014." Accessed July 6, 2024. http://www.uscc.gov/sites/default/files/Tanner_Written%20Testimony.pdf.

TAUBMAN, William. *Gorbachev: His Life and Times*. New York: Simon and Schuster, 2017.

THE STATE COUNCIL INFORMATION OFFICE OF THE PEOPLE'S REPUBLIC OF CHINA. "Opinion of the State Council of the People's Republic of China on Supporting High Quality Development and Construction of a Common Prosperity Demonstration Zone in Zhejiang." 2021. Here from: Dunford, Michael. "On Common Prosperity." Accessed July 6, 2024. https://socialistchina.org/2021/10/17/on-common-prosperity/.

THERBORN, Göran. "Dialectics of Modernity: On Critical Theory and the Legacy of Twentieth Century Marxism." *New Left Review* I/215 (January-February 1996).

TIEJUN, Wen. *Ten Crises: The Political Economy of China's Development (1949–2020)*. Singapore: Palgrave Macmillan, 2021. Accessed July 6, 2024. https://link.springer.com/book/10.1007/978-981-16-0455-3.

TIMASHIEFF, Nicholas S. *The Great Retreat: The Growth and Decline of Communism in Russia*. New York: E.P. Dutton & Co, 1946.

TOCQUEVILLE, Alexis de. *The Recollections of Alexis de Tocqueville*. New York: The MacMillan Co., 1896. Accessed July 6, 2024. https://oll.libertyfund.org/title/de-mattos-the-recollections-of-alexis-de-tocqueville-1896.

TOGLIATTI, Palmiro. "Social Democracy and the Colonial Question." *International Press Correspondence* no. 68 (October 4, 1928). Accessed July 6, 2024. https://www.marxists.org/archive/togliatti/1928/ercoli-sdandcolonialquestion.htm.

TRADING ECONOMICS. "China Average Yearly Wages." 2022. Accessed

July 6, 2024. https://tradingeconomics.com/china/wages.

Trotsky, Leon. "Manifesto of the Communist International to the Proletariat of the Entire World." March 6, 1919. Original Source: Protokoll des IV. Kongresses der Kommunistischen Internationale, Hamburg 1923. Accessed July 6, 2024. http://soviethistory.msu.edu/1921-2/comintern-texts/manifesto-of-the-communist-international/.

———. "Speech to the Thirteenth Party Congress on May 26, 1924." In *The Challenge of the Left Opposition: 1923–1925*. New York: Pathfinder Press, 1975.

Trump, Donald. "Excerpts from Remarks by President Donald Trump and Secretary General Jens Stoltenberg, June 11, 2018." Accessed July 6, 2024. https://www.atlanticcouncil.org/blogs/natosource/trump-believes-us-paying-a-lot-of-money-to-protect-nato-allies/.

Tse-tung, Mao. *A Critique of Soviet Economics*. With an introduction by James Peck. New York and London: Monthly Review Press, 1977.

———. "On Contradiction." In *Selected Works*, vol. 1. Peking: Foreign Languages Press, 1965.

Tucker, Robert C. *Stalin in Power: The Revolution from Above 1928-1941*. New York and London: W. W. Norton & Company, 1990.

Twiss, Thomas M. *Trotsky and the Problem of Soviet Bureaucracy*. Leiden: Brill, 2014.

Unger, Jonathan. *The Transformation of Rural China*. New York: East Gate, 2002.

UNICEF. *Levels and Trends in Child Mortality, Report 2013*. Accessed July 6, 2024. https://data.unicef.org/resources/levels-trends-child-mortality-report-2013/.

United Nations. *Declaration on the Granting of Independence to Colonial Countries and Peoples*. 1960. Accessed July 6, 2024. https://www.ohchr.org/en/instruments-mechanisms/instruments/declaration-granting-independence-colonial-countries-and-peoples.

van der Linden, Marcel. *Western Marxism and the Soviet Union: A*

Survey of Critical Theories and Debates Since 1917. Leiden: Brill, 2007.

VAN DER PIJL, Kees. "Democracy, Planning, and Big Data: A Socialism for the Twenty-First Century?" *Monthly Review* 71, no. 11 (April 2020).

VILLAROEL, Gilberto. "La herencia de los "Chicago boys."" BBC Mundo.com, América Latina, December 10, 2006. Accessed July 6, 2024. https://news.bbc.co.uk/hi/spanish/latin_america/news-id_3192000/3192145.stm.

VIÑUALES, Jorge E., ed. *The UN Friendly Relations Declaration at 50: An Assessment of the Fundamental Principles of International Law*. Cambridge: Cambridge University Press, 2020.

WALLERSTEIN, Immanuel. "Structural Crisis, or Why Capitalists May No Longer Find Capitalism Rewarding." In *Does Capitalism Have a Future?* Oxford: Oxford University Press, 2013.

—— *The Modern World System: Capitalist Agriculture and the Origins of the European World Economy in the Sixteenth Century*. New York: Academic Press, 1974.

WALTERS, Robert. *American and Soviet Aid: A Comparative Analysis*. Pittsburgh: University of Pittsburgh, 1970.

WARD, Chris. *Stalin's Russia*. London: Bloomsbury Academic, 1999.

WATERS, Mary-Alice, ed. *Rosa Luxemburg Speaks*. New York: Pathfinder Press, 1970.

WEBER, Isabella M. "Interview: How China Escaped Shock Therapy in the 1980s." *LeftEast* online journal, July 29, 2022. Accessed July 6, 2024. https://lefteast.org/how-china-escaped-shock-therapy/.

—— *How China Escaped Shock Therapy: The Market Reform Debate*. New York: Routledge, 2021.

WEINER, Michael. "COMINTERN in East Asia, 1919–1939." In *The COMINTERN: A History of International Communism from Lenin to Stalin*, edited by Kevin McDermott and Jeremy Agnew. Basingstoke: Macmillan Press, 1996.

WEIWEI, Zhang. "On Telling China's Story." *Peking Daily*, June 21,

2021. Accessed July 6, 2024. https://readingthechinadream.com/.

WELLERSTEIN, Alex. "A 'Purely Military' Target? Truman's Changing Language about Hiroshima." Note 11, January 19, 2018. Accessed July 6, 2024. http://blog.nuclearsecrecy.com/2018/01/19/purely-military-target/.

WERTH, Nicolas. *La terreur et le désarroi: Stalin et son système*. Paris: Perrin, 2007.

WHITSON, William W., and Chen-hsia Huang. *The Chinese High Command: A History of Communist Military Politics, 1927–71*. New York: Praeger, 1973.

WILKINSON, William John. *Tory Democracy*. New York: Octagon Books, 1980.

WILSON Center Digital Archive. "Meeting between Stalin and Kim Il Sung." 1949. Accessed July 6, 2024. https://digitalarchive.wilsoncenter.org/document/112127.

WORLD BANK. *China: Socialist Economic Development*, Vol. I. Washington, DC: The World Bank, 1983. Accessed July 6, 2024. https://documents1.worldbank.org/curated/en/192611468769173749/pdf/multi-page.pdf.

——— *World Bank Development Indicators*. Various years. Here from: Long, Z., and R. Herrera. "The Enigma of China's Growth." *Monthly Review* 70, no. 7 (December 2018).

WORLEY, Matthew. *Class Against Class: The Communist Party in Britain between the Wars*. London: I.B. Tauris, 2002.

WORRALL, Simon. "Clipper Ship Owners Made Millions. Others Paid the Price." *National Geographic*, August 31, 2018.

X, Malcolm. "Message to the Grassroots." In *Malcolm X Speaks*, edited by George Breitman, 4-18. New York: Grove Weidenfeld, 1965.

XIAOPING, Deng. "Carry Out the Policy of Opening to the Outside World and Learn Advanced Science and Technology from Other Countries." In *Selected Works*, vol. 2. Beijing: Foreign Languages Press, 1992.

——— "Interview by Oriana Fallaci." *The Washington Post*, September

1, 1980. Accessed July 6, 2024. https://www.washingtonpost.com/archive/politics/1980/09/01/deng-a-third-world-war-is-inevitable/a7222afa-3dfd-4169-b288-bdf34f942bfe/.

——— "Interview with Mike Wallace of CBS 60 Minutes." CBS, September 2, 1986. Here from: *All Asia Times*, December 13, 2006. Accessed July 6, 2024. https://china.usc.edu.

——— "June 9 Speech to Martial Law." 1989. Accessed July 6, 2024. http://www.tsquare.tv/chronology/Deng.html.

——— "Let Us Put the Past Behind Us and Open Up a New Era." Excerpt from a talk with Mikhail Gorbachev. In *Selected Works*, vol. 3. Beijing: Foreign Languages Press, 1984.

——— "Speech at the Communist Youth League Conference," July 7, 1962. *China Daily*, August 20, 2014. Accessed July 6, 2024. https://chinadaily.com.

——— "Speech at the Opening Ceremony of the National Conference on Science," March 18, 1978. In *Selected Works*, vol. 2. Beijing: Foreign Languages Press, 1992.

——— "Unity Depends on Ideals and Discipline," March 7, 1985. In *Selected Works*, vol. III, 1982-1992. Beijing: People's Publishing House, 2014.

——— "We Must Adhere to Socialism and Prevent Peaceful Evolution Towards Capitalism." November 23, 1989. In *Selected Works*, vol. 3. Beijing: Foreign Languages Press, 1984. Accessed July 6, 2024. https://dengxiaopingworks.wordpress.com/2013/03/18/we-must-adhere-to-socialism-and-prevent-peaceful-evolution-towards-capitalism/.

——— "We Shall Expand Political Democracy and Carry Out Economic Reform." In *Selected Works*, vol. 3. Beijing: Foreign Languages Press, 1992.

XIULING, Han, Liyun Zhang, and Xiulian Fan. "During the Difficult Days." In *Baoding City Selected Historical Materials*, no. 15. Baoding: Wenshi Ziliao Committee, 1998. Here from: Han, Dongping. "The Socialist Legacy Underlies the Rise of Today's China in the World." *Aspects of India's Economy*, no. 59 (October 2014).

Accessed July 6, 2024. https://www.rupe-india.org/59/han.html.

YAFFE, Helen. *Che Guevara: The Economics of Revolution*. Houndmills: Palgrave Macmillan, 2009. Here from: Lebowitz, Michael A. "The Struggle between the Future and the Past: Where Is Cuba Going?" *Monthly Review Online*, July 3, 2022. Accessed July 6, 2024. https://mronline.org/2022/07/03/the-struggle-between-the-future-and-the-past-where-is-cuba-going/.

YANG, Congmin, and Yang Liyuan. "A Survey of the Magnitude of the Rural Workers' Migration in Contemporary China." *Chinese Sociology*. Accessed July 6, 2024. http://www.sociology2010.cass.cn/news/131900.htm. Here from: Li, Minqi. *China and the Twenty-First-Century Crisis*. London: Pluto Press, 2016.

YANQI, Tong, and Shaohua Lei. "Large-Scale Mass Incidents in China." *East Asian Policy*. EAI Background Brief no. 520 (2013). Accessed July 6, 2024. http://www.eai.nus.edu.sg/Vol2No2_TongYanqi&LeiShaohua.pdf.

YAWEN, Cheng. "The Peace Dividend Is Over, and China Has to Prepare for a Full Decoupling." *Culture Vertical* no. 3 (June 2022).

YICHING, Wu. *The Cultural Revolution at the Margins*. Cambridge, MA: Harvard University Press, 2014.

YIYING, Fan. "China's Top Court Says Grueling '996' Work Schedule Illegal." *Sixth Tone*, August 27, 2021. Accessed July 6, 2024. https://www.sixthtone.com/news/1008375/chinas-top-court-says-grueling-996-work-schedule-illegal.

ZEDONG, Mao. "A Few Opinions of Mine." August 31, 1970. Accessed July 6, 2024. https://www.bannedthought.net/China/MaoEra/GPCR/Chinese/AFewOpinionsOfMine-1970-English.pdf.

——— "A Single Spark Can Start a Prairie Fire." In *Selected Works*, vol. 1. Peking: Foreign Languages Press, 1965.

——— "Analysis of the Classes in Chinese Society." In *Selected Works*, vol. 1. Peking: Foreign Languages Press, 1965.

——— "Annotations, Lecture Notes on Dialectical Materialism." In *Mao Zedong on Dialectical Materialism: Writings on Philosophy,* edited by Nick Knight. Armonk, NY, 1990.

——— "Concerning Economic Problems of Socialism in the USSR." November 9, 1958. In *A Critique of Soviet Economics*. New York: Monthly Review Press, 1977.

——— "Critique of Stalin's Economic Problems of Socialism in the USSR." In *A Critique of Soviet Economics*. New York: Monthly Review Press, 1977.

——— "Farewell, Leighton Stuart." In *Selected Works*, vol. 4. Peking: Foreign Languages Press, 1969.

——— "Letter to Jiang Qing." July 8, 1966. Accessed July 6, 2024. https://www.bannedthought.net/China/Individuals/MaoZedong/Letters/Mao'sLetterToJiangQing-660708-Alt3.pdf.

——— "Notes on the Report of Further Improving the Army's Agricultural Work by the Rear Service Department of the Military Commission." Letter to Lin Biao dated May 7, 1966. In *Long Live Mao Tse-tung Thought*, a Red Guard Publication, 1966. Accessed July 6, 2024. https://china.usc.edu/mao-zedong-%E2%80%9C-notes-report-further-improving-army%E2%80%99s-agricultural-work-rear-service-department-military.

——— "On Correcting Mistaken Ideas in the Party." In *Selected Works*, vol. 1. Peking: Foreign Languages Press, 1965.

——— "On New Democracy," January 1940. Accessed July 6, 2024. https://www.marxists.org/reference/archive/mao/selected-works/volume-2/mswv2_26.htm.

——— "On the Correct Handling of Contradictions among the People," February 27, 1957. In *The Secret Speeches of Chairman Mao: From the Hundred Flowers to the Great Leap Forward*, edited by Roderick MacFarquhar, Timothy Cheek, and Eugene Wu. Harvard Contemporary China Series no. 6. Cambridge, MA: Harvard University Press, 1989.

——— "On the New Stage." In *The Political Thought of Mao Tse-tung*, edited by Stuart R. Schram. Middlesex: Pelican Book, 1969.

——— "On the People's Democratic Dictatorship." In Commemoration of the Twenty-eighth Anniversary of the Communist Party of China, June 30, 1949. In *Selected Works*, vol. 4. Peking: Foreign Languages Press, 1969.

——— "On the Problem of Ideological Work," March 20, 1957. In *The Writings of Mao Zedong 1949-1976*, vol. II, edited by John K. Leung and Michael Y. M. Kau. Armonk, NY, 1992.

——— "Problems of War and Strategy." November 6, 1938. In *Selected Works*, vol. 2. Peking: Foreign Languages Press, 1965.

——— "Report on an Investigation of the Peasant Movement in Hunan." In *Selected Works*, vol. 1. Peking: Foreign Languages Press, 1965.

———. "Speech at [a] Conference of Members and Cadres of Provincial-Level Organizations of [the] CPC in Shandong," March 18, 1957. In *The Writings of Mao Zedong 1949-1976*, vol. II, edited by John K. Leung and Michael Y. M. Kau. Armonk, NY, 1992.

——— "Speech at the Conference of Provincial, Municipal, and Autonomous Region Party Secretaries," January 27, 1957. In *The Writings of Mao Zedong 1949-1976*, vol. II, edited by John K. Leung and Michael Y. M. Kau. Armonk, NY, 1992.

——— "Speech at the Tenth Plenum of the Eighth Central Committee of the CPC," September 24, 1962. In *Chairman Mao Talks to the People: Talks and Letters: 1956-1971*, edited by Stuart Schram. New York: Pantheon, 1974.

——— "Speech at the Wuchang Meeting of the Political Bureau of the Central Committee of the Communist Party of China." In *Selected Works*, vol. 4. Beijing: Foreign Languages Press, 1958.

——— "Summary of a Talk with the Representatives of Press and Publishing Circles," March 10, 1957. In *The Secret Speeches of Chairman Mao: From the Hundred Flowers to the Great Leap Forward*, edited by Roderick MacFarquhar, Timothy Cheek, and Eugene Wu. Harvard Contemporary China Series no. 6. Cambridge, MA: Harvard University Press, 1989.

——— "Talk with Edward Heath," May 25, 1974. In *On Diplomacy*. Beijing: Foreign Languages Press, 1998. Accessed July 6, 2024.

http://michaelharrison.org.uk/wp-content/uploads/2017/02/Mao-Zedong-On-Diplomacy-1998.pdf.

———. "The Chinese Revolution and the Communist Party of China." In *Selected Works*, vol. 2. Peking: Foreign Languages Press, 1969.

———. "The Question of Independence and Initiative within the United Front." In *Selected Works*, vol. 2. Beijing: Foreign Languages Press, 1967.

———. "The Role of the Communist Party of China in the National War." October 1938. In *Selected Works*, vol. 2. Peking: Foreign Languages Press, 1965.

———. "Three Rules of Discipline and Eight Points for Attention." Here from: Uhalley, Stephen. *Mao Zedong: A Critical Biography*. New York: New Viewpoints Publishing, 1975.

———. "We Must Prevent China from Changing Color." In the Ninth Chinese Reply to the Soviet Open Letter of July 14, 1963, published on July 1, 1964. This extract is included in Chapter III of *Quotations from Chairman Mao*. Accessed July 6, 2024. https://www.marxists.org/reference/archive/mao/selected-works/volume-9/mswv9_24.htm.

———. "Why Is It That Red Political Power Can Exist in China?" In *Selected Works*, vol. 1. Peking: Foreign Languages Press, 1965.

———. *On Diplomacy*. Beijing: Foreign Languages Press, 1998.

ZELIN, Madeleine, Jonathan K. Ocko, and Robert Gardella, eds. *Contract and Property in Early Modern China*. Stanford, CA: Stanford University Press, 2004.

ZEMIN, Jiang. "Speech at the Celebration of the 70th Anniversary of the Founding of the Party," 1991. Accessed July 6, 2024. http://www.qunzh.com/pub/jsqzw/xxzt/jd95zn/zyls/201606/t20160601_20990.html. Here from: Martinez, Gabriel. "Ideological Work in the New Era of Socialism in China." *The International* magazine, 2021. Accessed July 6, 2024. https://internationalmagz.com/articles/.

ZHENG, Z. "An Interactive Evolution between Capitalism and Statism in Modern China." *Chinese Studies in History* 47 (2013): 21–39.

ZHILIN, Pavel. *Recalling the Past for the Sake of Our Future: The Causes, Results and Lessons of World War Two*. Moscow: Novosti, 1985.

ZIYANG, Zhao. "Tiananmen Square Speech," May 19, 1989. Accessed July 6, 2024. https://web.archive.org/web/20110716222958/http://www.theasiamag.com/cheat-sheet/zhao-ziyangs-tiananmen-square-speech.

ZOUACHE, Abdallah. "Socialism, Liberalism and Inequality: The Colonial Economics of the Saint-Simonians in 19th-century Algeria." *Review of Social Economy* 67, no. 4 (December 2009).

www.ingramcontent.com/pod-product-compliance
Lightning Source LLC
LaVergne TN
LVHW042246070526
838201LV00089B/52